In Perfect Timing

Author's note

To avoid possible confusion or offence, the phrase 'the Findhorn Community' (capitalised) used throughout this book refers to the formal Community associated with the Findhorn Foundation, and not the residents of the neighbouring village of Findhorn which has its own quite separate identity and traditions.

As this is in part a history book, however, and much use is made of direct quotations from historical documents, the natural contraction of 'Findhorn Foundation' or 'Findhorn Community' to plain 'Findhorn' is unavoidable in places. Rather than try the reader's patience by qualifying each and every instance, we trust that common sense will prevail, and only add 'Foundation' or 'Community' where there is any danger of ambiguity or misunderstanding.

In Perfect Timing

Memoirs of a Man for the New Millennium

Peter Caddy

with Jeremy Slocombe

and Renata Caddy

First published in 1996

ISBN 1 899171 26 6

British Library Cataloguing-in-Publication Data.
A catalogue record for this book is available from the British Library.

Cover design by Findhorn Press and Posthouse Printing

Layout and setting in Times by Findhorn Press

Printed and bound in England by The Cromwell Press, Broughton Gifford, England

Published by

Findhorn Press

The Press Building
The Park, Findhorn
Forres IV36 0TZ
Scotland
tel +44 (0)1309 690582 / fax 690036
e-mail thierry@findhorn.org
url http://www.gaia.org/findhornpress/

This book is dedicated to Robert Ogilvie Crombie

— Roc —

my Friend.

As great a Magician, as humble as a Man.

In Gratitude,

Peter Caddy

Acknowledgements

Many hands make Light work: there is a play of words in this saying that is felt and appreciated when it comes to acknowledging all those who have contributed to *In Perfect Timing*.

Peter Caddy lived life to the full, and were the total tale of his experiences to be told, then you would be holding in your hands a volume at least three times longer and thicker.

Thanks must go to all those who out of love for Peter first began gathering material in order to help him with his memoirs, specifically Rue Ann Hass, Paul Schicke, and Leona Aroha Graham; then to those who worked on transcribing the raw material for the book from taped interviews and recorded collections: Kate Stokes, Helen Rubin who in addition helped Peter in his initial compilation and assembly of the material in a very dedicated way, and Dennis Evenson who worked through reams of written material to extract and sort out the reaches within them.

Many other contributed their insight and wisdom during the long gestation of the book, and deserve acknowledgements and gratitude for their support: David and Julie Spangler. Sir George Trevelyan, Donald Keys, William Irwin Thompson, Dorothy Maclean, Eileen Caddy, Muriel McVicar, Liza Hollingshead, Alice Weybull, Michael and Mary Jennions,Bev Walker, Robert Hargrove, Silvius Dornier, Paul Kluwer, Marianne Ricke, Maria Gabriele Wosien, Anke Maria and Rainer Leitzgen, Gisela Behrendt, Rose Küst, Erdmute Herden, Heidi Fieser, Edit Bernhard-Hess, Ingrid Maegle, Isabelle Duquesne, Ute Broll-Jonethal, Elisabeth Roesener-Valter and Derek Williams.

Deepest thanks go to Leonie Waldschmidt — Renata's mother — for all her love and support throughout the years.

Thierry and Karin Bogliolo at Findhorn Press deserve a special mention, because from the beginning they have been inspired to bring *In Perfect Timing* into the world, in perfect timing. Thanks too to Lynn Barton for her editorial assistance.

There are three towering figures who must be most acknowledged, as they have been with us since the book's inception — Roc, Peter Dawkins, and Shri Mishra Vishnu Dutt Shastri. Without these three — and their guidance and contributions on both inner and outer levels — this book would not be the work that it is.

Our heartfelt gratitude goes to all of the above.

Jeremy Slocombe Renata Caddy

17 November 1995

Contents

Preface

by Sir George Trevelyan, Bt.

...Come my friends,
'Tis not too late to seek a newer world,
Push off, and sitting well in order smite
The sounding furrows; for my purpose holds
To sail beyond the sunset, and the baths
Of all the western stars, until I die.
It may be that the gulfs will wash us down:
It may be that we shall touch the Happy Isles,
And see the great Achilles, whom we knew.
Tho' much is taken, much abides; and tho'
We are not now that strength which in old days
Moved earth and heaven; that which we are, we are;
One equal temper of heroic hearts,
Made weak by time and fate, but strong in will
To strive, to seek, to find, and not to yield.

THESE HEROIC WORDS from Tennyson's *Ulysses* spring immediately to mind when I consider the extraordinary life of my good friend Peter Caddy; they ably serve to describe the motivation behind his outrageous adventures, his indefatigable spirit and his very real achievements in the world. It is not given to all of us to leave something of lasting value on the shelf behind us when we quit this life, but Peter most certainly has, and with exceptional brio.

Here's the paradox of the man: an ex-Squadron Leader of the Royal Air Force, a conventional Englishman from a middle-class background who would not pay a halfpenny for convention if it got in the road of carrying out what his firm and formidable intuition required of him. He was a 'doer for God', as his younger friend and colleague, the American mystic, writer and philosopher David Spangler has written. After Peter's innocent and unfortunate death in a car crash in February 1994, his son Christopher noted, 'Few people become a legend in their own lifetime, but I believe that he did'. And in what is for many today a mad, bad and sad world, we need the freshness and power of new legends. We need those of heroic, almost mythological mettle who are not afraid of putting their hand into the fire and seizing the treasures to be found there. Peter Caddy was such a man.

It is fitting to record my first meeting with him. I was at the time Principal of the Shropshire Adult College, Attingham Park, which I directed and ran from its founding in 1947 until my retirement in 1971. This was one of a group of short-term residential centres for adult education founded after the war and it had developed into a fine centre. Our weekends there were often given to gatherings of a more exploratory, spiritual nature, certainly out of and beyond the cultural mainstream of the day, and lest we provoke the suspicions or ire of the public authorities who supported us we tended to eschew publicity of any kind: such gatherings were by personal invitation only. Therefore when in 1965 Peter got wind of a weekend conference at Attingham entitled 'Groups in the New Age', and rang to invite himself in another's place, my secretary gave him short shrift on the telephone—until a spiritually sensitive friend of mine, in the office with us at the time, nodded across to me that Peter should come. He leapt into his car and pounded down the length of England to be with us by nightfall; we had no bed-space for him, but in the meantime somebody else cried off from joining us, on account of the flu, so all was in order for Peter to be included.

I have never forgotten that amusing incident on his first night, where the session was given over to the subject of creating a charter for New Age communities and how to finance them: after hearing several speakers, and deciding no longer to control his impatience, Peter rose and claimed to be demonstrating with his small group at Findhorn what the rest of us were still only talking about. A sceptical Air Marshall Sir Victor Goddard interrupted to question his financial policy. 'We don't have one!', Peter replied breezily, and then, with greater gravity, added 'You give everything to God and give thanks that all your needs will be met to perfection, and then you just go ahead!' This was fighting talk, and it upset many people at the time.

Three years later, when I first visited his fledgling community at Findhorn, I was thrilled with what I found: the evidence was everywhere to be seen. This was the first time, I believe, that Peter confessed to an outsider the secrets of the garden's success — the cooperation with the invisible worlds that inform the nature kingdom, and the daily communion with God, whose 'voice' and guidance his wife Eileen received and recorded.

But the memoirs you hold here are not merely the history of the extraordinary phenomenon that the Findhorn Community came to be—that story is told elsewhere. Here you have the man himself, his perils and pitfalls as much as his triumphs (although he would boast of neither unless there were good and empowering reason to do so). Peter was indeed a man whose example is well made for the new millennium and a way of life for which we all hanker: easy, accessible and effective communion with the world of spirit; the translation of this into our everyday lives, even into the most seemingly mundane chores; finding our proper and correct and sensitive connection with the natural world and the planet of which we are only its sensory apparatus, its organ of self-perception. As Coleridge would have it,

...we receive but what we give,
And in our life alone does Nature live:
Ours is her wedding garment, ours her shroud!

But above all, if Peter's life is to teach us anything, it will be to make us more aware and effective as human beings, more conscious of our responsibilities to the world around us, and, I dare say, to find much more fun and fulfilment in our lives! His was a heroic heart and he leads us into adventure, whether in the high Himalayas or the imbroglio and shambles of the civil war in the former Yugoslavia, where Peter was supporting a peace initiative in the months before his death.

Courage is the key word that will lead us individually and collectively into the new millennium; as Samuel Johnson said, 'Courage is the greatest virtue, for without it there can be no others'. We have a sacred duty to encourage each other at this time, and Peter Caddy carried both personal courage and the encouragement of others wherever he went. You will find it in this book.

I am pleased to have known Peter and to have enjoyed his friendship; I am grateful that I was able to help him in serving a great cause that has helped and encouraged so many, throughout the world. But let us not allow the splendour and brightness of this man's adventure to dim our own. Instead we take a spark from his life to our own tinder-box, if it is not already kindled. I turn again to Coleridge—

Ah! from the world itself must issue forth
A light, a glory, a fair luminous cloud
Enveloping the Earth—
And from the soul itself must there be sent
A sweet and potent voice, of its own birth,
Of all sweet sounds the life and element!

By the end of his memorable life Peter Caddy's voice was certainly 'sweet and potent'. Enjoy the adventure of reading this book as you go along with Peter's great adventures—and may you find your way back from them determined to embark on your own, therein to find the sweetness and potency of your own voice.

This Preface was written in collaboration with Jeremy Slocombe

Introduction

by David Spangler

IN THE LATE twentieth century there can be no doubt humanity is in the midst of a profound transformation. Some see this as a cause for celebration and are optimistic about the future. Others view this change with discomfort and alarm and are filled with pessimism about the years ahead; while still others deny that anything is happening at all and try to maintain business as usual.

There is justification for each of these positions. New insights into our human nature and the nature of the world around us— whether arising from science, psychology, spirituality, or any other source— do offer us powerful tools to relate to each other and to our environment more wisely, compassionately and skilfully than before. On the other hand, mere change can unleash forces of fear and intolerance, destruction and hatred, as witness the rise of the brutal ethnic conflicts in Eastern Europe after the collapse of Communism and the Soviet Union. And no matter how political alignments or economic systems change or technology advances, the challenges of human relationships, of raising healthy children, and of caring for the Earth from which all our sustenance comes remain as they always have.

Whether our view of the future is optimistic, pessimistic, or indifferent, however, we may still miss a vital point: the future does not yet exist. It makes no sense to be optimistic or pessimistic about something that isn't there.

This is not to say that we cannot look out at the world as it is and see trends and habits which, if not altered, will bring either horror or blessing. But trends are not always reliable. Looking at world trends in 1988 would not have told us that two years later we would be living in a world without the Soviet Union, the Berlin Wall, or a communist-dominated Eastern Europe, and with a reunited Germany.

In his poem *The Second Coming,* Yeats asked 'what rough beast... slouches towards Bethlehem to be born', but in fact many things move towards potential birth, angels as well as beasts. What determines our future are our choices in the present; tomorrow emerges from the the things we do or do not do today, the opportunities we seize or neglect, the creativity and imagination we express or deny.

The challenge with the future is that it is easier to continue with the momentum of what is— the habits of yesterday— than to imagine what might be. Being imaginative, daring, exploratory, willing to change in the interests of a better future are not traits that are generally encouraged. They are not safe. That is why the past or 'trends' are so powerful: they are rarely confronted with the power of imagination and new vision.

Yet the challenges of the late twentieth century demand that we re-imagine our future and that we are daring in making changes personally and collectively to shape a more compassionate tomorrow... at least if we want angels and not rough beasts to define what our future will be like. We must dare to be skilled visionaries.

The New Age is an idea that reminds us that the future is ours to shape and that we have the power to do so. It is an idea that honours the role of transformation in our lives as a liberation from habits and trends. Unfortunately, much of the modern New Age movement does not fully grasp the power or challenge of this idea, often surrendering its creativity at the altar of prophecy, preferring to wait for a better future to arrive from some nebulous place where it already exists, rather than creating it through everyday actions.

One place where the New Age is being explored in depth, a place dedicated to empowering people in their ordinary lives to be creative agents of new vision and a better future, is the Findhorn Foundation Community in northern Scotland. This is a place where people are encouraged and trained not to wait for a New Age but to see it and create it in their lives right now, for in the choices they make to do so, they set into motion the forces that shape that New Age for their tomorrows.

The Findhorn Foundation Community is a place of hope and example for hundreds of thousands of people throughout the world. It has changed people's lives for the better. It has given birth both directly and indirectly to thousands of projects that build towards a compassionate future. It is a power for positive transformation that upholds the vision that today's choices create the future, and that we can choose with wisdom, with love, with faith, with imagination and with skill.

This place and the gifts it offers exist because three people dared to make visionary and imaginative choices in their own lives, risking all in the process. One of these three is Peter Caddy, whose life story you now have in your hand.

Peter Caddy was a remarkable man. Early in his adult life he gave himself completely and unconditionally to God. From this he gained an unshakable faith that served him in good stead throughout his life, and especially in being a co-founder of the Findhorn Foundation Community and a respected New Age leader.

He also gave himself completely and unconditionally to life, embracing it with zest, courage and delight. There was nothing otherworldly about Peter. He was a man of action who thoroughly enjoyed taking on an adventure, and the more challenging it was, the better he liked it.

As a consequence, his life reads like an H. Rider Haggard novel, filled with derring-do and spiritual wisdom. It is a ripping good yarn, which is all the more powerful because it is true.

For me, a principal message of Peter's life is that he was not afraid to change. He used his past as a source of wisdom and experience but never as a determinant of his future. He was not a man controlled by trends or prophecies. His view of the future was unswervingly optimistic because he was optimistic about himself. Even if it meant giving up all that he already had, if he needed to change in order to serve more effectively, he knew he could do so without a second thought. Because he could be positive about himself, he could be positive in his actions to create the future.

It was this positivity about oneself and the world that he wanted to give to others, for he knew that a positive future would not emerge from negative or fearful people.

He was not a philosopher, nor was he particularly self-reflective, but he was a visionary. He believed in people. He had a vision of what ordinary people could do when they aroused themselves and believed in their higher potentials, and he always sought to teach people how to do this. He built Findhorn to be a place where that kind of teaching and empowerment could occur.

Peter believed in demonstration, in setting an example; he never asked anyone to do anything he hadn't already done himself. For him, Findhorn was a place where ordinary people could demonstrate how to live a spirit-infused ordinary life that could change the Earth for the better so that others could come, see it for themselves, and go back to their homes to be agents of angels, not beasts, moving to be born. He wanted it to be a place where the power to create the future was embodied and demonstrated. This was his gift to the promise and challenge of the new millennium.

Peter was a master storyteller and in this book he tells his story. The best introduction to him lies in his own words, as well as in the ongoing creative actions of those inspired by him and by Findhorn to make our world a better place.

Part I

The Individual Responds to Love

The quotations at the head of chapters 1—30 are extracted from papers given to Peter Caddy as part of his spiritual training in the Rosicrucian Order Crotona Fellowship.

Chapter 1

First Things First

Faith and trust in yourself
are the only requisites in taking these lessons,
for as a soul you are a manifestation of power;
that power is named life

MY BIRTH WAS UNREMARKABLE. I was born on 20 March 1917, at Ruislip, Middlesex, about 16 miles west of London. The twentieth century was yet a troubled adolescent. World War I still had over a year to run its course; Britain had the mightiest empire in the world, America was only beginning its ascendancy, and few people realized how the impending revolution in Russia would have such an impact on the shape of things to come.

Ruislip was then a village. Frederick John Caddy, my father, had returned from service in East Africa, where he had contracted malaria, and was now working at Post Office Headquarters in London. He was the embodiment of traditional values: a strict disciplinarian, morally upright, a virtuous and solid member of society. Father was proud of his mental ability and had been brilliant at school. He came top out of 3,000 entrants in the Civil Service exam that led to his lifelong Post Office career. He had a critical mind and tongue, read from a methodically prepared list of books, and loved music.

Doris Mary Caddy complemented him. My mother was loving and sympathetic, devoted to Father and very much under his influence, doing only what he wanted. My sister Joan was born two years after me, and Mother looked after us all with a submissive but stoic personality: she suffered from very painful problems with her feet nearly all her life (she once commented that it was like 'walking on glass') but never complained.

I did not experience much fun and play as a child, but learned obedience, discipline and to ignore physical pain. While other members of my family were close, I was never interested in family history or my other relatives. I inherited characteristics from both parents: order and stamina from my father, disorder and a wish to care for people from Mother. Though my grandmother Mary Lees was a fastidious housekeeper, my mother was absolutely chaotic. She would forget where she put things and never keep her effects in order. Father, on the other hand, was meticulous and tidy. He kept records of how much water, electricity and coal we used, and could tell the exact cost of every item for any month and year. Every month he spent an evening putting money in small OXO beefstock tins in a cash box. Each tin was labelled for items like clothes, garden and holidays; only later did I realize that these frugal ways made our holidays in England and Switzerland possible.

For many years my father suffered from excruciating pains in his back, which orthodox medicine failed to relieve. Mother's compassion for his condition served to underline the great love between them. When he retired in 1947, my father said, 'For fifteen years or so I was never out of pain day or night. For many years I was so bad that I had to start getting out of the train two stations before I got to Ruislip[1] and on some occasions, I had to wait at the station until my wife could help me home. During that time, if she had not been completely cheerful, helpful and forgiving, I must inevitably have cracked. I don't know even now how I got through all those nightmare years, but I have forgotten the pain and remember only the selfless devotion of my wife.'

Despite his conservative nature, the agony drove him to try several unorthodox methods of healing. He went to chiropractors, osteopaths and homeopaths. He underwent three lengthy fasts, one of sixty days and two of ninety days, during which he consumed only water and one glass of orange juice a day. During these fasts he continued to go to work every day except in the last week, which shows the strength of his will and discipline. He had my sister and me fast one Christmas when we had developed colds — I would have preferred serious illness to missing my roast turkey and plum pudding! Joan and I were also made to have sun and air baths, naked on the lawn. I was embarrassed: what would the neighbours think?

Because Father also became a vegetarian we all had to become vegetarians. Joan and I did not approve. My mother would prepare brown bread, grated carrot and beetroot sandwiches, wrapped in greaseproof paper, for

1 Presumably because the motion of the train aggravated the pain

school lunch each day. By midday, they would become a smelly, soggy mess, so I used to throw them into a hedge on the way to school and at lunch time would scrounge delicious roast beef and ham sandwiches (made with white bread!) from my friends. The overcooked Brussels sprouts we were served during an occasional restaurant meal were far more enjoyable than the conservatively cooked, half-raw ones we had at home. This taught me the mistake of forcing children to eat foods they do not like, against their will — rebellion will be the only result. My mother, when giving me an unappetizing but 'healthy' meal would often say that it was 'good for me'; even today I refuse to accept anything I am told is 'good' for me if it doesn't look and taste good as well.

We went to church twice on Sundays, because my father was a Wesleyan Methodist. In my heart and soul I wanted to be out exploring the countryside, running in the fields and climbing trees; I suppose, however, that I did get a good grounding in the Bible. As part of his religion Father did not approve of the cinema, so we were very excited one day when my mother told us she was going to take my sister and me up to London to 'go to the pictures' (which in those days meant the movies). After a day seeing the sights we arrived at Piccadilly Circus and, as it was after dark, Mother pointed out the huge light displays advertising Coca Cola and other things. They were impressive but I was growing impatient. 'When are we going to see the pictures?' I demanded. These lights, apparently, *were* 'the pictures'. I was disgusted and felt really let down. By the time we were waiting for our return train home at Baker Street station, and my mother asked me if I had enjoyed the day, I had had enough. I started to cry, with great sobs. 'What's the matter?' she asked, concerned and not a little embarrassed. 'But we haven't even seen *Thames* station!' I managed to protest between sobs. 'There isn't one,' she replied. 'Oh yes there is,' I said, 'because every Sunday in church we say "Lead us not into Thames station".' Such was my understanding of the Lord's Prayer (and no doubt a desire to taste forbidden fruit as, subsequently, I often went secretly with friends to the cinema on a Saturday morning).

Curiously it was my father's back problems that led me to my first experience of a spiritual nature, when I was ten. Father had a very good singing voice and was a member of several choirs; among these was the church choir, and another of its members, Grace Cooke, received inner teachings from an American Indian 'guide' named White Eagle.[2] Despite his staunch

[2] 'Guides' are disembodied entities whose intelligence may be channelled through a human medium, whether in trance or not

Methodism, my father had tried so many healing methods without success that he was open to receiving healing from White Eagle if it could help.

Grace Cooke later became a well-known medium of the day, but some of her first channelling circles were held in our house and I was occasionally allowed to attend. Initially she came without her husband, Ivan Cooke, who wouldn't have anything to do with what he thought was nonsense. One day in the Cooke's home, while Grace was out somewhere, Ivan pointed to a glass-framed picture on the wall: 'I'd only believe in White Eagle if that picture came crashing down to the floor and did not break,' he declared. Crash! down it came, without breaking. After that he was a firm supporter and later played a key part in the growth and development of the worldwide branches of the White Eagle Lodge.

I remember on one occasion, just as Grace Cooke was 'bringing through' White Eagle, our pet dog Brutus suddenly lifted its eyes to a point just above Grace's head. It was clearly sensing something — I fancied it must be the feathers of White Eagle's headdress. The questions that I wanted to put to White Eagle were decidedly practical, such as how I could be helped with my examinations. On one occasion I asked, 'What do I do to win tomorrow's boxing match at school?' There was a ripple of laughter from the adults in the group. White Eagle, however, apparently took the question seriously. 'Look him in the eye,' he responded, 'and you will know when he is about to hit you.' I followed his advice and won my fight. So at an early age I was introduced to concepts of life after death and to receiving practical advice from other-worldly realms. I also realized that just because Auntie Ethel had passed on into another world, it didn't necessarily make her wiser than in this one!

My father's main hobby was gardening and we never needed to buy any vegetables. Despite his disability he often worked two hours a day in the winter, digging in the garden before catching his train to work in London. He won many prizes at vegetable and flower shows as a result of his hard work, skill and dedication to perfection. The extent of my gardening was weeding, particularly during the school holidays when other children were playing. I was rarely able to play cricket or other games or do any interesting things: it was just weeding, weeding, weeding. In fairness to him, however, I realize that he had difficulty in bending, and by observing him I did learn a great deal that I have put into practice in later life.

From my grandfather I gained an interest in nature on our long walks together. Father was also a keen walker, and our whole family went hiking and climbing, locally and later in Switzerland. These experiences gave me a love of mountains, the open air and walking, as well as a desire to travel, meet different people and taste various kinds of food.

Apart from enjoying such excursions, my father and I had little in common. I could not sing, did poorly at school, and felt that I was a disappointment to him. I know that my father loved his children but he never spent much time with us. Like many sons, I did not feel that he understood me. As he watched me go through my life, Father could never understand why, after faring so poorly in exams, I later did so well in the Royal Air Force and in business. It seemed to come so easily to me — perhaps he found it unjust because he'd had to work so hard — but as a youth, I felt that I was not really appreciated for the gifts that I had. My father didn't see them because he was judging me by his own standards and against his own talents. I know he was proud of my athletic prowess at school and in cross-country championships, but although he followed these achievements with pride, he never said anything to me — I only heard of it second-hand from other people. The only game I can remember that he ever played with me was 'catch' with a ball.

Much later, shortly before his retirement and after years of constant pain, in which he subjected all of us to eccentric diets and exposed us to increasingly unconventional practices, my father was diagnosed by a specialist as having a stone in his kidney. After a routine operation he was fine — both the kidney stone and the pain were gone, simple as that. Father went back to eating meat, white bread, etc., and reverted to his earlier, orthodox ways. But there was no turning back for me: as I had grown up with them, unconventional approaches like Grace Cooke's channelling seemed perfectly normal. Father had unwittingly gifted me an open mind, and in the years to follow, as my spiritual studies developed and my life often went off at a tangent to the mainstream, his disapproval turned to condemnation.

* * *

I was educated at the Lower School of John Lyon, Harrow, a private school (known in England, through some strange inversion, as a 'public' school). As I say, I was not an outstanding scholar, nor good at examinations as my father had been, but I did shine as an athlete. I excelled in individual sports, such as cross-country, middle- and long-distance running, and preferred these to team games like cricket and football. I was captain of the gymnastics and

— much to my surprise — easily won the school's annual cross-country race (maybe because of the early practice I'd had walking with my father). After leaving school, I joined an athletic club in London, the Polytechnic Harriers, and became the junior cross-country champion for three years, thus winning the cup outright. I also took part in the annual London-to-Brighton walk of 52 miles.

At most British public schools, boxing was considered a noble art, part of the school curriculum and of the regular programme in which everybody had to take part. If there were any disputes among boys, they would be ordered to report to the gym, put on gloves, and box three 3-minute rounds, shaking hands at the beginning and at the end. I was selected to be part of the team to represent the school in boxing matches.

In some ways I was set apart from other boys. I was not allowed to join the Officer's Training Corps[3] at school because my father was a pacifist and did not believe in it. I was banned from the school choir because I couldn't sing in tune (a great blow to Father, who, of course, loved singing). At home, there were not many boys living nearby; one, John Boltbee, with whom I loved to climb trees, was full of vitality but one day was caught using some swear words, and since his parents never corrected him, I wasn't allowed to play with him any longer.

One of the boys at school, Stanley Walton, was greatly feared. Nobody could beat him in a fight or at wrestling because of the bear hug with which he threatened to squeeze the life out of his opponent. But I discovered how to defeat him by rubbing my knuckles into his spine until he yelled and let go. We found then that we were equally matched, and became firm friends. Stanley was the only boy in the school who was able to climb the ropes twice in the gym without using his legs. During my four or five years at school we wrestled at every opportunity, all through the break period in the morning and all through the lunch hour. The headmaster used to watch our wrestling from a window overlooking the playground and called us Tweedledee and Tweedledum. Even my father encouraged this wrestling, although I wore out many pairs of trousers, because it seemed to him a manly thing for me to do.

Because I loved fresh air, I slept on the open veranda of our house in both summer and winter, and thus toughened my body. I was a very keen

---

3 Elementary training for service in the armed forces

Boy Scout and eventually became a King's Scout, selected to go to the jamboree at Godele, Hungary, where I caught typhoid fever and had to recuperate in a small village just inside the border of what was then Yugoslavia. I loved camping as a Scout, at weekends and during summer holidays. One thing I learned then was never to be uncomfortable when you could be comfortable — something I've put into practice ever since. Instead of sleeping on the hard ground, I'd go out and collect heather or straw to put under the groundsheet to make a softer bed.

During the jamboree at Godele a French boy asked how old I was, and to my disgust, I couldn't remember the French word for 'fifteen'. Later, when my father wanted to send me to live with a French family for a year to improve my grasp of the language, I refused; if after five years of learning French at school I still couldn't say 'fifteen', what hope was there for me? It was in the extra-curricular activities that I shone, not the forced, compulsory subjects like Latin and French.

My early life, then, was spent in many ways as a loner. My attention seemed to be on developing a strong will within a strong body. As I believe we choose our parents before we are born in this world, I later wondered why I had chosen mine: neither was really interested in spiritual matters, particularly my father, whose rigid and orthodox views were only relaxed if something unorthodox could bring relief to his physical suffering. I have come to realize that in order to break away from his ideas and way of life, I had to develop an even stronger will than his, which was considerable. It was like a chick breaking out of its egg. If the shell is thick, the chick has to develop greater strength to peck away until it can finally break out to find its own freedom. The thicker the shell, the stronger the chick must be.

* * *

In 1933, aged sixteen, I met an elderly clergyman in the British Museum who interested me in yoga philosophy and lent me books on the subject. These really opened my eyes: having been brought up as a Methodist, I had not realized that the truth of life, although dressed in different mental clothes in various cultures throughout history, is essentially the same all over the world. In studying yoga philosophy I began to question many of the things that had been taught by conventional religions, and started my own search for the truth through many 'ologies' and 'isms'.

Meanwhile more practical matters came to bear. Still at school, I could not make up my mind what I wanted to do with my life; I only knew that I did not want a routine nine-to-five office job like my father's. He therefore arranged for me to go to the Institute of Industrial Psychology where I spent three days being given various tests to find out what I was best suited for. The conclusion drawn from the results was a recommendation that I enter the catering trade. It seemed a wise and practical choice. The Great Depression was upon us; unemployment was high and even university graduates were unable to get jobs in their profession — whereas people always had to eat.

It was arranged that I should see the Managing Director of J. Lyons & Co., who were the largest caterers in the world. He offered me a five-year director's apprenticeship, starting with a year in the kitchens of London's Regent Palace Hotel. Thus I left school at sixteen; the Managing Director had explained to me that Lyons didn't want intellectual attainment in their senior staff as much as the willingness to work hard and to develop astute powers of observation.

At that time, the Regent Palace Hotel was the largest in Europe. Its kitchens were more cavernous than palatial, a hot, bustling bedlam in which every hour was rush hour with chefs, waiters and assistants shouting instructions at each other in almost any language but English, each one trying to be heard over the other. My training involved working in every department, observing how it functioned and getting hands-on experience of its activities. I wanted to become expert at one particular thing — making perfect French omelettes, which I loved, a difficult task because of the speed and dexterity it requires. Every evening for a year, therefore, whichever department I was working in, I would make myself an omelette for dinner until I had mastered the art.

Another early speciality of mine was potato soup, which served Stanley Walton and me in good stead when we went on a two-week climbing holiday in Switzerland — we had so little money that we practically lived on the stuff. I had an ambition to climb the Gornergrat, a mountain above the village of Zermatt, to obtain the spectacular view of the Matterhorn I had heard it afforded. Our plan was to do this hike on the last day before catching the train to return to London. A local person had told us that it would take three or four hours to Zermatt from Visp. We started walking up the valley. After several hours the Matterhorn, at the head of the valley, still seemed far away, and this struck me as strange. In all, it took us seven hours uphill to reach

Zermatt — I found out afterwards that the quoted time of a 'few hours' was by mountain railway!

I was still determined, and after a stiff climb we reached the summit of the Gornergrat, over 11,000 feet. The view more than repaid the effort. Then I realized that we would have to run down the mountain to be able to catch our train, which was the last one on the last day of the holiday. The frozen crust of the snow had melted and we kept falling up to our chests in the softer snow beneath. Eventually we reached the bottom of the mountain. Stanley wanted to give up and I had to prod him to run most of the 30 miles back to catch the night train from Visp. We had walked and run about 57 miles and climbed to 11,000 feet in one day. Even at that age, I was determined to achieve a goal no matter what the costs in pain or exhaustion; I could never contemplate quitting.

The next year we went to Bavaria, where we climbed three smallish mountains — the Tegelberg, Strausberg and Sauling — which we were told had not been done before in one day. Back in England, Stanley's mother was horrified to see how wasted our leg muscles were after these expeditions, and I often wondered whether she was responsible for the fact that Stanley and I saw less of each other from then on.

* * *

My apprenticeship at Lyons was long, hard work that left me little spare time and no social life. Six days a week I would leave home at 7.30 in the morning and not return until 10.30 that night. During the summer I spent the only break in the day swimming in the Serpentine in Hyde Park; during the winter I skated there. On the train to and from Ruislip, I read whatever books on occult and esoteric subjects I was able to lay my hands on.

This spiritual learning found its balance at work. There were two of us serving our director's apprenticeship at the Regent Palace Hotel, and on one occasion the Managing Director called us in to his office and asked us if we knew anything about liqueurs. 'Yes, of course, sir,' I bluffed, hoping to impress him. Without a word, he picked up the phone and asked for a bottle of every different liqueur in the hotel to be sent up; when they arrived, he turned his back to us and, one after the other, poured a small glass of each for us to sample and identify. Of the dozens of bottles, the only one that I got right was *crème de menthe*! The Managing Director then went on to explain where each liqueur was made, how it was made, and all about the bottling, but we were probably too squiffy by then to take it all in.

As apprentice directors, we were under the wing of a Mr Vivian, a retired army officer and a proper gentleman. When I was appointed assistant manager of a Lyons tea-shop in London, Mr Vivian would often visit to see how I was getting on. One day, as we were talking near the door, a smelly, down-and-out tramp who had bought a roll was leaving the shop. Mr Vivian instantly went to the door, opened it for him and addressed him as 'sir': a fine example for me of putting service into practice.

Four years into my apprenticeship, having served as a waiter, worked in the food factories at Cadby Hall, Hammersmith, and in the various departments of Coventry Street Corner House, experiencing every branch of catering, I became the manager of a large tea-shop with over fifty staff in London's West End. This was quite a responsibility for a twenty-year-old but as I learnt more about management, I began to develop my own strategies. For example, there was a young girl called Susan who cleaned tables in the tea-shop, and everyone seemed to be down on her. Nobody had a good word for Susan and this, of course, created a vicious circle — her work began to reflect the negative atmosphere she sensed around her — but it did not feel right to give her the sack. I watched her for about a week until I found something that she did well and then complimented her on it. She was so amazed and delighted that her attitude completely changed and she became one of the best workers in the establishment. From this experience I developed a practice of looking for the best in each person and acknowledging it with sincere praise. The dividends soon repaid the investment handsomely.

After gaining experience as a manager of several different establishments, I became an inspector responsible for five Lyons tea-shops in the West End of London and later in Manchester. My life beyond Lyons meanwhile had taken a dramatic turn.

Chapter 2

Food for Thought

All power and intelligence that
I can use are already mine

THROUGHOUT MY YEARS at an all-boys' school and the first couple of years of my apprenticeship with Lyons I had almost no social contact with the opposite sex. The closest I had come to losing my virginity, in fact, had been waving to a girl once from a bus stop on the way to school! My attention had been on sport and the outdoors, developing my physical body, and on my spiritual studies: in those years I was much more interested in reincarnation and karma than I was in girls. I still lived with my parents in Ruislip when working for Lyons in central London, so by the time I got home at around 10.30 pm I usually went straight to my bed.

In 1935, aged eighteen, I went on holiday with a fellow apprentice and his father to the Continental Hotel in Blankenberge, Belgium. One day from the window I saw two girls who were talking in French. A sudden intuition gripped me and I said to my companion, 'Leo, I'm going to marry that girl, the younger of the two'. To my logical mind this was absurd; for a start I didn't know how I was going to get over the language barrier, because I still wasn't any good at French. However, we went downstairs and followed them into the table-tennis room of the hotel where to my surprise I heard her ask in English, 'What is the score, Peggy?' Meeting Nora Meidling in this way and having an inner knowing that I was going to marry her is an example of the way my life functions. I do not dream, receive visions or hear voices. I am neither clairvoyant nor psychic. I experience an intuitive, spontaneous inner knowing which has guided me throughout my life, even though, in my youth, I had much to go through to accept it.

A few weeks after the holiday at Blankenberge, I visited Nora at her home in Ealing, West of London, where she lived with her mother and sister Peggy. The friendship gradually ripened. I met her other sister, Elizabeth, but it was with Elizabeth's husband Jim that I found an immediate and profound rapport. Jim Barnes shared my interest in spiritual and mystical subjects, and was obviously much more versed in them than I; he responded to my eagerness by offering the hand of friendship in my early spiritual training. He ensured that I read all the right material by giving me a list of books to study, and since my appetite for this material was voracious, I read nearly everything available at that time, including Madam Blavatsky's *Secret Doctrine*, the Arcane School books by Alice Bailey, and Max Heindel's *Rosicrucian Cosmo-Conception.*

For a long time I had been travelling alone in my studies and here at last was a man prepared to be my friend, guide and mentor —the first with whom I could really talk about matters so close to my heart. Although I badgered Jim with questions about reincarnation, karma, life after death, and a wealth of esoteric topics, his patience seemed inexhaustible. He was fifteen years my senior and our relationship became in some ways more important to me than Nora. I felt that my father was jealous of Jim (who was also in the Civil Service) because of the time we spent together; we would have long conversations about spiritual subjects of which Father thoroughly disapproved. Because of his narrow Methodist beliefs, my father and I never discussed his spiritual or religious outlook on life. Mother was interested in what I was studying but did not pursue the subject, due to Father's influence. This brought me closer to my friend than to my father.

I particularly remember Jim telling me that spiritual evolution was rather like going up a mountain. It would take thousands of lifetimes, gradually circling the mountain, getting higher and higher at each spiral, eventually reaching the top —self-realization and cosmic consciousness. Or one could, at this particular time in mankind's evolution, take the path of spiritual initiation and in a single lifetime make the direct, but steep, ascent from the foot of the mountain to the summit. This course would be very arduous and at times painful. Without hesitation, I made a commitment to the path of initiation, to climb unceasingly towards the top and reach it, come what may. Little did I know what this decision would mean.

In the meantime, my relationship with Nora was becoming closer. She was small, soft and delicate; not really pretty, but she had beautiful blue eyes and was always elegantly dressed. She was pale and did not like the sun or any kind of outdoors or sporting activity; she was more like an indoor house plant. When we went for a walk in the country, she would turn up in high heels and inappropriate clothes. At 4 pm she would be gasping for her usual cup of tea, when we would probably be miles from habitation.

I still had no doubts that I would marry her, although she was five years older than I. She came from a good family, was well-educated and had been to a finishing school in Switzerland. I felt that she was a good person to raise a family and would altogether make a satisfactory wife. This was the normal course of middle-class society in England between the world wars: it was expected of every young man that he marry and have children. Although love was somewhere in the equation, it was not automatically the most important factor.

Nora anyway preferred the company of her mother and sisters, and I think she was suspicious of men; and looking back, I realize that I didn't really have a clue what love was all about. But as I say, my intuition was very clear, and as it was the done thing anyway to get married and have children, I proposed to Nora and she accepted me.

Little did I realize that Jim Barnes had an ulterior motive for his enthusiastic encouragement of my spiritual studies. I did know that he and Elizabeth were very close to a certain Doctor Sullivan whom they obviously held in high esteem and for whom they had a great affection. This Doctor Sullivan lived at Christchurch in Hampshire[1], on the south coast, and they would travel down to see him each weekend. Over a year after we had become friends, Jim asked me if I would like to meet him.

So at the age of nineteen, I met Doctor Sullivan in London and it was to change my life. It is said that when the pupil is ready, the teacher appears; Jim had been preparing me for this meeting ever since he had first discerned my spiritual quest. It turned out that Doctor Sullivan was what is called in esoteric circles a Master, being the head (or Supreme Magus) of the Rosicrucian Order, Crotona Fellowship, which had chapters all over Britain. This Order had grown out of the original Rosicrucian mystery school which could trace its roots back to medieval Europe and beyond [2].

Doctor Sullivan was a big man with a shock of brown hair who exuded power and authority as well as gentleness and humility. I was particularly impressed by his great sense of humour — throughout my life I have found

---

1 Because of redrawn boundaries it is today in Dorset

2 Not be confused with A.M.O.R.C., the so-called Rosicrucian order that advertises heavily in the popular press and was founded by the American H. Spencer Lewis

that joy and lightheartedness are among the hallmarks of the advanced soul. Doctor Sullivan had many different names, among which he used *Aureolis* as his spiritual name, *Alex Mathews* as author and actor, and *Muser* as a poet. After answering his probing questions and meeting his inner scrutiny I must have passed muster, for I was invited to be initiated into the Order. I was thrilled. Soon afterwards I was initiated into the Francis Bacon Chapter Number 33 in London, and because the true Rosicrucian Order is a secret order I wasn't even allowed to tell my fiancée, Nora, that I was now a member. Fortunately, a few months later Nora too was initiated. We attended chapter meetings in London together and later at the headquarters in Christchurch.

There were several groups or departments of the Order: Masonic (symbology), Ordo (mental science), Temple (comparative religion, mysticism), Healing (therapeutics, healing), Drama (elocution, plays, oratory), a College of Psychotherapy and a School of Adepts. The theatre the Order later built was to become one of the best equipped on the south coast of England. Nora and I would go down to Christchurch at every opportunity, particularly during the annual two-week retreat, and it was a great privilege to be so close to one whom I considered to be a genuine Master living in our midst. He was a being of vast knowledge and seemed able to answer any question, but only if he felt it was right and appropriate to do so. He taught through lectures, drama, the church and Freemasonry, through fun and games, and by example. One had to remain alert during lectures and meetings so as to miss nothing, particularly the jokes. In spite of all his greatness, his wisdom, and his love, he would appear to the average person as an ordinary human being. Doctor Sullivan was a humble person and I discovered that no job was too menial for him. He was the one who emptied the chemical toilets in his ashram.

When (as *Aureolis*) Doctor Sullivan wrote and lectured, he often went back in time, recalling other incarnations (past lives in the world). He could travel to anywhere he wanted on the inner planes of reality. He was always examining our progress, whether he was there in person or not. Francis Bacon had written a code and cipher book for all the secret messages that had been hidden throughout the plays of Shakespeare; Doctor Sullivan had that original book, and I have seen it. He wrote many books and plays, as well as lectures, but these were only available to members of the Order and not to the general public, except for performances of the plays. He slept only three or four hours a night and seemed to function on several different levels of consciousness simultaneously. After World War II had broken out, he would also let drop many interesting things, such as what Hitler was thinking at the time, and I was told that even British Intelligence used his psychic information.

On the other hand, one could enjoy an evening at the cinema with him, or a picnic to some historical place whose story he could 'read' from his inner connections. He said very little about himself; one had to get personal information through one's own intuition. We would often play table tennis together, as he always stressed the importance of coming back down to earth after his lectures. He maintained a careful balance in all aspects of his life.

Although Doctor Sullivan added his power and the forces behind him to preventing World War II, war came and he knew that because of it, the work he had come to do could not be completed. He also knew that he was going to depart the physical world in 1942 — he reckoned he would be more useful operating on the 'other side' to combat the dark forces rolling across the world. Therefore to hasten the impartation of his teachings, he held an intensive series of lectures, designed for the more senior members of the Order, in which Nora and I were allowed to participate. It was thrilling for me to receive the papers every two weeks through the post.

This series of lectures, called *Soul Science* — concerning positive thinking and the power of the individual to effect change in the world — became the single most important foundation for my future life. As I studied the principles they established, these became part of my subconscious mind. I learned that nothing was impossible; that through the power of positive thinking, anything could be accomplished. We were trained in the use of spoken affirmations to bring about a change of thoughts, attitudes, and circumstances in our lives. *Aureolis* taught that by thinking, you direct your life into expression and that what you believe to be true moulds your destiny. You create every condition by your mind and that is reflected in your environment. By thinking, you make your life whatever it is, and are thus either consciously or unconsciously your own creator, designing your own fate.

A few examples will suffice to demonstrate how simple yet powerful these teachings are. The first lecture in the series contained the affirmation, ***'All power and intelligence that I can use are already mine'****. Constantly affirm this until it shall become part of your mental attitude and you unconsciously act from it. When you act from this affirmation, you will grow into the affirmation,* ***'I can',*** *whenever you think of anything you desire to do.*

You will, therefore, drop from your mind all thought of fear, and from your vocabulary, the words "can't" and "if". Anything you desire, you will know is possible to you, and you will speak of it with the same certainty of its coming, as you now speak of the New Year's coming. [It should be emphasized here that it is imperative that one gets his or her desires right, so that one does not follow personal whim but acts in accord with Divine intent. This involves the development of one's heart forces, as well as right thinking and the correct use of the will. In this respect, Doctor Sullivan urged us to] *Love whatever you do. Learn to love the place you are in, the people you are with and the work that you have to do. Find those things about the persons, places and labour that you can love, and ignore the rest. Make your affirmation,* ***'I am Love'****, and let Love radiate from you. You will thus create an atmosphere in which nothing but Love can come to you.*

Each lecture in the *Soul Science* series ended with practical exercises to be undertaken until the lessons were part of one's very being. These covered positive thinking, healing techniques, empowering others, and growing into self-possession and self-control. They included affirmations such as '**I am Power!** That power manifests in me, and is directed by my thoughts to do nothing but good!' I took these lessons to heart and gradually learned to gain mastery of my will, and the ability to respond immediately to inner promptings, unhampered by weaknesses of the physical body or vacillations of my mind or emotions. I became convinced that no task is too great nor any aspiration too far removed if a person utilizes the power and energy of the higher aspects of one's being in service to the overall will of God, whatever one calls it. These lessons later proved to be true and absolutely essential in the course of my subsequent life.

I married Nora when I was twenty-two, after a long engagement and a virtually platonic relationship that never went beyond somewhat clumsy kissing and cuddling. Doctor Sullivan performed the ceremony, which was an ancient one; he remarked that when a couple were married by such a ceremony, there would be an explosion within their beings if there was a strong link between them. When I asked him if he had seen such an explosion in our case, he avoided answering. I had a sneaking suspicion that there hadn't been one! But I knew it was right for us to be married.

After the ceremony, I invited him and Francesca Keen, the secretary of the Order, to lunch at a restaurant, where chicken and a bottle of wine had been ordered. Francesca was horrified but Doctor Sullivan silenced her protests — I did not know then that he neither ate meat nor drank alcohol. Since he had no wish to embarrass us, he consumed whatever was placed before him. The same was true of smoking: he would put a smoker at ease by having a cigarette without actually inhaling. (Some members of the Theosophical Society said that he could not be a Master because of this. Jesus, presumably, would similarly have been in their bad books by turning water into wine.)

Our spiritual marriage was legalized on 30 December 1939. We had an unremarkable few days honeymoon in a Bournemouth hotel and soon after this, I was called up by the Army.

My interview was with two old colonels who, despite my professional training and experience in catering, were only interested in looking for drivers. Sure enough, a few days later, I received my calling-up papers by mail, ordering me to report to barracks to become a driver in the Middlesex regiment. I did not relish the prospect, but fortuitously the same mail brought a letter commissioning me as an officer in the Catering Branch of the Royal Air Force. (I had previously been turned down as a pilot because I was slightly colour-blind.) Julian Salmon, a director of J. Lyon & Co. and Catering Advisor to the Royal Air Force, had selected me to be part of the first intake of catering officers drawn from various catering firms, in spite of my youth.

Doctor Sullivan gave his blessings on my joining the Royal Air Force (RAF). He advised me that all would be well, providing I didn't volunteer for anything.[3] On what was to be our last meeting, he gave me a copy of his play *Pythagoras* and wrote at the front 'There was a Peter who was great. Follow him and succeed.'

True to his own prediction, Doctor Sullivan passed out of this life on 3 June 1942. Few will know the scope or depth of the contribution he made, but then again he did not seek acclaim; I hope that in its own way this book pays tribute to his memory.

* * *

After initial training in procedures at the RAF School of Cookery at Halton, my first posting was to RAF Stanmore, about 15 miles from London. I lived in the Mess[4] there for some time before Nora and I rented a house and bought

3 In the event I never did. I did not see any fighting whatsoever and never heard a shot fired in anger; the only corpse I saw was hanging in a tree after a plane crash that I witnessed

4 In the British armed forces, a 'mess' is the social and recreational building where meals are served, entertainment and parties take place, and accommodation is provided for single men and visitors; during the Second World War in particular, the mess was a complete home for most serving officers

furniture. I think we were both more excited about being married and setting up our home together than we were by each other. For my part, I was also more absorbed in my Rosicrucian training and my duties and responsibilities in the RAF. After a year at Stanmore I was moved back to Halton, one of the largest stations in the Royal Air Force, in the beautiful countryside of Buckinghamshire, about 30 miles west of London. This huge station had a large number of messes, each with a different menu. There were twenty-six at Halton that competed with one another for diminishing supplies of food and trained personnel.

Julian Salmon, who had been responsible for my fortunate escape from driving army trucks for the Middlesex regiment, was now the Command Catering Officer at Headquarters. I discovered that he had selected me as the most suitable and qualified person to introduce centralized messing to RAF Halton so that one catering officer would be responsible for the whole station, with a standard menu. If successful at Halton, this system would be applied throughout the Command. There was great opposition to Salmon's plan. In peacetime Halton was a very conservative station with long traditions; despite the fact that we were now at war, life went on in the place much as before and the same resistance to change was met at every corner. Strangely, though, the strongest opposition to my appointment came from the Commanding Officer of Halton's RAF School of Cookery.

I learned of this when I came across one of his letters to the Air Officer Commanding. In it he had written 'not one of the young gentlemen who has passed through this School of Cookery would be capable of catering for a Wing (and there were six at Halton), let alone the whole station.' I thought, 'You bastard, I'll prove you wrong.' He was a career officer, popular and well-established in his position; here was I, a young outsider coming in to revolutionize the whole system of catering in the Royal Air Force. It was a tough challenge but I knew that I could and would rise to meet it.

I put my whole heart into the life at the station. Following the precepts of Doctor Sullivan, I applied myself to loving where I was, loving whom I was with, and loving what I was doing. Some people would have seen the posting as a dead end and a dull place, far from the exciting action of the war. Instead, I made the most of every opportunity to develop my personality — physically, emotionally, mentally and socially — as well as learning the many lessons the place had to offer. This helped me to discover in the RAF a wonderful spirit of love, cooperation, dedication and service.

In the first year at Halton I established myself as an athlete, becoming officer in charge of athletics and team captain, since I knew that this was a key to being accepted among the men. I ran competitive races every Saturday and Wednesday, and went swimming, horseback riding and played tennis on most days. I led a full social life, with dances and other activities, at the Officers' Club and in the Officers' Mess, a former Rothschild mansion known as the 'gilded cage' because its interior was covered with gold leaf. I spent time getting to know the commanding officers of the various units, and particularly the officer in charge of Administration, Wing Commander P.K. Wise.

'PK', as he was known, was a strict disciplinarian who ruled with a rod of iron. Many of the men feared him greatly. He was proud of his physical prowess and on one occasion at the swimming pool challenged me to hit him in his rock-hard stomach. Few would have dared to take him up on such a challenge, and I hesitated at first, but after he repeated the challenge I gave him a mighty wallop. He gasped in shock, and after that I think he liked me because he could see I didn't fear him. It proved a useful exercise; from then on, when it came to work, I used PK as a battleship in the background. If I was having difficulty with the commanding officer of a wing or unit over some proposal, I would only have to mention that I would discuss the matter with PK, and they would quickly agree with me.

I also learned how to get my way with him. When he had to approve and sign the first centralized messing menu, which I thought he would no doubt reject, I waited until he had had a good lunch and a few drinks, and then I went to his office. Knowing that in his contrariness he would take the opposite tack, I said to him casually, 'You don't want to sign this, do you, Sir?' 'Bring it here,' he replied gruffly and signed it without a murmur. He did not even look at it. Another encounter, however, did not end so happily. I usually tried to pack in as much activity as possible between finishing work at 5 pm and dinner at 9 pm. In a typical evening I would play a game of tennis, have a swim, cycle 12 miles to the horse stables to ride, and cycle back just in time to bathe and change for dinner. My batman (man servant) would always have my clothes laid out for a quick change, but on this occasion my riding boot stuck and took a long time to remove. I dashed down to the dining room, only to see Mr Baker, the head waiter, close the door on the dot of 9 pm. (Punctuality is a cardinal virtue in the Services.) I pleaded with him to let me in, just this once. He finally relented when I asked to see PK at the head of the table. When I reached PK and explained why I was late, he said, 'Caddy, you want to have it all ways, don't you? Well, in life, you can't.' I told him I was very hungry after all my activities and, if I could have dinner this time, I would remember what he had said in future. 'No,' he replied firmly, so I had to make do with a bar of chocolate for the evening.

The Officers' Mess was always a useful source of information. I loved swimming in the nearby reservoir, in spite of the large notice that it was out of bounds to all RAF personnel, and was surprised one day in the Mess when the Air Officer Commanding told me that he also swam in the reservoir; my surprise came from the fact that he himself had signed the notice declaring it out of bounds. He explained that this was just to cover us legally in case anyone was injured or drowned. I looked upon official notices and orders differently after that.

Often a group of middle-aged officers sat round a fire in the Mess with pints of beer in their hands, gossiping. I knew they criticized me and my activities. When I mentioned this to a wise old officer, who was also the athletic coach, he said, 'Peter, my lad, always remember that there are those who do and those who do not do, but criticize those who do.' It was advice well taken. Since then, if I knew from inner conviction that an action was right, I have always gone ahead regardless of opposition or criticism.

It took my first year at RAF Halton to establish relations with all the key officers, through athletics and social activities, before I attempted to introduce centralized messing. I chose as my assistant an officer who had been in the RAF for about forty years, Flying Officer Charles Rankin. He was very experienced and respected, and he loved my initiative and energy. Together we embodied a combination of experience and youthful enthusiasm, energy and sense of adventure. Charles Rankin was loyal and gave me good advice. With his help I was able to choose an excellent staff and inspire them to work together as a team; in this way all opposition was overcome with love, cooperation, and a great sense of fun. We knew that we were pioneering a catering scheme that would be applied to every station in the RAF.

My social life also flourished at this time. When I had been engaged to Nora, I had told my father that I was going to take dancing lessons. He scoffed at the idea and said I had no sense of rhythm whatsoever: hadn't I been turned out of the choir at school? Lessons, he continued, would be a sheer waste of time and money. His comments made me more determined than ever to master the art, so Nora and I did attend a dancing school. Sometime later, we were invited to attend Father's office ball, where Santos Casani, the most famous ballroom dancer in Britain, was to judge a dancing competition. Nora and I won it! From then on, if anyone said I couldn't do a thing, I often went ahead and did it, whatever the cost or opposition.

I love dancing, and at Halton I was able to attend a dance nearly every night. I had a wonderful time with many girlfriends, one for each activity: tennis, swimming, riding, and walking. None of these relationships was sexual, which I did not feel was appropriate at the time, but they were all warm friendships. One of these girlfriends was a very attractive and vital nurse, Maime, who gave me my first glimpse of real love. What a revelation! For the first time I understood the sentiment of that song, 'It's Love That Makes the World Go Round'. We never consummated the relationship and she was later posted elsewhere, but the experience made me aware of the emptiness at the core of my marriage with Nora.

Married life with Nora had never been very exciting. During my time at Halton, I rented us accommodation at a nearby farm; but Nora was not happy there and went back to live with her mother in a flat in Ealing. I would return at weekends on Saturday evening, having run a five- or ten-mile cross-country race, after which I felt more tired than playful. On Sunday we would have breakfast in bed and then go to a classical music concert at the Albert Hall in the afternoon. I then went back to Halton in the evening. We also attended chapter meetings in London and made frequent visits to the headquarters of the Rosicrucian Order in Christchurch. During this period our first child, Michael, was born, on 12 May 1942, at Fulham Chase Nursing Home, but even this happy arrival failed to bring Nora and me together in a way in which we both felt fulfilled.

Our geographical separation —me at Halton, Nora by her choice back in London —was not the root of the problem. A wise Frenchman once wrote that 'absence is to love what wind is to fire. It extinguishes the small, and inflames the great.' While at Halton I met an extraordinary officer, Walter Bullock, also known as the 'mystery man'. He had a massive head with a high forehead and penetrating eyes, and he spoke with a mid-European accent. Among his astonishing talents was an apparent ability to look into time, both past and future, and on one occasion he read my palm. He told me that my marriage was not a true one, it lacked that fire, and that when I reached the age of twenty-nine, I would meet someone with whom I would have a real marriage on all levels. This intelligence rather shattered me at the time, but in my heart of hearts, I knew that there was substance to what he said.

Looking back on the period of my life at Halton, I can now see that I was able to express myself fully there for the first time in my life. In addition to developing my physical body by taking part in a wide variety of sports, my will was also strengthened by running long-distance races of over 10 miles every Saturday and races of 1 mile or 3 miles during the week. So often in a cross-country race, when one goes flat out for the first 100 yards and then continues for the next 200 yards, then 400 yards, then 1/2 mile, 1 mile, 3 miles, continuing flat out the whole time, the body cries out to stop. It cannot go further than the next step. But the will tells it to go on just to the next tree, and when one gets there, the will again tells the body that it can make it to the next fence, and so on, until the course has been completed. For reasons I was yet to discern, this honing of the will seemed to me to be vitally important.

I was also very active at Halton in educational and cultural activities. For example, I ran a musical circle with weekly live or gramophone concerts. My social life became so hectic and so difficult to fit in with all my athletic pursuits that I hit upon the idea of forming an entertainments committee to coordinate the various activities- social, educational and sporting —with me as its chairman; only thus could these activities be so arranged that I could attend them all! I had a huge 'What's On' notice-board outlining the activities of the week, under the headings of 'Sports', 'Education' and 'Social', placed where five roads met in the centre of the base. (That board was still there nearly forty years later, in the early 80s, when I was travelling across England and invited to spend the night in the Officers' Mess at Halton. I also discovered just how strong traditions are in the Royal Air Force: nothing had changed but the people. The furniture, pictures, customs and atmosphere were all the same. I sat in my usual armchair, read my favourite magazine, and had the usual breakfast with a morning newspaper on a stand in front of me — and not a word was spoken during the meal.)

My childhood memories were mainly of weeding and dull school years, and my apprenticeship had been very hard work with long hours. Here at RAF Halton I was able to enjoy life to the full. I proved to my superiors that centralized messing *did* work; I proved to my fellows and subordinates what could be achieved through team spirit, cooperation, determination and having fun. The station provided all the facilities for developing my personality on every level but most importantly, it helped me prove myself to myself. I experienced the joy of really understanding my spiritual lessons and learning how to apply them in my daily life.

Chapter 3

Passage to India

I create every mental condition, and that condition reflects in my environment. Therefore, I create my life

AFTER THREE AND A HALF YEARS at Halton, I was posted to India to an RAF station at Cawnpore in the United Provinces (now Kanpur in Uttar Pradesh). This new maintenance base for the war in the Far East was the largest in the world and I was to be responsible for catering for about 10,000 personnel. Most people dreaded being posted to India, but I was delighted. I had always had a passion for mountains and climbing, and since early boyhood had longed to follow in the footsteps of such Himalayan explorers as Frank Smythe, Eric Shipton and Sir Francis Younghusband, the founder of the World Congress of Faiths. Along with my rucksack and all my climbing equipment, I took with me the intention to enjoy life to the full in India. I also hoped to visit Tibet, the mysterious land of the lamas.

We sailed from Liverpool on a large troop ship, the *Dominion Monarch*, on 16 October 1943. I looked forward to some leisurely reading while on board, something for which the press of my other duties and interests had left me little time. I sat on deck with *A Passage to India* by E.M. Forster. Halfway through the book I thought, 'What a damned fool I am! Here am I, *going* on a passage to India, and I'm reading about somebody else's experiences.' So I chucked the book away into the sea and from then on focussed on personal and not vicarious experiences.

Above all I was determined to enjoy myself. Dr Sullivan had taught me that the spiritual path did not necessarily demand renunciation or guilt about the acceptance of life's pleasures; *balance in all things* might have been his catchphrase. I was twenty-six and my personality was still developing. I felt I still had a lot of catching up to do after the all-work-and-no-play years of my apprenticeship with Lyons; my time at RAF Halton had whetted my appetite for the good life. In order to make the most of the voyage, I volunteered to become the ship's Entertainment Officer and enjoyed close contact with Geraldo, the famous dance band leader of the time, and with his celebrated orchestra. I shared a cabin with Brian Salmon, of the Salmon family who were directors of J. Lyons & Co., the catering firm with whom I had trained. Brian was a man of my own age, Jewish, and in many ways quite the opposite of me in personality: he disdained sport of any kind, enjoyed soft living, was obviously wealthy, shunned exercise and fresh air, and had an extremely sharp intellect. Brian would never stand if he could sit, and never sit if he could lie down. Thus we complemented each other and quickly became firm friends.

Several miles out of sea from Bombay we smelled the distinctive, spice-filled stench of the city, and upon disembarkation on 18 November 1943, we eagerly set out to explore it. After enduring years of food rationing and black-outs in England, Brian and I enjoyed the abundance of a city where food was plentiful and lights blazed into the night. Our first stop was tea on the lawn of the British Officers' Club, where we were served with large plates of delicious cakes. Mine included a large, fresh cream cake. Cream! I had not seen fresh whipped cream for about four years, so I carefully pushed it to the side of the plate to leave it until last, in order to work myself up to enjoying it. Just as I was admiring the cake, a kite hawk suddenly swept down and snatched it up. I was aghast. Ever since, I have always made a point of consuming the best that is set before me first.

We later had dinner at the famous Taj Mahal Hotel and then roamed the streets, growing heady on the rich, strange sights and sounds and smells of India. We toured (but did not partake of!) the red-light district. Throughout Bombay the extraordinary contrasts between rich and poor, squalor and luxury, holiness and beastliness, clamour and quietude were all woven into a single tapestry, of which the British Raj, which still ruled this sprawling, teeming sub-continent, was only another thread. We were thrilled to be there.

On 27 November 1943, I went to Cawnpore, and Brian to Group Headquarters in Agra, where although of equal rank he became my superior; any requests for equipment or supplies that I had would go to his desk. Our friendship therefore stood me in good stead, and with his acute mind Brian was a master at finding subtle ways of getting things done. He would come down to visit me and ask, 'Well, Peter, what do you need?' and when I had told him, he would write a letter, get the Station Commander at Cawnpore to sign it, and send it on to Group Headquarters — which of course meant that it was waiting on his desk when he got back. Brian would then approve it.

On one occasion I met him off the aircraft and he said, 'Oh, Peter, it's hot today. Let's just go and lie on our beds.' As we rested from the heat, I raved on innocently about a marvellously competent warrant officer under my command, describing him in glowing terms. When, a few weeks later, the officer was posted to be in charge of a School of Cookery in Southern India, I knew that Brian Salmon was behind the move. 'Right,' I thought, 'I'll fix you'. There was a sergeant whom I'd been trying to get rid of for some time without success; his work really was terrible. So the next time Brian came and played his trick of suggesting we go and rest on our beds, I enthused about this wonderful sergeant, saying how efficient and capable he was. Sure enough, the sergeant soon received a new posting. The next time I saw Brian, I had gone to meet him at the airport but he walked right past me without looking me in the eye and said, in passing, 'You bastard'. I think we understood each other, and we remained good friends.

I was absolutely delighted to be in India. I enjoyed my work and entered fully into the life of the British Club, with the swimming, dancing and parties. I formed a Rover Scout crew and each leave-period took them trekking and climbing in the Himalayas. The first trek was from 6 to 21 May 1944, to the Pindari Glacier, a place sacred to the Indians. The Station Commander, Group Captain Glaisher, read my printed account of this trek and was so impressed that he wanted to go on the next one. He was aged fifty-two, and had been in the Royal Air Force for thirty-five years; there were 10,000 men under his command. He insisted on coming; so I said to him, 'Well, sir, you know you'll have to take your orders from me, and just be one of the boys, having to peel potatoes and so on.' He agreed.

Each officer had a personal servant — a 'bearer'. Mine was a Pathan by the name of Muktha, who was about 6ft. 2in., and came from a fierce warrior tribe in the North West Frontier Province. He accompanied me on all my treks. Muktha always insisted that I was well-dressed and that I shave every morning — he would wake me up with a cup of tea and a mug of hot water for shaving, and watch over me to ensure that I did so — because his standing depended upon how well I was turned out. He wanted to make sure that I not only looked like a Sahib but *behaved* like a Sahib; he felt that it was his responsibility to keep me straight. Muktha once said to me, 'Sahib spends too much at Club'. 'What do you mean?' I demanded. Apparently he knew exactly how much money I had spent at the Club from his conversations with the servants; he was implying that if I spent less there, then he could be paid more.

Muktha could neither read nor write, and I have noticed that many people in this position compensate by developing a certain quick-wittedness. Muktha was no exception, but he had met his match in me. Ordinarily, many Muslim Pathans felt that it was their duty to steal from their masters. On our treks in the Himalayas, however, I found a solution. I made Muktha responsible for *all* the money, on his honour — which forbade him to steal any of it.

During the trek that Group Captain Glaisher joined, in October 1944, I took our party to the Valley of the Flowers, a hidden place in the foothills of the Himalayas. Ours was the first Western expedition there since it had been discovered by Frank Smythe, and despite it being the wrong season to enjoy the full glory of the flowers in bloom, we found the panorama, the sweep of the meadows to the snow-capped mountains behind, breathtaking.

On the way back, I read a little book, *The Call of Badrinath.* Badrinath is one of the four most holy places of pilgrimage in India; it is situated a little further north of the Valley of the Flowers. The book said that if you hadn't met the Master of Badrinath, then you hadn't really 'been' to Badrinath. The Himalayan climbers Eric Shipton, Spencer Chapman and Bill Tillman had each devoted a chapter in their books to him. They described meeting a holy man sitting in a loincloth at over 18,000 feet, meditating with snow all around him but remarkably well-informed about world affairs. I believed that his information came through out-of-body experiences, in which his mind was able to detach itself from his physical location and observe events firsthand elsewhere; but if those explorers were aware of this ability, they had never said so in print. I was fired by the possibility. Now that we were headed home, I felt a twinge of regret that I'd come all this way and not met this holy man.

On our return from the Valley of the Flowers our route happened to join the pilgrimage track to Badrinath. I was late in arriving at the guest bungalow, as I had been purchasing a goat for the coolies' meal. When I arrived the Station Commander said that there was a 'wonderful old Indian gentleman' who was also staying there, with a large retinue of servants; in fact, he was doing some shopping for us at the bazaar. I thought this strange at the time, because Group Captain Glaisher didn't get along with Indians at all and usually called them 'wogs'. This gentleman's Indian servant, who was immaculately dressed, served us Brooke Bond tea and Peek Freen biscuits, which was also odd — such Western comestibles were extremely rare in that part of the world. I thought that this must be an exceptional Indian.

Indeed he was. When he returned from the bazaar, he brought a powerful presence to the room. He had long white hair with a flowing beard beneath the most Christ-like face of anybody I'd ever met; I later learned that he was ninety-two years old. What surprised me more was that in the course of conversation he seemed to know the Bible much more thoroughly than I did, had great knowledge of other religions, and was up-to-date with all the foreign news.

Someone passed by with a camera, and when he asked them please not to take his photograph, I knew immediately who he was. 'You are Master Ram Sareek Singh,' I said, 'The Master of Badrinath.' Whenever Shipton or the others had met him, he had asked *them* not to photograph him, but each had surreptitiously taken a photo anyway. As a result, either the camera had broken, the plate didn't turn out, or something else had happened so that no picture of him resulted. He now smiled at me and said yes, he was Ram Sareek Singh. I mentioned having read about him in various books; to which he replied, 'Ah, my friend Chapman' or 'Yes, I remember Shipton'. When I asked him why he didn't want his picture taken, he replied that if people took his photograph they would put it up and worship him instead of God.

He had all the attributes of a great soul, in particular a wonderful sense of humour and true humility. Muktha was completely puzzled by the fact that Ram Sareek Singh was so interested in sampling our food. According to the people of India, a holy man is very strict about such things, but the Master of Badrinath was above such concerns and could eat what he wished. This holy man lived and breathed his philosophy. If he spoke of joy, then lightness and laughter would pour forth from his being. The great lesson that Ram Sareek Singh taught me was that the spiritual life need not be a pious, withdrawn, miserable existence; it is not necessary to wear sackcloth and ashes to realize God. God is life in *all* its aspects, including the abundance that is there to be used and enjoyed.

After this trek the Station Commander remarked that it was the finest holiday that he had ever had, being away from telephones and responsibilities. Some holiday! In spite of his age and lack of climbing experience, he had kept up with the best of us; despite his senior rank, he'd held true to his undertaking to be just 'one of the boys'. For me, the highlight of the trip had been my meeting with the Master of Badrinath. The suspicion was dawning on me that it was not by chance that so many of the places I visited or was drawn to in India, on this and subsequent treks, also turned out to be places of spiritual power, even if I did not know it at the time — Badrinath, for example, or the Amarnath Cave in Kashmir, where I found a constant line of pilgrims queuing up to stand in awe of a huge ice *lingam*, or phallus of the god Shiva, formed from water dripping from the cave's roof. On looking back, I see how important visiting these places was for my future work.

Meanwhile I was learning that one of the best ways of living life to the full was to maintain its contrasts. I'd have a wonderful time climbing and walking in arduous conditions in the Himalayas, and then thoroughly enjoy the luxuries of the Officer's Club and Mess on my return to civilization. I even managed to persuade the Station Commander to grant me a personal motor cycle that enabled me to get around to the various messes and kitchens on the base. It did wonders for my social life but caused a certain amount of jealousy, as I was the only officer to have one. Everyone else was marooned in the Mess with no other transport beyond the station buses, which only ran during work hours. Although I was diligent in my duties, it was sometimes difficult to remember that the War was going on; there was little time to think about it, what with working and playing so hard. Looking back over my appointment diaries for those years, I found only three entries, one in each year, that said 'early to bed'.

On 1 January 1945, after a year at Cawnpore, I was appointed the Command Catering Officer for the Bengal–Burma Front, with the rank of Squadron Leader. This was the biggest front during the War, and I was in charge of meeting the catering needs of nearly one million personnel — quite a responsibility. Doctor Sullivan's teaching that no challenge was too great, provided one's attitude was correct, once again proved itself to me. I saw no reason for making a big deal of it or suffering unduly. Our Headquarters were in Calcutta, where the weather was very hot and steamy; there was a swimming pool outside my office, so I had an extension put on the telephone and often conducted my business floating in the water.

Later in 1945 our Headquarters were moved to Rangoon, the capital of Burma, shortly after the city had been recaptured from the Japanese. I took my three junior officers with me. One of them, Bill Beckett, a well-trained, clever and efficient young officer, just couldn't understand how I seemed to sail through everything and enjoy what was either tremendous luck or a charmed life. I wondered, too, at the time; but now I believe that the secret of my success lay in the training I had received from Doctor Sullivan. I was being tested on it and given opportunities to put it into daily practice. One day, for example, in the Mess at Rangoon, shortly after our Headquarters had moved there, Bill and I were gazing out of the window. He looked down at the scene in front of him and said, 'Look at this bloody country, with all the dirt, the shit, the stink, the flies, the disease, the squalor. How I hate it! I can't wait to get back home.' All he could see was negative, the desolation and poverty made worse by the recent fighting. I turned to him and said, 'Yes, Bill, but look up'. There before us was one of the wonders of the world, the Shwedagon Pagoda, all covered in gold leaf that dazzled against a glorious sunset. Burma was noted for having some of the finest sunsets in the world. We were living in different worlds. *By thinking you direct your life into expression*, Doctor Sullivan had taught. *That which a man believes to be, moulds his destiny.*

On another occasion, my officers and I decided to go away for a holiday weekend to Puri, a small city and holy place of pilgrimage about 350 miles away on the Bay of Bengal. We planned to meet in the bar of a hotel in the evening. I travelled down by train with Muktha, my bearer, and had a wonderful journey. I lay on my bedroll, drinking tea that Muktha brought me at every station, and watched the colourful panorama pass by the window: green fields, young wheat, yellow mustard, rustic dwellings and attractive wells, all set off against a beautiful sky that gave way to sunset. When we stopped at a station I was captivated by the kaleidoscopic scene, full of interest and excitement — crowds of different races, pedlars, gurus with their chelas[1], fakirs with huge snakes around their necks, vendors selling sweetmeats, brahmins, beggars, betel-nut sellers — the whole sub-continent, it seemed, represented in a single setting. I was entranced by the whole journey.

When we met at the hotel in Puri, I asked my friend Bill what kind of trip he'd had. 'A bloody awful one,' he replied. 'There was so much rattling and yelling, the noise was unbearable; the flies were awful, the people smelt almost as badly as the shit — ' he went on and on about it.

[1] Literally meaning 'slave' or 'servant' in Hindi, chela is the word used for a novice or pupil under a spiritual teacher

I then discovered that we had both travelled on the same train. The fascinating sights that were obvious to me had been completely missed by Bill. *Look for the positive, and that is what you will attract to you; see only the negative and that is what you will get.*

Chapter 4

On Top of the World

Truth is mighty, and it prevails. All you have to do is treat it as you do the sunshine — let it shine.

WHEN HOSTILITIES with Japan ceased in 1945, it became apparent that I had only a few more months in the Far East in which to realize several ambitions. These were to visit Kashmir, take a trek along the western ridge of Sikkim to Phalut to see the sunrise on Mt Everest and Kanchenjunga, and to visit Tibet. In August, therefore, I made plans for a single journey in which I could fulfil all three ambitions — a seeming impossibility as I had only three weeks leave.

A simple ruse suggested itself. Now that the War was over, I had observed how officers and men were going to Calcutta to spend their accumulated leave-periods, only to find that they were then unable to get back to Burma on time because of the shortage of ships and planes. They were usually stuck in Calcutta for two or three weeks waiting for transport; but the War had been won and nobody seemed to miss them or care very much. I therefore could have two or three weeks up my sleeve if it were assumed that I, too, were waiting in Calcutta.

The expedition involved intricate travel arrangements, but I was soon on my way by air to Calcutta, on to Delhi, from there by train to Rawalpindi, and then by bus to Srinagar in Kashmir. I spent time on a houseboat on the Dahl Lake in the Vale of Kashmir, one of the most beautiful lakes in the world. I then went up to the Thajwas Valley — Valley of the Glaciers — to an Air Crew Mountaineering Leave Centre where crewmen could go to relax and get fit in the healing atmosphere of the mountains. Here I spent three weeks climbing mountains and glaciers and crossed the Loji La Pass for an excursion into Tibet.

I persuaded the Commanding Officer of the Centre to allow one of the instructors, Leslie Levy, to travel with me across India and then trek into Sikkim, and on to Tibet. In August, I had obtained the necessary permit to enter Sikkim and Tibet from the Political Officer in Sikkim. This could only be granted after a satisfactory medical examination, as the passes along the way were 14,000 feet above sea level. Rest bungalows and train and bus berths had to be reserved, provisions bought, arrangements made for coolies, equipment purchased, maps and guide books obtained and information accumulated. It was essential that careful and adequate preparations be made if the trip was to be successful.

Early in October 1945 Leslie and I set out on our five-day journey from Kashmir to Darjeeling, via Calcutta and Siliguri by rail. An advantage of rail travel in India is the opportunity it provides to meet people that one would not normally spend time with. One of our fellow travellers was an Indian industrialist, Mr Thakar Das, who had spent a great deal of time in England and spoke English well. We had some very stimulating talks. He made the interesting observation that Indians, suffering as they were from an acute inferiority complex, would forgive the British everything if only they would cease adopting a superior attitude and treat the Indians as equals.

From Siliguri we took the bus to Darjeeling, climbing higher and higher into the clear air of the hills. We had left behind the mosquitoes, the feeling of inertia and the damp, prickly heat of the vast plains of Bengal, which we occasionally glimpsed through a gap in the dense forest of bamboo and moss-festooned trees; these plains now appeared soft and indistinct through the damp atmosphere.

Darjeeling itself is completely walled off from the plains, clinging to the summit and sides of a spur which juts out from the northern face of an outer range of mountains. On the further side of the Rangest River rise other ranges, in gigantic, forest-clad tiers, each bathed in a hue of deeper and deeper purple, forming a vast amphitheatre which surrounds the little state of Sikkim, then an independent country ruled by a Tibetan maharaja.

Sikkim is less than half the size of Wales and lies north of Darjeeling, on the border of Bengal, south of Tibet, and between Bhutan on the east and Nepal on the west. Though small, Sikkim is the most mountainous country in the world. In a few hours, it is possible to ascend from tropical bamboos and jungle to alpine gentians. Peaks rise from 700 to 28,000 feet in a tumult of ranges, with the higher altitudes being nothing but snow and ice and rock.

The lower levels are a mass of tropical jungle ridges and precipitous gorges. Within its narrow boundaries is situated the most magnificent range of snow-clad mountains in the world, the Kanchenjunga Group, which reveals itself in varying moods according to the time of day and season.

Travel in Sikkim and along the trade route to Lhasa, the capital of Tibet, was made remarkably pleasant for us by good paths and well-furnished rest houses, called dak bungalows, set at easy stages along the way. They were invariably situated in well-chosen surroundings with superb views and furnished with beds, mattresses, carpets, curtains, chairs, tables, china, glassware, etc. Each bungalow was looked after by a *chowkidar*, or watchman, who usually provided firewood, milk and eggs, for a very small charge. Our first trek was along the western ridge of Sikkim. We started out with a Sirdar guide, five Sherpa coolies and a Tibetan woman.

Women coolies were quite common and, besides carrying the same loads as the men, were cheery and helped to keep the company in good spirits. All were well-equipped with nailed boots, warm clothing and blankets. The general population of Tibetan women dress in thick, long, navy-blue cloaks and red ornamental snow boots; they wear decorated fur-lined hats with ear flaps. The dark-eyed, well-developed Tibetan women spend several hours daily at their toilet and are quite attractive. Their appearance is not solely decorative however, as they preside over the stalls in the bazaars and virtually run the businesses. Since there are many more Tibetan men than women, and marriages are arranged, brothers are customarily wed to a man's wife, at yearly intervals. Tibetans love travelling, so it is usually arranged that only one brother–husband is at home at a time.

On our way up the Sandakphu trail, we could see the entire mountain range stretching for miles in an unbroken chain of snow-clad heights, dominated by Kanchenjunga and the saddle formed by the twin peaks of Mt Kabin. Kanchenjunga, at 28,156 feet, looked so still and serene that it was difficult to believe that a fierce wind was probably shrieking about its summit and avalanches were crashing down its steep sides. These are common to Kanchenjunga, and because of them it has been said that the mountain will never be climbed to the top.

After tea, we reached a vantage point where we were held spellbound by the most beautiful sunset I have ever seen. It was difficult to take in all the wonderful effects at once: the indescribable beauty of the drifting clouds constantly changing shape and colour in the west; the streaming light striking the snowy mountains, exaggerating every protruding spur and transforming the pure white snow into shades deepening from yellow to gold, to orange, to rose, and finally to red. From the east, darkness spread over the still plains, 10,000 feet below. Clouds gathered beneath us, filling the valleys with a sea of cotton wool. Slanting shafts of light were moving upwards, while range after range took on the purple hues of night, until only the summit of Kanchenjunga remained on fire. As the last rays left the highest peak, all was in darkness except for a pale green glow in the west. The stars were already out when we retraced our footsteps, feeling overawed and humbled by the glorious spectacle that we had just seen. Across an abyss, far away to the southeast, we could see the lights of Darjeeling, small luminous stars gleaming upon a background of black velvet.

It took two days to walk along the ridge, through Sandakphu, to Phalut. Our plan was to spend the night there and watch the sun rise over Mt Everest the following morning. On our way through a forest of pines, we came upon the bonzo, a species of wild dog. We were told that they hunt in large packs, moving with amazing swiftness to attack sheep, goats and cows in a disgusting manner: while some engage their prey in front, others attack from the rear, biting the backside of the unfortunate beast and disembowelling it with their paws. Animals soon learn to defend themselves by protecting their rear in front of a rock or tree.

Phalut means'the denuded peak', and so it is. Today people come from all parts of the world to Phalut for the view it affords of 'the kingdom of snows'; in 1945 there was no easy road to this extreme northwestern point of the then British boundary over the Singulela Range, and I felt privileged to be there. We arose very early in the morning and found our position in time to see just the tip of a mountain away in the distance, golden against an inky black sky, which gradually got lighter. Suddenly the whole helmet-shaped dome of Everest appeared, standing like a sentinel between the two closed lands of Nepal and Tibet. As the sun rose, the mighty peak changed in colour from the palest amber to the richest gold, and then a vivid crimson as the first rays of sun lit up the sky. Gradually the whole magnificent range came into view, a continuous chain of snow-topped mountains, clear against the blue sky. The plains lay sleeping beneath a wonderful quilt of billowy white clouds. Soon, however, Everest became shrouded in clouds, as if modesty prevented her beauty from being gazed upon overlong. There cannot be many places on earth that afford such a splendid sight as this jagged line of snows that skirt the vast tableland of Tibet.

Leslie and I set out with our coolies to cross Sikkim on foot, which took several days. Along this path we had our first encounter with leeches, the worst pest in the country. They are evil-looking things, one or two inches long and so thin that they can even squeeze through the eyelets on boots. They soon become bloated when feeding on blood. Leeches must never be pulled off, as the head remains embedded in the skin and can turn septic; the best way to remove them is to touch them with a lighted cigarette. Bleeding may go on for several hours, caused, I am told, by a liquid which the leech injects into the skin to prevent the blood from clotting so it will flow more easily. They prevented us from having a peaceful lunch by closing in on us as soon as we sat down — we had to consume our meals on the march. Leeches move with considerable speed, using their heads and tails, continuously reaching out to full length and then bringing up their tail to form a loop. It was an awful sight to see one standing on end, blindly feeling for my blood supply. On one occasion I went off the path to go to the toilet and squatted. To my horror, I spied a black mass of dozens of leeches moving towards me. These revolting creatures surrounded me and closed in on all sides. I hurriedly pulled up my trousers and beat a hasty retreat, knocking off the advance group that had begun climbing up my boots. Leeches even perch on the branches above paths and tracks to drop on unsuspecting people and animals passing by. Most of the natives we met had bleeding bites all over their bare legs, but did not seem to worry about them; our coolies were well protected with good boots and puttees[1].

Later the path took us through deep glades, with purple orchids hanging from dark trunks, and on past banks of moss and fern. All was damp and eerie, a rich tangle of leafage and a mass of trees engaged, it seemed to me, in a struggle for existence among so many species. When the barrier of the Himalayas was reached we climbed the 'Sikkim Stairs', where the mule track rises 10,000 feet in 9 miles between Rongli and Gnatong. The scenery became grander with every mile and the views were magnificent — the plains could be seen far in the distance.

To climb the 'Stairs', we began by trekking through the rhododendron zone, a forest of gnarled and twisted trunks not unlike a scene from Dante's *Inferno*. Then we joined the main trade route into Tibet and passed several mule trains carrying huge bundles of wool. The ponies were well-groomed and beautifully harnessed, with large red plumes on their heads and balls of

1 Strip of cloth wound round the leg from ankle to knee

red wool hanging from their necks. Bells also hung from their necks, making attractive sounds when the train was on the move. The muleteers were well-equipped, wearing fur-lined hats with ear-flaps, first-class fur-trimmed glare glasses, long thick woollen cloaks and calf-high felt and leather snow boots, all beautifully decorated.

Just before entering the village of Lingtu at the end of the 'Stairs', we had a look at the cemetery in which casualties of the 1902 British expedition of Younghusband are buried. It was noted that several died crossing the Jelup-La Pass, which still lay ahead of us. We pressed on and continued to climb through different climates and zones: sub-tropical, Mediterranean, deciduous, pine, scrub, moss and lichen to snow and ice. Finally we reached the summit of the Jelup-La Pass at 14,390 feet, from where we could see range after range of the mountains that form 'the roof of the world'. The most arresting feature of the view was the glittering peak of Chomolhari, at 23,390 feet, reputed to be the most beautiful mountain in the world. It appeared to rise in majestic isolation from the hard outlined stretch of mountains on the horizon. How I longed to be able to climb it!

A high, bitter wind starts to sweep across the plateau at 11.30 each morning and reduces the temperature to well below zero. In order to avoid this hardship, it was essential to start the journey by 4am. We had grown beards for protection and now wore every garment in our possession. There was no washing, showering or dressing, as water on the skin at those altitudes causes severe chapping and blistering; even breathing was difficult, and all movement laboriously slow. This was the toughest test of endurance that I had faced in my life, yet I recalled my cross-country racing experience and the trick of using the will to urge the body forward 'just to the next stage' — and then the next stage after that. It served me well here on the roof of the world.

At that altitude the sky has a black velvet appearance similar to the one in photographs taken by astronauts in deep space. After crossing Jelup-La we began our descent into the Chumbi Valley. More mule trains passed, and many interesting Tibetan characters: coolies, lamas, merchants and others. The path descended back through pine and later rhododendron forests; the leaves were still on the trees in all their autumn glory, and the ground was snow-covered, except for a few patches that had been melted by the sun and from which a delightful aromatic fragrance perfumed the air. Lower down, there were grassy clearings similar to Swiss Alpine meadows, where huge shaggy yaks grazed peacefully. We continued to descend through woods of pine, oak and walnut, and then over slopes covered with azaleas, berberis, clematis, and spirea. Large bushes of wild roses, covered with red rose hips, grew beside the river.

On some days we experienced heavy rain, blotting out the view. Occasionally, for a few brief moments, bright sunlight filtered through a fretwork of rich green foliage, lighting up splashes of colour where flowers were growing on the slopes of moss-covered banks. In the valleys, the air would be full of flying insects, dragonflies with bright red and blue bodies, beetles, flies and midges, and thousands of multi-coloured butterflies which came to life and flashed like living jewels from flower to flower under the stimulus of the sun. Everything would then dry up quickly and clouds of steam could be seen rising from the southern sides of houses, from the path and the rocks. This would be the time to take off our soaking clothes and hang them out to dry.

Besides the natural beauty of the valleys, there was much of interest. Tibet had been effectively shut off from the world by high mountains for centuries, and one did indeed notice a remarkable change as soon as the frontier was crossed: in the people, their clothes and houses, in the flora and fauna, and in the climate. The people were charming; they greeted us with smiling faces and frank curiosity. They asked where we came from and where we were going. Most of the men carried decorated swords or daggers, and all had a charm or amulet contained in a beautifully carved box of silver or copper. Even in this 'Forbidden Land', the children cheerfully begged, demanding their baksheesh!

En route we visited several monasteries. The word denoting a monastery is *gompa*, meaning a solitary place. A true *gompa* consists of a colony of lamas living round a collection of buildings and apart from the world. The *gompas* are often in lovely settings and the buildings conform to a standard design. The main building consists of a hall and vestibule, or house of prayer, which gives access to the main hall. Acting as guardians of the doorway, the Four Heavenly Kings of the Quarters are painted on the vestibule walls. The main square chamber consists of a nave and two aisles, and the walls and ceilings are covered with frescoes. These paintings are done in brilliant hues and depict events in the life of Buddha. The lamas sit on low stools on each side of the centre aisle, and near the altar are raised seats for the spiritual and the temporal heads of the monastery; the latter lead the service and the singing. The altar is hung with gold and silver cloth and crowned by three figures: Buddha in the centre, Guru Rimpoche, the founder of Lamaism, and Cheresi, the God of Mercy and the Patron of Tibet. Candles light the altar and it contains seven dishes of holy water, a censor, and various items for rituals. There are also musical instruments, such as horns, trumpets, cymbals and drums.

One-sixth of the Tibetan population were lamas, because it was customary for one son from every household to enter a monastery. We visited the famous monastery of Tashiding, standing in splendid isolation upon the summit of a precipitous and densely wooded ridge at the junction of two rivers. At its school for novitiates (boys aged about eight), I noticed a large whip above the door and asked what it was for. I was told that the pupils are tested periodically by a board of examiners, and if any fail the teacher is whipped, not the pupils! I felt that this practice might be put to good use in our Western schools. I was struck by the marvellous sense of joy and curiosity with which the novitiates crowded around us.

Our destination was Yatung, where a British trade agent was stationed with a guard of twenty-five Indian troops. We reached our rest bungalow there in time for tea with freshly toasted Tibetan scones. The bungalow was delightfully furnished with wall hangings depicting various scenes on the way to Lhasa, and was surrounded by a beautiful garden of flowering chrysanthemums and dahlias. It looked down into the valley, over the drifting smoke and fluttering prayer flags above the grey shingled roofs of the village, which appeared to be very prosperous, with trim, stone-walled fields, crops of potatoes and turnips, clusters of grey wooden houses like Swiss chalets, and wheat threshing in progress everywhere.

We visited another monastery called Donkar, where we saw several red-robed lamas engaged in weaving and woodcarving in the courtyard. One came forward to greet us, and I handed him our letter of introduction from the head clerk at Yatung. We were taken to a room next to the kitchen and invited to be seated on a richly carpeted couch. Set before us were three cups of the most delicate china, beautifully painted, and set on ornamented stands of silver. A bowl of puffed rice, apples, guavas, savoury pastries, and sweets moulded in the shape of fish were put before us. We had a look around the kitchen and ration stores, which were surprisingly well-equipped with urns, huge teapots, saucepans and ladles. Two gigantic pots, in which food for the poor was being prepared, were on a huge brick stove. I was impressed with the obviously high standard of culinary art.

Upstairs was the library, containing hundreds of old books, carefully preserved, each in its separate compartment behind glass doors. There were also a number of ancient printing blocks. Round the edge of the floor were thick woollen mats on which the lamas sat when reading, eating or meditating. Each lama had his own place, in front of which was his single wooden eating bowl. Folded on top of each mat was a heavy woollen cape or overcoat, and cap. I thought that it must be terribly cold at 13,000 feet in the winter, with little or no heating. About 150 lamas lived in this monastery, the largest in the district. It was almost entirely self-supporting, owning its own estate and cattle. The present Head Lama, a boy of eight, believed to be the reincarnation of the previous Head Lama, was in Lhasa; we were allowed to see his priceless robes of gold and silver Chinese brocade.

I was greatly impressed by the spirit of happiness, contentment and friendliness among these men who had devoted their whole lives to the service of religion and to religiously inspired art. The lamas were always ready for a joke, and for some reason found a great deal of amusement in our ice-axes. We were about to depart when a swarm of young probationers, whose ages varied from seven to ten, came rushing out of school and gathered round us, asking to have their photos taken. They were like a crowd of high-spirited, rosy-cheeked youngsters at home, except for their unwashed bodies and close-cropped hair. They usually came from large families and entered the monastery at the age of seven or eight, as soon as they were old enough to look after themselves.

I set down these observations in such detail because this way of life, unchanged by centuries, was thrown into turmoil by the subsequent Chinese invasion of Tibet. Since the power of the country was centered in its lamaseries, these were the invader's first target. I do not know, but doubt, that such a way of life still exists.

As Leslie and I retraced our steps and climbed back down the 'Sikkim Stairs' to India, I felt triumphant; I had been able to fulfil, in one trip, my ambitions of going to Kashmir, seeing the sunrise on Mt Everest and going to Tibet. The latter had particularly caught my imagination. I was determined to return — and to go further next time.

Back at Headquarters in Rangoon, I was glad to find that I'd got away with my long absence of five weeks. To establish an alibi, I had sent a telegram from Ladakh, Western Tibet: 'Regret return delayed. Snowbound in Tibet'. I believe now that there was a sneaking regard for such audacity.

From the roof of the world I came down to earth with a bump. Apparently the Commander-in-Chief himself had kept asking for me and had been put off with various excuses. We faced a major catering problem. There had been a mutiny in the ranks of the Army over food. To forestall similar developments in the Royal Air Force, the Commander-in-Chief wanted me to tour Burma and address all the RAF personnel throughout the country to explain the food situation to them.

I was called before my superior officer, the Air Vice-Marshal in charge of Administration, a man called Satterly, who explained to me the nub of the problem: there was no fresh meat to be had. Meanwhile the men were being issued with various soya products, like soya sausages, soya loaf, etc.; a scientist in England had discovered that the soya bean produced a very high amount of protein. When these were served to the army men, however, they mutinied.

This problem was not unfamiliar to me. Whilst at RAF Cawnpore, I had found a solution by having delicacies, such as ham and tomatoes, served on the men's plates. Then, in the centre of both of the two dining rooms, which each served about 1,500 men, I had a huge buffet prepared by my finest cooks, with grated carrot, shredded cabbage, beetroot and the various soya products. This was called the *baksheesh*, or free table. I asked the Station Commander to visit these airmen's dining rooms in turn. He then helped himself to a huge plateful of the buffet, and in a loud voice he pronounced that the food in the Airmen's Mess was much better than in the Officers'. The airmen, who didn't want to be done out of what they felt was their right, tucked in with relish — but if it had been served to them on their plates, they would have said, 'We ain't rabbits, giving us cabbage and raw carrots and soya'. So I had learned that if you allow people to do something of their free will, they feel that they have a choice, but when it is forced upon them they are likely to revolt — as had now occurred in the Army.

Therefore I was flown from station to station, addressing hundreds of thousands of Royal Air Force personnel, explaining the food situation and food supply and using the same tactics I had employed at Cawnpore. It was quite an unnerving experience, especially as I disliked soya sausages myself. The experience gave me good practice — it certainly quelled the mutiny — but it also strengthened my revulsion for all soya products!

The Air Vice-Marshal was known as 'How-when-where-why-Satterly', because he always asked those questions and paid great attention to detail.

In one of our regular morning sessions, he went back to the matter of fresh meat for the men. 'A supply ship with meat has just arrived in Rangoon harbour, Sir,' I told him, 'although I haven't seen it yet.' 'Then get in a boat, Caddy, see for yourself and report back when you have,' he growled. It was typical of the man. It was typical of me, too, that I got in the boat and reported back to him!

From my experience in the Royal Air Force, I found that an officer does not rise above the rank of Air Vice-Marshal (equivalent to a two-star general) without the love and loyalty of those beneath him. Satterly was absolutely brilliant at what he did; he worked about sixteen hours a day and had an excellent mind. He was liked and admired by almost all of us; yet he never rose any higher in rank. I feel the reason for this was that he truly expected everyone to be like himself: as dedicated, as hardworking and as brilliant. That was his failing. He was respected but not loved. The ability to inspire love and loyalty, rather than cleverness and efficiency, is the key to success, whether in the RAF or any other leadership role in life.

Chapter 5

Peak Experiences

Remember, only what you have
demonstrated in living is truth to you;
all else is possible truth.
Demonstrate by experiment;
live it: then you have knowledge

I WAS DUE TO RETURN to England in March 1946, three months away. Tibet still intrigued me; after trekking across its border, I was determined to penetrate even further into the country and reach Gyantse, a town on the trade route to Lhasa, 150 miles inside the frontier. The problem was, I had already more than used up my allotted leave. Then the idea came to me that I could form an RAF Mountaineering and Trekking Club and make such an expedition 'official'. I sold the idea to the Commander-in-Chief by explaining to him that it would be much better for the men than going on leave to the fleshpots of Calcutta and carousing; they could be given an experience to remember for the rest of their lives. I would put at their disposal the wealth of knowledge I had gained from my previous 2,000 miles on foot in the Himalayas, and even offered to lead the first party myself. He thought this an excellent idea and gave me his permission and support. In December 1945, I made my plans.

Once again, I had to obtain permission to enter Tibet. On a liaison visit to Delhi I stopped at Calcutta and went up to Darjeeling. I had heard that the British trade agent, Mr Richardson, who was based in Gyantse, was visiting. I went to see him on 16 January 1946, and asked him to approach the Tibetan government to sanction the entry of our party into Tibet and on to Gyantse. He wouldn't hear of the idea! The last time two British officers visited the small garrison based in Gyantse, one of them had died of a heart attack from crossing the 15,000-foot pass, and no further permission had been given to Europeans since. But Doctor Sullivan had taught me the power of positive thought; I was not about to take no for an answer.

While in Darjeeling I embarked upon a lobbying campaign. I went to see a Mr MacDonald, who had a Scottish father and a Tibetan mother and had advised previous Everest expeditions; he was probably the most knowledgeable man on Tibet. I managed to convince him that I had sufficient experience and sense of responsibility, and he agreed to approach Mr Richardson on my behalf. Finally, Richardson agreed to approach the Tibetan government on condition that I took a doctor. As a matter of fact, I said, I had already decided to include a minister of the church as well as a doctor, for good measure. Finally, a radio message came from Lhasa, via Delhi and Calcutta to Rangoon, giving permission for our entry as far as Gyantse.

Of over two hundred applicants to join the expedition, I decided that our party should number sixteen. I had read an account of the Younghusband expedition of 1902 and had found that most of the casualties had been from frostbite, as the temperatures could go down to 40 degrees below zero. It was therefore imperative that we were really well equipped. In fact, I don't think that any expedition to the Himalayas had ever been as well equipped as we were. With the Commander-in-Chief's blessing I was able to get the very best of RAF equipment, and in my position as Command Catering Officer I was able to lay in stores of the best food available, 4,800 calories per person per day, even including peaches and cream.

Two aircraft were put at my disposal to fly our party from Rangoon to Calcutta. The day before we were due to start, riots broke out in Calcutta and all passenger flights were grounded. Again, this seemed an insurmountable obstacle. I quickly rearranged our plans and transferred all our equipment and food supplies into one freight aircraft; I was determined that come what may, we were going to go ahead. I called Bruce Cosh, who had flown in from Bangkok, into my office.

Flight Sergeant Bruce Cosh, a bright Cockney lad, had been chosen by me to act as second-in-command on the expedition. He had been with me on all my previous treks; through our association, he was trained in the knowledge and power of positive thinking and was imbued with the same spirit as I. 'Bruce, we have to get this equipment to Calcutta and then up to Kalimpong, by fair means or foul,' I told him. 'Do whatever it takes!'

Bruce flew off in the freight plane. Within a couple of days the riots were over and the rest of our party were allowed to proceed in the second aircraft. When we arrived at Calcutta on 16 February 1946, there was a note to me from Bruce: 'Peter, for God's sake read this letter before going any further, otherwise I'll be court-martialled!' The letter went on to describe his adventures.

On arrival at Calcutta, he had indicated that the great pile of crates were supplies for an important RAF mission to Tibet and that they were to be straightaway escorted to the railway station. It was explained to him that this was impossible, owing to the riots: five RAF lorries had already been burnt in the city that morning. Even Mahatma Gandhi's hunger strike had so far failed to quell the unrest. Bruce wouldn't take no for an answer and demanded to be taken to the the Station Commander, to whom he explained the position and made out that this was a vitally important mission. In the end, approval was given for him to be escorted by a guard of armed warrant officers through the riot-torn city, and armed guards were even placed on top of our provisions and supplies on the back of the truck. At the station, the Railroad Transport Station Officer (RTSO) told him that there was no room on the train, but Bruce insisted that this equipment had to be transported without delay to Kalimpong (which was the starting point of our trek). He spoke in such an authoritative manner that an extra carriage was put on the train to take our equipment, which was in reality only for a holiday for sixteen people! On arrival at the railhead at Siliguri, Bruce again saw the RTSO, repeated his performance, and managed to get several lorries put at his disposal to transport the equipment by road up to Kalimpong. I was proud of him: Bruce had learned his lessons well, and a court-martial was quite out of the question.

From Kalimpong we were to travel by foot or on pony, donkey, mule or yak, and our baggage was to be carried by a mule or yak train. Before attempting the 'Sikkim Stairs', which as I've mentioned rise 10,000 feet in 9 miles, I explained to the party that this climb must be done slowly, steadily, and with a rhythm that I would set. It was most important that they fall in behind me and follow my example. The Padre (minister), who was a Squadron Leader and hence equal in rank to me, felt he knew better. He was young and strong and went storming ahead, stopping every now and again to get his breath. By the time we reached the top, however, he was exhausted, whereas the other members of the party, who had paced themselves behind me, were quite relaxed. Then we had to cross the plain to the rest house at Pharijong, and a snowstorm hit us. It turned into a blizzard. The Padre got further and further behind. I went on to find the route; meanwhile he was half dragged in, exhausted and in a very sorry state, by two airmen. He wanted to stay behind and recover for the next day, but we could not afford that delay. This illustrates a lesson that is very important to learn in mountaineering or, in fact, many other areas of life: at certain times, in certain situations, there must be obedience to those who have the authority and are responsible for the good of the whole group. Naturally, in mountaineering, disobedience can lead to disaster resulting in loss of life.

Mountains are great levellers when it comes to rank or social position. When you leave the plains, somehow you are forced to leave your dress uniform behind you. You measure your companions as men without regard for the status they held before, and your estimation of them relies on how they act rather than what they say.

One also finds, in the mountains, hidden reserves within oneself. On this expedition, after we had climbed the 'Sikkim Stairs' and crossed the Jelup-La Pass into Tibet, when we arrived at our destination, Yatung, I realized that three of our party were not with us. It was nightfall and there was a blizzard blowing, but I knew I would have to go back over the pass to find them. A large Tibetan coolie accompanied me. Eventually we found them at a dak (guest) bungalow, suffering from fatigue and mountain sickness; the Tibetan and I helped two of them back to the main party, again traversing the mighty pass. During that rescue we covered nearly 60 miles and three times climbed to over 14,000 feet. It was an effort of pure will, and the Tibetan, who had lived all his life at such heights, was even more exhausted than I was.

To climb in the Himalayas is rather like the path of spiritual initiation, for one sees the beautiful, snow-capped mountain in the distance that is one's goal. But before reaching it, there are as many as seven mountain ranges of increasing height. So one has to descend into the valley full of leeches and poisonous insects; there one loses one's vision of the goal, the mountain, until one reaches the next ridge. Then once again one sees it, before descending into another valley, though not as deep this time. The next ridge is higher, until the goal is reached — the mountain itself. Climbing the 'Sikkim Stairs' and being 15,000 feet above sea level for a month gave me the feeling of being on top of everything; as if I had risen above all the materialism, degradation and warring in the world below. It is easy to see why many spiritual teachers feel that the Himalayas are the place to live.

We arrived at Pharijong, a small village in the centre of the plain, in the middle of a snowstorm. One of our party, Tom, had blistered feet, and having ridden all day on a wooden saddle ended up with a very sore behind. He therefore had to have his supper standing up, eating off the shelf above the fire, with his teeth chattering and body shaking uncontrollably. I thought it was so funny that I couldn't stop laughing.

Retribution came swiftly, however, for I found on the following day that the ground was now composed of soft sand which made walking extremely difficult. Gyantse was still 30 miles away so I had to ride for the first time and for the whole day. During the journey the others had gradually become used to the hard wooden saddles, which are used either to carry packs or passengers; I had, so far, walked. As pack animals, the ponies and mules go about one-and-a-half-miles per hour. But to make them go faster when carrying passengers, there is an art of twirling a whip in front of their eyes so that they expect to be hit every now and again. That keeps them trotting. Well, I managed to do this, but my behind got very, very sore. I tried sitting on one side, then the other side, then forwards, then backwards. I was in real agony. I was also feeling very sorry for the poor mule, which was forced to trot. Then a wealthy Tibetan, a feudal lord with an entourage, came upon us and took pity on me because he thought I didn't know how to make the mule go fast. He continued to follow behind, whipping the mule every now and again, with the result that I was bounced up and down and was in excruciating pain. The final agony came when we were 2 miles out of Gyantse. Two army officers from the bodyguard of the British trade agent arrived to escort us into town; they galloped along beside me so that we arrived in triumph. I tried to put my best foot forward and look the part, although I was so sore I could hardly walk afterwards.

The small town of Gyantse nestled beneath the walls of a large monastery of between 4,000 and 5,000 thousand monks. We went to see the abbot, expecting to find a venerable old man, but instead found a young man in his late twenties. He was very vital, with mobile features, sparkling eyes and a great sense of humour. This, and his humility, convinced me that here was a great soul. He had a Parker pen and a pair of binoculars on his desk, which also surprised me: these are not the things you expect to find in the 'Forbidden Land'. The abbot enjoyed dressing up in our flying gear and asked us to take photographs of him in it; he took a great interest in all that we were doing, and wanted to try all our different items of food.

That evening he held a party for us. Realizing that we came from the West, he thought that the thing to do was to try and get us drunk on Tibetan barley beer; when that seemed to fail, he called for rum punch. Our Padre, was a teetotaller but nonetheless joined in, and became thoroughly inebriated — in fact, he ended up on all fours barking like a dog before the party was finished. We tried to get the abbot to have a drink, but our Tibetan cook, who acted as interpreter, made it clear that the abbot was not allowed to drink. Our host would have none of this — he got as tight as the rest of us!

There was no doubt about the authority that the abbot wielded. In taking us around the monastery, we entered what seemed to be a senior monks' common-room, where they were playing dominoes. The minute he entered the room, there was immediate silence and they all stood up. In visiting their temple, I was very struck by the resemblance to the Roman Catholic Church: they had incense, beads, candles, chanting, and a similar sort of atmosphere.

The time came to leave Gyantse. For the journey back, I wanted a reliable mule; I was sick and tired of the slow ones that had brought us there, even though I'd done most of the walking myself. In Tibet the feudal lords did not pay taxes but were required to provide travellers with transport: yaks, mules or donkeys. Whatever the beast, the problem was to make it move, and then to keep it moving at a reasonable pace; without the twirl of a whip before its eyes, promising further punishment, the beast would go at the speed of a pack animal.

I therefore chose a mule with a chain bridle instead of a leather one; surely this one must have some fire in it, I reasoned. Sure enough, no sooner had I mounted it when it took off in the opposite direction and I couldn't turn its head. The stupid creature eventually ran out of puff and I was able to coax it around and go back to the others, who were waiting patiently and trying to keep straight faces. I found the whole episode most embarrassing.

On our way out from Gyantse we were crossing a wide plain with mountains in the distance and, on the horizon, a monastery. I would have liked to visit it, but the Tibetan authorities had made it very clear that we were not allowed to deviate from our given route. The Good Lord must have had other plans, however; there was a tremendous blast of horns from the distant monastery, to which my mule instantly responded. It pricked its ears and then went off at full gallop across the plain towards the source of the sound. Now I knew why it was wearing a chain bridle — its temperament was obviously well-known, for a leather bridle would have snapped. I yelled to two of my party to follow us.

After a dash across the plain we came clattering into the monastery courtyard where the monks were in the middle of their daily service. I don't know who was more surprised, us or the monks, who had probably never seen Europeans before. However, some of the monks came to greet us and we were graciously offered Tibetan tea. This tea is made from China tea-bricks put in a cylinder made out of bamboo; then boiling water is poured over it, rancid yak butter and saltpetre are added and the whole ghastly concoction is churned up. The Tibetans drink, I had learned, between sixty and eighty cups a day of this stuff; it may keep out the cold but it has a revolting taste. Having sampled it before, I decided to get the experience over with as quickly as possible by holding my nose and drinking it down with one gulp, but this was a big mistake — Tibetan etiquette required that the cup be filled again promptly. One of my companions dashed out to get rid of what he had already forced down.

I later discovered that this monastery was the last one in which the Dalai Lama took refuge on his flight from Tibet when the Chinese invaded. Although he was forced to leave Tibet, I feel that there was a spiritual reason for his doing so. By coming out into the world, he and other great souls have brought with them an energy of love and wisdom that is sorely needed in the West today.

We rejoined our party, after thanking the monks for their hospitality, and proceeded on the homeward trek. On the way, Bruce Cosh and I made a detour to climb Mt Chomolhari. When we set out to do this, from a tea house where we had stopped, an icy wind was blowing, but by the time we were on the slopes it suddenly dropped, as if the mountain were welcoming us; we had a remarkably easy climb, made strenuous only by the altitude. The microscopically small figures we saw on the track leading across the Tuna Plain were the other members of our party, and our pony train appeared like a party of ants. We were treated to magnificent views of the mountain peaks across the plain and to our right rose the beautiful face of the main peak of Chomolhari.

We had climbed about 2,000 feet above the plain, taking us 17,000 feet above sea level. Once more we turned to the ascent and after a brief interval of scrambling up the by now heather-covered rock, we saw a pinnacle about 1,200 feet above us; we made this point our objective. It was rather disappointing on a couple of occasions to find that rifts in the rock caused us to descend 100 feet or so, in order to get on to a route that would lead us upward to our goal again. But by perseverance we steadily ascended and by 2.30pm, after a last scramble and long, panting effort we were there.

The view was spectacular and awe-inspiring; the summit of Chomolhari looked deceptively near. Away to our right spread out the route of a few days previous and in the distance we could see billowing dust storms between us and the huge, frozen lake of Dochen. Here we were above such disturbances of weather; Bruce remarked how puny man's efforts appeared when confronted with such terrific splendours of nature. We continued climbing as high as 18,500 feet — the highest I've climbed in my life — and ate our lunch there on top of the world. Bruce pointed out the lack of litter bins for our empty cheese tins and miscellaneous paper wrappings, and nonchalantly smoked a cigarette without suffering any ill effects. 'It seemed to be sacred to be able to stand on a point so high and so far away from worldly affairs,' he later wrote. 'I felt that the whole trek would have been worth the effort just to get this day alone.'

We returned to Kalimpong and then to Burma, exactly on the day planned, in perfect timing for me to catch my boat home to England. Everything had gone according to schedule, and it was only the sheer determination of will that had enabled us to cover the considerable distances. It was quite an accomplishment to travel 30 miles a day on foot, on very uneven terrain, often at heights above 15,000 feet. In answer to a challenge, I ran the last 21 miles in four hours — a fitting end to a 350 mile trek.

As far as I know, ours was the last Western expedition into Tibet before the Chinese invasion. The journey there was one of the highlights of my life. I had always been drawn to Tibet and had read every book on the country that I could find, little dreaming that I would one day come to be there. Of all the places that I have ever visited in my life Tibet had the greatest attraction for me. Not only the beauty of the land, with its snow-capped mountains, deep blue skies, rushing rivers, rhododendrons and azaleas in bloom, but also its people. They had a childlike simplicity, joy and vitality, which was different from the people of the plains.

On the other hand, I had looked upon Tibet as being central to the spiritual government of the world; therefore it had been disillusioning to see that just like anywhere else, many of the people had become crystallized in their thinking and customs. This led to the observation that the spiritual work of our times was not confined or concentrated in any particular creed or country, but must find its expression everywhere. The Chinese invasion has meant that many of the great souls in Tibet fled to the West; many of them used their teachings to found schools and centres, such as Samyê Ling in Dumfrieshire, Scotland. They brought with them the wisdom and compassion and knowledge of the East, and have learned about Love and the Christian ideals of the West. This spiritual meeting of East and West remains one of the significant impulses of my life and indeed of our times.

I left India and Burma with all my ambitions and aims for my time in India achieved. I had walked over 2,400 miles in the Himalayas, been to Kashmir, into Ladakh, seen the sunrise on Mt. Everest, and trekked in Tibet twice. No wonder I had felt thrilled when I heard that I was being posted to India. I had also experienced the life of the British Raj in India before the British pulled out. My whole time there was one of great experiences, fulfilment and training.

And I was exhausted! Utterly satiated from living life to the full. On 10 April 1946, I sailed from Rangoon back to England on board a troopship. On the way over, I had thrown away *A Passage to India,* the book that I was reading, determined to experience, rather than read about other people's lives. But this time I felt like reading. I climbed on to the top of a pile of rafts, made my bed there, and read Tolstoy's *War and Peace* from cover to cover all the way back to England.

Chapter 6

One Bloody Thing after Another

Everything which you find in your world without has been created by you in the world within

BEFORE LEAVING BURMA I had received the news that Doctor Sullivan had left his body, as he had foreseen, in 1942. On my return to England in 1946, I was surprised to find that Walter Bullock, the officer and 'mystery man' who had read my palm at Halton, was now the Supreme Magus of the Rosicrucian Order. I was the one who had introduced him to the Order; at the time, I had described him to Doctor Sullivan as 'a mystery wrapped up in an enigma'. 'Good,' my teacher had replied, 'That's the way I like them.' Many members of the Order found it difficult adjusting to the change in style of our Supreme Magus. Walter Bullock lacked Doctor Sullivan's warmth and fun; I felt that his heart was not fully developed. He had great knowledge and hypnotic power, however, and I resumed attending chapter meetings, church services and lectures each weekend.

I returned to Nora and our son Michael, who were living with Nora's mother in a bungalow at Christchurch in Hampshire, near Jim and Elizabeth Barnes and close to the headquarters of the Rosicrucian Order. After my exciting adventures in Tibet and the Far East I found it almost impossible to adjust to their way of life, which to me was dull and routine. The highlight of the week for Nora and her mother was to dress up in hat, veil and gloves and take Michael to a restaurant in Bournemouth, where the waitresses doted on him. I was expected to get dressed up and join them, when all I wanted was to remain in shorts and sandals on the beach, or in the garden, enjoying the open air. Furthermore, it was apparent that Nora put her mother first, her child second, and me third. She was not interested in the outside world and her whole life seemed to revolve so much around her immediate family that I felt like an intruder. We had never spent a great deal of time together, as we married at the outbreak of World War II and I had joined the Royal Air Force immediately afterwards. It was more a sense of duty than love that kept us together.

After three months leave, I was posted on 2 August 1946 to the Air Ministry in London, a desk job that chiefly involved formulating and implementing catering policy throughout the RAF. I lived in a small rented flat at Dolphin Square in Pimlico and returned home to Christchurch on weekends, where I spent time with the family and attended meetings at the Rosicrucian Headquarters; I would travel down on Friday evenings by train on the *Bournemouth Belle* and return to London on Sunday evening.

One Friday I missed the *Bournemouth Belle* and had to travel by a later train. I headed for the restaurant car, but the only empty seat that I could find was opposite a woman who was reading and appeared tired. She seemed to want to be alone. However, something impelled me to stop and I asked if the seat was taken. It was not, so I sat down and took out my own book, *The Aquarian Gospel* by Levi. After a while she noticed the title and we got into a conversation. Her name was Sheena Govan. She told me that she had also missed her train and caught this later one; she was going down to Southampton to visit and stay with a Miss Dowland, known as Nargis, a close disciple of the Sufi Master Hazrat Inayat Khan.

We started talking about the forthcoming Age of Aquarius, the so-called New Age in which spiritual truths would come to the fore and a 'World Teacher' was expected; also the fact that in this New Age, women would have a more guiding role. Sheena herself was running a travel agency specializing in unusual tours. Having just returned from Tibet and Kashmir, I spoke with her about the possibility of my leading a tour to Kashmir, and she warmed to the idea. She invited me round to her flat for further discussion about this over dinner.

On 12 March 1947 I had a superbly cooked dinner with Sheena. We immediately began talking about spiritual matters and never once referred to the proposed tour to Kashmir. The evening was interrupted by the arrival of a rather mysterious man by the name of John Wood, who appeared to possess great knowledge and wisdom, though he didn't talk much. (I later learned that John was the man who had given Sheena an esoteric or occult framework in which to interpret her mystical experiences; despite Sheena's biblical knowledge, she had initially had difficulty accepting them. John's help had been crucial. His wife, Dorothy — née Maclean — had known Sheena for years, as they had worked together in the British Secret Service in New

York during the War; Dorothy eventually became very closely associated with our spiritual work.) I assumed that John had been asked by Sheena to come and vet me, and I must have passed muster because it was arranged that Sheena would phone me to plan another meeting to discuss the proposed Kashmir tour.

Sheena rang me a month later, and this time I invited her to my place for dinner. Once again the talk was entirely on spiritual matters, and this continued when I escorted her home. At the end of the evening we were standing in front of the fire in her flat when our eyes met and we suddenly stopped talking; a tremendous surge of love swept through us both, on all levels of our being. This was a complete surprise, since our whole conversation and thoughts had been entirely of a spiritual nature. In that moment, we recognized a union more powerful than either of us had experienced before. It was as if our innermost beings had experienced a marriage and it was left to our personalities to follow suit. I moved into her flat the next day without a second's thought, because intuitively I knew that it was the right thing to do.

As it happened, we were well-matched on personality levels, although on spiritual and soul levels the relationship between Sheena and me was more that of teacher and pupil, mother and son. Sheena was one of the most remarkable and loving women that I have ever met. She had dark hair, radiant eyes and was a vivacious and extraordinarily beautiful woman, of medium height, slim build and finely chiselled features. Like myself she lived in the moment, saying 'God can only be found in the present, not in the past or the future'. Although she had had a previous deep relationship she was not married and was four years older than I. Sheena seemed like a very highly strung violin; she put her whole being into everything she did, with tremendous love, whether it was playing the violin or piano, or becoming a nurse, or going on the stage as an actress, or scrubbing the floor, or cooking a meal. The result was that she was highly successful in everything she touched.

Sheena came from a Quaker background; her parents had founded the Faith Mission, an evangelical movement with its headquarters in Edinburgh and branches all over the world. She had been brought up to a life of faith in God, dedicating her whole being to serving Him, no matter what the cost. As she grew up she began to experience God and the Christ Love within her own being and realized the deeper significance of the words *I and my Father are One:* God, the force behind everything, is found within and not outside of anyone. With her strong belief and faith, Sheena had a profound sense of her mission in life, which was to help transform the world through love.

Her flat was like a magnet. Throughout the day, people came for spiritual help and guidance; Sheena believed that at this time many people were going through an initiatory experience of self-realization that she called 'the birth of the Christ within'. She was like a midwife helping them to go through that process. This often required that an individual surrender the thing which he or she held most dear. What one person might find easy to give up, another might find extremely difficult. Sheena's older brother Frank, for example, was a good-looking man overly fond of quoting the Bible chapter and verse to back up his assertions; he was devastated when he had to give up such rendering of the Bible and stand in the light of his own truth.

I was privileged to be Sheena's scribe, recording the messages that, as a 'sensitive', she received in her meditations for those who came to her. She helped hundreds of people in this way, cloaking her words with her own wisdom and experience. The way she worked was to throw light on an individual's situation so that they could see the principle behind it and work out for themselves whatever action they might need to take — she never gave specific directions, only guidance and suggestions — and she knew that ultimately each person would have to go through the experience of this inner birth on their own. In every case, it was a question of renouncing something before the birth of the inner Christ child could take place. Little did I realize that I, too, was about to have to go through this experience.

She was not a spiritual teacher in the traditional sense. She had no programme, no classes nor meditation techniques, but would help people to see God in their lives. Since she was so busy with people, I slipped into the role of cooking meals, washing up, cleaning the flat and generally looking after her. This was an odd occupation for a Squadron Leader in the Royal Air Force working at Air Ministry, but it was marvellous training because I was given a unique opportunity to see the pattern running through people's lives, and how God's plan worked out for each of them.

Sheena was a wonderful balance of those aspects of God known as Light, Love and Wisdom. However this was not always comfortable to live with. She'd be all over me with love in one moment, and then she would whip out the sword of truth to cut away some part of my inflated ego. Then she would pour out love to heal the wound. When these three aspects were being embodied all in one person, it became very disorienting. Being thus pruned by Sheena enabled me to know what it felt like to be at the receiving end of the sword. Many years later, one of my tasks at the Findhorn Community was to wield the sword of truth, to prune old habits and ideas from the people who came to join us, so that new growth could take place. To do that, one needed to prepare the way with love, and then use the sword fearlessly and without hesitation.

One weekend, when Sheena came down with me by car to be dropped off at Southampton to visit Nargis, we stopped by the roadside in the New Forest for a picnic lunch and she recited by heart the 1 Corinthians 13 from the King James version of the Bible. She substituted the word 'love' for the given word 'charity'. This was the first time I had heard the word love used in this passage, and it had an overwhelming impact on me:

> *Though I speak with the tongues of men and of angels and have not love, I am become as sounding brass, or a tinkling cymbal. And though I have the gift of prophecy, and understand all mysteries, and all knowledge; and though I have all faith, so that I could remove mountains, and have not love, I am nothing. And though I bestow all my goods to feed the poor, and though I give my body to be burned, and have not love, it profiteth me nothing. Love suffereth long, and is kind; love envieth not; love vaunteth not itself, is not puffed up, doth not behave itself unseemly, seeketh not her own, is not easily provoked, thinketh no evil; rejoiceth not in iniquity, but rejoiceth in the truth; beareth all things, believeth all things, hopeth all things, endureth all things. Love never faileth: but whether there be prophecies, they shall fail; whether there be tongues, they shall cease; whether there be knowledge, it shall vanish away. For we know in part, and we prophesy in part. But when that which is perfect is come, then that which is in part shall be done away. When I was a child, I spake as a child, I understood as a child, I thought as a child: but when I became a man, I put away childish things. For now we see through a glass, darkly; but then face to face: now I know in part; but then shall I know even as also I am known. And now abideth faith, hope, and love, these three; but the greatest of these is love.*

Something clicked in me as she recited these words. Up to that time, things had been happening so quickly to me that I hadn't had time to evaluate the strange position I was in. I had been spending my week benefiting from Sheena's spiritual training and her presence, as well as exploring the depths of our relationship together. On weekends, I would return to Christchurch where my family lived and where I attended services and Walter Bullock's lectures at the Rosicrucian Order. Sheena, who was perfectly aware of my marriage, expressed only love toward Nora and our family, and never exhibited any jealousy or possessiveness. In fact her attitude made it easier for me *not* to evaluate the triangular relationship in which I was now involved. She would, however, be withdrawn whenever I came back from my weekend in Christchurch. She never told me that it was my double life that was creating this strain, but later I realized how dense I was being.

It was not flouting the social conventions of the time that bothered me, for society's morals are often hypocritical and reflect only the fears of the personality in relationships. My soul was seeking an understanding of deeper, spiritual law — God's law, not man's. According to this, I realized that what I was doing was wrong. In attempting to maintain the two relationships, I was violating a principle of God — Truth — when it came to Nora.

It was already clear to me that my marriage with Nora — if it had ever been a marriage in more than name — was over. She was obviously happier with her immediate, blood relations. The choice now facing me was between the Path of Love and the teachings which Sheena could give me, and the Path of Light, Knowledge and Reason represented by the Rosicrucian Order. Being with Sheena would automatically mean giving up the Rosicrucian Order since I would need to make a clean break from Nora who was, of course, also a member. Furthermore, I would be *persona non grata* in certain quarters, as my brother-in-law Jim was a high-ranking officer of the Order and would thoroughly disapprove of my actions.

My path had been one of learning spiritual laws and principles, but my time with Sheena marked the awakening of Love in my heart — and, as I was to learn, Love fulfils all laws. It was an agonizing choice. Duty to my wife and family weighed heavily on my mind and sometimes caused me grief. My career with the Royal Air Force was at stake, as well as my relationship with my parents, who would be deeply shocked at my actions and would not be able to understand them. I had wanted to tell Nora and her family about my relationship with Sheena, as soon as we had come together, but I had hesitated because Nora had recently given birth to our daughter Diana. I had also been advised by a 'sensitive' and healer, Kitchie, an old lady and friend of Sheena's, that I should not take action until Nora had finished breast-feeding.

A few weeks later, in September 1947, Sheena received guidance in meditation that the time had come for me to go down to Christchurch and break the news. The source of this message, a disincarnate being whom Sheena regarded as an inner friend, said that he would be with me, and indeed I did feel uplifted and supported in that which lay ahead of me. First I shared my news with Jim Barnes, who was disgusted with me, and Walter Bullock, who remained strangely silent. Then I explained to Nora, her mother, and her sister just what had happened. At the time, Nora appeared not to take it in and I was later told this was for her protection. I also went to Devon to tell my parents of the step that I had taken. They were indeed shocked and upset, because my father was a model of conventional high Christian morality.

I then travelled to Southampton to join Sheena, who had been staying with her friend Nargis, and I found her in tears. She had believed that we had been drawn together by God and that we were in fact two halves of the same soul. Nargis had just read her a passage from a book which stated quite categorically that 'soul halves' rarely came together upon Earth and, that if they did, it would only be momentarily. They would then be separated, to be reunited only when they had passed from earthly existence. Furthermore, unbeknown to me, while I was breaking the news to my parents, Sheena had been to Christchurch to see the Head of the Rosicrucian Order, Walter Bullock (who, you will remember, had seen in my palm that I would meet my 'real' partner at the age of twenty-nine. I met Sheena shortly before my thirtieth birthday). After hearing Walter lecture, Sheena had sought his blessing on the steps that we had taken — a blessing which he refused to give.

Giving up my home and family for Sheena allowed me to experience, in the system of biblical symbology that she had experienced and taught, the birth of the Christ within. I then realized I had to get rid of my entire library of mystical and ancient-wisdom books, like *The Secret Doctrine* by Madame Blavatsky and the Alice Bailey material from the Arcane School, and just follow the Path of Love. My years with Sheena were ones of continual learning, learning to do everything 'unto the Lord', as she put it, with love, and to do it perfectly. I was once suffering badly from hay fever and sought relief in a holiday by the sea. We rented a cottage, which was in a complete mess when we arrived; but before we left, everything had to be scrubbed, cleaned, polished and made perfect. I was not enthusiastic about doing all this work, as it was my holiday, but Sheena insisted that I do it, and do it with love. When everything is done with love, she explained, it raises the 'vibrations' — the quality of the atmosphere of a place and its conduciveness for spiritual work. In our flat, too, everything had to be perfect, shining and spotless. Sheena claimed that the resultant 'raised vibrations' helped her to contact higher and higher streams of intelligence in her meditations, until she was receiving from the Archangel Michael and finally had the ability to receive from the highest aspect of God, the **'I am'** within.

According to Sheena, it was now essential that I take the next step by which the Christ child may grow for, in her words:

> *His growth depends on that inner wisdom which enlightens our minds, enlarges our hearts, and teaches us the mysteries of man — 'Oh man, know thyself!'. How little time we have in the bustle of modern life to meditate and learn, through Divine enlightenment, the secret spiritual mysteries. Only when the heart is still can she reflect in her depths the light and truth of God. This stillness of heart will eventually be maintained in any circumstances of life, but before that it must be cultivated in solitude and separation of the mind and heart, if not of the body. In fleeing 'Herod', we renounce the dictates and judgments of the carnal mind forever. We give no further allegiance or attention to the maxims and standards of this world's reason or logic. The intellect now receives enlightenment from the source of wisdom.*

Try as I might, I could never gain direct access to this 'source of wisdom' Sheena was on about. She would have me sit down and meditate for hours on end, day after day, listening for an inner voice, but I never heard or received anything. She was very disappointed, but was only the first of many who tried to get me to meditate so that I would hear this voice within. I have tried until I was blue in the face, and not heard it. What I was developing, however, was a powerful intuition, without allowing mental or emotional considerations to interfere with it, and *that* was 'the source of wisdom' I learned to act upon: a deep inner knowing, beyond words and pictures, that prompted immediate action.

After the birth comes the baptism. Sheena identified this stage with the shadow of the Cross — a taste of trials to come — and a yearning that 'Thy Will be done'. As with most lessons in my life, it seems I had to learn this the hard way. The reason for Walter Bullock's refusal to bless Sheena's and my relationship soon became apparent: Walter had fallen in love with her himself and felt that Sheena was to be his wife and the mother of a special child. He represented Light and Power, he explained, and she represented Love. He felt that they had work to do for the future and it would be my role to serve them both. However much she may have disliked it personally, Sheena felt that Walter's vision was true.

The effect upon me was one of profound shock. I was devastated. Here I had given up everything — wife, children, home, the approval of my parents — for Sheena. I thought I may have to resign my commission in the Royal Air Force; I would certainly lose some of my closest friends, and the link with the Rosicrucian Order that had meant so much to me. I'd given it all up for Love, for Sheena. Now I was called upon to give up Sheena herself and to put God's Will first in my life — for Sheena felt that this *was* God's Will for her, despite the fact that she was in love with me, not Walter. She knew the great suffering it would cause me, but the only thing that really mattered in her life was understanding and executing God's Will.

The next fortnight was absolute hell. I was in the depths of despair, in tears, unable to eat; I didn't feel like going on living. Having developed a tremendous will through cross-country running, long treks in the Himalayas and Tibet, I was now called upon to give up that will and say, *Father, not my will, but Thine*. It appeared that God's Will for me was to serve the two people that I loved and respected most in this world, Walter and Sheena. I grew increasingly desperate as they began a courtship, but the worst was yet to come.

Walter had long had a conviction that one of his missions was to be the father of the *One who was to come*, the next Messiah. Since he saw Sheena as the mother of this child, a physical union was necessary. I was shattered, and for days wandered around in a state of shock until I grew tired of struggling. I can well recall lying in the bath one day, saying at last 'All right, Father, Thy Will be done; but there is one thing I will *not* agree to — that Sheena and Walter be sexually united.' Almost immediately I realized the grave error in making such a statement, and that this would be the one thing that I would have to face. Sure enough, that bath proved to be my baptismal font. The very next day I learned that what I feared had happened: Walter and Sheena had performed the act during the afternoon. Sheena found it very difficult; I was depressed for days afterwards. Since then, I have always said 'Let Thy Will be done' with no qualifications or provisos.

Because she loved me and not Walter, Sheena herself was going through 'a dark night of the soul' — the complete surrender of personal life and self — the 'crucifixion' in her symbolic system. Walter was a great teacher on the path of knowledge and ancient wisdom but had known very little of love. When he met Sheena, he experienced such a deep opening of the heart that he began behaving in some very strange ways; his behaviour, for all his worldliness, was like that of a moonstruck adolescent. Soon after their one sexual encounter, Sheena and I went to Sark to recover our relationship and she was given two visions to explain what had happened. One was of a man, like the giant in *Gulliver's Travels*, being held down by little people, and she was told that a giant needed the tests of a giant; I was that giant. In the other vision, she had seen the Supreme Magus, Walter Bullock, as a man on crutches with one strong leg and one tiny, withered leg that was just beginning to grow. The fit leg symbolized knowledge and wisdom; the undeveloped leg represented the Path of Love. The crutches indicated Walter's inner occult powers. When she saw those crutches being knocked away, he was in a most unbalanced state.

Sheena realized that the whole thing had been a test for all of us, and that she need not, after all, be married to Walter. It was enough for her to have served in her capacity as 'spiritual midwife' for the birth of the inner Christ in Walter. The most we could do was send Love to him, which we did. Sheena later discovered that she was pregnant and subsequently miscarried, but we never knew whether it was Walter's child or mine.

I remembered a day in Hyde Park, sometime before this, when Sheena asked me, 'Do you really want to go ahead with the path of spiritual initiation? Once one puts one's hand to the plough, there's no turning back.' I'd said, 'Yes, I am going to achieve this goal in one lifetime.' She had tears in her eyes, because she knew the pain and suffering of the path ahead, but she accepted my decision. I was at the beginning of this suffering, while she was approaching its end. Now I was beginning to see what she had foreseen in her vision of the giant. She had also added that the day would come when I would turn my back on her because my faith in God had become so strong, but I did not believe her.

When one is going through an initiation, as the three of us were, one is blindfolded. I realized this when watching Mozart's *Magic Flute*, when the couple are blindfolded before their tests. At the time I met Sheena, I had felt like a clear pool of water; then she came along with a great big stick and stirred up all the muck at the bottom, like scum rising to the surface to be cleared away. I was with Sheena for five years, day and night. Imagine what it's like to be with a woman who knows your every thought, your every feeling, and is always right. For me it was one lesson after another, until the time came when I felt I couldn't do anything right, and for a while, in Sheena's eyes I couldn't. I naturally questioned, ' What is it all for? What is the purpose of it? When are things going to start happening? When will this lesson-learning end?' There was always one bloody thing after another; love was the only thing that kept me coming back for more.

Chapter 7

From School to Staff College

The Rosicrucian method of acquiring happiness is to keep smiling. It is the only way to carry the Cross patiently, for otherwise the Roses will never bloom on it

I OFTEN had to make mistakes in order to learn my lessons, and Sheena sometimes suffered as a result. I learned faster when she *was* suffering from my mistakes: because I loved her, it hurt me to see her suffer. Once, after Sheena had been ill, we went for a month's tour in my open car around France. Sometimes we would get lost; I would ask the way, but with my chronically bad French we would end up in some strange places. Sheena suffered migraine headaches as a result, until she was told from a higher source that never again was I to ask the way: if I ever did, I would always be given the wrong information. I was to turn within, to follow my inner direction. This was a very important lesson for me in my future spiritual work.

Another, less dramatic lesson of this tour came during our visit to Montsegur, in Southern France, the last home of the Albigenses, also known as Cathars. It was their last stand and they were finally put to death by fire at the hands of the Roman Catholic Inquisition, during that Church's Albigensian Crusades. I had read in a book by Grace Cooke, founder of the White Eagle Lodge, about her expedition to locate the treasure of the Albigenses which was reputedly buried in the mountain below the castle. I was determined to find that treasure and spent three days looking for the entrance, until Sheena received a message in meditation that I was to stop looking for the external treasure, and seek instead the treasure within myself. We later attended a church service in a little Roman Catholic church near Montsegur, during which I felt overpowered by the beauty of the music, the incense, and the stained glass. Sheena received a further message that there was no longer to be war between the church and mystical orders, between man and woman, masculine and feminine, Light and Love, science and religion. In the New Age, they would come together in wisdom and harmony, as the Catholic Church and the Cathars were never able to do.

After Nora and I parted, I would spend as much time as I could manage with my son, Michael. Sheena and I did our utmost to give him an enjoyable time, taking him to sights like the London Zoo and the Farnborough Air Show. On 15 July 1948, however, Nora and I were divorced and I lost touch with both Michael and Diana.[1]

Sheena and I were married on 10 September 1948. There was much opposition to this from people of conventional mind, but we believed that whom God had joined together, no man can put asunder. People so often interpret God in this context to mean 'the church' (ie 'whom the church has joined together') but we felt that 'whom Love has joined together' is the correct interpretation when the Love is from God and occurs on all levels, as in our case; marriage is only the human recognition of what has already taken place. When marriage is to satisfy sexual attraction, social position, power, wealth, or for a hundred and one reasons other than Love, it is often little more than legalized prostitution. Even if they come to recognize it as such, many husbands and wives then stay together for the sake of the children, even if they are as incompatible as oil and water — as Nora and I were. Through Nora, I had met Jim Barnes and Doctor Sullivan and joined the Rosicrucian Order, although I knew of none of these when we first met; perhaps this was the reason we were brought together. To stay together just for the sake of children may sound noble, but I feel strongly that children suffer greatly if they are brought up in an inharmonious atmosphere, devoid of real love because of incompatible parents.

Sheena and I had bought a beautiful home on wheels, a Rollalong, 'the Rolls-Royce of caravans', which we left in the country so that we could spend weekends away from the flat in London. We also had a big Labrador dog called Brumas whom I used to exercise by allowing him to chase our car in Battersea Park. One country weekend, when we returned to the caravan after a long absence, Brumas slunk into his basket and howled. We could not stop him until Sheena meditated on the situation. She was told that as the caravan had been unoccupied, 'astral entities' — spirits formed from

1 In 1991, on a private tour of Britain, I was able to meet both Michael (and his family) and Diana: a time of review and reflection on the extraordinary twists that life had taken

unresolved emotions or thoughts, or departing souls who had not yet left the earth — had entered and taken up residence. These were now disturbing Brumas, as some animals are sensitive to such things. We cleared them out by lighting a blazing fire, playing good music and enjoying a lot of laughter, and Brumas was soon happy again.

Meanwhile I had decided to make my career in the Royal Air Force and obtained a permanent commission. I was posted as Command Catering Officer for Bomber Command, whose headquarters was at High Wycombe in Buckinghamshire. The job chiefly involved travelling and inspecting the various kitchens in RAF stations in the Command; post-war petrol rationing was still in force in Britain, so the petrol coupons that came with the job gave me the freedom of the road. After a brief stay at 'The Plough Inn', Sheena and I moved in to a charming thatched cottage nearby. We kept chickens, which Sheena adored — she had a great love for all life. One day her brother bought her a goose's egg, which we put under a broody hen. When the gosling broke its shell, the first person it saw was Sheena. Goslings believe that the first moving thing that they set eyes upon is their parent, so this gosling followed Sheena around everywhere. She was never without her. We named her Jemima. Even when Sheena was ill, I had to bring Jemima up to see her in bed, where the goose would nuzzle her neck and bite her hair. Sheena was always a great social success with people and didn't see why her new charge shouldn't join in the fun; so when we went to a ball at Bomber Command, Jemima had to come along too, with a pink ribbon tied around her neck. She sipped champagne and would waddle unsteadily across the dance floor — she became quite a mascot.

Another social occasion at Bomber Command taught me an uncomfortable lesson. The Commander-in-Chief had thrown a sherry party for the officers in the Command to celebrate his recent knighthood; afterwards, the Air Officer in charge of Administration, who was my boss, invited a few of us to continue drinking sherry at his quarters. I had never drunk so much sherry in my life. I drove my car back home at high speed, thinking it was an airplane, along the narrow roads of Buckinghamshire. At one point, I hit a ditch, and the bonnet of the car flew over the top and landed on the road behind. I stopped the car and laughed and laughed. I thought it was the funniest thing I had seen for a long time. I replaced the bonnet and arrived home at about four in the afternoon, just when Sheena was having a friend in for tea. She was not amused, particularly since we had found, on a previous occasion, how Sheena was so sensitive that when I had too much to drink, she was the one who felt the effects — even though she had consumed no alcohol herself. (I think that one reason Sheena was so often sick was that she seemed to take on not only the cares of others, but also, at times, their physical ailments.) I was now feeling very ill and went straight to bed. Never again have I ever had one drink more than I felt was wise, however hard pressed to do so by those around me; I had learned my lesson.

Whilst at Bomber Command Headquarters, I had an inner prompting to endeavour to go to the Royal Air Force Staff College, the elite school that prepares officers for the highest echelons of the RAF. Gaining admission necessitated passing a very stiff series of examinations; although I had never done well at exams, I was determined to pass these, and spent several years preparing for them. In preparation for the current affairs paper, for example, I went to every course I could find, in or outside the RAF, on current affairs. I made sure that I kept up to date with what was happening in the world by reading two or three newspapers a day, as well as various magazines. I also had been selected to go on the Officer's Advanced Training Course on administration, RAF law and discipline, and did very well at what was a difficult curriculum.

Early in 1949, I was appointed Commanding Officer for the RAF School of Cookery at Innsworth in Gloucestershire. Sheena was not well and had been in bed for some time. Nevertheless, I packed up our possessions, loaded up the car and the roof rack and squeezed in Brumas. We set off in the direction of Innsworth, a town near Cheltenham, full of faith that we would be led to the right place. I had no idea where we were going to go, particularly as Sheena was confined to bed and would need looking after while I was at work. I remembered the name of a hotel, Thirleston Hall, owned by the mother of a senior RAF Officer. I thought that we might be able to stay there for a while.

We eventually drew up outside the hotel only to discover to our surprise that it was a four-star hotel — probably the most expensive in town. Nevertheless, I went in to the Reception and asked to see the owner. She was dignified, gracious and very well-dressed. I explained my situation: I was posted to Innsworth, looking for somewhere to stay, with a sick wife and a large dog, and I had only a junior officer's pay. She said that they were full, and when would we like to come? I told her that my wife, dog and our possessions were outside in the car. She was taken aback but being the lady she was, she agreed that Sheena could stay there until she had recovered her health; and the cost was at a rate that I could afford. Sheena was served meals in her room and wonderfully looked after, while I enjoyed the facilities of the hotel and the superb food in the dining room.

The previous Commanding Officer at the School of Cookery had been good at catering but hopeless as a leader and disciplinarian. The result had been that inspecting officers reported unfavourably on the school and it became notorious throughout the service. Finally, the Commander-in-Chief himself inspected the school and wrote a damning report to Air Ministry. He said that he would not have another catering officer as Commanding Officer and recommended the post go instead to the adjutant, Flight Lieutenant Charles Arnett, a man in his forties from the General Duties Branch. Air Ministry did not agree with him, and said that they had just the right officer available who had recently completed the Officers' Advanced Training School, and whom they considered suitable for the job — me. Therefore it was against the wishes of the Commander-in-Chief that I arrived to take over command of this School of Cookery, generally recognized as the worst unit in the Royal Air Force. The adjutant, furthermore, who was nearly twice my age, was upset that *he* had not been given the job. It was hardly a propitious beginning. The set-up was perfect, however, for me to put into practice what Doctor Sullivan had taught in the series of *Soul Science* lectures, to *love where you are, to love who you are with, and to love the work that you are doing.*

I began my new duties by calling a meeting of all the instructors. Cooking is an art, a thing of the heart, not a science; therefore I wanted only those instructors who loved cooking, wanted to teach and loved where they were. When I asked those who did *not* want to teach cooking to raise their hands, about 60 per cent of them did so. Meanwhile I had discovered that Charles Arnett, the adjutant whom I'd pipped at the post to become Commanding Officer, loved bending the rules and was an expert at it. I therefore asked him if he could arrange for these unhappy instructors to be posted away. His eyes lit up and he replied, 'Just leave it to me, Sir'. I then combed the Air Force for more suitable instructors and leaders, many of whom I'd known earlier in my service career, and asked Charles to arrange for them to be posted to Innsworth.

Having gathered a dedicated team, I imbued them with my enthusiasm, work-methods, and ideas and plans for the future of the School. I refused to teach any airman who didn't want to become a cook; it had been RAF practice to draft almost anyone when cooks were needed. When the next new intake of about 200 arrived at the School, I addressed them and asked for those who did not want to become cooks to put up their hands. Once again, nearly 75 per cent did so; I had them posted away. This caused a stir at Command Headquarters and Air Ministry, as it was quite a revolutionary tactic in the RAF, but I stood firm.

As far as possible within the framework of strict discipline, the School was run on the principles of Doctor Sullivan's teachings. Once everyone *could* love what he was doing, etc., we all had a great deal of fun. I also learned that the stricter the discipline, the happier the unit. Some of the long serving non-commissioned officers (NCOs), however, found my style difficult to understand. When I asked them what they would like to do, their reply would be a stiff, empty, obedient, 'Anything you say, Sir'. They couldn't believe I genuinely wanted them to offer their opinions! After several months they were still well-disciplined, but became more relaxed and comfortable in contributing their own thoughts and ideas to the work of our team.

I divided the school into two units, 'A' School, and 'B' School, each with its own classrooms, barrack block, drill squadron, cricket team, etc., with a warrant officer in charge of each school. I shared my vision with them and put the teams to work. They competed with one another in a friendly fashion, and all I had to do was drop a hint that 'A' School was a little better than 'B' School, for example, and it was magical to see what happened. One evening, I went back at 9 pm and found all the lights on in all the classrooms. The men had voluntarily come back for extra classes in order to do well on their examinations and thus outperform the other school.

Cooks in the RAF had been notorious for being slovenly and poor at drill and discipline. When there was an Advanced Disciplinary Course for NCOs throughout the whole Royal Air Force, I had Charles commandeer enough spaces so that all my NCOs could eventually take it. They came back with a new pride in themselves.

Each year in the RAF, every unit in a Group is inspected by the Air Officer Commanding from Group Headquarters. In preparation, various specialist officers would come from Group Headquarters to inspect their particular field of responsibility and report on it. In our case, the senior officer in charge of administration was a Group Captain Goacher, who was notorious for taking a unit apart, opening everything and finding fault wherever fault was to be found. Everyone was afraid of him, so I decided to initiate a campaign called 'baiting the goat' and called a meeting of all the staff to explain my plan. Everyone was delighted and set about it with relish.

At my request, Charles Arnett was able to cut down the next intake of airmen by half. We closed one school, and I put a warrant officer in charge of preparing it for inspection. We arranged for each class to remain on for an extra week, so I had plenty of men to do the work. I asked the warrant officer to completely clean, scrub, and polish each classroom; when this had been done, I inspected each room and locked the door. (Some time earlier, arrangements had been made for the whole building to be repainted and repaired, and this too was completed.) The trainees were instructed to bathe and scrub their fingernails, and were issued a new set of clean 'whites' (cooks' uniforms). Everything was made perfect, and everyone entered into the spirit of the operation with fun, laughter and excitement.

On the day of the inspection, Group Captain Goacher arrived with his entourage. I saluted him, looked him in the eye and said, 'Sir, I challenge you to find anything wrong with this school'. He looked at me in amazement, grunted and said, 'Come on, then, we'll see about that.' Every drawer and every cupboard was open. He looked everywhere, but couldn't find anything wrong. He turned to his staff and said, 'Did you ever see anything like this?' and later submitted a wonderful report.

An even more impressive report was made by the Air Officer Commanding himself, when he made his inspection; he particularly commented on the drill, which was exceptionally good. He attributed my success to good RAF training. I wonder how he would have responded had he known the *true* source of my instruction.

During my time at the School of Cookery, Sheena had a friend, Janet Henderson, who was a psychologist and the wife of an army colonel; she had worked closely with the brigadier who had formally introduced psychology into the Army, and her field of study was applied psychology within the three armed services. She asked to visit the School of Cookery. When she came round, she inspected it very thoroughly, questioning officers, NCOs and the other men. She then said to me, 'I'm astonished, because this is the most perfectly run unit of any of the three services that I've visited. Peter, I know you never studied psychology — how have you done it?' 'I don't know,' I replied; it was only some time later, while out for a walk, that the verses from 1 Corinthians 13 returned to me. *If you have all knowledge, but have not Love, you are nothing.* Love fulfils all laws, psychological and otherwise. This unit had been shaped and run with love, within the strict discipline that service life demands.

Another thing I had introduced was prayers every morning, with the reading of a passage from the Bible. In reality, the School was inspired by the example of Jesus, the Christ, who gathered around him twelve disciples, inspired them with His vision, and put them to work. I had brought together a team and inspired them with my vision and method. Sheena had taught me the need for obedience as well as discipline. For example, when there was a crisis in the world, she'd have the group around her go on a fast, watch and pray for twenty-four hours, each taking two to three hour shifts, day and night. I don't know how much good we did, but I knew it was training in discipline. For her followers, Sheena's word was law, to be obeyed immediately.

When the Commander-in-Chief finally inspected the School of Cookery at Innsworth, he was so astonished at the improvement that he strongly recommended my selection to attend the Royal Air Force Staff College. With the support of my Air Officer Commanding, and having passed the entrance exam, I was selected.

Two months after we had arrived at Innsworth, Sheena and I had moved our caravan to a private site on the top of Combe Hill, on the edge of the Cotswold Hills. We had a spectacular view over the valley and went for many delightful walks. On most weekends we would return to our flat in London. We needed to get a new car for these journeys; I had an open sports car, but as Sheena had been ill, this clearly was not a suitable vehicle to take us back and forth to London — we needed a roomier and more comfortable car. The flat in London had just been redecorated and refurnished but we had not paid all the bills. We worked out that if I sold the sports car, there would be enough money to pay the outstanding bills and buy a more suitable car. I had my eye on a handsome, second-hand 4.5 litre Lagonda in which we could do the journey quickly, but I was not quite sure if it was just the 'little' me — my personality — wanting it. I asked Sheena to get guidance. Yes, this was the right car, so I bought it.

As we now had two vehicles, I set about selling the sports car. A very strange thing kept happening — I couldn't sell it. The harder I tried, the more difficult it seemed. So when I was posted to the Royal Air Force Staff College at Bracknell, we went there with two cars but no money. We even had to think twice about going out for a cup of tea. I thought that at least I would be near London and have a much better chance of selling the car, but again it was the same story: I could not sell that car. The bills for the flat started coming in, then came three summonses to appear in court, and finally letters threatening to write to the Commandant of the Staff College about me. If that happened, I would be in serious trouble: my whole career could be in jeopardy. I redoubled my efforts, but to no avail.

It then dawned on me that there must be some reason for this, so I asked Sheena to get inner guidance on the subject. I was told that, indeed, there was a reason, that I had to learn a lesson that would be of vital importance for my future: to learn to be dependent on God, and God alone, to meet my needs. First I was to make a list of all the bills and total them up. I did that — the total came to £375. Then I was to ask God the Father for that exact amount of money — no more, no less — and give thanks that it was already on its way.

My motto was to be *In quietness and confidence shall be your strength.* As with all things, it is one thing to know it in theory but quite another to put it into practice. I still had butterflies in my stomach: every day, it seemed, bills and final demands for payment came through the letterbox. It was about a fortnight before I could say, 'All right, I've handed this over to God. It is no longer my problem.' Once I could do that in perfect confidence, then — and only then — was the car sold for £375, the exact amount of money that was needed. From that time on, 'patience, persistence and perseverance' became one of my favourite catchphrases.

Attending Staff College virtually guaranteed that I would be completely secure in the rest of my air force career, particularly since so many senior and experienced officers had reported favourably about me. I was the first catering officer ever to have been selected for this course, which lasted for a year and was expressly designed to prepare the future leaders of the RAF. Although I didn't know it at the time, the training and experience I received was of inestimable value to my future spiritual work. It included the finer points of public speaking, writing, principles of organization, group work, and administration; the syllabus also covered local government, the political scene, affairs in the world, economics, and the importance of the spiritual side of life in the services. We were addressed by most of the leading commanders of the three armed services. It was rather like attending a university, a business management school and a teachers' college all at the same time.

There were no formal exams at the end of the course, but we were judged on two things: an essay and a half-hour lecture. We had been taught how to prepare for a lecture. It was to be written out by hand, with an introduction, a main body covering each important point, and ending with a conclusion. Then we were to learn it all by heart and have a few cards, each with a single sentence on, to remind us of our key points. This was the method Winston Churchill had adopted.

The training Sheena gave me in public speaking took an entirely different approach. I was invited to introduce a spiritual colleague who was giving a lecture at Caxton Hall in London. I'd written out my speech in proper Staff College style and showed it to Sheena, just before leaving. She read it and said, 'That's fine' — then tore it up into little pieces and threw it in the fire. 'Now, stand up and let God speak through you!' I was shocked, but Sheena was not a person to argue with. Life with her was always like learning to swim by being thrown into the deep end. Although I must admit that my first talk according to Sheena's method was only partially successful, since then I've never used notes or any other written help when giving lectures. I've just stood up and talked as the spirit moved me.

When it came time for me to give my lecture at the end of the Staff College course, I discarded what I had written and, at the last moment, took with me some artefacts that I had brought back from Tibet. I started by announcing the topic and saying, 'Most of you probably think that Tibet is an uncivilized country, but just look at this' — whereupon I produced a beer bottle from behind the podium, made of carved wood and intricate bronze binding. 'Compare it with our beer bottles.' Then I produced a Tibetan trumpet. It collapsed into short sections, and as I drew out each section a huge 15-foot trumpet was assembled. I then put it on the podium to draw attention to the beautiful large copper and brass work and said, 'Of course, it has many uses. For example, one can express just what one feels about the Directing Staff' (who were sitting at the back of the hall). I blew an enormous raspberry (a loud farting noise) which shook the walls. Everyone was stunned momentarily and then burst out laughing. They gave me a standing ovation, and for years afterwards I was known as the man who blew a raspberry at the Directing Staff of the Staff College!

The essay I was required to hand in, whose topic was of my own choosing, concerned moral and spiritual leadership in the Royal Air Force. I called it *Leadership and Morale* and based it on my training with Sheena and my experience as Commanding Officer at the School of Cookery; of course, in order to show that I had done the proper reading on the subject, I had to add a lot of quotes from leaders such as Eisenhower, Montrose, and others. The Commandant selected this essay as the best of the year, to be published in the *Royal Air Force Quarterly*. I used Jesus Christ as an example of a model leader, and the paper ended by calling for spiritual as well as military rearmament of the nation.[2]

The course, which had begun on 15 January 1951, ended on 14 December of that year. My spiritual training continued with Sheena throughout my time at Staff College, and she was very supportive and giving on all levels of her being. Her love was at times overwhelming. When we students visited a naval establishment in Northern Ireland I was confined to bed with the flu; as soon as Sheena heard of it she phoned the Commandant of the Staff College, asking if she could fly over to look after me. She was told that it would not be necessary, but it was an example of how, from the beginning to the end, ours was a beautiful relationship.

One day, totally out of the blue, Sheena announced that our relationship in the future was no longer to be that of man and wife, although we would continue to work closely together. This was a tremendous shock, because I loved her more than I'd loved anybody before. She was really my whole life — my wife, my teacher, my friend, my lover — and this was shattering news. I couldn't take it in, let alone understand it. For five years, through all our ups and downs, whether I had my back to the sun and walked only into my shadow, or when we sat together like children on a beach and believed that God was only Love, and we were in love, Sheena had never let go of her faith in me. Where Doctor Sullivan's teachings, spiritual knowledge and laws had honed my will and determination, Sheena had led me, sometimes kicking and screaming, into giving birth to the Christ child within, which is Love. *It doth not behave itself unseemly, seeketh not its own, is not easily provoked, thinketh no evil, rejoiceth not in iniquity, but rejoiceth in truth, beareth all things, believeth all things, hopeth all things, endureth all things.* Why was she now releasing me?

Around the same time Sheena made this announcement, I was posted to the Middle East. True to the spirit of my training, on the last night before leaving I gave the apartment a thorough cleaning, instead of going out to

---

2 See full text in appendix

dinner with Sheena. She received a message which said that though I wasn't her 'other half', our time together was not even the first chapter of a wonderful book, but only the preface. Then I realized that only the form of our relationship had to change, which did not affect the love we felt for each other. I also understood that my true 'other half' must be somewhere else in the world, and at the right time God would bring us together. With these thoughts in my head, I left on 17 February 1952, for the Middle East Headquarters of the RAF in the Suez Canal Zone in Egypt.

Chapter 8

God Spoke to Me Too

Life's first manifestation is an emotion.
The only emotion is love.

A SPECIAL JOB had been created for me. I was to be responsible for catering, in the air and on the ground, throughout the world, for all British service personnel who were travelling by military air transport. It was a wonderful job; in effect, as I was my own boss, it meant that I could go anywhere, top priority, as the spirit moved me. The work chiefly involved inspecting facilities and ensuring smooth lines of supply, so involved a great deal of travel. In the first year alone I flew over 70,000 miles, visiting the Gulf of Akaba, Habbaniyah in Iraq, Malta, Libya, India, Ceylon, Singapore, Hong Kong, Japan, Kenya, Cyprus, the Philippines, Aden, Jordan, Yemen, Pakistan, Sudan, Rhodesia, Malaya, Tunisia, Somalia and elsewhere. Often my military status gained me access to otherwise forbidden places, such as the Trucal States in southern Saudi Arabia.

I was thirty-five and determined to make the best of the opportunities my new job afforded. At Bomber Command in Wycombe I had been the Founder-Secretary of the RAF Mountaineering Association, and one of my climbing ambitions was to scale Mt Kenya, which rose 17,000 feet from sea level and was reputedly a spectacular climb. Now I was in a position to do so. The RAF station nearest Mt Kenya was in Nairobi, but the weekly plane only stopped there for a couple of hours. I decided that this was not long enough to carry out a proper inspection of the station, so I arranged to spend the whole week between planes — which of course would give me time to fulfil my ambition.

Since all RAF pilots are required to log up a certain number of hours in the air each month, the Commanding Officer at RAF Eastleigh in Nairobi gladly offered to fly me to Nanyuki, a town close to the foot of Mt Kenya. We had to buzz the landing strip several times to clear it of zebras and other animals. Once on the ground, the plane was met by an Army driver who awaited my instructions, but I hadn't a clue what to do next: there was the mountain, and here was I, but I was damned if I knew how to put the pair of us together. The driver suggested that I ring Anne Hook, the operator at the telephone exchange. Apparently she knew everything worth knowing in Nanyuki.

Sure enough, Anne proved extremely resourceful. She had two uncles living in the area, one of whom she was sure would help arrange the climb. The other, a former Royal Navy Commander, owned a famous hotel which boasted the longest bar counter in Kenya and had the equator running straight down the length of it. I spent a pleasant evening here. Later, from the Army Officers' Mess where I spent the night, I gazed in keen anticipation at the glaciers near the summit of Mt Kenya, glistening in the light of a full moon, and thought how wonderful it would be to see their beauty at close range.

Next morning I set out to find Anne's Uncle Raymond. He was a giant of a man, with a thick beard and blood running from scars on his arms: Raymond Hook caught wild animals for various zoos around the world, and also trained cheetahs to race against greyhounds. When I arrived at his ranch at the foot of Mt Kenya, a film crew was there making a documentary about this extraordinary character. 'So you want to climb the mountain!' he roared. 'Got any food?' When I said no, he made out a list and sent me down to the village bazaar, where I bought everything on the list except bully beef, which I dislike. Hook was waiting on my return. 'Got the bully beef?' he demanded. No, I replied. 'Dammit, that was our lunch,' he said, then casually reached for a rifle and shot a passing chicken, which he flung at the cameraman nearby. 'Here, pluck that!' he ordered.

After lunch he arranged for two native boys and a donkey to take me up the mountain. 'Plenty of clothes?' he asked; 'Gets damn cold up there.' When I said no he told me to take all that I had, including my best blazer and several dress shirts. Just as we were ready to depart, I asked him how I was to communicate with the two native boys, who spoke no English. Hook snorted. 'Just point up when you want to go up, and down when you want to go down.' We set out through tropical jungle to begin the ascent.

It was 11 March 1952 — a week from the vernal equinox — and extremely hot; as Mt Kenya stands on the equator, the sun was directly overhead and I climbed without a shirt. By the time we reached the edge of the jungle I was exhausted. We had come to a clearing by a stream, and using sign language I instructed my guides to pitch the tent. They protested vehemently — obviously they didn't want me to camp in that place — but I overrode their objections; this seemed the perfect place to spend the night and besides, I was incapable of further travel. Still protesting, the boys set up camp and then went back into the jungle with the donkey, leaving me there; I had no idea if they would be back but was too tired to worry about it. Only later did I discover the reason for their distress: the clearing was a watering place for tigers, elephants and lions, and highly dangerous.[1] On this occasion, however, I was so tired that I doubt whether a herd of elephants charging through the tent could have stirred me.

Raymond Hook had been right about the cold that night — but when I pulled out my best blazer, I found that it had been packed with the provisions, and the heat of the day had melted the butter all over it! I woke the next morning to the sounds of the jungle, feeling fully refreshed and ready to go. Fortunately the native boys had returned with the donkey, and we climbed through a wilderness of grass until we reached Two Tam hut, at a height of 16,000 feet. As I staggered to a bunk bed, utterly spent from the exertions of the day, I had to laugh: I couldn't even summon the energy to go to the door for a closer look, in the light of the full moon, at the glaciers I had so admired from a distance.

In the morning, I was able to take in the beauty of the glaciers, being now among them, and look down across the hot African plains whose horizon melted into haze; I felt an exhilarating sense of achievement. The boys returned and we began the descent. As we travelled through the jungle and approached the bottom, I noticed clothes strewn along the track. Somebody else, I thought, must be climbing the mountain that day. On closer inspection, however, I found they were mine; the donkey had disliked its panniers and tried to rub them off against trees and branches, unsuccessfully, but managed to dislodge the contents of one in the process. I could only laugh, despite the fact that they were my smartest clothes; it was a small price to pay for such a towering experience.

A month later I visited Baghdad and made a day trip to the ruins of Babylon in the company of a Doctor and Mrs Strong. He was an American

---

1 Years earlier a band of Italian prisoners-of-war had read about Mt Kenya and were so inspired that they decided to escape in order to climb it; they had stopped at the same place, but unlike me they had been forewarned of its dangers. They went to considerable risk to steal a gun so they could take turns staying awake through the night and keep the wild animals at bay

biblical scholar and prolific author, then writing a new book about Babylon, and wherever we went among the ruins his wife would make careful notes. We were excited to come across some bricks with cuneiform writing on them, which Mrs Strong duly noted; at another point, spying something myself, I reached down and picked it up. 'Look!' I cried triumphantly, flourishing my discovery, 'Babylonian barbed wire!' Mrs Strong's eyes grew in amazement and she dutifully added it to her notes. Some people can be delightfully gullible.

From there I went to RAF Habbaniyah, a very large base by the Euphrates River in Iraq. On arrival, I paid my respects to the Officer in Charge of Administration, Wing Commander Andrew Combe, whom I had previously met as a Station Commander in Bomber Command. He invited me to attend a lecture on archaeology in the Officers' Club that night. Still full of my Babylonian expedition, I found the talk fascinating and asked many questions. Andrew and his wife Eileen seemed impressed by the interest I was taking; Andrew made a beeline for me afterwards and asked me to dinner at their home the next day.

There I discovered why he was so interested in me. Andrew was one of the leading lights in the Oxford Group, or Moral Re-Armament (MRA), founded by Frank Buckman. He had read my article in the *Royal Air Force Quarterly*, on moral and spiritual leadership, and he was hoping to get me to join MRA. Andrew had dedicated his life to saving the world through the four Moral Re-Armament standards: Absolute Love, Absolute Truth, Absolute Purity and Absolute Honesty. The movement stressed the importance of sitting still and receiving God's guidance. His wife Eileen did not seem to share his enthusiasm. Among other things, MRA prohibited its members from wearing make-up or drinking alcohol; later Eileen was to tell me how uncomfortable this made her feel on social occasions. She herself came from a simple Christian upbringing. After her father died and her brother developed epilepsy as a result of an accident, Eileen was encouraged by her mother to join her in Christian Science, but she had done so chiefly out of love for her mother and a sense of duty.

At dinner with the Combes, I found Eileen to be a pleasant, motherly, somewhat shy woman leading a conventional life with five delightful children. Andrew did most of the talking during the meal; we discussed world affairs and the need for spiritual regeneration. Later, Eileen and I talked on the lawn while Andrew attended to some business. We had an easy, flowing conversation and found that we could talk comfortably about the things that really mattered to us.

After that, whenever I visited Habbaniyah, Andrew would invite me round to their home, where he continued his efforts to recruit me to MRA. I got on well with the whole family. Often Andrew wasn't there, so Eileen and I would sit and talk, with me holding forth on spiritual and esoteric subjects, while she knitted. I liked her. Not only was she a good listener, but she was practical, neat, tidy and obviously a good mother. Sometimes we took the children swimming at the Officers' Club pool; Eileen also enjoyed playing tennis, and was generally suntanned and fit. Ours was a pleasant, friendly relationship, and we liked each other's company, but there was nothing more than that between us.

In May that year, 1952, I was visiting Malta when a letter arrived from Sheena saying that she had something very important to tell me, but needed to do it in person. I immediately arranged a flight home on a transit plane and was back in London a couple of days later. I was dumbstruck by her news: she had fallen in love with another man, Jack, a Lieutenant Commander in the Royal Navy. I got no sleep that night; I felt as if my heart had been broken. The next day I went for a walk in Battersea Park and called my whole life into question. How could I go on loving Sheena? Could I ever forgive her?

I was desperately in need of consolation. A couple of days later, en route to leaving England again, I went to see Sheena's friend Nargis (the senior disciple of the Sufi Master Hazrat Inayat Khan). She sat me in the special chair that had only been used by him. I closed my eyes to meditate, and was immediately filled with what I can only describe as the power of the Holy Spirit — the dove of peace descended upon me and illumined my mind. Things that I had not understood or that had puzzled me suddenly became clear; for the first time, I understood Inayat Khan's teachings about Love:

> *There is, in a popular song in English, a beautiful line which says, 'The light of life dies when love is gone'. If you can no longer love, it proves that you never did love. Love that ends is the shadow of love; true love is without beginning or end. That living thing in the heart is love. It may come as kindness, as friendship, as sympathy, as tolerance, as forgiveness. The most beautiful form of the love of God is His compassion, His divine forgiveness. Love from above is forgiveness; from*

> *below, devotion. Love never asks for someone to love him, love is more independent than anything; it is love that makes one independent. Love that depends on being answered by the beloved is lame, it does not stand on its own feet. Love that tries to possess the beloved is without arms; it can never hold...Peace will not come to a lover's heart so long as he will not become Love itself. The best way to love is to serve.*

On the path of my initiation this, then, was the transfiguration. The great illumination my mind experienced lasted for days afterwards; anything that I wanted to know was revealed to me; even my conversation with others seemed to be inspired by the Holy Spirit. I flew back to Malta and spent a quiet time by St Paul's Bay, talking with a padre, swimming and walking.

In July I met and became firm friends with Paul Harris, the Group Captain in charge of the Establishment Committee which had created my post; he was also a keen member of Moral Re-Armament and a friend of the Combe family. We started to have swims together in the Suez Canal and discuss religious and spiritual subjects. Later that month the pair of us went to Habbaniyah where I was introduced to Flight Lieutenant Johns, a catering officer who was also interested in MRA. The three of us had dinner with Andrew and Eileen Combe and, although I was not yet prepared to become a member of MRA, the conversation impressed me enough to accept that there was something in it. On occasion I would join the Combes and others for their MRA 'quiet times', periods of reflection in which one wrote down messages from God. As usual, I didn't hear anything — and neither did Eileen, who confessed to me that she would write down the first thing that came into her head, so as to avoid the 'unblocking' process that members who wrote nothing were subjected to. I saw a lot of Eileen during this visit and continued to enjoy our friendship, although I note today that in my diary of the time she is still referred to as 'Mrs Combe'.

Three months later I was in Amman, Jordan, and decided to make a side trip to Jerusalem. I spent a busy day seeing all the sights, particularly those associated with Jesus, like the Dome of the Rock, but the only one that truly attracted me was the 'garden tomb' — all of the others seemed too overlaid with man's presence and projections. I had a strong feeling that Jesus had been buried in that garden. With these thoughts I climbed a mountain on the outskirts of the city and sat on the top, in the sun, looking down over Jerusalem.

I was pleasantly tired after the climb. The October sun was still warm; the traffic and bustle of the city were a distant hum. Suddenly, quite clearly, I heard a single sentence that is the closest I have ever come to hearing an inner voice: 'Eileen is your other half'. I rejected the idea immediately, finding it preposterous. Eileen was married to a senior officer, and had five children. There were no signs of any romantic love between us; all I felt with her was a warm friendship. 'Besides', I told myself, 'soul halves only meet once in a blue moon!' Yet try as I might to shake off the echoes of the idea that Eileen was my 'other half', they persisted.

I pondered on this throughout my journey back to Amman. After a while, I realized that I was not entirely unreceptive to this astounding revelation. I remembered the wonderful message from Sheena before we separated, that while she wasn't my 'other half' after all, God would bring me together with the one who was. Although Andrew, Eileen and their children were viewed as a model family held together by the four principles of Moral Re-Armament, several people had hinted to me that the marriage was on a rocky foundation. I began accepting the possibility that Truth had spoken and perhaps Eileen *was* my 'other half'.

I knew, from Sheena's training, that one can always ask God for confirmation of what one receives from within. Therefore I prayed now that either Andrew experience the birth of the Christ within, which would enable him to give love to his wife and family, or be asked to give up Moral Re-Armament and focus on his family. I felt neither of these was likely, but if Andrew *were* to be asked to give up MRA, and refused, perhaps this would be the confirmation I sought.

It was my custom in those days, as I moved from one RAF station to another around the world, to 'hitch' a ride on the first available military aircraft; it was uncanny how often there was a seat available as soon as I arrived at the airport. After my trip to Jerusalem, I had planned to travel on to the Far East, but when I arrived at Amman there was no space on any flight in that direction. For days I waited for a seat, in vain, and finally felt that there was a strong reason for it; perhaps I should be flying in the opposite direction, to tell Eileen my news. Therefore I abandoned my plans and flew back to home base in the Canal Zone — and there was a seat on the very next plane.

There I found an urgent telegram that had just arrived: Sheena was dangerously ill and already in hospital. I was immediately granted compassionate leave and flew on to London, where I rushed to the hospital. Just as I arrived, the surgeon was about to operate: Sheena was already under an anaesthetic. The doctor explained that she had an ectopic pregnancy in a Fallopian tube, and an operation was necessary to save her life; otherwise she could die in a matter of hours. 'No,' I said, to my surprise as much as the doctor's, 'I refuse permission'. I felt inwardly that surgery was wrong. Although divorce proceedings had begun, Sheena was still my wife and, as next of kin, I had the right to refuse permission. I felt with the full force of my intuition that Sheena would die *if she had* the operation. The surgeon paled and broke out in a sweat, protesting vigorously, but I was adamant. I still felt that it was wrong to operate and said so, and again refused my permission. That night, the doctor moved his bed into Sheena's room, certain that she would not live to see the morning. I went home and slept in the deep faith that all would be well.

Sheena not only survived the night, but quickly began to recover, much to the surgeon's amazement. The experience strengthened my faith in God's guidance and reminded me of the importance of putting it into action when one *knows* that it is right.

During her convalescence, Sheena was the first person I told about my extraordinary revelation in Jerusalem. She listened carefully and encouraged me to let God steer me in the right direction. I later told Dorothy Maclean about it, too, as we were driving across London one evening. 'Look up in the sky, Peter,' she said, smiling. There, hanging delicately over the city skyline, tinted by the smoke and the mist from the Thames, was a 'blue' moon.

Sheena had recovered sufficiently by the beginning of December for me to resume my duties in the Middle East. I arranged to spend Christmas in Habbaniyah and, upon arriving on the 18th, I immediately sought out Eileen. Sitting at the opposite end of the sofa from her, I explained what had happened to me in Jerusalem. She expressed surprise and said she didn't feel anything, but if it was so, God would bring it about. 'Let's leave it at that, shall we?' she concluded. I agreed, and we dropped the subject.

The next week was a busy one, with Christmas parties and dances in all six of the Officers' Messes. I went to see the Combe children in a nativity play, and had several meals with Andrew and Eileen, including Christmas dinner with the family, but even when we were alone, neither Eileen nor I referred to our earlier conversation.

I was having a wonderful time that Christmas; Eileen, on the other hand, generally stayed at home. She felt uncomfortable attending social events because of Andrew's high moral principles. There was one, however, that she couldn't avoid — the Flying Wing Ball on the 27th. I was determined to see her enjoying herself, and devised a plan to this end. I drew together a small group of officers who sympathized with Eileen and, like me, did not approve of the way Andrew treated her. He was not affectionate, and absolutely forbade her to wear make-up, to smoke, or drink alcohol. At the ball, we planned that these officers would engage Andrew in discussions about moral and spiritual matters for several hours; when one had run out of subjects, another would take over. Meanwhile, I would have most of the dances with Eileen.

On the night of the ball I hid some John Collins cocktails, containing gin, in tall glasses so that they looked like lemon squash. Eileen and Andrew were very late in arriving. Apparently she had put on some lipstick, and Andrew had refused to take her to the ball until she took it off. She stood her ground. Finally, around midnight, he gave in, because it would look bad if they didn't attend. Our plan worked like a charm: the party was still going strong at 2 am, and people were surprised that Eileen was still there, *and* enjoying herself. We had a wonderful evening dancing nearly every dance together. I had previously asked God how, if Eileen and I were destined to be together, we would overcome the complete lack of emotional or physical attraction; well, during the last dance, that attraction suddenly blossomed. I knew then that if we were to have a relationship, it would certainly work out on all levels.

Four nights later, the New Year's Eve Ball in the Officers' Mess promised to be the highlight of the social season. I wanted to attend this ball very much, but there was a conflict — I was scheduled to leave the very same morning for Singapore. I therefore asked God if the aircraft could be held up until the next day, as often happened, if I was meant to go to the ball.

Although I knew that Eileen had felt the same attraction as I had during that last dance at the Flying Wing Ball, she was still wary of taking our relationship any deeper. Fair enough, I thought, all in God's timing, but I saw no reason to hide my own feelings. When I went to say goodbye to her on the 30th, I added, 'I really won't be going tomorrow. The aircraft will be held up, now that I know that it's going to work out between us. We'll see the New Year in together.' The following morning I boarded the aircraft, looked around at the other passengers as the engines were revved up, and thought 'Ha! You think we're going to take off, but we're not.' We then roared down the runway — and we took off, much to my surprise! I felt that God had really let me down, but I reminded myself that this must mean there was a very good reason for the trip.

Chapter 9

Taking Flight

Remember that the larger and deeper your emotional nature, the more your power is manifested

TEMPTATIONS IN THE WILDERNESS were to be the next step on my path of initiation. Because of my enthusiasm for spiritual subjects, Andrew Combe felt that in all but name, I was already part of Moral Re-Armament, so before I left Habbaniyah he gave me letters of introduction to all the key people in the movement. During this tour of the Far East, I was to be fêted by the MRA people wherever I went. Earlier, while on compassionate leave in Britain, I had realized that if I wanted, I could become a big noise in Moral Re-Armament, as its members seemed to pay me more attention than Andrew. On the other hand, I could humbly serve Sheena as a disciple, doing her bidding to obey God's Will, even though our relationship had changed. I had chosen the latter path.

The first stop on my way to Singapore was at Colombo, where I stayed with a well-known dancer, Surya Sena, who was a key person in Moral Re-Armament. A group of MRA men were also visiting, on their own tour of the Far East — a group of clean-shaven, morally upright men with big chins. They invited me to one of their meetings, where I remember sitting in a circle, according to their practice of 'quiet time', waiting to get inner guidance from God. Everyone but me was busy writing; then each person shared what he had received. Of course when my turn came, I hadn't written anything down. They pressed me, trying to uncover reasons for my 'blockages' to receiving the word of God, but I could only shrug and tell them I heard nothing. In the end they concluded that I must be thoroughly out of alignment with God.

I was upset with their conclusion so I told them what I did 'get': Eileen Combe was my other half, God would bring us together and we would marry.

Afterwards I realized that my statement was very unwise, because it could get back to Andrew, but they were all so self-righteous and judgmental that, at the time, I couldn't resist. There was a shocked silence, particularly as they felt that the Combes were a model family of Moral Re-Armament. Not surprisingly, I was asked to leave the next day!

While at the Far East Headquarters of the RAF in Singapore, I had a strong feeling that I should go to Japan, a country I'd never visited. I was told that it was almost impossible to get there, and that there weren't more than half a dozen officers at Far East Headquarters who had been able to do so. One first had to obtain permission of the Air Officer in Charge of Administration in Singapore, then the Air Officer Commanding for Hong Kong, and then the Liaison Officer with the American Forces in Japan. My spiritual training came to the fore: *Never take no for an answer, for with God, all things are possible.*

I thought about ways and means of getting there. As the Korean War was at its height, I hit upon the idea of joining a casualty evacuation aircraft on its regular flight from Japan to the United Kingdom. The aircraft would be calling at many stops along the route — staging posts, where refuelling could take place — and the thought came to me to report on the catering system. What usually happened was that at every stop, the passengers would be given a meal. This needed to be cooked at a moment's notice, since arrival times were quite erratic. Fried eggs, chips and tinned fruit were the quickest to prepare. The trouble was, every staging post had the same idea, so that during the flight between Japan and England, about thirty-four eggs were being served for each person on board! Everyone thought a reevaluation inspection was an excellent idea, and permission was granted for me to join the flight.

The night before leaving Singapore, I was talking to an officer who told me that I would be passing through Clark Field, an American air base in the Philippines, and suggested that I look up a delightful family with whom he had spent Christmas. On landing at Clark Field I made my way to the address that he had given me, but the major I was there to visit had gone out for the evening. Instead, I was greeted by a grey-haired lady, Anne Edwards, who was his mother-in-law. She invited me in and offered a drink.

Within a short time, our conversation came round to spiritual matters. I mentioned that I had been to Tibet, and we talked about books that had been written by the Tibetan Master, Djwal Khul, through Alice Bailey. It was then that Anne Edwards — whose spiritual name was 'Naomi' — said that she was a sensitive, and that she too received from this source. Her news thrilled me; tingles went up and down my spine, and I knew we had met for some special reason. I asked her if she could receive an inner message on the purpose of our meeting.

We were told that we had been together in many previous lifetimes, and had now been drawn from the opposite ends of the Earth, she from Lexington Fields, near Chicago, in the USA, and me from the United Kingdom, to perform a specific work together in this life. Naomi had received many messages from beings in space, concerning their space ships, their purpose and mission. Her work had also been to form a group of seven in Lexington Fields, to contact, telepathically, groups of people all over the world, forming a 'Network of Light'. There were, within this group, both those who 'received' and others who 'transmitted' telepathically; in all, some 370 different groups had been contacted. The purpose of this Network of Light was to receive energies which were being poured down upon the planet. These energies were then transmitted and transformed, or stepped down, through a system of triangles from one level of power to another — much as electricity in a national grid goes from one generating station to another, then to regional stations, local sub-stations, and finally fuse-boxes in buildings for individual use. Naomi gave as an example a high overlighting group covering the whole of Africa, which radiated to three overlighting stations or groups. These people then radiated to key stations or groups, and from these key stations to three other stations. That's the way the energy was stepped down by the system, or relay of transformers, so that it could be used in the everyday world — just like electricity when it finally reaches the home, and appliances can be plugged into it. The energy in the Network of Light, of course, was spiritual.

Naomi's message went on to tell us that we were to share with each other our spiritual experiences to date. This was strange, because neither Naomi nor I had ever spoken completely with others about our spiritual work. How could it be done? There were only a few hours left before my aircraft was due to leave. I needn't have worried, because the aircraft was grounded and unserviceable, and so takeoff was delayed indefinitely. We spent the next seventeen hours together, with Naomi receiving messages from higher levels and both of us relating our experiences. This established an extraordinary bond between us; true to the direction of Naomi's guidance, after this meeting, we kept in touch with each other over the years by writing long letters, once or twice a week, nearly every week.

On my way back from this trip, I stopped in Habbaniyah for a week, chiefly to see Eileen. The day I arrived we went to a church service together; afterwards, I raved on excitedly about my experience in the Philippines, telling her all about Naomi, the messages she'd received, and the Network of Light. Eileen listened politely as she sat there sewing, with a slightly fazed expression. I didn't mind whether she was taking any of it in or not, I was just happy to be with her.

During the next six months, I saw more and more of the Combe family, and felt more comfortable and loving toward Eileen and her children, whom I really liked very much. Andrew was still trying to convert me to Moral Re-Armament; obviously no word had filtered back from the big-chinned MRA men in Colombo. The relationship between Eileen and me remained very friendly, but only that.

My friend Paul Harris and I spent the last day of May 1953 at the beach in the Canal Zone, swimming and talking as we often did. Paul told me that he had received guidance that Andrew was to give up Moral Re-Armament and concentrate on loving his wife and family. He was worried about the family. (Later I discovered that there were severe strains created by the way Andrew related to both Eileen and the children, and as a result the Combe family had all the stresses and secrecy of a troubled and unhappy family.) As Paul spoke, it suddenly dawned on me that this was the confirmation that I had asked God for: if Andrew now refused to give up MRA and focus on his family, I would know that Eileen and I were meant to be together. I urged Paul to share his guidance with Andrew.

The very next day, I was sent for by the Officer in Charge of Administration and asked to go on another visit to Habbaniyah, to check on their reserve supply of food. It was quite extraordinary, the way I was moved around the world, seemingly by chance, to be in the right place at the right time. I'd always conducted my travels in the implicit faith that God would arrange things that way. On several occasions aircraft schedules had been changed in order to keep me in one place, or enable me to travel to where I had to be. Having had the confirmation of the rightness of the guidance that I'd received in Jerusalem, concerning my being Eileen's other half, I expected that I would stay at Habbaniyah for a while, and all would develop to bring us together.

As soon as the plane landed, I sought Eileen out and asked her if Andrew had heard from Paul Harris. She said he had. I eagerly asked if he had agreed to give up Moral Re-Armament, and she said, 'Good Lord, no!' 'Eileen,' I said, 'don't you see that this is the confirmation that I had asked for?' 'I'm sorry, Peter, I can't,' she replied. 'Besides, we're both married, and I have five children.' Well, we talked nearly every day for the next ten days and she still didn't want to see it, but I knew it was so. I returned to the Canal Zone trusting that we would be brought together.

While walking along the beach one day, I was full of inspiration as to what would happen when the two halves were brought together. It would not only be a balance of male and female, but of Light and Love, mind and heart, intellect and intuition, action and being. I was very excited by this revelation, and shared my thoughts in a sixteen-page letter to Eileen; I enclosed a large number of photographs I'd taken of her family as a covering excuse. I wanted to get it to her without the embarrassment of Andrew seeing the letter, so gave it to an officer from Habbaniyah who was visiting the Canal Zone. I asked that he please personally hand it to Mrs Combe only. Andrew was away in South Africa and hadn't yet returned; I further made sure that he wasn't on the passenger list of the same aircraft as the officer flying back to Habbaniyah.

As it happened, Andrew *was* on that plane — he flew as supernumerary crew and therefore his name did not appear on the passenger list. The idiot of an officer gave this thick letter to Andrew to give to Eileen. When Eileen received it, she was so terrified and embarrassed that she hastened to the bathroom, where she quickly read through it, tore it into small pieces and flushed it down the toilet — an untimely end for an inspired letter.

It seemed as if I were getting nowhere, but my faith never wavered. I longed to see Sheena and ask what she could make of it all, since right from the start she had given me her full support in following my guidance about Eileen. Then, in August, I was called to London for a conference. At the same time, I heard that Andrew, who was nearing the end of his tour of duty, had decided to send Eileen home to England six weeks before his return. She was to bring the children back by air to get them established at school and make the family home ready for him. The timing was too good to be coincidence. I planned to meet her at El Adam near Tripoli, in Libya, and join her aircraft there so we could return to England together.

I went to El Adam early, to prepare the way. There I made elaborate plans for Eileen's well-being: these included flowers for her room, hiring a car, and organizing a programme of swimming and supervision for the children. I arranged to take her out to the best restaurant in town, the Ristorante Romagna, to sample the food and wine of the country. When I wrote to Eileen describing these preparations, she was reluctant to come and did all that she could to avoid being on that aircraft. I think she may have had some premonition of the pain and suffering that might lie ahead; but Andrew, unaware of my plans, was adamant that she take the flight. I asked God that if it was His Will, I would overcome any obstacles in getting on this flight, and that all would work out perfectly.

I was due to catch a plane from Fayid in the Canal Zone at 3.30pm to take me to El Adam where I would meet Eileen. I arrived at the air base early and decided to inspect its kitchen facilities; when I returned to the departure lounge at the specified time, nobody was there. On inquiry, I was told that the aircraft was taking off early and that all the passengers were on board. The aircraft was already at the end of the runway, revving up the engines, so I stopped a jeep, jumped in as the aircraft began to move, and said to the driver, 'Chase after that plane and stop in front of it. Stop it!' We sped across the runway and managed to head the plane off. It stopped and I got aboard, thanking God that so far, so good.

Another challenge was waiting for me at El Adam. On arrival, I was told that Eileen's plane was already 2,000 pounds overweight and there was no chance of my getting a seat. I remained unperturbed. I knew that if Eileen and I were meant to come together then there *would* be a seat on the aircraft, and all would be well. Eileen and the children arrived on schedule; all the arrangements that I had made in El Adam worked smoothly and we spent a pleasant evening, returning to the airport for a departure time of 11.30pm. Sure enough, not only was there a place available for me on the flight, but the only vacant seat was next to Eileen's. To this day, I have no idea how it came about.

We arrived at RAF Lyneham in Britain on 24 August 1953. I had arranged for my Lagonda car to be waiting at the airport, so I drove Eileen and her children to their beautiful three-storeyed home in East Cheam. I then went to stay with Sheena in our London flat; although we were no longer together as man and wife, I always enjoyed being with her — there was never a dull moment.

Eileen's thirty-sixth birthday fell a few days later and Sheena proposed that we take her out to celebrate. When the day came, Sheena was laid low with a migraine headache, and she suggested that I take Eileen out, alone, on the following night. We had a pleasant evening at the theatre seeing a play called *Worms Eye View*, with dinner afterwards at the Trocadero; when I took Eileen back to her home, as it was late, she invited me to spend the night. We were both surprised by what happened then: a tremendous surge of love engulfed us both, overwhelming and uniting us, its intensity amazing us; it was something beyond passion, it came from the source of our beings, and we were able to celebrate it on every level.

The next day, Eileen wrote to Andrew telling him what was happening between us and asked him to release her. She felt that she would like to break the news to her aunt, who had brought her up, and to her sister and brother-in-law in Leicester, so Sheena and Dorothy Maclean came to look after the children while we drove to Leicester on 8 September. (It might seem a strange situation, but Sheena truly believed that Eileen and I *were* soul halves. She gave us help and strength; without her support, I doubt that we would have been able to overcome the fierce opposition that our actions provoked. She had an overall vision of Eileen and me being brought together by God for a deep purpose, as yet unrevealed.)

Andrew turned up on 9 September, having received Eileen's letter and flown back from Iraq on compassionate leave. He evicted Sheena and Dorothy as accomplices in the drama that was taking place and sent Eileen a telegram demanding she return. She had not expected him to fly to England so soon and had been hoping to have the children with her before he arrived in the country. Now *he* had the children. With tremendous courage, Eileen replied to Andrew's telegram with a letter saying that she would not go back to him. He responded by forbidding her to see the children, which upset her very deeply.

We returned south and went to stay in the caravan, which was still in the countryside. Fortunately I was now on leave. A week after her letter to Andrew, Eileen was missing the children so badly that she wrote again, this time begging to be allowed to come and look after them; he refused.

It was a harrowing time for all of us, and we decided that Sheena, Eileen and I should go down to Glastonbury, in Somerset, to find peace and guidance for our next steps.

Chapter 10

Footprints Off the Path

Never contend! Let truth, good, life, God do all the work

GLASTONBURY has long been recognized as a place of spiritual power and pilgrimage, the Isle of Avalon in Arthurian legend, the place where Joseph of Arimathea planted his staff into the ground and watched it take bud. Sheena had always gone there to renew her inspiration; years ago, I had been led to a book there called *The Winds of Truth* and traced its source to a nearby group of Solar Mystics, in whose private sanctuary the book had been 'channelled'. We went to this sanctuary now for a time of quiet meditation. As the three of us sat there, Eileen heard a strong, clear inner voice for the first time in her life: *Be still, and know that I am God.* The voice went on:

> *You have taken a very big step in your life, but if you follow My voice, all will be well. I have brought you and Peter together for a very special purpose, to do specific work for Me. You will work as one, and you will realize this more fully as time goes on. There are few who have been brought together in this way. Don't be afraid, for I am with you.*

When Eileen shared these words with Sheena and me, we were both thrilled for her, but Eileen herself was very shaken and could not be consoled. She thought she was going crazy. From then on she began to receive daily messages from this inner voice of the God within; with (sometimes severe) encouragement from Sheena, she gradually came to accept it. This was the clear source that was to guide us step by step along a very difficult and intricate path.

While I was still on leave, Sheena shared her London flat with Eileen and me, and Dorothy Maclean would often visit. Ours was an extraordinary tangle of relationships. Eileen was married to, but separated from Andrew.

Although I was legally still married to Sheena, Eileen and I were now living together as man and wife — with Sheena's blessing. Sheena's relationship with Jack, the naval commander, had passed into history, although Jack remained friends with all of us. Dorothy had divorced John Wood.

Little wonder Sheena was fond of saying 'God chooseth the foolish things of this world to confound the wise'! One day my parents came into London and we invited them round to dinner. They were rather puzzled when they found that Eileen was sitting at the head of the table opposite me, and Sheena was on my right; I had not let them know exactly what was happening. I later felt really sorry for my father. It seemed that as soon as he had got used to my leaving Nora and marrying Sheena, here I was in another relationship, with Eileen. It was very tough on him, but I hoped it all helped to break down his rigidity.

Eileen and Sheena got along well together at the start, but it soon became apparent that there was stormy weather ahead. Just before I returned to the Middle East on 4 October 1953, Eileen had guidance that she was to be with Sheena, who would be her teacher. Eileen was told that she had much to learn from Sheena and time was very short. I had spent five years receiving intensive training from Sheena, but there was a great love between us which would often cushion the blows she delivered; I also knew, from deep within, that what she was doing was right, for she was an instrument of God and her words came from her Higher Self. Eileen was to have a much shorter time, therefore her training would be even more intense.

It was bound to be a painful process. Sheena would cut away the lower self — the desires of the personality — whenever it raised its head. I was able to go through it with love; Eileen, alas, was to go through it with fear.

One evening, when the three of us were out to dinner in a London restaurant, Eileen caught a glimpse of what I had gone through in my training with Sheena. We had eaten a delightful meal and were now sitting in a lounge enjoying our coffee. Halfway through my cup, I had a sudden inner prompting to go and see Jack, the naval commander, who lived nearby. I leisurely finished my coffee and stood up, saying to the others 'I'm just off to see Jack, I'll be back shortly'.

I walked around the corner to the block of flats where Jack lived, and to my amazement the hall porter told me I had just missed him by a few seconds. Sheena was very angry with me when I returned to the restaurant and told them what had happened. 'Jack had a revolver,' she said, 'and while you were sitting there finishing your coffee, he went off to commit suicide!' She railed at me for not following my inner prompting *immediately*; because I had waited to enjoy my coffee, Jack was now *dead*. Eileen was shocked and I felt terrible, about three inches tall. As it turned out, Jack didn't kill himself, but I had to believe at the time that he did, in order to have the lesson rammed home: *always act on an inner prompting immediately*.

But for the constant reassurance of Eileen's guidance, the force of her love for me and her conviction that we really were soul halves, I doubt whether Eileen would have stuck it out with Sheena while my RAF duties kept me abroad. Spiritual and esoteric matters still confused her; she remained desperately concerned about the happiness of her five children; she found it hard to believe that Sheena had really given me up so that I could be with her. To make matters worse, Eileen also had to look after Sheena, who was often unwell; this was very difficult for Eileen, whose Christian Science instruction had taught her not to recognize or believe in illness. Although Sheena was capable of tremendous love, she could also be a martinet. She demanded discipline and obedience, a vital lesson to learn, and everything had to be done perfectly, 'unto the Lord'.

The first lesson Eileen had to learn from Sheena was discipline in receiving guidance, and she experienced Sheena's wrath if she kept God waiting for even a minute at 9am, noon or 6pm, the appointed times for meditation. Eileen had to write down not only the words she heard at these times, but also her visions and other inner experiences, and share them all with Sheena, who for some reason had stopped getting guidance for herself. At the time, Eileen had no idea what Sheena was training her for and resented the way Sheena treated her, but — as I had earlier found — obedience to Sheena had to be learned; it was preparation for obeying God without hesitation. Eileen, however, was full of fear, and afraid that if she did not do as she was told, I would be taken from her.

I had returned to the Canal Zone in October to resume my job of arranging the meals of military travellers throughout the Middle and Far East. My correspondence with Naomi in the Philippines continued; by 1954 I had amassed a wealth of material that she had received telepathically. This included a series of many messages from our 'space brothers' — extraterrestrial beings concerned with the welfare and evolution of the Earth — giving, in scientific terms, information about why they had come to our planet, details about their craft, and their methods of operating. Much of this material was difficult to understand and needed revising. I had an inner prompting to use the training that I'd received at the Royal Air Force Staff College to produce a paper entitled *An Introduction to the Nature and Purpose of Unidentified Flying Objects*. The aim of the paper was to provide an introduction to the study of the reality of 'spaceships', why they exist, their composition and their significance for mankind; it was written with the help of a fellow catering officer who'd been trained as a scientist, and we completed it just prior to my being called home to the United Kingdom for a conference.

Eileen had guidance that twenty-six copies of this paper were to be made, and I was to ensure that each copy reached a key person. I was given the names of Winston Churchill, the Prime Minister; Clement Atlee, the Leader of the Opposition; Lord Alexander, the Minister of Defence; the Deputy Director of Intelligence at the Air Ministry, who was responsible for the study of UFOs; Col. Lester, Chairman of the Churches' Fellowship for Psychical and Spiritual Studies; Air Chief Marshall Lord Dowding; His Royal Highness Prince Philip; President Eisenhower; and several prominent people in military, scientific and spiritual circles.

Dorothy Maclean, who lived near Sheena, kindly offered to type the manuscript, but the appendix, which was oversized, could not be done on her typewriter. This part was vital and could not be omitted. I was desperate because I had an appointment to see Air Chief Marshal Dowding the following Saturday; then I remembered that the Air Ministry had a department that reproduced large maps and other top secret material. I managed to get past the guard, by indicating that I was from another Air Ministry department, and said that this important document was for the Prime Minister and the Minister of Defence, and that I needed twenty-six copies the day after tomorrow. I was told that such a rush job could only be done on the authority of the head of the department. I demanded to be taken to him. I explained the urgency and importance of the document for the Prime Minister and he gave his permission for its immediate reproduction.

I returned on the appointed day, wondering if anyone had read the report, which certainly wasn't official, as it was about UFOs. I needn't have worried: it was there waiting for me.

I had no idea how it was going to be possible to distribute this paper. In each case, I was either inwardly guided or Eileen received direction as to the steps that were to be taken. For example, I was brought into contact with someone who knew Clement Atlee's aunt very well and was sympathetic to the subject. After she had read the paper, she wrote that she would insure that Mr. Atlee would receive the copy, and, furthermore, she would insist that he read it!

I eventually met Lord Dowding at his club in London. Sheena had insisted that every night for two weeks prior to the appointment, I travel by train and bus, to stand outside his house, beaming Love and Light to him in preparation for our meeting. He was called 'Stuffy Dowding', and he was difficult to talk to. He was Commander-in-Chief of the Fighter Command, and had been largely responsible for our winning the Battle of Britain, which had saved the country and ultimately led to victory in World War II. We discussed the paper, which he took away with him, later writing to me, 'I am personally convinced of the existence of spaceships, and I think it highly probable that they are manned by extraterrestrial crews...I think that the government ought to take the subject of spaceships very seriously, and to let some senior and responsible official take on the task of collecting evidence as a preliminary step to formulating an opinion, and perhaps a course of action.' However, he declined to take action himself at the time. (Much later he received a great deal of press coverage of his belief in the reality of UFOs.)

Colonel Lester invited me on two occasions to the Dorchester Hotel to meet the chairman of a publishing company, with a view to doing a series of articles about UFOs in *Picture Post* and another publication. I told him that I felt the time had not come to present this material, which had been received telepathically, as the public was not yet ready, but suggested instead that a more factual series be done on the subject. As a result, *Picture Post* ran a very good series of articles, complete with photographs of suspected UFOs.

I was wondering how I was going to get the paper into the hands of Prince Philip, when I remembered that I'd been to the Staff College with his Air Equerry, Squadron Leader Peter Horsley. I arranged to meet Peter at Buckingham Palace, and said that I believed that Prince Philip was interested in the subject of UFOs. Peter said that indeed he was; all the staff were, including General Browning, the Controller of Prince Philip's household. I told him that I had written a paper on the subject and wondered if Prince Philip would be interested in reading it, and if so, how could I get a copy to him. He replied that the best way to ensure that Prince Philip received and read my paper would be to get it to him before he embarked on the Royal

Yacht, which would be bringing him and Queen Elizabeth home from North Africa after a tour to Australia. As part of my duties, I was responsible for their breakfast at El Adam, the air base where they were to end their flight and go on by sea on the Royal Yacht from Tripoli. Peter Horsley suggested that I contact Commander Mike Parker, Prince Philip's private Naval Equerry, and give the paper to him.

During their breakfast I was the only officer present in the dining room with Queen Elizabeth and Prince Philip. Later I had an opportunity to converse with Commander Parker, and mentioned that I believed that Prince Philip was interested in UFOs, and that I'd written a paper on the subject. He said, 'Oh, good! Anything to have a crack at the dome-headed boys,' meaning the scientists. He asked how he could get hold of a copy. I'd been standing with my hands behind me, holding the paper and I produced it immediately. He said that he would give it to Prince Philip and make sure that he read it — in fact, for the rest of that day, he carried it around with him under his arm in company with King Idris and other officials.

I also saw the Deputy Director of Intelligence at Air Ministry, whose department was responsible for the study and sifting of all UFO reports in Britain. After reading the paper, he said that really he was the last person who should deal with such a paper, because he was a 'nuts and bolts' man, an engineering officer, and a very down-to-earth person. He would first have to have a UFO land in front of him, so that he could take it to bits before he would believe in its existence.

Eventually, all twenty-six copies of this paper reached those for whom it was written, in person. This was a wonderful example of God's guidance working out in practice, against seemingly impossible odds; we found the experience greatly encouraging, particularly as it increased Eileen's faith in her guidance.

As the early indications foretold, Eileen was finding life with Sheena increasingly challenging and difficult. Sheena was an exacting teacher; she also felt that Eileen was putting her love for me before her service to God. In order that Eileen learn the meaning of service, Sheena arranged for her to move in to the attic of a young couple who had recently had a baby and were finding it difficult to make ends meet; Eileen was to help them. Meanwhile, divorce proceedings had begun between Andrew and Eileen. Since adultery was one of the few grounds for divorce allowed by English law at that time, I joined Eileen in this tiny attic room, which was furnished with only a bed and an orange crate beside it, so that a detective could confirm that we were living together. We spent some of our happiest times together there, despite the cramped conditions; we learned that happiness was not dependent on material surroundings or comfort.

Towards the end of my tour of duty in the Middle East, Eileen wrote to me that she was pregnant. This horrified her, because we were not married and she had had a very orthodox upbringing. I cabled her to reassure her that I was delighted. Sheena, too, was delighted, for she had seen the child on the inner planes and felt that although Eileen was carrying it, it was the baby she should have had. (After her ectopic pregnancy by me, Sheena had been advised on medical grounds against trying again to have a baby. This had upset her greatly.)

I was posted back to England on 24 August 1954, as Command Catering Officer to Home Command near London. In October, Eileen, Sheena and I went to St. Patrick's Chapel in Glastonbury where Sheena performed a spiritual marriage for us; in the same chapel, Eileen received in meditation *His name shall be Christopher Michael*, so we knew that the baby would be a boy!

The birth of our first son in Sheena's London flat on 9 March 1955, was an easy one and a wonderful experience. As the baby had been conceived in love, so he was born in love. I was able to be there throughout the process, with a doctor and a district nurse. Sheena was in Ireland at the time; when Christopher was six weeks old, she phoned me and said she would like Eileen to come over to Killarney with the baby, as she wanted to see him. My new post once again involved a lot of travel, so with some reluctance Eileen took up Sheena's invitation.

A few weeks later I took some leave and suggested that Eileen meet me in Dublin. Eileen badly wanted to see me and accepted Sheena's offer to look after Christopher; this would allow the pair of us to spend some time together alone. After a couple of days in Dublin, we went on to London.

Sheena received guidance that the time had come for me to leave the Royal Air Force, that I had learned all I needed to learn there, and that I needed to be free to do God's work. Up to then, I'd thoroughly enjoyed my time in the Royal Air Force — it had enabled me to travel widely, meet many new people and learn important lessons for the future. My intuition, however, told me that Sheena was right.

At the time, it was extremely difficult for an officer to leave the RAF, particularly one who had been to the Staff College for training which had cost the country many thousands of pounds. Circumstances had provided me with nearly the only reason for which the Air Force would countenance my resignation: I had fallen in love with the wife of a senior officer and wished to marry her. This was accepted and I was relieved of my commission. Instead of getting a pension, I received a substantial gratuity; I gave half to Nora and half to Sheena in lieu of paying alimony. Eileen and I were thus left without a regular income and had very little money.

In September, Sheena announced that Eileen and I were putting each other before God: in place of our spiritual work, we were allowing our relationship to develop too strongly. Therefore she suggested that we split up for a time, and she directed me to go to Ireland. The only job I could find there was as a kitchen boy in a small hotel, preparing salads under the orders of the proprietor's wife, a pernickity woman who knew very little about cooking and food preparation. This was a hard blow to my pride, after training with Lyons and having been a Command Catering Officer for twelve years.

Eileen was sent to Dorothy's flat. Originally, our separation was intended to be brief, but it was not to be so. It was easier for me because of my training under Sheena in complete obedience, but Eileen had not had the same training to the same degree. She found even this brief separation very difficult, in fact, intolerable; at one point she attempted to commit suicide. Sheena felt that Eileen was not in a fit state to take care of Christopher, so she had taken him away from Eileen to care for him herself. I felt that this was quite right, for at that time, Eileen was experiencing 'the dark night of the soul': she was not receiving guidance as she had been earlier, and was hardly able to look after herself, let alone a child. During her suicide attempt in Dorothy's flat, she was about to put her head in the oven and had turned on the gas, when her brother Paddy arrived unexpectedly. He was shocked by the state he found her in and took her back to the farm where he was working. (Andrew lived nearby with the children, so that Paddy and his wife could look after them.) Our intended short separation hence became an extended drama.

This, too, was my 'dark night of the soul', the crucifixion experience. Life without Eileen was hell, made worse when I felt that she had turned her back on God. I seemed to have lost everything — my life with Eileen, home, money, career in the Royal Air Force, my spiritual path and inner direction.

I was going around like a blind person. Above all, I felt that we were both failing God and His plan for us within His greater Plan. I knew that eventually Eileen and I had to work together to fulfil an important part of this Plan, but the work could only proceed if we *were* together. What's more, I was worried that Eileen was bringing upon herself a heavy karmic burden that would take lifetimes to work off.

This was a time of great suffering. When Dorothy Maclean saw me on my return from Ireland, she found me almost unrecognizable: I had lost 2 stone (about 13 kilos) in weight, and although I was only thirty-eight, my hair had turned white. I found work making hay on a farm in Cornwall and was able to visit Sheena, who was now living in our original caravan in the New Forest with baby Christopher, whom I wanted to see. When I heard that Eileen had returned to the children (and, I thought, to Andrew), I immediately phoned her. She said she would not return to be ruled by Sheena, but she did want to be with me and have Christopher back.

I determined to use all the power of my will to bring Eileen and me back together to do God's work. One evening, against Sheena's wishes and without her knowledge, I got in the car and drove all night to the farm where for the past six weeks Eileen had been staying with her brother and her family. I hid in a nearby ditch, waiting for Andrew to go to work, and finally entered the house at about ten in the morning. Eileen was shocked by my appearance. 'Pack your things and get in the car,' I told her, 'I'm taking you away'. This she did in rather a dazed state, and we returned to the New Forest.

Sheena received us coldly, because Eileen had made it perfectly clear that she had not come back to me because of God, His Will, or His Plan, and she was no longer turning to Him to receive guidance. She'd come back to live a normal life with a normal job, and to put me first, before God. Sheena would have none of this and said that from now on we would have to go it alone. Eileen and I left in the Lagonda; since we had no job nor place to live, Eileen reluctantly agreed that it would be better for Christopher to stay with Sheena for a little longer.

We found employment at a girl's school near Lymington, in Hampshire: Eileen as a kitchen maid, under a young and rather dominating cook, and me as a groundsman and odd-job hand. Our joint wage was £8 a week, and we lived in a caravan in the school grounds. After we'd been there a few weeks, Sheena returned Christopher to us, much to the surprise of the children attending the school — instant baby! The period of simple work with the soil and domesticity was absolutely vital to restore ourselves after the severe emotional and mental strain that we'd been through.

After we'd been at the school for about six months, I felt that I had to look for a more permanent position — Eileen was expecting our second child. Peter Merchants, the largest industrial caterers in the world, offered me a job, and after a two-month training course with them I was appointed manager of the Club at the Air University at Hamble, Hampshire. People came here from all over the world to learn to fly, and the problems of catering for the tastes of sixty or so different nationalities had nearly driven the previous manager, a retired colonel, mad. I quickly diagnosed the problem. The colonel had planned menus that were more suitable for a first-class restaurant; whereas the majority of the Club's patrons were lads from working-class backgrounds who had simple tastes in food. I decided to offer on the menu the sort of fare that they were used to and would like: fish & chips, egg & chips, sausages & chips, and baked beans, as well as different curries and rice for those from the East. This food was a great success, and also much cheaper.

Eileen remained at the girls' school in Lymington until I could find us suitable accommodation. As we had so little money, I thought another caravan would offer the best short-term solution, and soon found a promising model. Although it was second-hand and in poor condition, it had been custom-built and was 30 feet long — large enough to accommodate Eileen's children, whom we hoped would come to visit. The asking price was £720. I told the owner that I could only afford £650 and he agreed to sell it at that price; I then explained that I'd just come out of the Royal Air Force, and needed a place to live, but all I had was £l0. Since I had obtained a job managing the Club at the Air University, I could pay him £16 a month. He said that he'd been through some hard times himself and agreed to let me have the caravan for a deposit of £10. As it was a time of hire-purchase restrictions, he had his own solicitor draw up the contract. After I'd moved and repainted the caravan Eileen joined me, and this was where Jonathan was born on 18 June1956. I was there for the birth, which was a difficult one.

Part II

The Community Responds to Clarity

Chapter 11

Dark Nights, New Dawn

Think nothing that you do not wish to be real in the objective life

SHEENA HAD MOVED, with her nephew Douglas, into a very simple croft in Glenfinnan, on the shores of Loch Shiel in Scotland. It could only be reached by the daily mail boat. Since it was here that Bonnie Prince Charlie had placed his standard, round which the clans gathered to move forward and reconquer Scotland, Douglas felt that this was the place for Sheena and her followers to establish a base. The symbolism was not lost on Sheena; she truly felt inspired to spread word of the coming New Age throughout Europe and beyond.

I considered Douglas an impractical romantic who followed the Path of Love. Sheena also now felt that the world could be saved by Love and Love alone; she had voluntarily renounced Light and Wisdom, leaving herself completely unbalanced. As a result, she and Douglas together demonstrated — often in a dramatic way — just what a pickle Love can get into on its own, without the balancing guidance and protection of Light and Wisdom. On one occasion, for example, Sheena was ill and entirely dependent upon Douglas for bringing food supplies to that remote and inaccessible place. At the time, Douglas had a job as a shepherd; one day he saw a cloud in the sky, a lovely silvery cloud, and he felt that it was leading him. It led him into a boat, and he followed this cloud all the way down Loch Shiel, until he came to the rail head at the end of the loch. There he got an inspiration to travel down to London, and then on to Hamble, to see Eileen and me. He thus left the sheep without a shepherd, and Sheena without any provisions, and she nearly starved.

During my summer holiday, I took the train up to see the pair of them. Sheena felt that Douglas and I, one representing Love and the other Light, needed to learn more about each other and to work together in harmony. She suggested that he and I go on a quest, a shared adventure. We decided to make a pilgrimage to the island of Iona, off the west coast of Scotland, where St Columba had landed, bringing Christianity to Scotland from Ireland in the sixth century. I had long wanted to visit Iona, one of the major centres of spiritual power in Britain: the veils between the worlds seem thinner on Iona, and many people have had mystical experiences there.

Reaching Oban on a Sunday, we thought it would be a simple business to get the ferry across to the island of Mull and hitch-hike to the other side of the island, where we would get another ferry to Iona. But there were no boats on the Sabbath. I eventually found one old woman who crossed to Mull in a small dinghy to deliver the Sunday papers. Douglas grew impatient and decided that he'd had enough; he turned back, leaving me to go on alone.

Once on Mull, I looked at the map and found a road that went right across the island to the Iona ferry. I thought finding a lift would be easy, but obviously I did not know the islands — absolutely nothing moved on Sunday except to go to and from church. I walked along this road for miles and miles; it was rather like walking 'in the valley of the shadow of death', so bleak and empty was the terrain. The road climbed, becoming more and more isolated and narrow, through a valley with clouds coming down on the mountains, with neither houses nor trees — a dreary and desolate spot. At last a car appeared, but it was travelling in the opposite direction. I decided to take the ride anyway, retrace my steps and go the other way around the island. Again I started walking, and covered a good portion of the 36 miles. I stayed overnight at a farm house, where I devoured huge quantities of food, for I'd walked about 30 miles that day. (Years later, when I asked if that farmhouse still did bed-and-breakfast, I was told, 'Oh no, some years ago a young man came and ate them out of house and home. After that, they felt it wasn't worth it.')

I eventually reached Fionnphort, on the following day, but had to wait for the ferry to Iona. I spent my time walking to a little cove at Kintra where I found a few cottages, one of which was empty; I thought this would be ideal for Sheena, who was looking for a retreat within the spiritual aura of Iona, and made arrangements to rent it for her. I also explored south of Fionnphort, and was strongly attracted by a row of cottages on a small tidal island called Erraid, just a short distance off the coast of Mull, but there was no way to reach it at the time.

Eventually, the ferry took me across to Iona. All the available accommodation had been taken by the hundreds of summer pilgrims who visit this sacred island daily, so I went to the Iona Community at the abbey and asked to see its founder, the Revd George (later Lord) MacLeod, a great spiritual leader in the Church of Scotland. Fortunately, a bed was found for me, and for the next few days I played my own small part in the ongoing rebuilding of the abbey.

I returned to Oban, feeling that I should contact Douglas again, and tell him about the haven that I'd found for Sheena at Kintra. But where was he? My intuition told me that at the current stage of his evolution, he was seeking humility and would take the lowest possible job available, so I visited various hotels in Oban, asking if they had a kitchen porter by the name of Douglas. At last I came to one where, sure enough, the hall porter told me Douglas had been engaged but had left two days ago, heading in an easterly direction. Ah, I thought, he's probably run away to seek asylum on some lonely island. I bought a map of the islands and set off east to find him.

I reached the first island by train, bus and boat. As we approached, I saw a lone figure working outside the island's only house. The boat drew nearer and I could see that it was Douglas; I hailed him across the waters and said that Sheena needed him. His face blanched and he put down his tools with a resigned air, leaving there and then, without a word to his employer, and meekly returning with me to Glenfinnan, where I left him.

I returned to Eileen at Hamble after this holiday and went back to work, but not for long. I was not at all happy working for Peter Merchants. The directors were mostly accountants who were more interested in profits than in their staff, and I felt that I could not give my heart and services to such a company — especially after my happy time in the Royal Air Force, when men and women and their welfare were given such a high priority. I had done my best at the Air University to love where I was, the job I was doing and the people I was doing it with, and succeeded in this — the results spoke for themselves, the Club had become very successful — but I was shocked at the directors' attitude and refused to work for a company that put money before people. Therefore I tended my resignation.

Our time in Hamble had been a useful experience. I had learned more about leadership; Eileen had realized her dream of us both living together with the children, having a normal job, not having to turn to God for guidance three times a day, and being far from Sheena's influence. But I was fundamentally dissatisfied. I felt at the core of my being that we were cheating God and His Plan for us. After all, it had been made abundantly clear that the link between Eileen and me was on a soul level; far beyond our personalities, we complemented each other as part of a *bigger picture*; we had been brought together to achieve a *purpose*, even if that purpose was yet to be revealed. It seemed as if I saw things more from a spiritual perspective than Eileen's rather normal, human perspective, at that time, and I was damned if I was going to settle back into a comfortable, middle-class, mundane existence.

I told Eileen that I felt our future lay in Scotland, and that I was going up there to seek a job. Douglas, meanwhile, was arranging to move Sheena from Glenfinnan to the cottage at Kintra. I went back to Oban but found that there were no suitable jobs available for me there. This was the first of several journeys I made between Hamble and Oban, hitch-hiking on each occasion. There is nothing quite like hitch-hiking for learning to follow one's intuition. On one occasion, outside Glasgow, I was picked up by a commercial traveller and, in the course of conversation, I told him about Sheena. His name was Fred Astell, and he was so inspired by the conversation that he was later prompted to go to Mull and make contact with Sheena; he ended up staying with her and became one of her followers! This was to have surprising ramifications.

Sheena once again became ill during this time, and asked if Eileen would come up and look after her. At this point, Eileen had still not returned to God and was not receiving His guidance; she was still putting me first, and therefore Sheena felt that we should be separated once again. Eileen was to go to Kintra, and I was to go to Glasgow to seek a job. Despite Eileen's protests, I knew in my heart that it was the right course.

And so Eileen packed up our caravan at Hamble and made the long journey north to Kintra by train, boat and bus, with our two children. She arrived exhausted. Douglas missed meeting her off the ferry, although he had been asked to do so. Sheena welcomed Eileen and the children (whom she adored) and, for a while at least, they seemed to be getting on well together.

On my arrival in Glasgow I needed to find accommodation, so I went to the notice board of a kiosk in the railway station, which advertised rooms for let. The first one to catch my eye was in Baliol St; I went round to ask if they had a vacant room, and they did have one. The woman who answered the door was Lena Lamont, who was to be closely connected with our future work. She lived there with her husband Hugh, two children and her mother-in-law. I arranged with Lena to move in immediately.

Looking for a job in Glasgow, I found that I was climbing out of the depression occasioned by Eileen turning her back on God, and the avarice of the directors of the Club. As the Light returned, it brought with it an appreciation of the lessons I'd learned. One weekend, still unemployed, I went down from Glasgow to Oban to meet Eileen and Sheena. Whilst we were having a cup of tea in a cafe, I had a sudden, inner prompting to go down to Hampshire to see the man I had bought our caravan from, whom I had promised to pay £16 a month. I felt that I owed him an explanation for my present inability to meet those payments. Although I was only halfway through my cup of tea when this prompting came, I well remembered that other time in a London restaurant when Sheena had berated me for waiting to finish a cup of coffee ('Jack has a gun and has gone to kill himself').

I had only a shilling in my pocket, but I immediately got up and said, 'I'm off down south to see the man who sold us our caravan. See you when I return, whenever that is,' and walked out of the cafe without finishing my tea.

There, coming down the main street, was a Rover car with a woman driving it. I stopped her and asked her if she was going to Tyndrum, which was the next village, 24 miles away. She said that she was. I asked her if I could go with her, and she replied 'Yes'. I found that she was going all the way to London, and she was interested in spiritual matters — we had marvellous talks on the way down. She also had a beautiful hamper of food! We stopped by the side of the road and spread out a rug, where we ate a whole chicken, drank a bottle of wine and continued our conversation. If I'd stopped to finish my cup of tea, I would have missed this wonderful ride and superb picnic, and probably would have had to wait for hours or even days for another lift.

On arrival in Bournemouth, I explained the situation to the previous owner of the caravan. He quite understood and said that he fully trusted me; he might not have, he added, had I not taken the trouble to see him, so the journey was well worth my while. On the way back, I managed to get a lift on a lorry at Marble Arch in London, going up the Great North Road. When we got as far as Grantham, the traffic lights were red; I looked down to the right and saw a fast sports car with an empty seat, and a girl driving it. I immediately said 'Cheerio' to the driver, climbed out of the cabin and asked the girl if she was going up to Scotch Corner. She said she was, so I jumped in the car and off we went. If I'd hesitated and thought, 'Well, it's a bit of a cheek...', she would have been away and the opportunity would have been lost.

This immediate action without any hesitation is so important on the path of spirit. I found that my driver was not only going to Scotch Corner on the east coast route, but all the way to Carlisle on the west coast route, and we went between 80 and 90 miles per hour all the way. She too had plenty to eat, masses of sandwiches, so again my needs were met. On top of that, she was very pleasant and attractive company: *Seek ye first the kingdom of Heaven, and all else will be added unto you!*

When we arrived at Carlisle, it was getting dark and I wondered how I was going to travel on to Oban. 'Ah,' I thought, as one came towards me, 'a fish lorry — they travel fast all through the night'. I stopped it and asked the driver if he was going to Oban. When he said 'Yes', I climbed aboard, but after a while, I found he was almost falling asleep over the wheel. He said he'd been driving for seventeen hours. 'Why don't you let me drive?' I offered. He looked at me dubiously: 'Well, can you?' 'Certainly!' I replied (never having driven a lorry in my life), and took over from him; as I pulled on to the road, I remembered the instruction from Doctor Sullivan's *Soul Science* series: *Eliminate the words 'if' and 'can't' from your language*. While the driver slept, I drove all through the night on the winding Scottish roads, arriving at Oban at 7.30 in the morning; the driver was so delighted that he bought me a huge Highland breakfast. By following that inner prompting to take immediate action, all my needs had been perfectly met throughout the journey; and I doubt whether the fastest public transport could have taken me there and back again in so short a time — for a shilling!

I took my farewells of Eileen and Sheena and went back to Glasgow to resume my job-hunting. Lena Lamont's family needed a lot of support. Her husband Hugh had been spoiled as a child by his mother, and had grown into a lazy adult as a result of her lack of parental discipline; he slept in every morning, and was always late for appointments. When Lena asked me to help her sort him out, I took a bucket of icy water to his bedroom one morning and warned him that unless he got up immediately, he was for it. Others had threatened him before, but a threat is no good unless one is prepared to carry it out, and they had never been. Hugh ignored me, so I threw the water all over him, soaking the bed clothes.

On Mull, Sheena recovered quickly from her illness and soon left for another cottage, taking Christopher with her because she felt that Eileen was still in no state to look after him. Eileen was left in the cottage at Kintra with Jonathan, who was still being breast-fed. She had a very tough time on the island, in midwinter, separated from me, separated from her friends, alone except for the tiny baby Jonathan, and cut off from God. She felt that everyone had deserted her: God, me, *everyone*. She did not want to listen to that still, small voice that had at one time brought such comfort and reassurance; she now felt that it was all illusory rubbish. To make matters worse, she had no money to get off the island — I had not yet found a job in Glasgow, and could only send her a pound or two from my unemployment benefit. Eileen tried to get a job on Mull as a housekeeper, but having a baby was a handicap; the only position she was offered was with a farmer, who was single, and she did not feel comfortable accepting it. She and Jonathan were helped to survive by a simple village lad who saved some of the meals from his mother's table to take down to her, with pieces of fuel for the fire.

Shortly afterwards, when Dorothy Maclean went through a similar 'dark night of the soul' on Mull, this lad was also her benefactor; his role, it seems, was to serve us all.

Toward the end of her stay at Kintra, while I was in Glasgow and unaware of the hell she was going through, Eileen, in desperation, turned back to God and started to hear His Voice again. She wrote to tell me about it. As much as I felt for the anguish she'd been going through, I couldn't help seeing God's hand in the setting up of this drama.

When I finished reading Eileen's letter, I knew that the time had come to return to her; I felt that both of us were now ready to get on with our real work, that I should go to Mull and spend Christmas with her. I went and found to my joy that yes, through all her trials, she had reestablished her contact with God. I had brought a chicken and other food with me and we had a wonderful reunion and Christmas dinner together. The next day, Boxing Day, Eileen had guidance that we were to leave Kintra and go to my first caravan, the Rollalong that Sheena had lived in, which I had brought up from the New Forest and placed on a beautiful site a few miles away from Oban, by the sea. As we met the ferry that would take us back to the mainland, there was Dorothy Maclean stepping off it on her way to see Sheena and to face the final challenges of her own 'dark night of the soul'.

It later dawned upon me that Eileen, Dorothy Maclean and myself had all been — or were going — through the experience of the crucifixion around that time, despite the fact that Sheena had told us that in the New Age there was no longer any need to go through it. It seems we had chosen this way. It took years and it was very difficult; everything was stripped away, and it was only when I was coming out the other side of it that I realized that scaling high Himalayan passes was a Sunday stroll in comparison.

Our tests and training with Sheena were now over. To this day, I feel that she has been much misunderstood and often misrepresented in published accounts of the Findhorn Community story; the fact is, I doubt very much that there would have *been* a Findhorn Community without her. The training which Sheena gave each of us — Dorothy, Eileen and myself — was to be vital for its establishment. Attachment, rigidity, crystallization, disobedience and sloppiness, of thought, word and deed, were not allowed. As soon as they appeared, they would be broken down so that we were flexible and fluid and could follow the guidance received from within, moment by moment. This training ensured that there was no focus on the little self; Sheena made quite sure that when the time came for us to wield power, it would not be taken to inflate the ego.

Whom the Lord loveth, He chasteneth was one of Sheena's favourite quotations, and by the end of our time with her I think we all felt like latter-day Jobs. It was as though one had to be put, like a steel sword, into the fire, taken out and examined, and if there were any flaws, back into the furnace that piece of steel would have to go, until it was finely tempered, strong and yet flexible.

Up to this time, Sheena had been completely selfless and dedicated. With each of her followers she encouraged the birth of the Christ child within, and helped each of us through the various spiritual experiences leading up to a symbolic crucifixion, when we were indeed stripped of everything: our hopes, our ideals, everything had to fail. Her mission was to bring each one of us to God so that we heard His Voice clearly, or (as in my case) through inner certainty knew His Will and were empowered to act on its direction. All the time, I knew that there was purpose behind this training — we were being prepared for some work, to play some role — but when our faith wavered, or we were disobedient to spirit, Sheena's relentless perseverance carried us through.

Now, however, it became clear to me that the time had come for a parting of the ways with Sheena, who had also been going through some changes. The tremendous power she channelled was taking its toll at last; she was beginning to become unhinged and to lose her discrimination; she developed a monomania about Love and its ability to save the world, forgetting that the Light of Truth would always be needed to balance it, to serve and uphold it. It was distressing to see her subsequent deterioration but there was nothing we could do about it. I will always remember Sheena, however, as she was at the height of her powers, full of life and the love of God, ceaselessly searching for spirit in all its manifestations.

These thoughts came to me as I walked up a hill outside Oban near the caravan where Eileen, Jonathan and I were staying. Having released Sheena, in my heart, I assured Eileen that Christopher would soon be returned to us.

After a few happy days together in Oban we went to Glasgow, the three of us sharing my room with the Lamont family while I continued my job search. It was January 1957, and as surely as the days were growing longer after winter had touched her deepest point, so the Light in our lives was growing daily ever stronger.

Chapter 12

The Heavenly Hotel

Remember this: all that others can do, you can do.

AFTER HER 'dark night' experience on Mull, Eileen was now turning to God several times a day and writing down the messages she received. I never doubted the purity of their source for a second: their content was so far removed from the doubts and difficulties of Eileen's personality! Years earlier, when Eileen had first started hearing the Voice and I wrote to Naomi in the Philippines to tell her about it, Naomi's questions concerning its source had drawn a sharp reply from Sheena:

> *No other person would dare to use the first person singular, as you'll no doubt realize from your knowledge of such things. Not only did the words themselves of such absolute love, certainty, power, gentleness, patience, confirm their source, but their effect on the lives of those who receive them, believe them and act upon them. These writings rest on three things. They are based on three truths or realities. The first and foremost is their Source, who is God the Father, as is stated countless times in them. Second is the Son, the Christ, through whom, and only through whom, God Himself is thus able to contact the tiny erring mind of man. The third truth is the infinite Love that pours through them, to whoever will receive that Love, but the third is dependent upon the acceptance of the two previous truths. Deny one and you deny all. You are not with us and cannot see with your own eyes the indelible signs of the truth of these three things, but you have accepted and been greatly helped by these teachings. This can all be revealed to you, very deeply and fully, when you are rightly oriented to the great Light, when self is forever behind, forgotten, and before your face, the Glory of God.*

In addition to special messages which concerned the state of the world, humanity's likely fate if it resisted making certain changes of consciousness, and general advice on how to conduct our lives, Eileen's guidance would sometimes be surprisingly specific; no question seemed too small or trivial to be taken to God, and when the answer came I would then take action. It was a perfect partnership.

The time had come for me to secure a stable, income-producing job. Because of my catering training and leadership background in the RAF, the job that I felt I could do best would be to manage a hotel, so I went to see the head of the Hotels and Catering Department of the Labour Exchange in Glasgow. She said that the only suitable positions then available in Scotland were with one company which had twenty-one hotels, but they treated their staff so badly — particularly their managers — that she wouldn't dream of sending me for an interview.

It so happened that the General Manager of this company, Mrs Bruce, would be visiting Glasgow the next day. Intuitively I knew I had to see her. When she asked me what experience I'd had of running hotels, I had to admit that I had none; but I quickly added that I'd been trained in catering, and had held most of the major responsible catering jobs in the Royal Air Force, including being Command Catering Officer on the Burma Front, the biggest of the War, with 250 catering officers under me. 'Oh,' she said, not seeming overly impressed. 'that may well be, but we're in this as a business. How do we know that you can run a business?' 'Well,' I replied, deciding to pull out all the stops, 'I know how to run things in accordance with spiritual laws and I have found that if things are right on *that* level, they will be right on all levels, including the financial.' She considered this for a moment, and then said, 'Yes, I could believe in that — but my directors wouldn't.' I replied that if she gave me a hotel, I would prove it for her directors.

I made it clear that I had three conditions. After my soul-numbing experience of Glasgow, I needed to love the place I was working in if I was to give it my best; second, because our two small boys needed looking after, Eileen would not be joint manager with me (husband-and-wife joint managership was standard practice); and third, I had to love the person for whom I was working. I indicated that she would do. I think by then she thought I was a bit odd, but to my delight she offered me a position as manager and then showed me photographs of two hotels. The first was of Cluny Hill Hotel in Forres, Morayshire, and it looked most attractive: a large

Victorian palace of a place, standing like a sentry halfway up a thickly-wooded hill. I knew I could love such a place. The other photograph showed a hotel at the Trossachs, a place of spectacular natural beauty in a glen near Loch Lomond. Mrs Bruce gave me the choice of either, but as I sensed she was an intuitive woman, I left it for her to decide. She chose Cluny Hill.

Because the hotel was closed for the winter, my presence was not required there until March; in order to have an income until then, I managed to get a temporary job as a door-to-door salesman with the Kleenezee Brush Co. This soon taught me how little I knew, after my sheltered life as an officer in the Royal Air Force, about how others lived. As I went round knocking on people's doors and glimpsing tenement life in a big city like Glasgow, I was appalled by the grey faces, eyes full of suspicion or fear, and the grim surroundings I found.

Once more I experienced the truth of Doctor Sullivan's training in the power of positive thought. Selling brushes was tough and exhausting work. I would get very tired, after carrying a heavy case up six or seven flights of stairs in each building, and when I knocked at a door, if my face said, 'You don't want any brushes today, do you?' the door would be slammed against me. On the other hand, when I was fresh and full of vitality, I would knock on the door with an expression of 'What brushes would you like today?' and make a good sale.

During this time, our past association with Sheena came back to haunt us. Fred Astell, the commercial traveller whom I had told about Sheena when he picked me up hitch-hiking, had been to meet her, seen the Christ in her, and decided to give up his wife and family so that he could follow her. He told his wife Sylvia of this decision and went to join Sheena on the island of Tiree, but he had not taken into account his unhappy and determined mother-in-law, Elsie Moss, a little woman with a will of iron. She got in touch with the newspapers and, with reporters in tow, set forth to find her errant son-in-law — either to bring him back or at least tell him (and the world) exactly what she thought of him.

Thus began a madcap chase round the islands of the Inner Hebrides, including Mull, with newspaper reporters hounding Fred and Sheena, and his mother-in-law in hot pursuit. Some reporters even located Dorothy, who was now living in our caravan at Oban while she worked as a secretary: twenty of them turned up at breakfast time one day, all hungry for information about these unusual people and their goings-on, involving an alleged woman cult leader, her disciples, and the 'messages from God' they claimed to receive. It must have been a very slow time for news!

The reporters descended upon the Lamont household at Baliol St when I was in bed with the flu, and they hung about outside for days; at one time sixteen of them invaded my bedroom, where they plied me with questions. Some bright reporter struck upon the idea of calling us 'the Nameless Ones' because, of course, our 'group' didn't have a name — it wasn't even a group! Yet the label stuck, and soon the story of 'the Nameless Ones' was headline news on the front pages of most Scottish newspapers. A Sunday paper published a series of full-page articles by several 'disciples' of this remarkable woman, Sheena Govan, who according to the press, at least, was looked upon by many as the Messiah who had come to save the world through Love.

In the middle of all this, I suddenly remembered that Eileen and I were not legally married. If this were discovered, it would create difficulties with Mrs Bruce and the hotel chain. I got up from my sickbed and dressed, but found there was no way out of the house — the reporters and photographers were still waiting outside the front door. Eventually we left through a back window, clambered over a wall and hailed a taxi to the Registry Office, where we were married, with the taxi driver as a witness. On our return, we climbed over the wall again and I went back to bed, without anybody discovering us. What a story that would have made, had we been spotted! Shortly afterwards, Sheena returned Christopher to us, again escaping the watchful eyes of the press.

This hurricane of publicity lasted for about two weeks, the twists in the story growing daily more bizarre as the reporters ran out of 'facts' and hence had to invent their own. In a way, it was good training for Eileen for the days ahead, because she often had to stop in the middle of cooking or tending Jonathan to seek guidance on our best response to the latest developments. Mrs Bruce was naturally alarmed to find her new manager enmeshed in such nonsense but we managed to convince her that we had severed all ties with Sheena at that time, and promised not to involve her in any way with the hotel.

* * *

The town of Forres is an ancient Royal Burgh in the north of Scotland, sited 26 miles east of Inverness, the capital of the Highlands, on the busy main trunk road to Aberdeen. Shakespeare set the three witches in *Macbeth* 'on a heath near Forres'; the town today retains its medieval high street, market cross and tollbooth. Its most arresting feature, however, and that which sets it apart from neighbouring Nairn and Elgin, is Cluny Hill, a tree-covered eminence that dominates the landscape for miles around and is used as a navigation point by sailors in the Moray Firth. Nelson's Tower, built in 1812 to commemorate the Battle of Trafalgar, stands at its top like a finger pointing to heaven above the beech and birch trees that surround it; from here, there are spectacular views of Findhorn Bay and the Moray Firth, the mountains to the north, and woodlands and farms to the south.

I caught my first glimpse of Cluny Hill from the train as we approached Forres in March 1957. I don't know why, but I found the sight thrilling; perhaps it was because Eileen's guidance had promised to lead us to 'the land flowing with milk and honey'. We were met at the station by Graham MacDonald, the hotel's General Assistant, who had been looking after the hotel during the winter. He drove us across town and along the tree-lined drive to our future home.

Cluny Hill Hotel nestled in dense woods on the southern slope of the hill, overlooking the greens of a golf course fringed by darker conifers, with hazy, heather-covered hills in the distance. Formerly known as the Hydro, it had been built at the end of the 19th century as a health spa for Scots and English gentlefolk who came, with their servants, to enjoy a range of water cures and treatments, play golf over the road and enjoy other leisure activities.

Its outside appearance confirmed the promise of its photograph: in the late afternoon sun, it did indeed look like a palace of light, particularly after our grim experience of Glasgow. Our first impressions inside were also favourable, as Graham MacDonald gave us a tour of the building. We saw luxury suites of rooms, beautiful furniture, spacious public rooms, grand bathrooms with huge bathtubs, and a large, wood-panelled, bay-windowed dining room jutting out towards the golf course so that one appeared to be floating above the trees in the grounds below.

Then we were taken round the back and shown the manager's quarters: two poky, dark rooms. I said we couldn't possibly live there with two children, but Mr MacDonald said that he was sorry, these were the manager's quarters and we would have to make the best of them. Since we were now taking all our questions to God, I asked Eileen to find out what we should do. Her guidance told us that the whole success of this venture depended on the health and well-being of the manager — therefore we were to have the best rooms in the hotel, and not the worst. This was indeed wonderful news! Out we went, round the hotel on the first floor, and selected a suite with a lovely large room, with bay windows, as our sitting room; a double-bedded room next door for Eileen and me; a twin-bedded room for our two boys; and at the end, a luxurious private bathroom. It distressed Graham MacDonald when we moved into these quarters. He was afraid of Mrs Bruce's reactions, for she usually ruled by fear.

Very soon, at her headquarters in Aberdeen, Mrs Bruce heard what had happened. She immediately came storming across to Forres, demanding to know on whose authority we had made this move. 'Mrs Bruce,' I told her calmly, 'you must understand right from the beginning how this hotel is going to be run, because I will not be running it.' 'Oh!' she said, taken aback. 'What do you mean?' I said, '*God* is going to run the hotel, through me.' Then I explained to her how we operated, and read her the guidance that Eileen had received about our rooms. Well, that rocked her in her tracks — she didn't know what to reply. In the end, she burst out laughing and said, 'Well, I can't compete with that!' And, of course, she couldn't. So, round one had been won, with Mrs Bruce saying, as she left, that she didn't know how she could explain it to her directors.

Although I had been trained in catering and had considerable experience in personnel management, I had no idea how a hotel was run, let alone a large one like Cluny Hill employing over fifty staff. I hadn't a clue about what was a fair wage to pay them, whom to engage, or how much to charge our guests. When we had settled in, a few weeks before the start of the season so we could prepare the place for the arrival of our first guests, I realized the magnitude of what we had taken on.

There was a further challenge beyond my lack of experience. Although the hotel looked great on the outside, closer inspection showed it to be very run-down. It was known locally as 'the morgue', and with good reason: the atmosphere inside seemed dead. This lack of life was reflected in its takings. In all the years of its operation under this company, I suspect that the hotel had rarely made a profit, and I was sure that the fault lay in the policy of the chain that owned it.

After World War II, social attitudes and behaviour in Britain had undergone a revolution. The greatest empire in the history of the world had crumbled in little over a decade; previously rigid class distinctions were breaking down; the Welfare State, offering free health care, housing and other benefits for all who needed them, liberated millions from the chains of birth or circumstance. Before the War it had been customary for many members of the English gentry to spend a part of their summers in the Scottish Highlands, enjoying the clean air and the pleasures of hunting, shooting and fishing; grand hotels like that at Cluny Hill catered perfectly for their needs. After the War it was all different. The rich and upper classes increasingly holidayed abroad, while the lower and 'working' classes were able to take holidays for the first time. Coach parties and package tours within Britain became popular, and the large hotels, deserted by their former clientele, became available at knock-down prices to accommodate them. Quantity of turnover, and not quality of custom, became the order of the day.

Thus the chain that owned Cluny Hill and twenty other hotels throughout Scotland had every reason to keep them 'cheap and cheerful' (although how much they achieved the latter was open to doubt). This bargain-basement approach was cannily planned to take advantage of different social groups at different times in the April–October season that the hotel was open. Old-age pensioners, for example, would prefer to come before the summer crowds with children arrived; the well-heeled or well-bred families, if they came at all, would visit at Easter and again in the autumn. The Automobile Association (AA) rated every hotel in Britain according to a number of stars from One (which meant very basic) to Five (de luxe), depending not only on the number of rooms and facilities available, but also on its standards, particularly of food; at the time Eileen and I arrived at Cluny Hill Hotel, it had three stars in the AA guidebook.

I was determined to change all this. As only the best is good enough for God, I reasoned, why not have quantity of turnover *and* quality of service? I knew that we could make a success of it, and Eileen's guidance seemed to confirm this conviction:

> *My son, I want this hotel to be a four-star hotel and you are to do everything you can to make it so. Simply ignore what Mrs Bruce told the Automobile Association man, as she would be quite satisfied for this place to remain a three-star hotel. It is up to you to prove to Mrs Bruce that this is no ordinary*

> *place and you will never be satisfied until you've seen it made into a four-star hotel. You have My full blessing with this and you go ahead with My authority, stopping at nothing.*

Eileen's guidance more than made up for my lack of hotel management experience: I sought her inner direction on every detail of running the place, no matter how small the question was or how obvious the solution. We were told that we were to establish Cluny Hill as a 'Centre of Light', and soon learned that Light quickly throws up shadows — dark forces that were determined to snuff out our efforts right from the start. The heads of our five departments were alcoholics, for example, and if they got drunk at the same time, all hell would be let loose throughout the hotel. I had to tackle this by taking one problem at a time to Eileen and then carrying out the written instructions she'd receive. She learned to be able to get guidance no matter what the turmoil was; she would also have to drop whatever she was doing, such as cooking a meal or changing the baby's nappies, and immediately turn to God for an answer.

My overall guiding principle, however, remained to love where you are, love whom you're with, and love what you're doing. As time went on, my own intuition about running the hotel developed, but I still went to Eileen for confirmation that my chosen course of action was correct. Usually it was; on some occasions the timing of it would be wrong; less often, I would be barking up the wrong tree altogether. In the early days at Cluny Hill, however, I took *every* question to Eileen and we worked together as one. She received the guidance, and I took action accordingly. Neither the staff nor the guests knew that this was how the hotel was being run, because we didn't talk about it, but they *did* know that it was a hotel with a difference.

Love was the other ingredient vital to the success of Cluny Hill Hotel. Eileen had explicit guidance to this effect:

> *I want you to realize now as you have never realized before how terribly important it is that whatever you do in this My chosen place you do with love. I want you to take time to look around you. Study the staff you have here and you will see, whatever their job is, they are doing or learning to do it with love. If you ask them why, they could not tell you, but the reason is I can only have those who work with love in their hearts here. The atmosphere is so very important. You will see*

> *several go from here and the main reason will be they were working without love.*

We had a good example of this with a kitchen porter whom I employed shortly after the hotel opened for the season. When he complained about the management behind our backs, as is usual in hotels, none of the other staff responded. He found this very odd. The obvious love and goodwill among those working for the hotel made him so uncomfortable that he left soon afterwards.

Eileen and I were often reminded of the importance of keeping the love flowing in our relationship. We were both extremely busy. I worked from the morning until well after midnight, seven days a week; in addition to caring for the children, Eileen arranged all the flowers throughout the hotel and sometimes worked by the hot plate in the kitchen, receiving the orders from the waiters and waitresses and calling them out to the kitchen staff. Not surprisingly, both of us could become tired and stressed, and this would strain our relationship; sometimes I failed to let Eileen know what was going on, which caused further resentment. Guidance told her:

> *My child, it is more important for you and Peter to be united than anything else. Peter has much on his mind but that need not stop him from being civil to you when you ask him a question. Peter, My son, to brush aside these questions with a wave of the hands is very unloving. Allow My child to be part of all that is going on... In this way, she knows when prayer is necessary. She can feel when help is needed. Peter, I placed you and My child side by side. Remember, you complement each other. One cannot do without the other. You are the perfect whole, when you are operating together. The atmosphere you create affects everyone. You are united only in My divine Love. So keep very close to Me.*

After we'd been at Cluny Hill a short time, Dorothy joined us; she became my secretary and also worked as a receptionist. Lena Lamont came up from Glasgow with her children, to look after the staff. Eileen, Dorothy, Lena and myself were able to achieve great unity at Cluny Hill with the heads of departments and the rest of the staff, partly because of the hard and strict training we'd had under Sheena.

It is people that matter became my personal motto. Almost everyone who came to the hotel received my personal attention, even if they were only dropping in for a cup of tea or a drink in the bar. I would usually talk about the hotel and, if possible, take them on a tour of it; often they were so impressed that they would book to come for their summer holidays. I liked to meet every guest as they arrived, preferably as they were getting out of their car; I would show them to their room myself, all the time making a personal connection with them. After that they would see everything through rose-coloured spectacles. Throughout the day, I spent as much time as possible in the hall at the centre of the hotel, like the captain on the bridge, instead of hiding myself away in the office.

Every letter that came to the hotel was answered immediately. When the morning post arrived I would sit down with Dorothy and, as I opened each letter, dictate an answer before opening the next. In fact I would not even open a letter unless I was prepared to reply to it immediately, because the first reading produced a freshness of impressions and insights that was hard to recapture later. Normally when people wrote to hotels, they got back a form letter filled in by the receptionist, but I made a point of writing a personal note to each one. Dorothy would then type the letters throughout the rest of the day; I would come back in the late afternoon to sign them, and they would be sent by the 5 o'clock post. Thus every letter was answered on the day it was received, with an immediate and personal reply from the manager.

One method I employed to make people feel welcomed and at home was to keep a card index on each guest, noting down little personal details about them, what they liked to eat and drink, about their families and so on. When next they visited, I would then be in a position to ask something like 'How is your daughter Sally doing in school? Has she passed her chemistry examination this time?' They would be amazed at the interest shown in them and, as a result, come back to the hotel year after year.

The non-story of 'the Nameless Ones' returned to haunt us in our first season at Cluny Hill — for some reason, we hit the newspapers again under the headlines 'Heavenly Hotel', with a far from heavenly picture of me in bed when I'd had the flu in Glasgow. The article described how this 'luxury hotel for millionaires' was run by God; it was all journalistic nonsense, of course, but the hotel chain's Chairman kicked Mrs Bruce over it, so she kicked me. I had to give them both a firm undertaking that there would be no such publicity in future, and that we were no longer involved with Sheena, whom the newspapers called 'the Messiah of the Nameless Ones'; Mrs Bruce's real fear was that Cluny Hill Hotel would end up as the headquarters of this 'group'.

Despite this hiccup, we were well pleased with the results of our first season at Cluny Hill. Most of the staff, who were used to being treated like dirt at other hotels, cheerfully took their leave and promised to return next year. Normally only the manager and his family were allowed to spend the winter months at the hotel, but Eileen was pregnant again, so Dorothy occasionally stayed the night with us as 'mother's help'; she would also type up the voluminous guidance Eileen had written down every day in a series of notebooks.

Earlier in the year, Eileen had written a letter to Naomi in the Philippines:

> *Please don't thank me for sending God's Word. It is Dorothy who so faithfully types and sends it off to you. As you know, I am but an instrument that God uses to receive these messages. Of myself, I am, indeed, nothing. The only reason I am an instrument is because Sheena has suffered as no human being could suffer to take my tremendous burden of sin from me, to free me to do God's work. Naomi, my dear, I don't think you have any idea what that weight of sin was like. I don't suppose you know what it is like to sink down to the very depths of hell, to have rejected God and to have rejected Sheena completely, and yet, despite all this, to be lifted up into God's wondrous Love and Light again. It is the most wonderful thing that could possibly happen to a soul, and that is what happened to me. Sheena, who is Love, had to sink even lower to lift me out of the darkness. Do you wonder, I have been willing to give up all to serve her? If she is willing to do that for me, the very least I can do for her is to offer myself to her, to use in the service of Love. This has not been an easy path to tread, but it has been my own fault it had to be so difficult at times. It is generally the resistance in me that makes it difficult. When I've been free and willing to follow God's guidance without a second's hesitation, there has been no pain and suffering, but when I've kicked against the pricks, then not only have I suffered, but others as well. If only we could all realize this quickly, and*

cease resisting and do as we're asked, how easily God's promises would come about.

Sheena had been in touch with us by letter and phone. She was still with Fred Astell, whom she thought represented the Light aspect of God, while she embodied Love. Eileen, Dorothy and Lena all received in meditation that this was not true — at that time — and Eileen's guidance went on to suggest that Sheena should send Fred away and place herself in our hands, that we might look after her. Sheena refused. She told us that she now only accepted a thing if it was 'given in Love', in other words, through a spontaneous prompting of the heart — not as a result of Eileen or anybody else getting guidance to give it to her, since such a gift would then be 'of the Light'. Thus shunning the Light, Sheena sank further and further into darkness, getting into one mess after another and suffering tremendously.

In December 1957, Eileen's guidance told us to break off further contact with Sheena, who had been writing asking for money and wanting Christopher to visit her. Then one snowy day she turned up at Cluny Hill without warning, wanting to stay. She looked tired and distraught and told us she'd spent the last of her money to travel up by train. I knew then that I had to turn her away: quite apart from the injunction of Eileen's guidance, we had given Mrs Bruce an undertaking that nobody else would be staying in the hotel when it was closed. I told Sheena that we had written to her, talked to her on the phone, and asked her to come to us so we could look after her when the hotel was open, but she had refused. Now I had to turn her away in the snow. She was angry. She hit me in the face, turned round and left. Later I recalled the time when we were walking in Hyde Park in London and she had said to me that in the end, I would be so close to God that I would turn against her. At the time, I had not believed her; now it was happening, just as she'd prophesied, and I watched with great sorrow the lonely figure of the woman I had loved and served, walking away down the frozen drive.

Chapter 13

New Life at the Morgue

You are to think, affirm and act from this thought: life is infinite and I have all I desire

FOR THE SIX MONTHS of our closed season, Eileen, Dorothy and I often worked in the garden, raking up leaves and weeding, and above all putting in as much love and positive energy as we could. As in all things, if one is working with a spirit of love and joy, with attention to detail and a sense of perfection, the energy of this spirit flows into the object of one's work; the same happens if one is angry, depressed or out of sorts, when a negative energy is transferred. If you prepare a meal when you are in a bad temper, for example, those eating it afterwards are also partaking of that energy. If you bring joy and fun into your housework, it will have a cheering effect on people later entering the room. Some people are more sensitive than others and can describe these vibrations accurately, but everyone is affected by them whether they are aware of it or not; therefore the energy which one brings to any task is of vital importance. I would not allow any of us to work in the grounds or building at Cluny Hill unless our spirit, temper and attitude was positive, loving and correct; we had been told time and again, in guidance, the necessity of this in all our work.

During the winter, I decided to bring up to Scotland the large caravan that Eileen and I had lived in at Hamble. It was fortunate that my Lagonda was such a powerful car, for we could not afford to pay a haulage contractor to do the job, but it was still a mighty challenge towing a 30-foot caravan all the way from the south of England to the north of Scotland. Along the way, local police outriders often escorted me through narrow town or village streets and I arrived at Forres without incident; just as I entered the town, however, in a final spurt like a horse that has smelled its stable, I took a right-hand turn too sharply and knocked over an illuminated 'Keep Left' sign on a traffic island. This fused the lights, and the whole area was plunged into darkness.

(Today, as you drive into Forres from Inverness, you will find my legacy: a roundabout on the road, built by the council as a result of the accident.)

I parked the caravan in the hotel's large garage, repaired the damage to its side and generally refurbished it over the winter. I planned to sell it, as we still owed money on it, but Eileen's guidance was firm on the subject: *My son I do not want you to sell the caravan no matter how good an offer you get for it.* This surprised me, for I thought we would do better having the money, but I had learned the lesson of obedience well enough by then.

Our third son, David Jeremy, was born on 13 January 1958 at Cluny Hill Hotel. For some weeks before, the doctor had confined Eileen to bed because there was a danger of a miscarriage and he had wanted her to move to the local hospital for the actual birth. But God said that the baby should be born in the protected environment of Cluny Hill, so I refused to give my permission. The doctor was very angry and hardly spoke to us again; true to God's Word, however, the birth was an easy one.

When the staff arrived at the beginning of the new season, Eileen arranged flowers in all their rooms and Lena made sure that these were as sparkling clean as the guest rooms. The love with which this work was done shone out from every corner; it made the staff feel very welcomed, and led them not only to respect and look after their quarters, but also to spread the same care throughout the building. As I had learned, when one works with love, one wants to do the job perfectly and bring joy and a sense of fun into it. The housemaids had a friendly competition to see who could put the most love into their bathrooms, polishing the linoleum floors until they gleamed, and soon the whole hotel shone.

After our first year the head chef had left to become a hotel manager, so I advertised for another. One day a young man called Charles Campbell came to apply for the job. He was quietly spoken, fresh-faced and had innocent blue eyes; he appeared to be little more than a boy and I felt sure that he couldn't have sufficient experience. 'I'm sorry,' I said, 'but this is for a three-star hotel, and I intend it to earn a fourth.' He gently replied that he had been head chef at Cluny Hill Hotel two years before. Just at that moment, Graham MacDonald, my General Assistant, phoned and confirmed Charles's story: he told me what a good chef he was and, furthermore, that he had been head chef at one of the best railway hotels in Scotland. I wondered then why he was out of a job, but because of Graham's recommendation I decided to engage him.

Charles moved into the kitchen with quiet authority and was indeed a wonderful chef, a wonderful person — and a dreadful alcoholic. We never knew if he would be sober enough to serve dinner. On one busy Saturday evening, for example, I went into the kitchen and found him drunk and demanding another whisky. I immediately went to Eileen to get guidance, because I didn't know how to handle alcoholics. She opened up her notebook, picked up her pen and immediately wrote, *My son, if you want the dinner served, give him another whisky*. I thought this was very strange advice but I went to Charles immediately and obtained for him a generous dram, because I had learned absolute and implicit obedience to God's word. He pulled himself together and served an excellent dinner. Mrs Bruce was always at me to fire Charles, but I finally said to her 'Mrs Bruce, what would you rather have - a chef who drinks and is a first-class cook? Or one that doesn't and is a poor cook — like the ones you employ in your other hotels?'

One day, Charles asked if he might have a few days off to visit his wife and family on the west coast of Scotland; I agreed. He borrowed a van and left with one of our hall porters. That evening the police came and asked me if we had a Charles Campbell employed as chef. When I said that we did, the sergeant told me that Charles had been involved in a slight accident and they discovered that he had hidden a quantity of food, which included half a sheep and tins of ham and other meats, in some nearby woods. I checked the stores and confirmed that these items were missing. As the police wanted to charge him with theft, I asked Eileen to please get guidance on this situation. She received that we were not to charge him as he was at a crossroads: *Give Chef all the help you can, he is well worth fighting for. He will never let you down again.*

We waited for Charles to return. He came back in the middle of the night a month later to collect his things and to give himself up to the police. I asked him why, as I hadn't preferred charges. He was astonished and bewildered, but he agreed to stay. If he went to prison, he would continue in a life of crime, but I put it to him that together we could demonstrate that Cluny Hill Hotel could be run with love. And we could prove to Mrs Bruce, who ruled through fear, that a hotel could be run in this way, that any business could prosper when run with love and in accordance with spiritual laws.

Charles returned to the kitchen in a very quiet and gentle way. Once again he proved himself to be a master chef, but above all, and in spite of his frequent drunkenness, it seemed that everybody loved him and loved working for him. During the first season that Charles was with us, a medical student had come seeking holiday employment and the only job I could offer him was washing pots and pans in the kitchen. He accepted this and so enjoyed working with Charles — where there was never a dull moment — that he came back year after year for more.

Traditionally the head chef and head waiter in any hotel are usually at war, at loggerheads. This was not the case between Charles and our head waiter, a Mr Lovey, who had been at Cluny Hill for sixteen years and was formerly a gentleman's gentleman. Mr Lovey was devoted to his dining room and never left it during the season, not even to visit the local town of Forres; he would be in the dining room most days from 6 am until after midnight. Both staff and guests had great affection and respect for Mr Lovey, who was something of an institution, but the greatest bond of all was between Charles and Mr Lovey, who would do anything to help each other: their relationship was key to the success of the dining room. As the hotel's custom increased dramatically, however, Mr Lovey could no longer cope; he started taking to drink surreptitiously and was obviously unsteady at times. Finally, Charles came to me with tears in his eyes and said, 'You know what you've got to do, don't you, sir? You have to fire Mr Lovey, for his own sake.' He did this out of love for his friend. Because I had treated Charles with love, he wanted to repay me and was always watching out for my interests. Like Lena, he was very sensitive; sometimes he would come to me and suggest that I get rid of some member of the staff, if not for their own sake then the good of the hotel. Often I felt I should give the person concerned another opportunity but I found that Charles was always right. In the end, you could say that I hired them and he fired them.

Charles Campbell was an incredible mixture of light and dark. He drank, gambled and was a terror with the women, but he had an amazing understanding and insight — a sixth sense — about individuals, and an often clairvoyant awareness of forthcoming events. Without him and his help and support, Cluny Hill Hotel would have been a very different place.

Once on a very busy Sunday, I went into the kitchen about an hour before lunch and found only one member of staff there. 'Where's Charles?' I demanded, 'Where are the rest of the staff?' Apparently Charles had been filled with guilt about being drunk the previous day and had taken eight of the staff away in a taxi to repent in the local church. Somehow they got the wrong time for the service, so they couldn't go to church but went to a pub instead. There they thoroughly enjoyed their repentance and came back to Cluny Hill just in time to serve the lunch. I must say that before they left, they had made sure that everything was ready, but it never ceased to amaze me how grown-up people could follow Charles in such a way. He was a born leader.

I never let a meal go by without passing some comment on to Charles. As was my practice with the rest of the staff, I was always careful to express appreciation before suggesting improvements; I might say, for example, 'That was a *magnificent* dinner, Charles — next time, how about making those colour combinations even better?' Cooking is a thing of the heart, and it is so important for chefs and cooks to know that you do take notice and appreciate their efforts. Otherwise the heart goes out of the cooking and the food becomes dull.

Charles excelled in preparing banquets. One year a millionaire gave a big dinner party, and Charles created a multi-course dinner. When the host received the bill, he told me it was much too low and I could have charged more; so the next year, when he came, I took him at his word. Charles prepared a magnificent dinner, with caviare, smoked salmon and other delicacies, and, of course, tanked up while doing so. At the end of the meal the millionaire wanted to toast the chef and asked for him to come to the table. I was horrified, as I knew that Charles would be totally inebriated by then. But Charles changed into immaculate whites, had another drink, and responded to the toast with a most eloquent speech, unlike his usual incoherent mumbles. He was always full of surprises.

Like a lot of head chefs, Charles tried to get into any racket in which he could make money behind the manager's back. One of his schemes involved the old water tanks on the hill behind the hotel: he put several hundred little duckling chicks into these tanks and told the hotel butcher to feed them with scraps from the kitchen. This involved climbing a mound which happened to be a place of great power and spiritual energy; we had been warned that only those who had attained a certain degree of inner awareness and purity should go up there. Eileen's guidance had been quite specific: *Places of such power will tend to intensify those things within people which are already slightly out of balance, in order to bring them into our awareness to be corrected or dealt with.* It was hardly the place for a picnic, let alone a dodgy sideline.

Neither Charles nor the butcher knew anything about the energies of this power point. Charles was all right — God had previously said of him, *Some of the staff will come and go but there are certain ones I need here and Chef is one* — but it seems that repeated exposure to these powerful energies unbalanced the mind of the butcher, for he went very strange. He fell in love with Dorothy — not that that in itself was strange, but on one occasion he presented her with a bouquet of plastic flowers which he'd collected off the graves in the nearby cemetery. Given Dorothy's love of nature, it was like offering a ham sandwich to a vegetarian. On another occasion, completely naked except for his thick-lensed glasses, he chased a girl around the kitchen with a meat cleaver; we had to capture him and put him in a room downstairs with our head hall porter, who had been a psychiatric nurse and knew how to deal with him. I phoned the doctor, who came with another doctor to certify the unfortunate butcher for a mental home. God knows what happened to the ducklings.

Charles had a great sense of honour and would avenge any misdeed against a friend, but he never held a grudge. One Saturday, three members of the staff — our resident photographer, our new head waiter and the barman — had gone out for the afternoon in the photographer's car. It was at the height of the holiday season and we were very busy. The car with these three key members of staff was still not back by dinner time, and I anxiously awaited their arrival. What had happened to them? When at last I saw the car coming up the driveway, and hurried to the back door to find out why they were so late, I was met instead by a police sergeant and constable. They had followed the car and wanted to identify the driver, so that drunken driving charges could be preferred. As none of the three would admit to the charges, they were taken away to the police station for further questioning.

I went into the kitchen and asked Charles what was going on. 'What do you mean?' he asked. I told him what had happened and he grabbed the telephone. 'Give me the best lawyer in town!' he said, and then 'My friends are in trouble. Meet me at the police station in ten minutes time.' He ordered a taxi and was gone. Some time later they all arrived back in a taxi, in obvious high spirits; the police had put them in three different cells and questioned them but had not been able to find out who was driving. Of course, they had to celebrate their victory with a few drinks before they returned.

The next day Charles was missing again, before dinner, and this time I was really getting angry. I waited for him at the back door. Finally a taxi raced up the driveway and Charles got out with a big man who had cauliflower ears and a broken nose — he was a former boxer and at least a foot taller than Charles. His heavily bandaged arm was in a sling. Charles ignored me and led this stranger off to the kitchen, where he sat him down and gave him a beer and a steak. I followed, more bemused than angry now. 'What's going on?' I demanded, but Charles didn't answer me. I later found out that he had spent the afternoon trying to find the man to whom his friends had given a lift the day before; they had dropped this man near the police station and he had apparently told the police that the driver had been drinking too much. When Charles finally found him, he had beaten up the ex-boxer, broken his arm, and taken him in a taxi to the local hospital to have the broken limb set. He then took him to have a drink and brought him up to the hotel, where he treated him like a respected guest. Honour had been satisfied; now, from his heart, he poured out love to him.

Like Charles, Lena was a very sensitive person and often knew what each of the staff was thinking and feeling. She would let me know what was happening in their inner lives so that I could take appropriate action when there was trouble. In all I had a wonderful collection of sensitives — Eileen, Dorothy, Lena and Charles — to keep me informed of what was really going on amongst the staff and guests. Cluny Hill quickly became a powerhouse of Love and Light, and we were told that hotels like it were to replace the monastic sanctuaries where people sought solace from the chaotic world. Those who came would leave refreshed in body and spirit, often without knowing why, but always hoping to come back.

One of our visitors was the Countess of Mayo, a remarkable woman with dynamic energy, known as the Lady in Lilac because she always dressed in that colour. In the middle of dancing a quick waltz with her in the ballroom, I learned to my astonishment that she was over eighty years of age, for with her clear skin, bright eyes and dark hair she didn't look more than fifty — and she was a very good dancer. The secret, she told me, was that she rejuvenated herself through fasting, diet and — above all — by positive thinking, in which she had commanded her body to obey her positive thoughts. This naturally endeared her to me.

Lady Mayo was a great character and had travelled widely; she had complete faith in God, and told some wonderful stories to illustrate the power of positive thinking. One of these was set just after the War, when foreign currency was short; Lady Mayo wanted to travel to America but had insufficient money. She advertised her flat on Edinburgh's Princes Street, a prestigious address, in exchange for a house in Miami, Florida, for a few months' holiday. Eventually she was offered what she considered a satisfactory arrangement: in exchange for her flat, for six months, she was to enjoy the use of a house which had servants, racehorses, a swimming pool, etc. Just as she was boarding the *Queen Mary* to sail to America she was handed a telegram calling the whole thing off. She stopped still for a moment, then said, 'Father, you own all the houses in Miami, I therefore go ahead in faith! Thank you, Father.' She had very little money with her when she arrived on board, but very soon won several hundred dollars in a sweepstake. When she disembarked she was met by a small group, and someone asked her where she was going to stay; she named the most expensive hotel in the area. Just then, a quiet elderly lady came up and said, 'Lady Mayo, I have a house for which I am responsible. It has a swimming pool. The owners are away — it would be a great honour if you would come and share the house with me.' She immediately accepted and said, 'Thank you, Father.' The house was even more splendid than the original one that she had been offered.

On Lady Mayo's first visit to Cluny Hill Hotel, we decided to have tea on the terrace outside. The waitress came and laid the table, and just as we were about to start, I looked up and saw a dark cloud which was about to obscure the sun. 'I think we will have to go inside, Lady Mayo. It looks as though it's about to rain,' I said. 'Nonsense!' she replied imperiously. 'I will command the cloud to go back.' So she did, and the cloud moved away. We enjoyed our tea in the sunshine.

If the Countess of Mayo personified positive thinking, we also had examples of its opposite. One of our coach parties, who stayed with us for a week, was dogged by bad luck. Their coach broke down several times. They obtained another coach; this one went into a ditch. I came to the conclusion that one of their party must have powerful negative thoughts that were attracting all these mishaps. One afternoon, a woman in the group stayed behind when the coach went off on an excursion; everything went well for the rest of the party, while she went pony riding, fell off and was badly bruised. She was the same woman who had said it did not surprise her to be given a back room at the top of the hotel, because she had told herself, as she approached Cluny Hill, 'I expect they'll stick me up at the back somewhere.' I said it served her right; if she had expected a room on the first floor with a lovely view, she probably would have got it. The woman thanked me and said she would try this out in future. *Think nothing that you do not wish to be real in the objective life.*

We had two examples among the staff of how impossible it is to help with either Light or Love when the person concerned is determined to go their own way. The first involved Hugh Lamont, Lena's husband, who joined us as night porter. He had more effort, more Light, more Love poured into him than any other person I know, with no effect whatsoever. He seemed hell-bent on self-destruction; he was lazy, irresponsible and a liar, and were it not for Lena I would never have employed him. Hugh had the benefit of God's direct guidance through Lena as well as Eileen. But still he just went his own way, which was always the opposite of what God wanted him to do. He was so full of himself and his own desires that Love and Light could not reach him. Hugh decided to leave us and go back to his doting mother in Glasgow, where he resumed a life of self-indulgence; he ended up in a mental home.

At first, I could never understand why so much had been given to Hugh. For month after month, Eileen received guidance for him; Lena poured Love into him; I had spent weeks and weeks trying to help and train him. If I said, 'Hugh, go in *this* direction,' he would always go in the opposite direction. He was so off-beam and in the dark that if I was not sure of the right course of action or the truth in a certain situation, I had only to ask Hugh, because I knew that the *opposite* of whatever he answered was bound to be right. Later, I did see the purpose behind our experience with Hugh — it taught us that since every individual has free will, no amount of positive thinking, Love or Light can do anything to save a person from destruction if he or she so chooses.

I was sometimes accused of being callous when wielding the sword of truth with people like Hugh, but I was more disinterested than uncaring; I would only unsheathe the sword in the first place if there was a very clear need and I had the best interests of the other person at heart. Truth sometimes does hurt, and the Love that accompanies it may not always be immediately apparent, but if one is acting from the source of one's being, and not the lower self, there is never any lasting damage and nothing but good can come of it. In February 1960, Eileen received for me

> *You can help so much to lift others to a higher state of consciousness. As you expound on any subject always it is with the aim of lifting and broadening the consciousness of those you are talking to and writing to. But always it is to seek and*

find the Truth and only the Truth in everything. You will never rest until the false has been exposed and the Truth revealed. One of your roles in this respect is a very unpleasant one for no one likes having the false exposed in them, but you have been trained in such a way, that the reactions, no matter how violent, slide off you like water off a duck's back. There are very few who can really perform such an unpleasant role without being hurt in one way or another. The reason for this is because in most there is still that part of the lower self which is evident and it is that part which gets hurt...there is nothing in you to be hurt. People have thought at times that there was a hardness in you to the point of being unfeeling, but realize now that this is not so. What you are doing is the Will of the Most High. Therefore nothing is allowed to stand in the way of that Will, whether it means exposing the false and doing battle to do this, you will forge ahead regardless. This characteristic of yours is priceless. You can see now why you have been called many times the rock, immovable. Your training has been really thorough and no stone has been left unturned, no chink has been left uncovered and unprotected.

Various of Eileen's recorded messages stressed the importance of sending Love to those who had rejected the Light. This was to act in part as a protection from their desire to do us harm; this desire, of course, boomeranged back on them. Hugh's mother and sister, for instance, sent many negative thoughts towards Lena and ourselves. With no action on our part, they were returned to them a hundredfold; one calamity after another seemed to bedevil them. We noticed over and over again that if anyone tried to do harm to Cluny Hill and those who lived there, it rebounded in similar fashion. God did indeed protect His 'chosen place'.

Paddy Heffernan was the second example of one of the staff shunning the Light, although his was a personal tragedy and he intended no ill against anybody. Paddy was a close friend; we had been squadron leaders together in the Royal Air Force and I had known him for years, including the time he had been Command Catering Officer for India while I was Command Catering Officer for the Bengal–Burma Front. He was a self-effacing person with a delightful sense of humour and a great personality. Paddy gave up a good job in Canada to come and be with us at Cluny Hill Hotel, where he became our distinguished and delightful barman; we loved him dearly, but when things started going wrong for him and he turned to us for help, we were powerless to do anything for him because of his stubbornness in accepting it.

Paddy fell in love with a woman, but because she was a blood relation his Catholicism forbade a consummation of the relationship. He asked Eileen if she would get guidance for him; when she did, however, he refused it, as he also refused to respond to the love and support that we gave him. He said he preferred to be miserable in his own way, rather than be happy in anyone else's way. His stubbornness could become ludicrous; throughout the winter, for example, he continued to wear tropical trousers indoors and out, and was constantly complaining of the cold, but obstinately refused to wear warmer clothing *just because* we had suggested it. Here he was, in a Centre of Light, in an atmosphere of Love, among tried and trusted friends, yet he was lifeless and utterly miserable, and we could do nothing to help him. It was heartbreaking because we were so fond of him, and he was the sort of person who would never cause anybody any harm. He went steadily downhill until in the end, after he had left the hotel, he committed suicide.

In May 1959 we had a visit from my parents, who stayed for two weeks. They spent a lot of time with the children and it was a very successful visit in every way; my father was obviously very proud of the way that I was running the hotel. Eileen received:

> *My son, the visit of your parents is just one of My many, many promises being brought about. Your father is a new man. So much hard news and bitter news simply dropped from him. His heart, which he has been afraid to use because he has been afraid of being hurt, is wide open and very great love is flowing through him. The children have worked wonders with him. This visit is the happiest time they've ever had in their lives. They are not sure why but can feel so much about this place. The children are working wonders with them. Love is the greatest healer and the love within the children and the grandparents will work wonders with them, especially with your father.*

And then, just before they left:

> *My son, your mother and father are going away feeling entirely different people. For the first time for years and years*

> *your father is free of resentments and because of this he is a really happy man.*

When we first arrived at Cluny Hill, I had discovered that the ballroom opposite the cocktail bar was never used. Little wonder the spirit of the place seemed dead! My aim was to have something going on there every night of the week; by our second year, in addition to evenings of ballroom dancing and Scottish country dancing, one of the weekly highlights was a ceilidh — an evening of Highland dancing, Scottish music, puppets, singing and stories. The ceilidh was performed by local artists, whom I brought together after scouring the surrounding area during the winter for talented performers; even the staff formed a skiffle group, a band with various unlikely instruments such as a washboard. All this had great appeal to visitors from England and abroad. Some journalists visiting on one occasion said that it was the finest show they had seen anywhere; their praise puzzled me at the time, because they were a hardbitten lot who must have seen scores of entertainments all over the world. Then I realized that since the show was being done out of love, it gained an extra dimension. The performers enjoyed doing it — they were not paid entertainers — and they considered it a privilege to come up to Cluny Hill Hotel and perform what they loved doing most. The atmosphere brought out the best in them. Beyond the currency of appreciation, their only payment was a free drink from the bar and, at the end of the season, a festive dinner at the hotel.

Forres is close to the world-famous 'whisky trail' along the River Spey, so each year the Scottish Whisky Association would bring a party of between twenty and thirty top journalists to stay at Cluny Hill, using it as a base for daily visits to various distilleries in the district. Their week would end with a special dinner, to which Eileen and I were always invited. I had always let it be known that whatever a guest wanted, I would see to providing it (barring ladies of easy virtue); I would get in the car and go out to buy a particular brand of spirits, for example, if the hotel didn't stock it and a guest requested it. One year, John Hope, the public relations officer who organized the Whisky Association week, decided to take me up on this boast. He was telling a hilarious story at their final dinner about a horse called Brown John, and towards the end he turned to me and said, 'Peter, can you arrange for Brown John to be brought into the dining room?' 'Certainly!' I replied, immediately getting up and excusing myself, 'I won't be long'. I left the dining room, jumped in my car and went in search of Leslie Klein, whom

I'd helped set up a pony-trekking business; when I found him I asked him to bring his brown horse up to the hotel as quickly as he could.

The horse came galloping up the hill, arriving a bit out of breath outside the hotel, and I told Leslie to bring him inside the hall. This made Leslie very nervous, but the horse behaved itself and I said, 'Now bring him into the dining room.' So, much to the surprise and delight of the journalists, there was 'Brown John' being led round the room. I had to ask them not to clap or make a noise in case the horse bolted, but despite a round of appreciative laughter, all went well. I have often wondered whether the subsequent press advertisement for White Horse Whisky, which featured a horse in a dining room, was inspired by this occasion. That evening, when the boys were told about it, our eldest son Christopher said, 'Mummy, what did Mr Lovey say? A horse in his dining room!' Mr Lovey, who was still with us at the time, ruled the dining room with just a look, a raise of the eyebrow, and woe betide any diner or member of staff who misbehaved. Fortunately the horse had got the message.

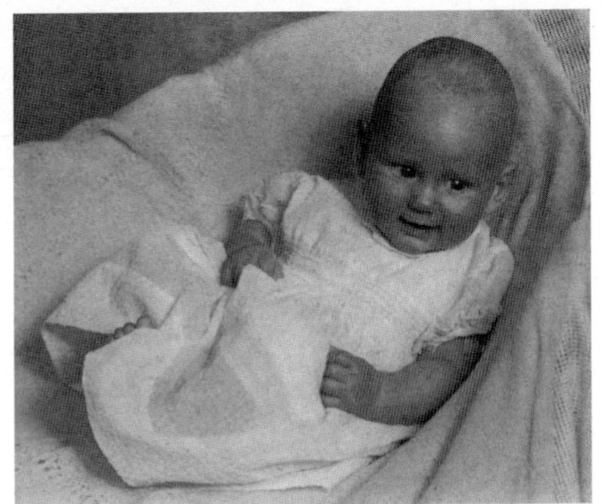

Peter Caddy as a baby

Peter (right) with fellow Boy Scout

Dr Sullivan — Aureolis — in theatrical garb and (right) at his Christchurch headquarters

Peter in the RAF

Peter's parents at their golden wedding (1966)

With Nora, his first wife

Peter with baby Michael

Peter (at front) in the Himalayas

Sheena with Peter and Eileen's son Christopher

Aerial view of Cluny Hill Hotel, Forres

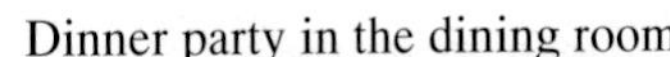

Dinner party in the dining room

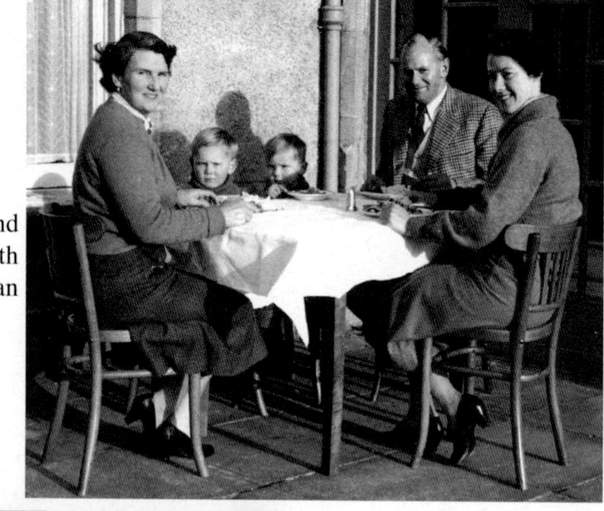

Eileen, Peter and Dorothy with Christopher and Jonathan

Jonathan, Christopher and David at play in the grounds of Cluny Hill Hotel

The Trossachs Hotel, Perthshire

Peter's Lagonda and the caravan

Dorothy, Eileen and Peter: the patio and the original garden

The caravan with Dorothy's annex

Peter,
the new bungalows (1968),
the new gardens
(and inset, same around 1970)

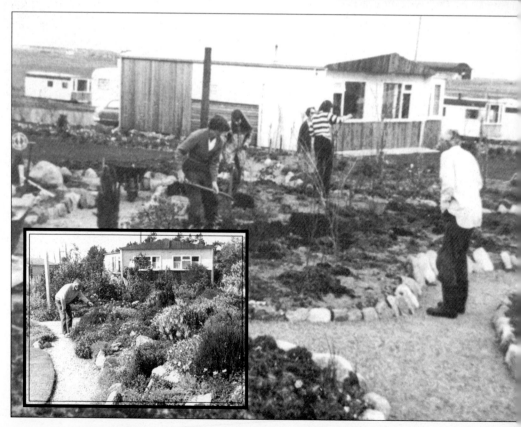

The Community Centre under construction

Roc
(Robert Ogilvie Crombie)

'Man of the Trees'
Richard St Barbe Baker

David Spangler

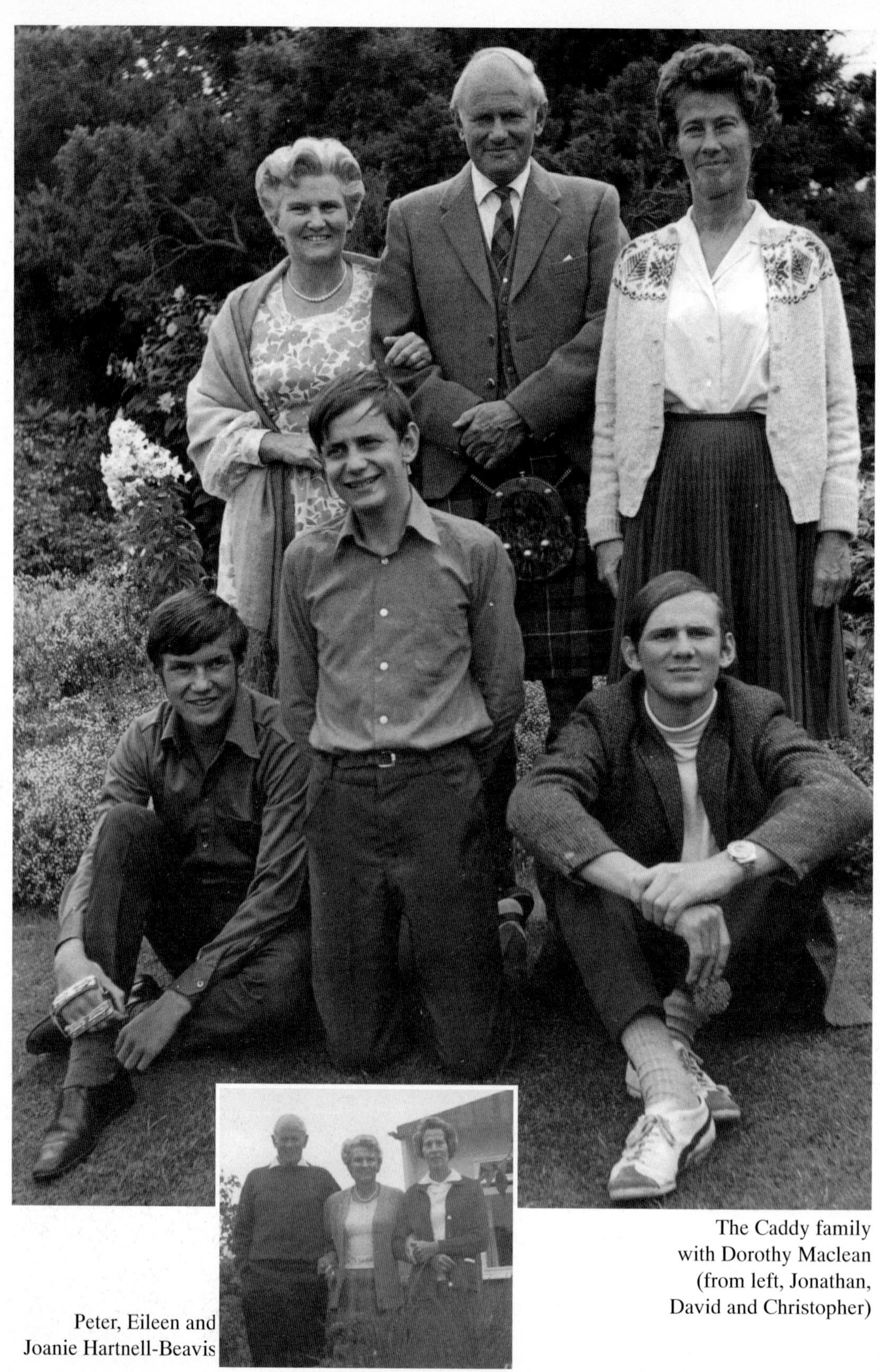

The Caddy family
with Dorothy Maclean
(from left, Jonathan,
David and Christopher)

Peter, Eileen and
Joanie Hartnell-Beavis

Chapter 14

Flying Sauce-boats

Always suggest from the ideal.
Seek and live the ideal

ALTHOUGH EILEEN'S GUIDANCE always referred to Cluny Hill as 'this My chosen place', we little suspected at first that there was a specific meaning behind the phrase. Some years after I had written the paper, *An Introduction to the Nature and Purpose of Unidentified Flying Objects*, Eileen had seen with her inner eye the word LUKANO written in letters of fire. Since neither of us knew what it meant, we were told to write and ask Naomi, who was a remarkable sensitive and could be in instant telepathic contact with any name given to her, whomever it belonged to. She was in immediate contact with the being called LUKANO, who said that he was the captain of a 'mother ship' from Venus and wanted to make contact with us, because mankind was in great danger and may need help from our space brothers. Now, at Cluny Hill, we were told the time had come to make that contact.

The Cold War was beginning to hot up in the late 1950s, with both sides testing thermonuclear weapons of ever-increasing power; there was a real danger of total nuclear holocaust if the wrong finger was on the wrong button at the wrong time. Planetary crisis on such a scale would affect the balance of the whole solar system, so certain contingency plans had been made by extraterrestrial beings, and among the more desperate of these plans was one in which groups of people were to be evacuated from chosen places around the world. Over the next few years, therefore, we were in daily contact with these beings through Dorothy, Lena, Eileen and later Naomi. During the months that the hotel was closed each year, Lena and I would go down to a landing site that had been chosen on a beach near Findhorn, every night for a week either side of the full moon. It had been stressed that there was to be utmost secrecy about this operation, so we went down after midnight, taking with us blankets and cushions, so that if we were spotted, it would be said, 'Ah, there goes Peter Caddy with one of his staff, having an affair.'

One day our photographer, Marcus Johnson from Aberdeen, visited us with a journalist friend to discuss plans for pictures of the hotel and its activities. They had somehow heard, I think from Colonel Lester of the Churches' Fellowship for Psychical and Spiritual Studies, that I was interested in unidentified flying objects, and they knew of the paper I had written for the Air Ministry three years earlier. Their whole visit seemed so extraordinary, and they were so sympathetic to the subject, that it seemed to me that they both might have a role to play when the time came to tell the world about the space brothers' mission and their message for mankind. I therefore told them just enough of the story to prepare them, and accepted their promises to keep the matter secret.

When the reporter returned to his Sunday paper, however, he wrote a confidential memo to the news editor. Somehow this knowledge was leaked to others in the press; in order to keep up with the opposition papers, the news editor felt obliged to print the full story, and he did. We all did our best to stop him — the reporter even threatened to resign — but to no avail. An article was published with huge headlines, on the front page, about a landing site for UFOs on the top of the mound behind Cluny Hill Hotel: and what a stir it caused! We were inundated by reporters the next day and I refused to see them, explaining that the story was based on a paper written for the Air Ministry years ago and that it should never have been published. We did receive many letters of support from all over the country, and the reporter who had given me his promise did resign, but the damage was done.

The Chairman of the company was furious, because I had apparently broken my undertaking that there would be no more publicity about the hotel. What particularly got his goat were reports of 'little green men' scampering about one of his hotels; he came in for a lot of ribbing from his friends, some of whom uncharitably put the phenomena down to his fondness for treble gin-and-tonics. This was the last straw: he came down with the Company Secretary and Mrs Bruce to give me the sack. I refused to listen to him, however, and just kept on talking about my future plans for the hotel in a most positive way, as if there were no question of our leaving. Mrs Bruce caught my enthusiasm and began supporting me in a subtle manner. In the end, they gave up; such was the irresistible power of God and positive thought.

The whole incident had an amusing postscript at the Scottish Whisky Association gathering in 1960. One of the party at the closing dinner was the chief newscaster at the British Broadcasting Corporation; music from BBC radio was being relayed over the loudspeaker system in the dining room as we ate. It faded out, and a familiar BBC voice came over the speakers to say that an urgent message had just been received: strange little men had been seen after the landing of a spacecraft in the vicinity of Forres, in Scotland, and they were moving towards the Cluny Hill Hotel. A few minutes later, the windows of the dining room were raised and men in spacesuits climbed in to the room, much to everyone's delight.

My constant battles with Mrs Bruce continued. She tried to browbeat and bulldoze me as she did everyone else, but I don't think she was used to dealing with a manager who refused to be treated in this way. Sometimes when she arrived in a bad mood, she'd go through the hotel like a dose of salts, with the staff scuttling out of her way in fear. I asked her not to do this, not to speak to staff individually, but to come to me: I was the captain of the ship, and if there were changes to be made, I would ensure that this happened in the proper way. It was not my practice to interfere in the internal running of the various departments or to correct, directly, a waiter or waitress, or a chef or cook in the kitchen. I only communicated through the heads of the departments, and gave *them* the authority to take action. My RAF experience had taught me the value of clear lines of command, authority and communication.

One particular feud with Mrs Bruce provided great sport. Each month over a period of several years, I had placed an order for more silver sauce-boats for the dining room. They never came, but with patience, persistence and perseverance I kept ordering them every month. At last one dozen sauce-boats were delivered. The van driver brought them into the kitchen but when I opened the box I found that they were cheap china sauce-boats, probably from Woolworth's. I knew that the van driver acted as a spy for Mrs Bruce, to keep her informed about what went on in the hotel, so I took the sauce-boats one by one and smashed them on the floor. 'How dare Mrs Bruce send these *china* sauce-boats, instead of silver ones, to Cluny Hill, a four-star hotel!' I fumed, secretly enjoying my performance and knowing that my actions would be reported back to Mrs Bruce. Charles was very upset and begged me to stop. I never had any reaction from Mrs Bruce, no doubt because she wanted to retain the secrecy of the van driver's role.

Mrs Bruce did respond to love, however, and after her visits she usually left all smiles, kissing the children and waving goodbye. She was a very powerful woman with a strong character, and deep down had a very spiritual side to her. Standing up to Mrs Bruce was chicken-feed compared with Sheena, whose onslaughts had no equal; they had taught me to stand rock-like against the buffeting of lesser forces.

The grounds of the hotel, when we had first arrived, were an overgrown wilderness; whole areas had never been cultivated and the beauty of the drive was obscured by overcrowded trees. I visualized how the grounds could be made into a garden and explained this to Mrs Bruce in detail, but she was opposed to many aspects of my plan, including taking down the trees — apparently the Chairman was very fond of these. A great storm arrived one day, however, and blew down many of the trees across the drive, giving me a good excuse to cut the others down. (Most of them were old and dying anyway.) James MacLeod, the head gardener, was also not very keen on some of my ideas for the garden, but I found that if I held the vision and kept my thoughts positive, he would carry out the plans thinking they were his own.

James MacLeod once told me you can always tell a good gardener by his silence, and the slowness of his speech and movements, because you can't hurry nature. Another thing I learned from him was the importance of looking after garden tools, which should always be of the best quality. It used to annoy me a little that the gardeners would leave the grounds at a quarter to five, fifteen minutes before the official end of the working day; then I discovered that during this time they would collect the tools, clean and oil them, and hang them up in their rightful place. If any tool was missing, they would not go home until it was found. Such care of tools was a lesson I was not to forget.

The garden and grounds of the hotel had been completely neglected since the War, and we were blessed to have two of the best gardeners in the region. James MacLeod had served a seven-year apprenticeship at nearby Darnaway Castle, home of the Earl of Moray; he was joined by the former head gardener at Scotland's famous Gleneagles Hotel, who had retired in Forres but grown restless and wanted to resume the work he loved so much. Although older and far more experienced than James, he took care to defer to James's position as head gardener at Cluny and would never undermine his authority. They made a magnificent team; I learned much from them as they created a vegetable and fruit garden and a 150 yard herbaceous border along the road at the bottom of the hotel grounds.

During our fourth year at Cluny Hill, we worked for months revitalizing and greatly extending the lawns on the slope in front of the hotel so that, by the following spring, visitors coming up the driveway would turn the final corner and find the hotel in an oasis of brilliant emerald-green grass. We also created several gardens in a sheltered fold in the slope of the grounds: a rock garden, with a waterfall that went into a small pond with water-lilies and goldfish, and a scree garden beside it, which led into a marsh garden at the bottom. My plan was to be able to provide an environment for every type of plant.

* * *

In the summer of 1961, tension between the USA and the Soviet Union was so high that nuclear confrontation seemed imminent, and extraterrestrial plans for a rescue operation were set into motion accordingly. Eileen, Dorothy and Lena were not only receiving messages and instructions from the spacecraft involved but were also in telepathic contact with scores of others groups around the world who were also involved in the operation. Three years earlier, Eileen had received:

> *My son, this is not the only oasis from which people will be rescued when destruction comes, but it is the only one in this country. There are others in other countries. You will hear of them in time but at present leave all this alone.*

On the same day, she had been given a vision in her meditation:

> *I saw a silhouette of the head and shoulders of a soldier with a tin hat on his head, and the point of a rifle showing. Ahead of him was a brilliant light and it seemed to be beckoning him, but he seemed incapable of moving, so he shot at it and kept on shooting at it; every time a shot was fired the light was completely blotted out. Then I saw the head and shoulders of the soldier fall forward and it was something like a steamroller which went over him and then all I saw was the light blazing ahead with nothing in the way.*

Eileen's guidance offered an interpretation:

> *This picture represents mankind's refusal to accept My Light, My Truth, and because he refuses to accept it he wants to destroy it and thinks that by blotting it out and ignoring it, he can destroy it. The steamroller is the destruction which is to come rolling over mankind and destroying him so that nothing but My divine Light and Truth remains. All else is destroyed.*

This was stern stuff, sandwiched as it was between more prosaic messages like *My son, put forward the suggestion of a supper license but do not push it,* and *Pay Mrs Brussene £5.10 per week — she will do well on tips*, but over and again it was made clear to us that despite the apocalyptic nature of these warnings, humankind still had free will and could avert disaster; furthermore, we were to concentrate on the work at hand: *I want you to put all you have got into making this place a success...build up all the time, and never slack off or feel that it is not worthwhile if destruction is inevitable.*

Now, it appeared, the world *was* on the brink of destruction. In the summer of 1961 we were told, *Each one of you should be in readiness, you will be given very little warning.* As an example of how seriously we took the import and urgency of these messages, which were confirmed by several independent sources, I had had the trees cleared from the mound behind the hotel in preparation for the landing. This horrified Mrs Bruce, who feared her tree-loving Chairman's wrath, but by the time she found out about it the trees were already gone.

A landing had been attempted on the mound on Christmas Eve 1960 and then again on the first night of 1961, but both attempts failed. We were told that this was because of climatic conditions and, more importantly, the radiation from a recent atomic test explosion in the atmosphere. A third attempt would have to be made before the next atomic test; for weeks, Lena and I — and sometimes Eileen — would patiently keep vigil on the landing site at one o'clock in the morning, for an hour or two. It was damned cold! Meanwhile our inner work was to concentrate on radiating Love to the other centres in the Network of Light, as well as the spacecraft trying to land, and to direct our positive thoughts into all that we were doing.

Throughout that year, the intensity of this inner work naturally found its outer expression, although the vibrations could only be stepped up gradually else there would have been chaos. Light shone throughout the hotel and this had an impact on individuals, particularly members of the staff, which at times was devastating. It affected each one in a different way. All their faults, failings and weaknesses surfaced as they were brought into contact with the Light; those who could not stand it left of their own free will, while those who had their weak points spotlighted, but chose to stay, received a great deal of Love. It was an extraordinary time for all of us.

The hotel not only made a handsome profit that year, but I found that we had trebled the takings since the time we first moved to Cluny Hill. True to God's Word, it also became a four-star hotel. We had built up a clientele of regulars who came back year after year, drawn to this 'hotel with a difference' even if they could not name that difference. I had shown Mrs Bruce and her directors that a business *could* be run according to Love and spiritual laws. The brand name of the blue duplicate-books in which Eileen faithfully recorded her guidance every day for five years was 'Challenge', highlighted and underlined by the manufacturer. At Cluny Hill Hotel, I felt, we had met and mastered the challenge.

Chapter 15

From Morgue to Graveyard

Whenever there is discord in any case, cease contention. Stand still

IN DECEMBER 1961 Eileen's guidance told her to *keep radiating Love, Love and more Love to Mrs Bruce, remembering always that she is the key to many things*. This puzzled me; of course, Mrs Bruce, being the General Manager of the chain that owned Cluny Hill Hotel, was 'the key to many things', but why this should merit special mention, and why Eileen should be asked to radiate Love to her, put me on my guard. Clearly something was in the air.

One would have thought that the success of Cluny Hill Hotel would have pleased Mrs Bruce, who could turn to her directors and claim that her (albeit reluctant) support of me had been vindicated, but in fact the opposite was true. The harder I worked at Cluny Hill and the more I improved it, the less pleased she seemed to be, presumably because it showed the other hotels in a bad light. In many ways I was a thorn in Mrs Bruce's side. In other hotels in the chain she was the absolute ruler and had all the ideas; at Cluny Hill, I was the ideas person and always implemented them, whether she approved or not — and, as she often didn't approve, I would have to find the money for them myself. Once, for example, I mounted a display, in the public rooms and corridors, of hundreds of pictures of Scottish scenery by a well-known photographer; when these were sold, the proceeds were used for projects in the garden. Mrs Bruce probably suspected that I was pocketing the money but I wasn't interested in the profit, only in the success of Cluny Hill Hotel — God's hotel. She was wary (and, I think, not a little envious) of the fact that management decisions so often came from Eileen's guidance. She was embarrassed when she heard so many comments comparing the other hotels in the company unfavourably with Cluny Hill.

For some time, Mrs Bruce had been pouring money into one particular hotel, the Trossachs, and had tried many of my ideas from Cluny Hill there, but without the right person as manager, the right staff, and — most importantly — the right spirit, it was doomed to fail. The Trossachs Hotel had been going from bad to worse and was developing a very poor reputation.

Perhaps, then, in order to kill two birds with one stone, Mrs Bruce told me early in January 1962 that she wanted to transfer us to the Trossachs Hotel. This was even larger than Cluny Hill Hotel and was situated in the heart of the Trossachs country north of, but accessible to, both Glasgow and Edinburgh. In spite of its beautiful position overlooking Loch Katrine the hotel was a disaster. It was known as 'the graveyard of managers' and could never keep its staff, who would leave and be replaced at the rate of at least two a day. No manager seemed to be able to make a success of running the hotel, no matter how well he started.

This then was what Eileen's guidance had been preparing us for, and I was aghast. The newspapers of the day were confirming the grim warnings of Eileen's guidance about the danger of nuclear war. At that time, January 1962, Cuba was ousted from the Organization of American States, and this intensified the sabre-rattling between the USA and the Soviet Union; the French and the Chinese were also developing thermonuclear weapons. Like Prometheus stealing fire from the gods, mankind had secured an awesome power, but in dealing with it was now more like a child playing with matches, and the prospects were terrifying. We took the warnings and our work with the space brothers at this time very seriously — and key to that work was our position at Cluny Hill.

Of course, I was reluctant to share the details of this with Mrs Bruce, so instead reminded her of my first condition when she hired me, that I needed to love the place that I was working in if I was to give it my best. She argued that I could do this equally well at the Trossachs Hotel. She certainly sweetened the pill: I was to have an assistant manager, and there were speedboats, water-skiing, a fleet of dinghies for sailing on the lake, pony-trekking, an excellent resident dance orchestra, and beautiful countryside for walks. In stark contrast to the poky rooms we had originally been offered at Cluny Hill, Eileen and I were promised, for our accommodation, the hotel's Royal Suite, so called because Queen Victoria used to stay there; we would have a magnificent view over the lakes and the mountains of the Trossachs. Mrs Bruce painted a wonderful picture to persuade us to go there in good grace.

'That's all very well,' I said, 'but I can only work with love, and I love Cluny Hill, not the Trossachs Hotel.' I explained that you can put a man and a woman together and tell the man to love the woman, but 'love floweth where it listeth'. This fell on deaf ears, however, and Mrs Bruce remained adamant that we should go.

Although she said that the decision had already been made, I doubted it; I felt sure that I could persuade her to arrange for us to stay where we were. Eileen's guidance was that she continue radiating Love to her: *This is a fight for life or death and must be fought with all you have got, and My divine Love is your greatest and most powerful weapon.* I took this to confirm that if the worst came to the worst and the space brothers *were* to mount a rescue operation, we would need to be at Cluny Hill in order to take part in it. We were expecting Mrs Bruce to return the next day, but when she failed to appear we were told to keep our spirits up: *the longer everything is postponed the better, so do not worry about delays. Just keep that Love flowing to her.*

The following day, 17 January, I was prepared for my meeting with Mrs Bruce by the following:

> *My son, as you feel inspired by Me, talk. You need not feel your hands are tied as you did last time. Very much Love has been radiated to Mrs Bruce preparing her, so you can feel free to talk to her as long as you are alone with her. You will know exactly what to say and how much to tell her. I am not going to tell you to be cautious, but simply guided. If you are sensitive and feel her need you will know exactly how much she can accept; watch her every reaction with gentle care. The things that you accept as natural are like a foreign language to others. Learn to put yourself in the other person's place — that will help both of you greatly.*

When Mrs Bruce arrived and was shown into my office I decided to lay all the cards on the table. While it was true that my heart was in Cluny Hill Hotel, I explained, there was a more vital reason for staying there. The darkness in the world was spreading, and therefore there needed to be places or fortresses of Light; Cluny Hill was one of these Centres of Light. Over the past five years we had been carefully guided to build up that Light, which we had done, and she could see the physical results for herself. On a higher, inner level the results were even more impressive; God had chosen this place for a special purpose, and we were the ones responsible for carrying it out. Mrs Bruce considered this for a moment and then replied that she didn't believe it at all: God was everywhere, she said, and I could do at the Trossachs Hotel everything that I had done at Cluny Hill Hotel. The decision was final.

After she left, Eileen had guidance that Mrs Bruce would never be the same again after all that had been revealed to her, but that she could not now change her mind about moving us, even if she wanted to: *There is so much involved which she was unable to disclose to you. She has been put on the spot, My son, regarding this place and you.* We were to accept going to the Trossachs Hotel on a year's trial, on the understanding that if I was unhappy about the whole situation there, Mrs Bruce would arrange for us to return to Cluny Hill at the end of the year. We had 'lessons to learn' by going to the Trossachs.

Eileen was asked to continue radiating Love to Mrs Bruce, and I was told to assure Mrs Bruce that whereas at Cluny Hill I had been working for God, at the Trossachs Hotel I would be working for her. The guidance went on:

> *Tell Peter he is not to try and copy what he has done here and apply it at the Trossachs — it just will not work. Tell him to start afresh with new ideas for the staff as well as the guests. All this will become very clear to him once he gets to the Trossachs but I just do not want him to waste time planning something that will not work out. It would simply leave him very frustrated.*

The date set for our move was 9 March 1962, and there was a lot of sorting out and packing to do before then. When I asked Eileen to get guidance on what should be done with our 30-foot caravan in the hotel garage, thinking that we should either sell it, take it to the Trossachs or at least rent it out, I received a rather puzzling reply:

> *Put it on the Findhorn caravan site for this summer. You will be able to find somebody to clean it during the summer, it is not a very arduous job once a week or fortnight. By the end of the season you will know what the next move is to be...*

* * *

The Trossachs is a 5-miles-wide area of outstanding natural beauty in West Perthshire, sometimes called 'the Highlands in miniature' because of its dramatic concentration of mountains, moorland, lochs and glens. Artists like John Everett Millais and John Ruskin were inspired by the soft light and idealized the landscape; Sir Walter Scott set his novel *Rob Roy* there, as well as a poem, *The Lady of the Lake*, the lake of its title being Loch Katrine. These have given a romantic appeal to the area since Victorian times, when the queen herself was only one of many tourists. In this century the American musical *Brigadoon* about a Scottish village that appears out of the mists for one day in every hundred years, only to vanish the next, was likewise inspired by the Trossachs, and British television viewers would recognize the town of Callander as the 'Tannochbrae' of the original *Dr Finlay's Casebook*.

The Trossachs Hotel was some 7 miles by road from Callander, set in splendid isolation on the shores of Loch Katrine. Like 'Brigadoon', it came in and out of the mists that were formed in the wooded glen where the mountains met the loch; the moistness of the atmosphere and delicacy of light gave its surroundings a soft, verdant appearance, as if some kindly power had blessed it with perpetual fertility. The hotel itself was even more palatial than that at Cluny Hill, a Victorian concoction of towers, spires and gables that seemed straight out of a book of fairy tales. The interior had been designed on a similar grandeur of scale, and the Royal Suite — which was to be our quarters — was the *pièce de résistance*. True to her word, Mrs Bruce had delivered us to a seeming paradise.

It was hard to imagine the ill rumours we had heard of the place, but in any case we felt sure that with God's help we would be able to make a success of the hotel. We brought with us five heads of departments and twenty-five of our staff from Cluny Hill Hotel, including Dorothy, Charles and Lena. With such a tried and tested team, to complete a total of some eighty members of staff, and all the recreational and other facilities that Mrs Bruce had laid on, I looked forward to achieving even greater results.

I had been given a free hand to run the hotel as I wanted. We had everything material that we could have wished for, which promised to make life so much easier after the battles with Mrs Bruce at Cluny Hill Hotel. A short distance from the hotel, the staff had a beautiful house of their own, 'Woodlands', which was comfortable and had been done up for them before they arrived. Again we had Lena to look after it, which she did beautifully.

Our three boys were enrolled in a lovely little village school where they were able to do well because the teacher could give them a great deal of individual attention.

To begin with I endeavoured to weld all the staff into a team. This produced an inevitable sifting process, with some leaving and being replaced, but somehow it did not happen with the same ease or grace that had marked our later years at Cluny Hill; I encountered an air of hopelessness and negative thinking about the place. I tried to counter these with positive thoughts and actions. We managed to get the inside of the hotel clean and tidy, and at one time had nearly all the staff working in the gardens, before we opened for the season, yet something was wrong and I couldn't put my finger on it.

Shortly after we arrived, I called some of the key members of the staff that I had brought with us into my office and told them that we were going to forget about Cluny Hill Hotel: the task before us was to bring in to the Trossachs Hotel the same qualities of Light and Love that we had achieved there. Charles, the head chef, regarded me shrewdly. 'The evil is in the very bricks of this place,' he said, ' and you will not get it out.' I had found that he was never wrong in his prophetic utterances, drunk or sober, but this time I did not believe him. Time seemed to prove him correct, however. There was so much discord among the staff that they were not happy and many of them left. One after the other of those I had brought with me went downhill, physically, morally and spiritually: they took to drink, drugs, theft and promiscuous sex. No matter how hard we tried, we did not seem to be able to do anything about it.

Part of the trouble was that we were far away from the nearest town and there was no public transport. To counter this I laid on a hotel bus for the staff but it had little effect on boosting morale — all too often it simply provided them another opportunity to drown their sorrows in the local pub. The staff had all the conveniences we could possibly give them, including radio and television, yet there was always strife, particularly with the kitchen staff. Charles, as head of the department, often set them a very poor example. All the faults we had found in him at Cluny Hill Hotel — his drinking, womanizing and racketeering — were magnified at the Trossachs. On one drunken occasion he took a knife to threaten Eileen; on another, she was called away from the ballroom where we were dancing one night, to help fish him out of the loch. Apparently Charles had heard of a sunken ship whose cargo contained gold, which he had naturally taken an interest in recovering; so he had downed a good deal of whisky, decided to practise his diving skills, donned a wet suit and diver's weights and thrown himself off the end of the boathouse jetty, too drunk to remember that he couldn't swim. With a great deal of struggle, Eileen and his girlfriend Madge managed to pull him to safety.

Due to his essential integrity, Charles was always ashamed of himself when he had drunk too much, for he felt that he was letting me down; he would then redouble his efforts to please me. He was devoted to Eileen and me and would do anything for us. I never raised my voice to him, because I knew that he had a part to play in God's plan — certainly at Cluny Hill Hotel I had found that he was key to the success of the place. One night at the Trossachs, when he'd had a bit too much to drink, I found him by the hatch where staff members could get drinks from the bar; he leaned against it unsteadily and said to me in a slur, 'You bastard, if only once you *would* raise your voice or be angry with me, I'd know how to treat you, but now I don't.' He had never been treated with love before and just didn't know how to handle it.

Try as I might, managing the Trossachs Hotel was like wading through treacle, every step a slow and sticky effort. The atmosphere, too, was oppressive. Despite the hotel's beautiful location, it always seemed to be raining, and even when it wasn't, the mists came down physically as well as psychically, making it a depressing place to live. I pined for the sparkling clarity of air, sky and sunshine we had enjoyed in the north of Scotland.

My relationship with the guests, which had been so important and delightful at Cluny Hill, also withered at the Trossachs because of essential differences in the clientele. The Trossachs was a tourist hotel which most of the guests used as a staging post for one or two nights only, dinner, bed and breakfast, as they passed through the district; there was little or no opportunity to develop a rapport with them (nor, I must admit, had I a great desire to do so). I was no longer 'the captain on the bridge' and spent more of the time in my office. Eileen too was missing Cluny Hill Hotel, even though the boys were now old enough for her to spend more time with the staff and guests; in April her guidance gently warned, *As long as there is that tiny feeling of 'well, we shall go back to Cluny Hill one day', I cannot use you fully.*

If it was hard to put a finger on the apparently negative energy that dogged every step we took at the Trossachs, undermining our morale and outlook, pulling everything down, it was even harder to lift up the spirit with which to surmount it. All the extras should have made the job enjoyable, but somehow they did not. Looking back I wonder that I tried so hard; in my heart of hearts at the time I *knew* that my best would never be good enough, but determination and no doubt a degree of pride kept me going, whereas I could have been content just to do my job and take the occasional day off to spend time with the family. Eileen's guidance told her, *you know that unless Peter's heart is in whatever he is doing, he cannot do things 200 per cent — he will do it 99 per cent or even 100 per cent, but you cannot expect him to give that extra plus* ... and the truth is that my heart *wasn't* in it. Even the application of my Rosicrucian training seemed of little avail.

As the season drew to a close I knew that it wouldn't be fair to ask the staff that I had brought with me to come back for another summer. I therefore told Mrs Bruce that I was not prepared to return to the Trossachs Hotel and asked if I could go back to Cluny Hill Hotel. She did not reply. As the weeks went by I kept on asking her by letter if she would visit the Trossachs, as I had several things I wished to discuss with her. (For example, I had invited Naomi, the sensitive I'd met in the Philippines and who was intimately involved in our work with the space brothers, to come over and join us — I wanted her to be able to stay with us at the Trossachs Hotel through the winter and then at Cluny Hill, where I expected to return.) But Mrs Bruce continued to ignore us. *My tests are very severe,* said Eileen's guidance, *because they have to be. This is a final test for each of you.*

On the morning of the last day of the season before the hotel closed, Eileen received an even stranger piece of guidance:

> *I want you to keep very, very positive about tomorrow over everything. If you are in constant touch with Me you can change quickly in midstream without it throwing you out, and you must be ready to do this. You must be willing to change your plans at a moment's notice. None of you can become rigid and forge ahead with a plan no matter what happens. If I tell you there is need for change, do it without arguing or questioning the whys and wherefores. I know none of you find this an easy matter and yet how vitally important it is. Now and again you try and form a picture of what it is going to be like here in the winter and you find you cannot see further than one day at a time. This is just as it should be. If you could see too far ahead you would become*

rigid and if I would ask you to change plans quickly you would find it even more difficult..

The next day, 11 October, Mrs Bruce arrived with a posse of stocktakers who went over the books and checked the stock inventory from ceiling to cellar. While they were doing this, she brusquely informed us that the company no longer required our services: she gave us a cheque for a month's wages, and four hours to pack our things and leave. She offered no explanation for this drastic decision, beyond it being 'a change in company policy'. It had nothing to do with our running of the hotel; the books were found to be in order and the stocktaking could account for every last pepper-pot. When I protested that we had nowhere to go at such short notice, Mrs Bruce offered us, as a sort of sop, three nights free accommodation at any one of the company's twenty-one hotels in Scotland — providing, of course, that it too had not closed for the season.

I had never before been sacked from any job in my life, and this sudden, unexpected and curt dismissal came as an utter shock. With only four hours to clear out, however, there was no time for a post-mortem. Somewhat dazed, we went to our rooms and sorted through our belongings, throwing out all but the essentials. We packed as much as we could into the car and tied more to the roof-rack; everything else had to be chucked out because we had no idea where we would go or what we were going to do.

I phoned my parents, told them what had happened and asked them if they could put us up until I got another job and a place to live. They were not at all helpful and did not want to have us in their Devonshire home, even though it was a huge, six-bedroom house that could easily accommodate us for a while. This hurt me but I consoled myself with the thought that God must have something else in store for us.

Then I remembered our caravan on the public site at Findhorn and Eileen's guidance that *By the end of the season you will know what the next move is to be...* We decided that after we had collected the boys from school, we would take Mrs Bruce up on her offer of free accommodation and drive to the Stotfield Hotel at Lossiemouth, about 10 miles east of Findhorn along the coast. We could stay there while I prepared the caravan. Dorothy was to come with us. The boys were bewildered when we picked them up at school, but children take changes better than adults: what was for us a crisis, they saw as an adventure. Here was something new and exciting — we were going to live in our caravan until I got another job.

The six of us set out just before lunch — it was a tight squeeze with all our luggage — and while I was driving I tried to take stock of our situation. It seemed to make no sense at all. Eileen's guidance had told us, time and again, that we were to return to Cluny Hill, and I was so *sure* that we would. I had put everything into making the Trossachs Hotel a success and on the surface — from the company's profit-making point of view — it was, although not nearly as much as Cluny Hill Hotel. Why had I been sacked? What was going on? I suddenly pulled the car over to the side of the road and asked Eileen to get guidance on these matters.

She sat quietly and began writing in her notebook. We were told, as before, that we had many lessons to learn and that the tests at the Trossachs were important for our future. We were assured that 'all was very well' and what had happened was all part of God's Plan for us. Furthermore we were to send Love to Mrs Bruce because she had an important part to play in that plan.

This was the final straw. 'What, send Love to that bitch?' I exploded. 'I have worked day and night, week after week, month after month, year after year without a single day off — and this is how she treats us! How on earth can such a woman have a part in God's Plan?' When I had cooled down, however, we did our best to follow the instruction and sent her Love.

It was late afternoon by the time we reached the north east coast but instead of driving directly to Lossiemouth I made a detour into Forres and up to Cluny Hill, where I parked the car. The boys amused themselves while Dorothy, Eileen and I climbed the mound behind the hotel, the 'power point' of which her guidance had said I was the guardian. The sun sets early at that time of year at such a northerly latitude, and the sky was a blaze of light; the air was crisp, clear and dry, in total contrast to the dank, oppressive atmosphere we had come from. It seemed suddenly symbolic and made a great impression on me: I felt filled with Light, as if a tremendous burden had been lifted from us. The Trossachs Hotel had disappeared into its shroud of mists, like Brigadoon. Here we had come home, had stepped back into the Light.

Chapter 16

Fancy Living in a Dump Like That

Your protection at all times will lie in your faith in yourself and in the All-Good

OVER THIRTY YEARS after our depressing and seemingly disastrous experience of the Trossachs, I still find myself drawing a veil across my memories of that time. Of the 'lessons we had to learn', according to Eileen's guidance, only two particularly stand out. One was the importance of a united staff. When we arrived there the assistant manager and the head receptionist had already been at the Trossachs for some time, and really belonged to Mrs Bruce — I later discovered that they both undermined what I was doing, particularly the assistant manager, whom I strongly suspected had been after my job.[1]

The other, greater lesson was that it is a waste of time trying to turn an apparent centre of darkness into a Centre of Light. There are some places that are inherently gloomy, cheerless and dismal on a physical level; others that may seem quite beautiful physically but have those same negative qualities at a psychic level, and I have always felt that the Trossachs was one of these. With the best will and heart in the world — and if enthusiasm counts for anything — we had tried our best to lift this enervating gloom from the hotel but failed and had to admit defeat. If I had only been giving 50 per cent I would have blamed myself for the lack of success but that was not the case; despite the melodramatic tone of Charles's statement that 'the evil is in the very bricks of this place', I have to concede that there may have been something in what he said. It certainly accorded with my experiences of our time there.[2]

---

1 Years later his son — who was a Findhorn Community enthusiast — confirmed my suspicions

2 I have never returned there since we left in 1962 and in no way wish to suggest or imply that the conditions we experienced then still pertain. (Jeremy Slocombe adds:) The

My spiritual training had taught me that on the planet there are certain centres of natural power which can be likened to the chakras[3] and acupuncture points on the human body. An energy of one kind or another is concentrated at such points and has a subtle but profound effect on whoever or whatever happens to be there. Like many people I am insensitive to a physical perception of such places — just as I discovered, when called up for the Royal Air Force, that I was slightly colour-blind — but there are many others who *can* sense their energy and describe it accordingly. Many of the great cathedrals and holy places were deliberately sited to take advantage of those power centres conducive to spiritual work. At some point in their lives, most people have found a 'special place' with which there was some resonance in their being.

Just as the energy concentrated at some of these centres can have a positive and benign effect on people, so the energy at others can tend to have a negative and malign effect. Some places seem to draw out the best in people, others the worst — *but it all depends on the susceptibility of the individuals concerned.* I think that many of those whom I employed at the Trossachs had their weaknesses compounded there; the place was testing all of us, but it would be unfair to blame the place and not the person if he or she failed to pass those tests. Strength is gained by confronting opposition, as one gains strength in the body by use of weights as resistance.

Eileen's guidance referred to this testing process as the 'powers of darkness' — in July 1962, for example, she was asked, *Can you withstand the powers of darkness or will you succumb to them?* — but it was never suggested that we were helpless in the face of them. *I have given you each the power to protect yourselves if only you will use it.* The choice was always

---

Trossachs Hotel was totally gutted and rebuilt as self-catering holiday units in 1993. According to past and present management, there was a long history of malevolent hauntings in both the main building and, worse, in Woodlands (the staff house); poltergeist activity and other supernatural occurrences added to the sense of 'evil in the very bricks of the place' that Charles had warned of. The suspected cause was the ghosts of two people killed on the hotel staircase during a fire in 1864. The staircase was subsequently removed and rebuilt elsewhere, thus incurring the ghosts' wrath at the loss of their 'place'. 'It was the most heavily haunted of all our properties', says Geoffrey Baber, managing director of Holiday Property Bond, the group that now owns it, 'Even the security guards' dogs refused to enter the building during its reconstruction.' Mr Baber called in a priest to conduct holy communion and a blessing before the building was reoccupied, and since then there has been no further trouble.

3 According to many ancient Eastern traditions, chakras are the seven main energy centres of the body. These must be activated or fully 'opened' in turn before enlightenment can be attained

ours. I believe that we did maintain our integrity but could not have done more at the Trossachs Hotel, and once we had learned that lesson it was time to move on.

When people ask me today for advice on setting up a centre or community I always stress the importance of the location they choose. The physical attractiveness of a setting may be beguiling — as we found at the Trossachs — but the fact is that some places are simply more conducive to spiritual work, to creating a Centre of Light, than others, and one should take great care to seek out and locate such a place.[4] Of course, in 1962 we had no intention of starting anything, but by obeying Eileen's guidance we were led, step by step, to exactly the right place for our future work, though we didn't know it then.

Looking back through Eileen's guidance and with the benefit of hindsight, there are further clues to the significance of that time. We were told, *you are now in this place which could represent the state of the world...you are in but not of this place.* I was too busy managing the hotel to pay much attention to this, but the state of the world was indeed perilous: the beginning of the Cuban Missile Crisis, in which US President Kennedy issued an ultimatum to the USSR to dismantle and remove all its medium-range ballistic missiles from Cuba, coincided with our dismissal from the Trossachs. It was the superpower showdown that everyone was dreading and the closest the world has come, before, and probably since, to the nuclear holocaust that Eileen's guidance had been explicitly warning us about for over a year.[5] Little wonder that we were so keen to be in the protected environment of Cluny Hill, where the Light had been built up and there was a landing place for the space brothers if their rescue operation was needed! At the time, however, this was not a mental or emotional reaction to world affairs, to which I paid scant attention; it was simply obedience to God's Word through Eileen long before the crisis was made public.

Whether there be prophecies, they shall fail. Thank God they did on this occasion although we were not to know then, as we discovered later, just how close to the edge of destruction humanity came in those dark months. I have subsequently learned that no matter how high or pure the

---

4 The Chinese have developed a whole art of doing this, *feng shui*

5 The official ultimatum was publicly issued on 22 October1962, and the US Navy imposed a sea blockade on Cuba. The USSR finally backed down six days later and removed the missiles

source of prophecy, no matter how clear or specific the prophecy is, no matter how often the same prophecy is voiced by however many different sources, whether the prophecy be of good things or bad, enlightenment or earthquakes or the end of the world itself, we as humans have free will and a free hand to help shape the things to come, to overturn prophecy — if we choose to do so.[5]

* * *

The Stotfield was a stolid, unpretentious hotel in the fishing port of Lossiemouth. We spent two nights there, and during the day I drove across to prepare our caravan at the Findhorn Sands Caravan Park overlooking the Moray Firth — a bleak site in the sand dunes, exposed to freezing winds that blew out of the north east. We knew that we would not be able to stay there permanently, as it was a seasonal caravan park.

I was still in a daze after our apparent dramatic fall from grace, but we did receive some reassuring words from God:

> *I know that yesterday was a very grave shock to all of you, but I have tried to prepare you very gently. I want you to know that only the very best can result from this. You may not be able to see it at the moment but you will. Your faith will be strengthened in a new way. You'll be drawn together. Now there is little time to do all that has to be done, but as you take one step at a time you'll find that things will work out perfectly. Your immediate action is to get housed.*

The following day, 13 October 1962, we packed up the car again and drove the 10 miles from Lossiemouth along to the caravan. Eileen was told:

> *My child it would be best to stay as near Findhorn as possible for the time being. Findhorn radiates great Light and you need the protection of the Light.*

The village of Findhorn lies on the tip of a peninsula bound by Burghead Bay, the Moray Firth and Findhorn Bay, into which flows the Findhorn River after a long, meandering journey from its headwaters in the Cairngorm moun-

5 'The Hawaiians possess a great natural insight into things, and they prophesy and prognosticate. There is a certain group of Hawaiians who will get together and tune in impending influences. If they perceive an influence that is not of benefit, they turn it over to another group who work against it, and it never manifests. The Hindus say that one man can prophesy and another God-man can stop fulfilment of the prophecy.' — *The Life and Teachings of the Masters of the Far East*, Vol 4, Baird T. Spalding, De Vorss and Co

tains. Findhorn was once a major port for the whole of Moray, with tall ships sailing into the bay and trading their cargoes of fine cloths, wines, spices and comestibles for the grains, salmon, whiskies and deerskins of the area. It is the third village to bear the name Findhorn — at least one of its predecessors having been washed away by the river's flooding. The coming of the railway and the gradual silting-up of the bay ended the present Findhorn's role as a port and it became a popular holiday village, its long, often cloudless summer's days earning that stretch of the coast its nickname as 'the Riviera of the north'.[6] When summer and the crowds have gone, however, the long, cold nights steal in to redress the balance. The clear skies bring heavy frosts and fierce winds whistle in the wires.

I connected the electricity to our caravan in the dunes and set about making us as comfortable as possible, but on the day we moved in I suddenly realized that our American friend Naomi was on the *Queen Mary*, in mid-Atlantic. She was coming over to join us for three weeks, we had thought at the Trossachs Hotel, and in the drama of the past three days I had completely forgotten about her. With a hasty farewell to the family, I jumped into the car and drove down to Southampton, England, to bring her back.

As it was a time before modern motorways, the journey took three days each way. I met Naomi off the *Queen Mary* in perfect timing and took a scenic route back, wanting to show her the traditional, 'olde worlde' sights so beloved of American tourists. We stopped at Glastonbury where I arranged for us to stay the night in the quaint seventeeth-century Pilgrim's Inn with worn, rickety stairs, low-beamed wooden ceilings and a big old-fashioned bathroom at the end of the corridor; for lunch en route to Scotland I avoided featureless roadside cafes and took her instead to traditional pubs with their oak pannelling and views over the village green. Imagine my disappointment, then, when on our last night before reaching home, all I could find for us was a gaudy, modern roadside motel utterly lacking in any character or charm whatsoever. I apologized to Naomi, but disappointment turned to dismay when I discovered that she loved this place best of all: forget 'olde worlde' charm, all she'd wanted was a decent en-suite bathroom!

We managed to find Naomi a place with Miss Harrold, an elderly woman who lived in the Findhorn Village. The room was very small and not warm, but — accustomed as she was to enjoying her American creature comforts

6 In fact I had coined the phrase, for publicity purposes, when Chairman of the Moray and Nairn Tourist Association during my years at Cluny Hill Hotel. It caught on and is still used today

— Naomi was good about accepting the situation. She was with us in our caravan during the day and I took her back to her room at night. We all came to know each other well. She was a remarkable sensitive and received channelled messages from a variety of sources. One of these messages was that I would never again have to undertake such an onerous task as that at the Trossachs: now was the time for my real work to begin. Since I didn't know what my 'real work' was, this didn't help all that much.

During this time, Dorothy received guidance that she was to stay with us, but as there was no room for her to sleep in the caravan we had to find somewhere for her. The local hotel had a small hut attached to it which was used by relief staff during the summer; it had a bed but no form of heating. With the agreement of the hotel owner, Dorothy moved in, bought herself an electric underblanket and spent every night there throughout what was to be a bitter winter.

During her stay with us, Naomi joined Dorothy, Eileen and me every morning and evening as we resumed our inner work connecting with the various groups and stations in the Network of Light. I would read out a list of the key stations to which we would radiate Love or Light (or sometimes both, depending on our perception of the needs of a particular station). While the boys were away at school during the day, the three women would share the various messages or visions they had received. On the surface it paints an odd picture — four adults sitting silently in a caravan surrounded by sand dunes, in a lonely spot in the north of Scotland, at the height of the Cuban Missile Crisis — but in heart, mind and spirit we were connected with a network of others that literally spanned the globe.

This work continued after Naomi returned to the States, and meanwhile we had to cope with the practical realities of our situation. 'Trust God — and keep your powder dry' was a useful maxim of the Duke of Wellington in the Napoleonic Wars. I was forty-five, unemployed, and had a family to support. We had very little money. Hotel managers are poorly paid, as accommodation and meals are provided as part of one's salary; I had also poured my own money into various projects at Cluny Hill Hotel, such as the landscaping, and therefore had no savings. Dorothy — having no dependents — had managed to set a little money aside and generously offered to share it with us, but I felt strongly (and told her) that she should keep it in reserve.

Eileen was shocked when Dorothy and I signed on at the Labour Exchange in Forres in order to find jobs and to draw Unemployment Benefit (and later National Assistance). She wondered how much lower could we sink. From my point of view all our needs were wonderfully met — the boys, for example, who attended the local school in Findhorn village, had free milk and a hot meal at lunchtime every day — but Eileen was horrified that in order to get my unemployment money I had to stand in a queue in the Labour Exchange along with many members of my former staff. I had once been the biggest employer of labour in the district.

The ritual had its lighter moments. One day when I was standing in the queue I met a fat, elderly woman named Babs who had washed pots and pans in the kitchen at Cluny Hill Hotel. Her Scots accent was so broad that I'd never been able to understand what she was saying and Charles was always called in to translate for me. Misfortune makes strange bedfellows. On this occasion she explained, through a friend, that although I had spoken to her nearly every day at Cluny Hill she also had never understood *my* speech. No wonder she had always only grinned in reply and cheerfully banged her pots!

I felt buoyant in those days. Life had suddenly become very simple. The day after we'd left the Trossachs, Eileen's guidance had said:

> *Never try to rush ahead and make plans. I just want you to live from day to day. You can do this in everything you do, even to your catering. At this time I want you to have a complete change. Whereas you have lived far from simply, now I want you to do so — and enjoy it. Really have fun doing it.*

That wasn't a hard prescription for me to take. After the initial bewilderment at our sacking from the Trossachs Hotel had passed, I had an inner conviction that we were in the right place, at the right time, doing the right thing — following God's Word to the letter. Eileen's guidance also said, *Always keep very positive about your return to Cluny Hill...*, which I took to mean a change in Mrs Bruce's policy that would have us reinstalled at the hotel in time for the next year's season. For some reason, however — perhaps because my attention was elsewhere — I failed at the time to take proper notice of the second half of the sentence, which concluded *...but not under this company.*

At the end of October 1962 we had to find another site for our caravan, as the Findhorn Sands Caravan Park was to close for the winter. We were quite determined to find a secluded, private place, thinking we'd only be there for a short time; therefore I went to see the Sanitary Inspector, whom I knew at County Headquarters in the nearby town of Elgin and who was responsible for caravan sites in the area. I had found a private site at Findhorn, but he would only give permission for us to stay there until Christmas — we would then have to move to one of the large residential parks in the district.

The one place we knew we could never stomach was the Findhorn Bay Caravan Park a mile outside the village. For years we had driven by this park on the way to the beach at Findhorn, and I had often made a remark like, 'Fancy living in a dump like that, cheek-by-jowl with a lot of other caravans.' It was a bleak, treeless and dreary place, with row after row of mobile homes lined up like shabby privates on parade along the concrete lanes that had served as dispersal bays for aircraft from the adjacent RAF base during the War. RAF Kinloss was still a functioning station with Nimrod reconnaissance planes thundering in and out both day and night.

'Never' is a dangerous word in anybody's vocabulary, particularly if one is living according to the direction of spirit. After weeks of fruitless searching throughout the area, we were told of one vacant site for our caravan — down by a hollow in the Findhorn Bay Caravan Park. We went to see this site, and what a dump it was, beside an old garage with broken windows, and surrounded by old tins cans and broken bottles, blackberry bushes and gorse. At least it was away from the other caravans on the site. Eileen had clear guidance that it was the right place; we still thought that it would be only a matter of weeks before we returned to Cluny Hill or found other employment.

Thus on a snowy day, 17 November 1962, the owner of the park towed our 30-foot caravan to the site where it still sits today. Jonathan, our second son, was ill at the time, so he stayed in bed while the caravan was being towed. My first job was to get the caravan jacked up and put on a firm foundation of sixteen concrete blocks and fixed up with electricity; the pipes were frozen and we had to fetch and carry all our water from a nearby standpipe. All we had to live on was £8 a week Unemployment Benefit with an additional £1 10s per week of Family Assistance; when I brought the money home each time, Eileen would first pay the ground rent, then put shillings in the slot for our electricity, set enough money aside for gas for the cooker and anthracite for the fire, and the rest into a bowl on the mantelpiece for food. The first winter was so cold that we had to keep the fire lit throughout it — there was snow on the ground for nearly three months.

We were told, *This situation will show you exactly who your real friends are.* I found this guidance most interesting, because it did feel strange to return in such a manner to the County of Moray after being away for a year. At the time we left, we had been people of some social significance. Not only had I been the manager of a four-star hotel, but I was the Founder-Chairman of the Moray District Hoteliers Association, the Moray and Nairn Tourist Association, and the Forres and District Hoteliers Association. We had been frequently invited out to dinner and parties. After we moved to the caravan park and were living on Unemployment Benefit, nobody wanted to know us; in fact when rumours began that I must have been sacked because I was robbing the hotel chain, some people in Forres actually crossed the street to avoid meeting us. The only people who came to see us were two women, reformed prostitutes, who had left the latter occupation to work at Cluny Hill and really loved us.

Looking back, of course, this was all part of the plan. One could not take part in an active social life and at the same time lay the foundations for a spiritual centre. Furthermore we needed to be isolated from the world, to concentrate on what had been given us to do. We were really living like hermits. When people asked me if it didn't hurt my pride to line up for Unemployment Benefit, I realized that my only concern was, were we doing God's Will? I felt that we were, though the whole situation did not make sense at the time.

In November 1962, Eileen received:

> *Try to understand, Peter sees the goal, and seeing the goal, he does not see the many obstacles in the way. As far as he is concerned, all those obstacles are as nothing. Today he expects you to reach that goal. This my child is where he has to learn patience and gentleness. His very forcefulness frightens you, and makes you want to pull back ...These gifts Peter has received are priceless, and there are very few who have been given them, but they need to be balanced with wisdom. Let Peter help you at this time. He is the rock, strong and unshakeable and his faith is the same. He will sustain the outer. Let him do this willingly. You, Peter and Dorothy will achieve a new unity as you put Me and My work before all else. The rest will fall into place. Your roles will be made very clear. Work nothing out with the mind. I will reveal all. Wisdom is where*

Dorothy can help Peter, while you are a channel for Love. Step ahead fearlessly into the new, knowing I'm with you, and all is very very well.

During the long cold winter there was little that we could do, so we spent much time in meditation continuing our inner work with the Light Centres all over the world. Eileen or Dorothy would sometimes have the vision of a certain centre or they would have a telepathic contact and describe it as it happened, which for me — since I could neither see nor hear their connections — was rather like listening to a one-sided telephone conversation! Less than a fortnight after we arrived, Lena and her children moved in to a caravan next to ours, and she joined us in this work.

The children thoroughly enjoyed their new freedom after their rather restricted life in a large hotel. When we arrived at Findhorn they had plenty of fresh air and sunshine and were able to play on the beach; now they loved the cold, snowy winter weather too, and really enjoyed going to school — they would take the sledge and take it in turns to pull each other along the footpath into the village. Their friends would come and talk and play with them in and around the caravan. On the whole, the boys adapted well, and learning to tidy up their tiny room was a useful discipline.

Theirs was a good example for us adults. Soon after we moved on to the caravan park, Eileen had received:

Learn to count your many many blessings and give Me constant thanks for them. There are times when each of you becomes so weighed with burdens that you fail to see your blessings. At times like that it is well to just start counting your blessings one by one and you will soon see how mightily blessed you are.

It would have been so easy at this time to be full of pessimism, despondency and resentment. We had been kicked out of the Trossachs, had to move into a caravan by a rubbish dump, and were dependent upon Unemployment Benefit. We could have had a lot of self-pity, but instead we counted our blessings. We were grateful for the clear air, the beautiful countryside, the freedoms, the peace, the love between all of us, and many other blessings. We were told that we were now to learn to live as a group and that our strength depended upon our unity — above all, we had to focus on loving one another, as Love is a shield against negativity and depression.

We were all so different that this was not always easy, especially in such a confined living space. As the guidance suggested, in an archetypal sense Eileen represented Love, myself Light and Dorothy Wisdom, three very different aspects of the Divine trying to create oneness. This uniting of Light, Love and Wisdom was the foundation of the establishment of the group and later the community at Findhorn. During Naomi's stay with us we had received many messages on this subject; one of them was to the effect that it needs three people to hold a 'Centre of Light', each representing one of these three aspects in balance with the others, like an equilateral triangle. One without the other is useless, although ideally in personal evolution a person learns to embody all three within the self.

Another thing we learned was that it was important in the beginning to be without any routine, so we could start an entirely new life under God's guidance. On 22 December 1962, Eileen received for me:

> *You and Eileen do work as one in Me. Your inspiration, your guidance comes direct from Me, the Lord your God. Only use the written word through Eileen, when you are in any doubt and need confirmation. Let me work through you more and more.*

One vital step was to clean the caravan thoroughly, inside and out, so Dorothy and I began by scrubbing the interior, stripping off the paint and repainting it throughout. Eileen had guidance that if we couldn't do this with love it would be best to stop and go for a walk along the beach, or meditate, because it was important that the energies of Love and Light were put into the very fabric of the caravan. This process was called 'raising the vibrations' and would act as a protection for the sensitive inner work to be done there. At the Trossachs Eileen had felt that she was unprotected, like a snail without a shell, and it hindered her ability to get guidance easily; here at Findhorn that protective shell was being formed. I believe that this cleaning and painting is necessary when preparing any centre for spiritual work, and that the worse the state of the building, the better, for it means that more Love and Light are needed to be put in to add to the protection. Order and cleanliness allow no room for stray, chaotic or negative influences.

We also had more mundane reasons to be neat. Though large for a caravan, our home was very small. Its main room served as our bedroom, dining room and sitting room; before we could pull the bed down from the wall, the dining room chairs had to be stacked and the armchair placed on top of the sofa. Everyone had to walk through this 'bedroom' to get to the bathroom, with a tiny tub in which we bathed and where Eileen did the washing on her knees. Another door led to the kitchen, a door to the left was for the toilet, and ahead was the three boys' room, where there was a three-quarter bed and a single bed with a bunk bed above it. There were two doors between the bedrooms, which cut down on noise. On Saturday afternoons the boys and I would watch wrestling on television while Eileen cooked the dinner in the small kitchen between our rooms. Then I would clear away the furniture and they would wrestle, two at a time, while the other watched. One of them would usually get hurt and go running to Eileen crying, and the other would take over; then as the wounded one returned he would have another chance. I acted as the referee and after two or three hours they would be completely exhausted. We thoroughly enjoyed ourselves.

Eileen got very worried about my not obtaining a job. I searched diligently during the day and spent the evening and bad weather days poring over garden books of every conceivable point of view— organic and non-organic, traditional and progressive — looking forward to a time when I might start my own small garden. I intended to grow our own lettuces, radishes and parsley, in order to supplement our food supply, but had no intention of it becoming a major project.

We had no money to spend on sending Christmas cards. Formerly we had received and sent 300–400 cards at Cluny Hill Hotel, but these had been from social and business acquaintances and hardly what I would call 'soul links'. For Eileen, however, this was tangible evidence of our apparent fall from grace. When she went into Forres and its 'busy' High Street, she would return with a headache, so she stopped going. She really appreciated where we were living and what a special place it was, but breaking with the old and emerging into the new was a very painful process, especially as there was so much of the old to be done away with. We were like butterflies struggling out of cocoons. They struggle and then emerge wet and drab, until the light of the sunshine brings out their full glory. That is what we were trying to do — emerge into the new, and we needed God's strength to enable us to do it.

Chapter 17

Breaking New Ground

There is a world within,
a world of thought and feeling and power,
of light and life and beauty
and, although invisible,
its forces are mighty

ON 14 JANUARY 1960 — when we were still at Cluny Hill Hotel — I had written a curiously prophetic paragraph in a letter to Naomi:

> *Dorothy's work is developing and she has just obtained a book about fairies and nature spirits.*[1] *I am sure you will be interested in the following message received today: 'The responsibility which I give to My nature spirits is directly theirs; though all power comes through man, yet like Love and Light are the two necessary in creation. When the worlds were formed I breathed My breath of life and through the ages built up a world and all upon it for the use of My child man, but now that the child will destroy My creation, he will also rebuild it for habitation. And so cooperation between man and nature is necessary as never before. A great work this is, to be done in the joy of the Lord.' This throws more light on the work of the nature spirits, which you and I seem rather to have left out of the scheme of things in the past. This is where Dorothy and her work will fill in the gap.*

During this period Dorothy, Eileen and Lena were all receiving pages of messages every day, and while this particular message would have been duly noted along with all the others at the time, my attention was elsewhere and I had forgotten all about it by the time we were at Findhorn three years later.

---

1 In 1993, Dorothy writes 'I expect the book was *The Kingdom of the Gods* by Geoffrey Hodson, from which I heard of the word "deva".'

In fact the day after we arrived at the caravan park, 18 November 1962, Dorothy was given another message related to nature:

> *All nature's forces have a different feel. Even the wildness of the wind has been used; in creation great powers are needed, of all sorts. [...] Feel into the nature forces behind, and go with them...It is a matter of feeling into nature's conditions and becoming one with them. As you are in harmony with them, you can be used to forward their purpose...These are mighty forces and man can cooperate with them. Feel into them and the co-operation can start.*

But even her inner voice admitted 'all this is vague' and Dorothy simply took it to mean that she should enjoy nature during her daily walks over the dunes between Findhorn village and our caravan.

In February 1963 Dorothy decided to spend some of her modest savings and buy a prefabricated annex which we built on to the side of the caravan so that she could be with us. We painted and decorated the annex, and now Dorothy had not only a place to live but also a work space in which she could type and file the messages that were received in meditation by Eileen, herself and Lena. Throughout our years at Cluny Hill Hotel and the early days at Findhorn, Dorothy was totally dedicated to typing and organizing not only this material but also my weekly letters to Naomi — and thanks to this, there are very clear records of all that happened at the time.

We were told that nothing, no matter how small, was to be done without first seeking God's guidance; when this was not done, the consequences were unfortunate. For example, Dorothy was looking out for a carpet and I discovered that there was a sale of shop-soiled carpets in town. Dorothy saw one that she liked, and being in rather a hurry bought it without first asking for inner confirmation. Only later did she discover that not only was the pattern wrong for the room, but it was made of cotton and not wool — she had, in fact, been taken for a ride. This may seem to some a trivial instance, but it is often in the minutiae of daily life that we learn lessons to prepare us for dealing with the big issues.

By March 1963 it was obvious that we would not be returning to Cluny Hill Hotel that season; it became increasingly clear to me that it was not right for me to get a job that year, as the steps that we were taking to create a Centre of Light could only be made in seclusion away from the world and its influences. This did not mean that I was unprepared to take a job or refused to apply for any position offered me. Throughout these early years the Labour Exchange did its best to find employment for me — the manager was Graham McDonald, who had been my assistant at Cluny Hill Hotel. I went to one interview after another, but every time something would happen and I wouldn't get the job. Of course, it didn't help that I had no references: the Royal Air Force doesn't give references and Mrs Bruce steadfastly refused to supply one, despite my persistent requests.

During this first spring at Findhorn, we noticed that the dirt and sand which surrounded the caravan was being brought to the front door, leaving foot marks on our blue carpet. Therefore I had the idea to put a concrete slab in front of the caravan for a patio, and a path right the way round the caravan and between the caravan and the garage. I also wanted to put in a fence to give us some privacy and protection from the winds. The children and their friends often would play noisily nearby, and this made meditation difficult. (David, our youngest, would warn his friends that we were having our 'peace'; being Scots, they misheard this as having our 'piece', ie a piece of bread or cake with afternoon tea.)

Making concrete is an expensive business because of the cost of the cement, and there seemed no way we could afford it. I decided to go ahead in faith, however; Eileen's guidance had told us that *when the first step is taken in the right direction all the rest will fall into place.* On the day I started this work and was wondering where on earth the cement would come from, somebody mentioned in the course of conversation that a quantity of cement in bags, slightly water-damaged, had been dumped just outside the caravan site. I immediately collected it and found that there was more than enough for our needs — its cash value was the equivalent of over three times our weekly income! Such apparent coincidences became commonplace; I was amazed how God was looking after us in small and seemingly strange ways.

I stored several tons of this cement in our garage and then spent weeks levelling the ground and surrounding it with wooden boards. Dorothy and Eileen collected sand and small stones from the Findhorn River. When all was prepared, the three of us set about the back-breaking job of mixing the sand, cement and stones, making the concrete with spades. By teatime at 4 pm we had laid a 12-foot concrete square for the patio and, utterly exhausted, decided that we'd done enough for the day — we would finish the paths on the morrow.

The next day came but there was something else to be done, and the day after, and the day after that... there was always something new to create, each with its own new energy. In fact it was six years before the path round the back of the caravan was completed! Here we learned an important lesson in creating a community, or anything for that matter: to complete one job at a time and to do it perfectly before moving on to the next. It is extremely difficult to go back and complete a job to perfection once the energy involved in its conception has been redirected.

I erected a six-foot high slatted fence around the twelve-foot concrete square, with some ground to spare, giving us complete privacy and protection from the wind. That little patio was to give us much joy in the years ahead: it served as a 'dining room' and a space for meetings and meditation when the weather permitted.

Since I was still without a job, I decided to begin a small garden. Inside the fence was a patch of ground, 11 feet by 6 feet. I wanted to grow a few radishes and lettuces to supplement our meagre income. There was only about 2 inches of turf on top — really just a tangle of couch grass — and the rest was sand and gravel held together by the long, creeping roots of the couch grass. Before I could plant anything I had to remove this turf, turning it upside down into the bottom of trenches 18 inches wide by 12 inches deep, and chopping it up thoroughly. Then the fine sand was replaced on top. This 'soil' was so devoid of humus that water would not sink in; I tried to water the seedlings every day, but bubbles just formed on the top and the water ran off.

It was here that the Findhorn garden was started. Before I had sown a seed, I knew that it would be useless without a good supply of compost or manure. That very day on the caravan site I discovered a large pile of black matter which turned out to be the rotted remains of cut grass — perfect for growing vegetables when added to the soil. The way different materials just 'appeared' for the garden when they were needed sometimes made us wonder;[2] it made me think that this must be a very important project, but I was too busy to spend time guessing why. As far as I was concerned it was enough to be growing our own food. Not only would this make what little money we had stretch further, it would also (and more importantly) return the 'vibrations' we were putting into the land, in the form of nourishing food to help refine our bodies. Eileen's guidance had been quite specific about the need for this.

2 We later called this phenomenon 'manifestation': see Chapter 19

If they were not literally 'manna from heaven', as far as the garden was concerned the compost materials we found were the next best thing. One day, I was told that a bale of straw had fallen off of a lorry and was lying by the roadside. I immediately jumped in to the car and drove off to collect it. On the way back I gave a lift to a man whom I knew slightly; I explained that the bale of straw in the back of the car was to make compost for the garden. As we passed a field of horses he said, 'Why don't you collect the horse manure from that field?' 'I can't do that,' I replied, 'I don't know the owner.' He told me that *he* was the owner and I was welcome to the manure! After we had collected it, he put his horses in a field adjacent to the caravan park, so that the supply was continued; the sight of Eileen and Dorothy following the horses with shovels and buckets to collect that precious fresh manure was a source of some amusement to passers-by. We would carry it home in an old tin bath in the back of the car.

We became remarkable scavengers when it came to gathering other ingredients for the compost. A local shop gave us spoiled fruit and vegetables; grass cuttings came from the caravan park. We fetched peat dross and cummings (the germ of barley, which is a potent fertilizer) from a nearby maltings for the whisky distilleries. If I saw smoke rising on the horizon, I would fetch my binoculars to locate its source, knowing that the ashes of wood fires contained potash, another crucial ingredient. Sometimes during the hard, cold work of cutting seaweed off the rocks by Findhorn Bay, Dorothy and Eileen would find a dead salmon or swan washed up on the seashore, and these too would be added to the mixture. Even the caravan's 'night buckets' were emptied on to the compost heap — no wonder our neighbours considered us a little strange!

By May I was able to write to Naomi that our compost heap was 'steaming away like an ocean liner'. The first vegetables I had planted — radishes, lettuces, peas, beans, carrots and spring onions — were thriving on the mixture and the boys thoroughly enjoyed watching them come on. One night I planted out a batch of small lettuces which I had bought in nearby Elgin; when the boys saw them the next morning they wondered if they had grown overnight!

Behind the caravan was a steep slope covered with gorse and brambles. I wanted to cultivate this so I could add turnips, celery, leeks, swedes and a few other vegetables to the garden, but upon investigation I discovered that the ground was even less suitable than the original plot. It was mostly gravel;

any 'soil' there was had been washed down the slope. With shovel and wheelbarrow I began the arduous task of swapping the two: the sandy soil went back up the slope and the gravel was used to fill in the gap between the caravan and the garage at the bottom.

There was a vitally important reason for this hard labour, which took several months. Eileen received for me, *Know that every time you put a spade into the ground you are putting in radiations*. By working in total concentration and with love for what I was doing, I could imbue the soil with love, and this in turn would create a protective barrier, like a force field, around the caravan.

One day during this period I was visited by Phimister Brown, a solicitor who was company secretary to a number of hotels. He had been interested in me for several years and, in fact, had offered me the management of a hotel in Aberdeen the previous October, shortly after our dismissal from the Trossachs. (I had turned it down then, so sure that we would be returning to Cluny Hill.) He took us out to dinner, which was a special treat, and then repeated his offer but with a new twist: if I built up the Aberdeen hotel in a short time, then he could sell it and buy Cluny Hill Hotel (which was going from bad to worse) and install me there as manager, because he knew that this was the only place I was really interested in. It was a tempting offer. Eileen's guidance was for me not to turn this down, but be prepared to take it if the present manager cracked under the strain of running the hotel in Aberdeen. Meanwhile I had more than enough to be getting on with in the garden.

Dorothy had always been a great nature lover but the earlier intimations that she could be used to 'forward the purposes' of the nature kingdom returned with startling clarity one morning in May. In her meditation she was told to 'feel into the nature forces', to 'be positive and harmonize with that essence'. She thought this would be a good excuse to lie in the sun and and take rambles over the dunes, but I put a different interpretation on it — perhaps it meant she could get information to help in the garden.

My spiritual training under Dr Sullivan had included information about the elemental spirits of earth, air, fire and water, and their role in creation; the possibility of conscious cooperation with them had always intrigued me. Was this now an opportunity to do so? I pressed Dorothy on the subject, and the next morning she received:

Yes, My child, you are to cooperate in the garden. Begin this by thinking about the nature spirits, the higher nature spirits who overlight, and [by] tuning into them. That will be so unusual as to draw their interest here, and they will be overjoyed to help and to find some members of the human race eager for that help. That is the first step; the smaller individual nature spirits are under their jurisdiction.

By the higher nature spirits I do not mean just the one that geographically overlights the area but the spirits of the different physical forms such as the spirits of clouds, of rain, of the separate vegetables. In the new world their realms will be quite open to humans — or I should say, humans will be open to them — and when rain is needed, for example, it will be brought about. It is even possible with you now, if the faith were great enough and there were no sense of limitation. Now just be open and seek out into the glorious realms of nature with sympathy and understanding, knowing these beings are of the light, willing to help but suspicious of humans and on the lookout for the false, the snags. Keep with Me and they will find none, and you will all build towards the new. [3]

Two weeks later, after a lot of badgering from me, Dorothy directly contacted a spirit of the plant kingdom, the angel or 'deva'[4] of the garden pea. She was as much surprised by the suddenness of the contact as she was by its message:

I can speak to you, human. I am entirely directed by my work, which is set out and moulded and I merely bring it to fruition, but you have come straight to my awareness. My work is clear before me, the force fields are there to be brought into manifestation regardless of obstacles, and there are many many on this man-infested world. You think that slugs, for example, are a greater menace to me than man but this is not so; slugs are part of the order of things and the vegetable kingdom holds no grudge against those it feeds, but man takes what it can as

[3] This is the original, uncut and unedited message as typed by Dorothy at the time; other published versions vary in some small but significant ways

[4] 'Deva' is a Sanskrit word meaning 'shining one'. Dorothy writes: 'To me, "angel" was full of Christianity, harps and haloes. Angels and devas are exactly the same thing.'

a matter of course, giving no thanks, which makes us strangely hostile.

What I would tell you is that as we forge ahead, never deviating from our course for one moment's thought, feeling or action, so could you. Humans generally seem to know not where they are going, or why, and if they did, what a powerhouse they would be and how, if they were on the straight course of what is to be done, we could cooperate with them!

I have put across my meaning and bid you farewell.

My excitement at this breakthrough is preserved in a letter I wrote to Naomi at the time:

... This is only the beginning and what infinite possibilities this opens up. To be able to grow vegetables with the direct help of the Archetypal being in charge of the vegetables! Co-operation between man and the nature forces! I have not heard of this being done before but of course in days gone by when man was nearer to nature it was probably done instinctively...I am eagerly awaiting further contacts.

I did not have to wait long. Dorothy repeated the experiment, this time attempting to contact the being responsible for the general area of the garden, which she called the Landscape Angel: she had equal success with this. We came to understand that every species of plant has its own deva, an intelligence that holds the overall pattern of the shape, characteristics and development of plants within that particular species — much like an architect has a blueprint for a certain type of building. The devas also direct energy towards bringing individual plants into physical form according to that plant's pattern, just as the architect hands his plans over to the builders.

I seized this opportunity to ask the devas, through Dorothy (who knew less about gardening than I did), for practical advice to solve many of the problems I had encountered in the garden. Before coming to Findhorn I had very little gardening experience; the books I had read were comprehensive, but the problem was that they were written for gardens in the fertile south of England or the Midlands, and not for those in the north of Scotland — especially not for such harsh, unpromising conditions as surrounded us in the caravan park. Furthermore these books often contradicted each other, and this is where I had to turn to the devas for answers.

When I wanted to grow watercress, for example, one book said that this wasn't possible without running water, and another said it could be grown in the shade, if well watered; yet another said it should be grown in full sunshine. This was very confusing. When I asked, the Watercress Deva said (with an uncharacteristic lack of help), 'Experiment'. I dug a trench and put in a lot of compost to hold the moisture; half of the trench was in the sunshine and half was in the shade. As it happened, we'd found the perfect solution. The watercress that was in the sun came on early and went to seed, leaving us with the watercress in the shade for the rest of the season.

Usually, though, the devas were enthusiastic and specific in their advice. Our working relationship was a two-way affair — this experiment in conscious cooperation between humans and the nature forces was as new to them as it was to us. I did not always or automatically turn to the devas for *every* answer, however; I would only give Dorothy questions after I had tried something my way and was obviously not having any success. Had I been an experienced gardener I might have known many of the practices that the devas recommended, but as I later discovered, some of their suggestions went far beyond the ken of conventional gardening.

While my chief interest in the devas lay in the practical advice they could give me, Dorothy was more attracted to their ethereal, philosophic communications and resented my pestering her for down-to-earth information. She was also upset by what she saw as the 'brutality' of my weeding, thinning out, cutting back and similar actions required to keep any garden in order. This led to a friction between us that sometimes sparked heated arguments. I maintained that as man was the creator of the garden, he must have the final say; it was not always possible or appropriate to follow the devas' suggestions, given the time, labour and material resources we could afford; left to their own devices, the nature forces would quickly return the garden to a wild state. Dorothy conceded that a garden was anyway an artificial creation but argued that the devas could be trusted to render weeding, pruning, etc., unnecessary once we had found the right level of cooperation with them.

The devas themselves seemed disinterested in human squabbles but warned us that our thoughts and states of mind *did* affect the garden when we were working in it. The love with which I handled the soil and tended the plants was more important than sentimentality; positive thoughts were more powerful than doubts about what we were doing. At this time, Dr Sullivan's *Soul Science* series of lectures on positive thinking played a great part in helping Eileen, Dorothy and Lena come to terms with the extraordinary events taking place in our lives. The four of us would go over the course-work of a particular lesson every night for two weeks, before moving onto the next, and the three women often received in their own personal guidance supplementary 'instruction' related to the current lesson.

These teachings, and our daily times of silence together when we invoked the God within, helped us to transcend (if not resolve) personality differences or clashes of opinion. This was important not only for us to be able to work and live effectively together in such cramped quarters, but also to enhance our sensitivity to the needs, both material and spiritual, of the plants in our garden. I learned, for example, that the type of music that was played affected the growth of the plants; therefore I constantly played classical music on the radio (though this sometimes annoyed Dorothy, who preferred quiet).

Dorothy received messages from the devas of trees, shrubs, vegetables and flowers; also from the Landscape Angel that directed the life force into the whole garden so that the devas of individual species could use it in the fulfilment of their particular work. This angel often offered practical advice on general matters such as soil and compost:

> *No, it is not necessary to put the peat in the garden. What good it does in protection is more than offset by the harm of having a dead weight, so to speak, which has to be amalgamated into the life being of the garden. Better in the compost; we are greatly speeding up the compost for you. Mix.*

These beings did not speak to Dorothy in an audible 'voice'. She contacted them (or they her) telepathically, so that the message was communicated in a stream of consciousness which her own mind translated into the nearest equivalent English words. As with Eileen's guidance, I would only consider the messages received *if they were written down*, as a safeguard against them being coloured further by the mind and emotions in a spoken rendering. But Dorothy was a highly sensitive channel, carefully and strictly trained by Sheena, and even if she herself sometimes doubted the information she received, it was uniformly sound (and very useful). Without Dorothy's stoical service to the garden I was creating, I doubt whether many people outside Scotland would have heard of the name Findhorn today. Her autobiography, *To Hear the Angels Sing,* was published in 1980.[5]

---

5 Reprinted many times and available at this time of writing (1995) from Lindisfarne Press

Chapter 18

The Magic Garden

Harmony in the world within
will be reflected in the world without
by harmonious conditions,
agreeable surroundings,
the best of everything

AS I CONTINUED developing the garden, it became an intensive one in which every inch of space was used. Parsnips, for example, would be sown 18 inches apart, and between the parsnips two rows of lettuce, and between the lettuce and the parsnips, a row of radishes. The radishes would mature first and be picked, leaving space for the lettuces, and by the time they were cut there would be room for the parsnips to expand. There was so much life and vitality in the garden that it became a showplace and people began to come from the lower caravan site and then the surrounding area to have a look. They were surprised and impressed by this fertile spot in an otherwise bleak environment, and wondered at our secret: was it green fingers? Why were we establishing a permanent garden around a temporary home in the first place? Sometimes I sold our surplus produce to them, in order to buy more plants, but I never discussed the true nature of our work.

By the end of our first summer a garden had been created, step-by-step, right around the caravan. Eileen felt that more and more protection was being added; the shell around us was becoming stronger and we felt more secure. She also received in her guidance that what we were doing in this garden was very important for the world, and that tens of thousands of people would one day come and see it. This made no sense to me at the time. I did feel, however, that in consciously working with the devas we were learning the very secrets of creation.

Although we were using neither artificial fertilizers nor pesticides, the plants in our garden were vibrant and had developed a natural resistance to disease and pests. In the first year, 1963, we learned that our cabbages and Brussels sprouts were the only ones in the neighbourhood that had survived a plague of cabbage root grubs (which, as their name suggests, destroy the roots of the plant). The devas had told me to bring the soil up around the plants' stems and keep them watered — as a result, the plants put out extra roots and thus survived.

At this time, Eileen received:

> *Tell Peter, all the work that he has put into this place and is still putting into this place will bear vegetables in abundance. Radiations and all he has put into the soil to nourish it [are] making this place a very special place. His reward will be to see how greatly this place is to be used in the days to come.*

In that tiny garden surrounding the caravan I eventually grew sixty-five kinds of vegetables (including many varieties of each), forty-two kinds of herbs and twenty-one different kinds of fruit. Although we were living on Unemployment Benefit, our food was magnificent — the vital, vegetarian fare from the garden grown with the help of the devas, who seemed to be queuing up in their eagerness to cooperate with us. Once the first crops were ready, Eileen began receiving specific instructions about refining our bodies through eating our own produce, as well as fruit, honey and wheat germ.

Every day we had a big salad, which we took in turns to prepare, each person picking the herbs of his or her taste to add to a variety of ingredients; finally I tossed it with an olive oil dressing. In the evening we would have a vegetable stew, including potatoes, carrots, onions, leeks, turnips, parsnips, artichokes, celery, cauliflower, swedes, tomatoes, garlic and marrows, all seasoned with a variety of herbs. For a sweet we would often eat the over-ripe bananas that I'd collected from the greengrocer's for the compost heap, and we used the top of the milk as cream. Another important addition to our diet was potatoes: I collected sacks of damaged ones from a shop, ostensibly to add to the compost, but we cut out the bad bits and made soup out of the remainder. We had potato soup nearly every day.

This gradual refinement of our physical bodies through diet and exercise, we were told, meant that our intake of food would diminish and we would begin to absorb more energy directly from the sun — even our skin would become more absorbent. I must say that after days in the sun and fresh air, with a daily run along the beach followed by a dip in the icy waters of the Moray Firth, I *did* feel the difference, but who wouldn't? We made the most of good weather, wore the minimum of clothing and had regular picnics on the beach. *All this is helping you and preparing you for the future,* said Eileen's guidance, *but whatever you do, it is so very important you really enjoy doing it.*

The need for physical fitness soon became apparent. Building up the soil in our garden had become almost an obsession with me, and by the end of the summer we had nearly used up our supply of manure. I began casting covetous eyes on a pile of manure on the farm next door to us. It seemed that the farmer had no use for it, preferring to use artificial fertilizers which were subsidized by the Government, so after a couple of months of seeing it just sitting there I went to visit him.

This was in October, when the 'tatties' (potatoes) — a staple food for Scots — are ready for harvest. I offered the farmer our help picking tatties in return for as much manure as we could cart away. The farmer protested that surely our labour was worth more than that, but I assured him that this was all we needed. In the end he agreed, as he was short of labour and could do with the extra hands.

It was backbreaking work bending down all day for two weeks picking tatties, but Dorothy and I persevered for the sake of that precious manure. The farmer still felt he was paying us too little, but his embarrassment turned to dismay as, over the next few months, he watched the entire pile of manure carted away in tin tubs, rubbish bins and buckets. This four-year-old dung was ideal for the garden and I lost no time applying it liberally.

* * *

Despite the growing importance my work in the garden seemed to be assuming, I could not shake off the certainty that it would not be long before we returned to our 'rightful' place, Cluny Hill Hotel, although this made no sense given Mrs Bruce's implacable opposition even to giving me a reference. In order to be eligible for Social Security benefits, I was obliged by law, however, not to refuse any 'reasonable' offer of employment in the meantime and my obvious qualifications were in the hotel management and catering fields.

During our first summer at Findhorn, the Ministry of Labour asked me to go to Glasgow for an interview for the post of manager in either of two large hotels in the resort of Strathpeffer in the northern Highlands. Before I left, Eileen received:

> *It is not right for Peter to have a job yet. He must be willing to go for an interview. You need not give it any force, and it will not come about. By his thoughts he can bring about or reject a job. If he has to go for the interview, he will have to take one step at a time, and let Me guide him in action. Always, you are to affirm that you are going back to Cluny Hill Hotel and bring that about. Never waste time wondering how this can be brought about and sweep all negative thoughts aside. See My hand in all that is happening. Nothing is by chance.*

At the interview the next day I kept Cluny Hill firmly in my mind but I did not see how I was going to get out of accepting either of these jobs, as the Managing Director of the company wanted me to start right away. While I was in his office, however, there was a telephone message to call at the Ministry of Labour Hotel Section in Glasgow. When I went there, I discovered that another company with first-class hotels in Scotland wanted a manager; the General Manager was coming that afternoon from Edinburgh to interview me. I went to meet him. He immediately offered me one of the best hotel jobs in Scotland, at North Berwick near the English border, with a very good salary; he proposed to take me there immediately. That got me out of the jobs at Strathpeffer, but how I was to get out of this one? I was not left long in doubt. While we stopped over in Edinburgh en route, the General Manager phoned Mrs Bruce in Aberdeen and she brought up all the publicity about 'the Nameless Ones'; she said that she'd come to Edinburgh straight away (a four-hour journey each way) to discuss it with him. We waited for her to come, but by the afternoon of the next day I suggested I return to Findhorn and that he could get in touch with me. Mrs Bruce must have put him off, because I never heard from him again.

I returned to Findhorn, where Eileen had received:

> *Be not distressed at all about what is happening at Peter's end; as he follows out My guidance step by step, only good can come out of it. He can only take one step at a time, and that is the way My Plan will open up. Realize that My hand is in all that is happening at this time, and there is a pattern running through it. You cannot see it just now,*

because you are too close to it, but you will see it. Whatever Peter feels strongly about, go with it. He will know what the next plan of action is, and give him full support, whatever it may be. Watch My Plan open up as surely as does a flower in the warm sunshine.

The day after I returned, we heard a rumour that Cluny Hill was doing very badly and that they had had a disastrous season; James MacLeod, the gardener, confirmed to us that it was half empty. Again Eileen received:

You are all to know that you are to return to Cluny Hill, your rightful place. How or when or under whom, remains to be brought about. Many times I have told you that Peter is guardian of Cluny Hill. A guardian can go away from a place, but he must eventually return, and this is what will be brought about. Leave it all in My hands and relax.

In Glasgow I had agreed to go to Strathpeffer where the two large hotels were, to see them for myself and to meet the Chairman of the company again. Eileen received, *Go to Strathpeffer tomorrow, all of you, make it a family outing, take a picnic with you, see all there is to see. Tell Peter to be noncommittal, just to await developments.* We went, but I could not imagine myself working there — nothing felt right about it. The Chairman and the General Manager showed all of us around and we had a discussion afterwards, but they fully realized that our hearts were at Cluny Hill and that we would return there at the first opportunity. In any case, the Chairman had not heard from Mrs Bruce, to whom he had written about me. The offer of a job was withdrawn.

I later heard from Naomi that her sources were most anxious that I did not, in my usual dynamic way, mess things up by going out and getting a job when my energy was required elsewhere. It was not my personal choice to refrain from really pushing to get a job, nor was it easy for me: there is nothing I like better than being in the centre of activity and organizing things. It appeared that Mrs Bruce's part in God's Plan was to prevent me from getting a job so that I could concentrate on the work in the Findhorn garden and — although we did not know it at the time — the development of a community.

Over twenty-five years later, I happened to be in Edinburgh on my way to Findhorn and decided to go and see Mrs Bruce. Having first phoned to make sure she was there (and replacing the receiver as soon as she answered), I took a taxi to her flat and heard a voice say, 'Come in, the door's open.' I thought this strange and went on in; as we met I asked if she remembered me. 'Of course, I remember you, Mr. Caddy, do come in,' she said, and offered me a cup of tea. She told me she'd been expecting her son and that was why the door was open.

Several of her friends were gathered in the dining room, so I followed her into the kitchen to talk as she made the tea. 'Mrs Bruce,' I began, 'I've long wanted to tell you that without you and the part that you played, the community at Findhorn would never have been created.' She was astonished and said, 'Oh? Tell me more.' I replied, 'Well, by not providing me with a reference you effectively prevented me from getting a job. I was upset with you at the time, but if you hadn't taken this action I would have been given work and the community could not have been founded.'

She smiled sweetly and said, 'Well, we all have to follow our guidance, don't we?' It was my turn to be astonished. I left soon after to catch my train, having parted on the best of terms with her.

* * *

On 8 September 1963 we had a visit from Sheena. Dorothy was typing on the patio and I was painting inside the caravan; I came out for a moment and saw a woman walking along the path towards us. I did not at first recognize her. She was leaden, drawn and drably dressed. It was Sheena, but not the Sheena we had known — only the shadow of her former self, come like a grey ghost from the past to see how we were getting on. It was an awkward and strained reunion. She asked both Eileen and Dorothy to go into meditation and find out what God had to say about her unexpected reappearance.

The message Eileen recorded was blunt and to the point:

> *The past is past and finished...Sheena has no part in your lives...She does not fit into the plan I have for each of you. She knows this, but refuses to accept it, like a drowning man who clutches at any straw. That is why she has come today.*

Dorothy's guidance, though gentler, was equally clear:

> *You only feel immense gratitude for all that Sheena has been instrumental in doing for you — and I alone know the*

> *extent of that — and you want her, and I want her through you, to know that. That is an ever present truth.*
>
> *Your various forces, the various persons, came together for a purpose and that purpose was only partially fulfilled. The original perfection of it is impossible now, and your ways are plotted apart. Whatever works for Me comes together on My levels. Leave it at that.*

After this was read to her Sheena got up and left, angrily denying that she was 'clutching at any straw'. It was illuminating for us to see what we had been told before: that the part of Sheena — the high, fine, sensitive spirit — that had once taken each of us to personal heavens and hells, had now been withdrawn, leaving only an empty shell. Dorothy's guidance after this latest bristling parting of the ways sums up, I think, what we were all feeling:

> *You have often wondered how Sheena, being what she was, could be what she is, and now you understand more. The force has been withdrawn, the sensitivity dulled, even the memory shattered...The heart has returned to Me, and understands. Remember Sheena as she was, part of My heart, and let your gratitude go towards Us.*

I was saddened — without Sheena's training and her bringing us each to God, we would certainly have not been entering a new world at that stage — but I could only agree with Dorothy that we owed her great gratitude. Some years later she died of a cerebral haemorrhage in Edinburgh.

* * *

At such a northern latitude the nights grow very long as winter approaches; there is less time for outer work and more for taking stock. Here we were, still at Findhorn. I was still without a job. I had created a garden, but to what end beyond our need to feed ourselves? We had established a working relationship with the devas, but they were solely concerned with the plants under their particular jurisdiction and offered little or no glimpses of the larger picture. Regardless of our financial situation, we were fit, we were healthy and we were happy: but what were we doing there?

One morning the answer came to me: *we were pioneering something new*. We had been stripped of everything except our faith. We neither regretted the past nor feared the future. We were finding God in an apparently God-forsaken caravan park and creating, with what little means we had, a demonstration of the fact that with God all things are possible.

That evening Eileen received in guidance: *Tell Peter that what illuminated him this morning was indeed so...What is now happening is something new, and this is the way the world is to be re-created.* This was later amplified with an explanation of my role in the garden:

> *Peter is the one who is creating it, and who is being inspired all the time... inspiration comes and he sees a picture of what should be put in such and such a place. He can bring about that vision. If it means buying fruit trees, trees are to be bought. The vision he has of the garden is to be perfected. He will find that he will only get a little bit of it at a time. Therefore, he will not be able to plan the whole of it at once, but bit by bit it will be revealed to him...*

In fact once I woke up in the middle of the night with the very clear realization that just as at Cluny Hill Hotel I had planned every different kind of garden, so here at Findhorn every kind of fruit, vegetable, salad and herb that could be grown in that part of the world should be represented.

It seemed clear, then, that we were to continue exactly where we were. The guidance that Eileen was given in December 1963, clarified this:

> *I want you to look upon this place as a permanent home and know that all effort that is put into it will bear an abundance of fruit, not only material fruit but spiritual fruit as well. Remember, this is a vast work. Peter will need the help and cooperation of each one of you to bring it about on all levels. It is only when you seek that you find. Therefore, never sit back and expect anything to fall into your lap.*

When Christmas approached we wondered if the children would feel a sense of deprivation, as we had little money to spare. But they enjoyed this Christmas more than they had ever done before. Various people were prompted to give us just what we needed, and all the children's presents seemed perfect and brought them much joy. We invited Lena Lamont and her family to join us for dinner, but then the expected bird did not arrive and we found we did not have enough food; at the last moment, Eileen's brother sent us a lovely turkey. We were eleven sitting down to Christmas dinner —

Dorothy, Eileen and I, our three boys, Lena and her three children, and Miss Harrold (the old lady in the village with whom Naomi had stayed) — and the smoothness of the team effort was our first real experience of the advantages of living as a group.

My only disappointment was that Naomi was not there to join us. For some months we had been trying to persuade her to leave the States and join us at Findhorn, where as we had found the year before, her physical presence could contribute to the inner work as well as complete the 'four-square foundation' required before building could commence[1] (although we had no idea of *what* it was we were building — we were simply following inner direction, step by step). I also planned to edit the vast amount of material Naomi had received from various sources and prepare a book for publication[2]. In September 1963 I had even obtained a caravan for her but she continued to dither over the decision to come, worrying about having insufficient funds, and eventually we had to let the caravan go.

---

1 Naomi herself had received that it takes three people to anchor the spiritual energies in a Centre of Light — representing the aspects of Light, Love and Wisdom — and four to begin building

2 For various reasons this never happened; some of Naomi's recordings were finally published in 1981 in *A World Within a World / X-7 Reporting* (Neville Spearman, Jersey), telepathic transmissions received from a group of prisoners of conscience down a salt mine in Siberia — now published by Findhorn Press, March 1996

Chapter 19

Manifestation

As we become conscious of the wisdom in the world within, we mentally take possession of this wisdom and, by taking mental possession, we come into actual possession of the power and wisdom necessary to bring into manifestation the essentials necessary for our most complete and harmonious development

BY THE SUMMER OF 1964, our second year at Findhorn, we were growing about 70 per cent of all our food. The garden continued to be created according to my spontaneous intuition; Eileen sometimes asked me what my next step in the garden was, but I would inevitably reply that I had no idea — only when I put the spade in the ground did I know. At this time, for example, I had a lot of small lettuce seedlings which I planted everywhere — in the bottom of the celery trench, in mounds, between other plants — so that eventually there were hundreds of them. I didn't stop to think how we were going to eat all those lettuces! Well, due to early cold weather that year, the local lettuces grown in greenhouses had all been used and the ones grown out in the open were not yet ready. We were the only suppliers of lettuces in the whole area and I was able to sell them to local shops; the money from their sale was used to purchase more plants and fruit trees. I had not planned this venture but had followed my intuition.

We found that the garden was sometimes damaged by a strong southerly wind and we didn't have the money to buy cotoneaster plants to make a hedge. Each plant cost ninepence, so I grew surplus cabbages along where the cotoneasters were to be planted and sold them for ninepence each; this just covered the cost of the hedge. We called it our 'cabbage hedge' and it was a protective wall on the southern side of the garden, 100 feet long. There was a row of wallflowers in front, another row of spring cabbages on the inside, followed by a 6-foot-high wire fence, and within that, a row of raspberries.

There was difficulty in finding room for all the various species I wanted to plant, and whose devas confirmed their eagerness to join the experiment. As it was, I planned a fruit garden of apples, pears, plums, greengages, cherries, blackcurrants, red currants, gooseberries, raspberries, strawberries, peaches, apricots, boysenberries, and loganberries. Working in the garden from just after eight every morning to ten o'clock at night, I was so close to it that I did not realize how extraordinarily strong and vigorous the plants had become. It was not until one Sunday afternoon when we visited Cawdor Castle nearby, whose gardens had been established and carefully tended by professionals for several hundred years, that it dawned on me how potent were the results of our cooperation with the devas.[1] Our vegetables were much larger and in better condition than those at Cawdor, and we could only marvel.

Dorothy had meanwhile taken a job as secretary to a man in Forres who was planning to develop the fish products of the area for sale in the UK and abroad. Since Charles, our ex-head chef, was an expert at smoking salmon, he was brought in to experiment in the processing; once that was perfected, I was to join the team as sales manager. Charles had often come to stay with us after we settled in the caravan park — usually to sober up and settle down between various jobs and rackets — and he and Christopher would share a tent. He helped me in the garden during these visits. Sometimes he would come back at night raging from a fight he'd started with one of the locals to protect my name; there was still gossip going around that I had been sacked because I had robbed the till at Cluny Hill Hotel, and Charles — who had often tried, without success, to involve me in one of his rackets there — knew more than anyone how absurd such rumours were. (Another story had it that we were Mormons and that I had five wives!)

One weekend, however, against his employer's wishes, Charles went home to the west coast; he got very depressed and decided to commit suicide. He threw himself off the end of a pier and — much to his annoyance — he was rescued. The result was that he got the sack, and that was the end of the fish project; but as I had had a prospective job with this venture, it kept the Labour Exchange quiet for nearly a year.

---

[1] For more information about the devas, see *To Hear the Angels Sing* (Dorothy Maclean, Lindisfarne Press), and *The Findhorn Garden* and *The Golden Web* (see bibliography)

By the end of the summer of 1964 I wanted to extend the garden. When I asked the owner of the caravan park if I could add another 15 feet, he said that as far as he was concerned I could extend it right up to another caravan 200–300 feet away. I set to work. The almost constant, year-round winds at Findhorn were the chief obstacle to creating a garden, and I realized that the early vegetables in particular needed protection; to provide this, I estimated that I'd need about thirty-six cold frames made of glass or polythene (preferably the latter, since it was lighter). For the back and sides, I scrounged railway sleepers from various sources, and then a few days later happened to be looking for something in a junkyard when I came across a pile of polythene frames — and there were exactly thirty-six, which I bought for the ridiculously low price of two shillings and sixpence each. Once these were in place I prepared the soil inside the frames so they would be ready to protect next season's early crop against wind and frost.

Another use for the cold frames was for growing mushrooms, a favourite plant of mine that we did not have in the garden. To make a suitable growing medium, we collected fresh manure by following the horses around a neighbouring field with buckets and spades! The experience showed us that the devas had a sense of humour: in retelling the story, I cannot improve on my original account in *The Findhorn Garden:*

> *Attempting to do everything perfectly, we got fresh horse manure and prepared it by laboriously turning it several times, read books and followed the instructions with utmost accuracy. We even bought a thermometer to take the temperature of the horse manure — a high extravagance in those days. Dorothy contacted the Mushroom Deva who said that we would see 'astonishing results'. In passing, Dorothy mentioned that this deva had felt sort of round and as if it had a sense of humour.*
>
> *We did everything for those mushrooms, carefully putting some in the garage and some under frames. All the while the Mushroom Deva was reminding us:* Growth depends on many factors which we cannot foretell, and therefore we — any of us — always grow where possible. *More care went into looking after those mushrooms than anything else we had ever grown. After all, we were expecting astonishing results. After weeks and weeks of this, our mushroom beds produced two tiny offspring. But all over the garden where that four-year-old horse manure had been spread was a magnificent crop of mushrooms!*

In the caravan next door lived an antagonistic man who had a large, delightful but unruly Dalmatian puppy. One day this puppy climbed over the new cold frames and broke all of them. At first I was very upset about this — I felt some dark force was trying to prevent our growing food, which was vital to us — and I spent the next three months constructing a strong wire-netting fence around the whole of the area that I intended to cultivate, to keep both Dalmatians and dark forces at bay. As soon as it was finished, the site owner happened to sell the caravan park; when the new owner asked him how much I was paying for all the land that I was using, he said that we should be getting paid for improving the land! Thus was the garden extended on land that we neither owned nor had to pay for, thanks to the puppy's destruction.

* * *

Once again, in 1964 Naomi received inner direction that she was to come from the States and join us, but her lack of faith prevented her doing so. She wrote and said that she never believed that God required all of our time dedicated to service. I replied that He does require just that, and the only kind of service that matters is whole-hearted dedication to Him. He wants all of us and not just part of us. When we give our all, all is given back to us and more, and God sees that all our life is balanced between the inner and outer activities. I reminded her that at Findhorn we had such a balance.

Eileen had guidance that she was now to learn the 'laws of manifestation', and that she was to 'manifest' the money to buy a caravan for Naomi, who was dependent upon an old-age pension. These so-called laws were based on my Rosicrucian teachings and were put into practice right from the beginning of our time at Findhorn; they were to become a cornerstone of our work. David Spangler has given the most elegant and concise description of these laws of manifestation:

> *Give up all of the little self so that one can have a clear vision of the will of God and of what constitutes a true need and not simply a personality desire. Look to God and God alone to meet that need. Have a precise vision or idea of what it is to be manifested, if necessary sharing that vision so that all involved in the process have the same idea and are united in their thought and imagination. Ask once, knowing in faith that the need is being perfectly met. Give thanks that this is so and release it. If action is required, go ahead*

in faith, keeping in mind the positive thought and image of the need being met. When the manifestation occurs, gives thanks again. Realize that what you have manifested is not your possession but is part of God placed under your care and trust. Treat all you have as if you were their custodian, willing to release them when their work is done. Care for all you have with love and skill, recognizing them as gifts from God.

As a 'warm-up' exercise in applying these principles, Eileen was first to manifest £72 for a garage bill for repairs we'd had done before we'd left the Trossachs. That seemed a lot of money in our present circumstances. In meditation she was told to write to a trustee of her marriage settlement to see if it would be possible to use some of its capital; the answer came back that it could not be touched, but the solicitor asked if she'd tried to get a repayment of the income tax paid on past dividends. We hadn't thought of that, so we went to see a solicitor in Forres and filled out the necessary forms. In due course we received a cheque from Inland Revenue for £72, the exact amount of money to pay the garage (which was our only outstanding bill at the time).

Eileen was overjoyed with this and it strengthened her faith regarding the laws of manifestation — but we still hadn't the money for the caravan for Naomi. In the meantime, I proceeded in faith that the money would be there. I felt that the ideal caravan for Naomi would be one like ours and Lena's, a Rollalong, the best commercial caravan available — it would also be warm and comfortable. (I had not forgotten, from her last visit, Naomi's love of her creature comforts.) Lena had rented her Rollalong from a Mr Cameron, who owned a number of them, and one day he told her that he had a larger one for her and the three children. I then realized that her present caravan would be perfect for Naomi. I asked Mr Cameron how much he wanted for it, and he replied £750. I said that that was far too much and whittled the price down to £650; finally I offered him £325, and we compromised on £350. To make sure this was a fair price, we asked a local caravan dealer to come in and value it, which he did — at £275!

Eileen was then told, in meditation, to write to my father and ask him for a loan of £275. Father was very much against what we were doing at Findhorn. He had been proud of my career in the Royal Air Force, and also when I was manager of a four-star hotel; but now he was bitterly disappointed, not so much that his son was on the dole but that I should regard my position with such 'apparent complacency', as he wrote in answer to Eileen's letter. He later wrote to me,

> *I've spent the days since your letter arrived resisting the temptation to tell you exactly what I thought of the contents. But writing you my first letter caused me quite enough worry and distress. And no good purpose would, I'm afraid, be served by another attempt on my part to wean you away from your delusions... I had hoped to find some justification for helping you in regard to a second caravan, but it would not be in your own best interests and, in any case, such an action would be misinterpreted. The rebate of income tax received by Eileen was granted as a result of Inland Revenue routine and was hardly the result of divine intervention.*

The letter revealed the deep hurt and sadness in my father; he knew that whatever he said or did, he would never be able to change my way of thinking or living, of which he did not approve. The letter made it quite clear that Father had no intention of loaning us the money and that I ought to get a job[4]. Eileen was devastated by this letter and wept, but her guidance told her

> *Don't worry about the money for the caravan. I will open another door for you. Never give up. Know that I want you to have that caravan sooner or later... have patience, persistence and perseverance and all will be well.*

She was then advised to write to her sister and ask her for a loan of the money. Her sister and husband were both school teachers; they were quite well off — every year they had holidays on the continent and bought a new car — but in spite of their material comforts I found them to be rather miserable. They too disapproved of the way we were living. The letter that came back released a lot of fury: how dare we ask for a loan of £350, when I wasn't even working and was quite capable of working? It was just as though a boil had been lanced and a lot of poison released (so much so that we were able to visit them a few weeks later); but we still didn't have the money for this caravan. Patience, persistence and perseverance.

Dorothy's brother Don was coming over to Scotland on his way from Canada to Russia for a holiday. He was coming for one night, and Eileen had

[4] What he *did* do was to make an arrangement by which our three boys would receive £10 on their birthdays for the next seven years, and with income tax relief that came to just about £350.

guidance that she was to ask *him* for a loan of £200. That was a bit hard; she had never met this fellow before, and Dorothy had said that he was very close with money. Somehow Eileen managed to pluck up the courage to ask Don for the loan; he hummed and hawed and said he would have to think about it. He left the next morning. We had done all we were asked to do and left the matter in God's hands.

About two weeks later Don sent us a cheque for £200. We were filled with joy — our needs were indeed being met — and I asked Eileen to get guidance on the next step. We were told that I was to offer Mr Cameron £200 because this was all the caravan was worth, and that he knew it. I went down with Dorothy and offered him the £200. He looked surprised and asked, was it part payment? I said: 'Oh, no, it's full payment.' He said that this was unacceptable: he had already been offered £350 for it by another person. His wife was there, however, and as she had a soft spot for Dorothy she whispered afterwards 'You leave it to me, I'll work on him.'

The next day I went down to see him again and said, 'Well what about it, Mr Cameron?' At the time, he also owned a big old gypsy caravan next door to us, used for storage, and its paint was peeling off; I knew that Dorothy, who loved painting, had been itching to take a brush to it. Imagine my surprise when Mr Cameron said, 'I'll tell you what I'll do. I will let you have the Rollalong for £200 if Miss Maclean would agree to paint that old gypsy caravan.' And so it was joyfully agreed. Within a week, though, Mr Cameron had had a row with the owner of the caravan park and had taken all his caravans off site, including the gypsy one — so Dorothy didn't have to paint it after all. The Rollalong caravan needed a new carpet and new curtains which came to £50, and just at that time Dorothy was left £50, so the remaining money to complete the manifestation was there. Even the caravan park owner waived the rent on its land until Naomi arrived, in exchange for my help in preparing two other sites.

* * *

One day our family doctor, Dr Spence, came to see me but I was out. He asked Eileen if I was all right. She said that I was fine, but he asked if she was quite sure. Bemused, Eileen replied that I was very well indeed, and why was he enquiring? To begin with he was very reluctant to tell her, but then the truth came out. Apparently my sister Joan, who was working for a psychiatrist in New Zealand, had written to ask Dr Spence to visit me to see if I needed psychiatric treatment! After reading my parents' letters to her, she must have felt that I was out of my mind to be living with a family in a caravan, with little money and no apparent prospects. I wrote to Joan to reassure her that I had never been happier or more content in my life:

> *There is one further point, one which I think upsets Mother and Father, and that is if I had my life to live over again, I would not have it changed in any way, and I have no regrets whatsoever. I have been through many deep experiences and have led a very full life, and the experiences I have been through have taught me many lessons. One of the most important is that an individual soul must be left to lead his own life without being influenced by other people's ideas and desires.*

Even though my father disapproved of what we were doing, we were told to keep the contact with my parents. In the late summer of 1963 we drove south to enjoy a lovely holiday with them in their Devonshire home, and it healed many of the earlier misunderstandings. There was a second, equally important reason for the visit; as Eileen was told in meditation,

> *Very often when you are in the process of learning lessons, you cannot see the wood for the trees. It is later, when you can stand back and view it from a different angle, that you realize exactly what the lessons were that you were learning. You will find that you will be able to look back at this time, and see what amazing lessons you have been learning.*

After our return to Findhorn I could see clearly how true this was, and the thread that had been running through our holiday. One after another, our experiences there enabled us to see just how far we'd moved into a new way of living, and that the gap between the old and the new was increasing all the time. If one watches a rosebud, one cannot see it opening into a perfect rose; there appears to be no movement at all, but if one goes away and looks a day later, one can see a change. We were able to do the same, by staying for a time in the outside world.

The first thing that struck us forcibly was the completely materialistic approach to life so many people take. Eileen's relatives and my parents could not understand or accept the way we were living. To them it seemed madness, for they measured success by material possessions and money in the bank. We realized just how strong our faith in God was, as we knew that He would provide for us perfectly. Having once placed our whole life in God's hands, there was no need to worry about the future. Having passed on the responsibility to God, we knew that we would never be let down. At Findhorn we were living in the moment with little regard for the past or future — God can only be found in the moment — and in this way were leading a much richer life. It would have been pointless to explain our approach, open as it was to misinterpretation.

We were also shaken by the noise and frantic bustle of the world, and it was a shock to find that even people who were on holiday were still in a rush. Most people seemed to have homes that were too big for them and cluttered up with useless things that had to be cleaned and looked after but served them in no real way. In our caravan we had the bare essentials: only those things that we needed to survive and make ourselves comfortable.

When we returned to Findhorn, we realized that we had a window on the world through television, but even that didn't convey just how bad the general atmosphere in the world was.[5] We had no desire to dwell on that, however, striving instead to keep our thoughts and conversation positive. At the birth of a baby, it is wiser for the mother to focus on the beauty and perfection of the child who is being born, rather than on the pain and suffering involved. In the birth of a new age, it is important to concentrate on the positive and so help to create and build it, rather than get caught up in the destruction of the old.

After our journey we had no desire to leave Findhorn. Our lives were complete, with more than enough to do. I felt very much like Noah, building an ark under God's detailed instruction, even though Noah was miles from water and the people around him thought him utterly mad. He himself must have wondered from time to time, but he kept on building and ignored the criticisms and jeers of those around him.

Our aim in all we did at this time was perfection, as only the best was good enough for God's work. We focussed on sparkling, radiant cleanliness in our environment. We were attuned to God, letting His Will be heard and acting upon it; we had a simple diet that built clean, strong bodies worthy to be temples of the spirit. We were working in a form of conscious cooperation with the nature kingdom. Our service was to God, with love flowing through our work and play, making life, as best we could, a joyous, harmonious experience, whether working in the garden, cleaning a caravan, having a picnic or going for a swim in the sea. We were *doing something*.

5 The US began its entanglement in Vietnam at that time, for example

Chapter 20

Foundation Stones

All growth is from within:
this is evident in all nature

AS THE GARDEN flourished, more and more casual visitors would drop by to have a look around: it was a startling oasis to come across in an otherwise barren caravan park. One day in August 1964 a man brought a friend of his to see the garden, but as they could only stay briefly the friend returned with his wife and children the next day. They spent a long time looking around and asking detailed questions. At the end of their visit the man told me that he was a professional nurseryman, and how impressed he was with the amount of food we were growing, the planning and organization of the garden, and most of all the quality of the produce. He felt that it should be on television and that a book should be written about it. (Later, the man who had introduced us told me that his friend could not get over his experience of the garden and had talked about it for hours.)

I longed to tell the nurseryman the real secret of the garden, namely the cooperation with the devas and God's guidance, but prudence dictated that I put the amazing results down to hard work and compost. In this connection, Eileen received in meditation:

> *This garden is My garden. You are fully aware of this, you see My hand at work everywhere you look. Always remember, you are in this world but not of it. On no account are you to talk to those who would never understand the way this garden has been created by the constant help of the devas, by My constant guidance. You know how it has been done but it is never to be talked about except to those you know will understand.*
>
> *Tell Peter this is not the time to have the garden televised. I will make it quite clear when it is to receive publicity. On no*

> *account is it to have it now. You have only started, wonder upon wonder will emerge from this place, and at the right time it will be brought to the public eye; timing is so very important. Something done at the wrong time can cause an unnecessary set-back, and we do not want that at this time when everything is working out so perfectly. Yes, Peter can always say it is the compost which has really helped the garden and soil.*

That same autumn I asked the County Horticultural Adviser, a Mr Berridge, if he would come and take a sample of the soil to analyze it. When he arrived he said that he knew this soil already, and it needed an ounce of sulphate of potash per square yard. I said that I didn't believe in artificial fertilizers and used wood ash instead, but he replied that it was no substitute. After an hours' discussion he had nearly convinced me; but when he returned with the results of the analysis, he had found that the soil was balanced and completely adequate. He couldn't believe it. To me, however, it proved the devas had kept their promise that they could create all the trace elements that the soil would need.

Mr Berridge was so impressed that he suggested that I take part in a radio programme with a professional gardener who was also a broadcaster; Berridge would be in the chair asking questions. The proposed date for this was some months away, and I agreed.

I was encouraged by Berridge's enthusiasm. The horticultural advisor had seen for himself the huge cabbages, weighing as much as 42 pounds, and the great vitality of all the vegetables in the garden. I had planted cabbages in between the gooseberry bushes, but one was actually a broccoli plant which grew almost into a bush — it provided us with broccoli for three months. When it was finished, it was almost too heavy to carry so I dragged it along the ground to the compost heap.

Our second season in the garden was even more successful than our first. As it drew to a close I turned my attention to preparing for Naomi to join us. I prepared the site for her caravan and, when the caravan was in place, established a lawn in front of it with a rose garden and protective fence to surround it. (We had been told that red roses were the only flowers we should grow at that time.) As the soil was almost non-existent in that part of the garden — just poor grass on sand — we had to build it up from old turfs and compost; every square inch of soil was handled several times. Eileen had a busy time making up curtains and chair covers, while Dorothy scraped down and revarnished some of the wood surfaces and re-enamelled the bath. Each of us had something to contribute and I saw it as a good example of our working as a group[1] to create the right atmosphere for Naomi's spiritual work.

I wanted everything to be perfect for Naomi. She was an old lady in her seventies and was accustomed to a high standard of living, enjoying certain foods, fine coffee, and cocktails in the evening that we would not be able to provide; she also enjoyed the flattery of being placed on a pedestal by the group around her in America. In addition to the anthracite fire in her caravan, I installed an electric thermostatic space heater and paraffin stove to ensure her warmth. I placed my last two possessions from the past — a beautiful blue tea set from Hong Kong and a delicate Kashmiri lacquer bowl with matching finger bowls — at her disposal. The compost heaps in the garden were screened off so that she would not see them, and I spent several days fitting new linoleum in her kitchen.

The reason for all this was that Naomi and I were to spend the winter going through the thousands of pages of inner messages she had received throughout her life, with me sorting them into order so that a series of books could be published. Intuitively I knew that after this winter we would never have the time again to do this, so as Naomi kept postponing her departure from the States I grew increasingly frustrated. Christmas came but Naomi didn't. I passed the time reading gardening books, watching television and working in the garden when the ground wasn't frozen.

Eileen had a vision of Naomi flying across the Atlantic to join us, but when Naomi finally confirmed that she was coming, it was by a ship due to arrive in Southampton (in the south of England) on 21 January 1965. I left a week early to travel down and collect her, stopping en route to visit several old friends and acquaintances. Among these were Lady Mayo (the 'Lady in Lilac' we had met at Cluny Hill Hotel), with whom I stayed a night in Edinburgh, and Grace Cooke's son-in-law, who supervised the publication of her messages from White Eagle; he gave me some very valuable advice about preparing material for publication. When I arrived at Southampton, however, there was no ship and no Naomi. Hers was the only passenger vessel to have been cancelled as the result of a dockers' strike in New York, two hours before it was due to leave, and Naomi had gone home in a state of shock.

[1] Although she and her boys still lived beside us, Lena was not at that time considered part of our group. She was struggling to write an interpretation of the book of Revelation in the New Testament and largely kept to herself; we were told in meditation to leave her alone

I was fazed too, and wondered what opposing forces were preventing Naomi's joining us, but by the time I returned to Findhorn there was a letter awaiting me with news that she would fly after all. She arrived at Glasgow's airport nearly three weeks later.

I picked Naomi up after recording the radio programme that Mr Berridge had arranged between a professional gardener and me. Berridge introduced me by speaking in glowing terms of our garden at Findhorn, and wondered aloud about the secret of its success. Mindful of Eileen's guidance I felt it unwise to talk about what would sound like fairies at the bottom of the garden; instead I attributed the phenomenal growth to the use of compost. I did manage, however, to make the point that man and nature seemed to me to be seriously out of balance and that artificial fertilizers only made the matter worse, devitalizing the food that we ate. This was a red rag to a bull as far as the professional was concerned: we spent fifteen minutes debating the virtues of compost versus fertilizers.

The programme was broadcast a week later and served many purposes. Those spiritually-minded people we had met at Cluny Hill Hotel might now know what we were doing and where to find us, if they wanted to. All the local newspapers featured the broadcast and in some eyes we became 'respectable' again — the number of local visitors increased. Lady Mayo sent us a cherry tree to join the small orchard I had planted. Above all, I received a payment of 12 guineas[2] for my services, a princely sum in those days! I declared it to the National Assistance Board, however, so lost most of it.

* * *

Before proceeding with the narrative, it may be useful to explain some of the terminology used in this and subsequent chapters. In some esoteric cosmologies, including those I studied in my early spiritual training, the universe is seen as emanating from a single source or Godhead. This emanation expresses itself in three distinct qualities: Will; Love/Wisdom; and Intelligence. Sometimes they are referred to as creativity, life, and mind, and they are also analogous to the Trinity in the Christian tradition of Father, Son, and Holy Spirit. If one accepts that God is Love, then these three are really the Will (or Power) of Love, the Wisdom of Love and the Intelligence of Love.

---

[2] In the pre-decimal currency of the time, a guinea was worth one pound and one shilling: so 12 guineas was over half as much again as our weekly benefit payment.

These three qualities interact and blend with each other in seven ways altogether, sometimes called 'the Seven Rays'. One or more of the three qualities is predominant in each Ray, just as the three primary colours of red, yellow and blue in different combinations make up the seven colours of the rainbow. Hence it is generally held that the First Ray is Will; the Second, Love-Wisdom; the Third, Active Intelligence; the Fourth, Harmony-Beauty; the Fifth, Objective Knowledge or Science; the Sixth, Devotion; and the Seventh Ray is Ordered Activity, Patterning or Synthesis.

The qualities of Will, Love, Intelligence, Harmony, Knowledge, Devotion, and Synthesis are thus the seven emanations from Godhead that form the basic archetypal threads which weave together to form the tapestry of creation.

In certain esoteric and occult traditions each particular Ray is channelled by and personified as a 'Master' who takes his or her place in a Hierarchy of great beings, dedicated in service to the unfoldment of the Divine Plan. The Master of the Seventh Ray, for example, is variously known in the Western mystery tradition as St Germain, Prince Rakoczi, the Lord of Civilization, or (a favourite title, lest all this be taken too seriously) the Master of Mirth. It is not important (in fact, it can be foolish) to get caught up in the glamour of the terminology; the words and symbols date from a time when to speak openly of such matters was to invite ridicule, persecution and sometimes even death.

As one age gives way to another, however, what was previously hidden is gradually being revealed, and to speak of Masters and Rays is no more of a mystery to many people than when the physicists, in their own esoteric language, speak of quarks, wormholes and superstrings. In neither case should unfamiliarity with the terminologies put people off or ensnare them in flights of fancy — they are simply a form of shorthand to describe otherwise complicated matters, and any good bookshop is likely to have volumes on the subject.

* * *

Naomi did not find life at all easy at Findhorn, particularly on the physical and personality levels. She had been pampered and spoiled by her husband and her group: she was a very sensitive and delicate soul, and needed looking after and protecting. It was Eileen who mostly cared for her. When Naomi expected me to wind her watch every day or cut up her chicken for dinner, as her late husband had done, I refused — I had far more important things to do. Yet she was the best sensitive I had ever come across.

For many years Naomi had worked with the Network of Light around the planet, telepathically broadcasting to and receiving from the various 'Magnetic Centres' to which, we believed, people were being drawn to prepare for the nuclear destruction that so many sources were predicting. If Naomi were given a name to tune in to, she would be in immediate contact with that being, whether a space brother, a prophet of old, a member of the Hierarchy, or a person (living or deceased). It was as though she had a highly developed antenna through which she received an enormous amount of information that was of great help to our spiritual development and understanding, and hence the advancement of our work at Findhorn.

This was a time of much inner practice. We met at 11 am every day, when Eileen, Dorothy and Naomi would share the early morning message each had received in her individual meditation. This was followed by a time of group meditation and the receiving of more messages; it was also a time of linking with many groups, Magnetic Centres and people throughout the world, radiating Light and love and making telepathic contacts. This was repeated at 5 pm, with Naomi and Dorothy concentrating on our extraterrestrial links; there was a final session later in the evening, with more radiating and telepathic work.

Basically we were laying the 'four-square foundation' upon which we could build. We were told that it was as if we were building a temple and a place of refuge, a Centre of Light in the coming darkness. Just as in the original Dark Ages there were isolated places, like Iona and Lindisfarne, whose small spiritual communities kept the light of truth and knowledge burning, so we came to understand that our purpose at Findhorn was to establish a place that demonstrated a God-centred lifestyle and would be prepared, if necessary, to aid the reconstruction of civilization in the event of catastrophe. I never spent time thinking about any of this, however. I was too busy carrying out the instructions that each of us, in our own way, received from the source of divinity within.

For those four foundation stones to fit perfectly, the rough edges had to be smoothed (and occasionally knocked) off. This was not always easy. There were often personality clashes among the four of us. Naomi at least had her own caravan, but Eileen, Dorothy, myself and the three boys were living on top of each other in very cramped conditions.

When there were disagreements between us, we didn't discuss them, other than sharing what they were. We would then have a time of silent attunement to the God within, reaffirming our essential love for one another, and the problem would vanish. Whereas Eileen, Dorothy, Naomi and Lena were all psychically sensitive, and I wasn't, they all lacked faith (to begin with) in what they were receiving. Naomi was often full of fears; Dorothy would find intellectual arguments against a certain course of action; despite years of receiving pages of clear and precise guidance every day, Eileen still had trouble accepting that it came from God. What I lacked in sensitivity I made up in faith and the ability to take instant action on the guidance received.

It was vital that we maintained a balance of Light, Love and Wisdom among the four of us if the foundations were to be solid. I have found that more groups and communities have failed because these qualities were out of balance than for any other reason. When Love opens the doors to all comers without the discrimination of Light, communities fail; when Light is not tempered by Love it can become hard and sometimes ruthless, lacking the latter's attracting and unifying power. Wisdom — sound judgement — negotiates between the two, but if left unchecked it can stifle boldness of action and mire vision in intellectual debate. Thus in our early years at Findhorn we were each tested on our particular qualities and our ability to blend them into a balanced whole.

My faith was tested shortly after Naomi joined us in early 1965. She started getting inner messages that I should go out and lecture on a public platform and 'go into the highways and byways' to gather people in. I knew with an unshakeable conviction that this was not my role, however, and that at that time I had to stay at Findhorn; the people would be drawn to us here. I told Naomi that even if the whole Hierarchy of Masters manifested in front of me and told me to go out and speak in public, I would not do it. This challenge, apparently, was taken up: for the next three months Naomi received message after message from different members of the Hierarchy ordering me to go out and bring people in. This bewildered both of us. I recognized that Naomi's psychic ability was of the highest quality, and her messages had invariably rung true, but I could not accept these present ones and I stood my ground. Then it dawned on me that the whole thing was a test, and that I'd needed to be tested by someone in whom I had such great faith. The messages ceased as soon as I had this realization.

My faith was also tested when I came across a book called *The One,* containing messages supposedly received from the Archangel Michael. As it concerned a group living near us in the north of Scotland, I was excited and read it immediately. I then wrote and told them enthusiastically how we were receiving not only from the prophets and the Archangel Michael, but also from God Himself, and that the whole theme of our work was one of cooperation between like-minded groups. I received a fairly cool and patronizing reply. It said that in view of the possible destruction to come we could move our caravans to their place at Glen Rossal, a place of protection.

I wrote back that we too were protected, that we were being guided step by step and that we had work to do where we were; I also told them about Eileen's seeing an image of the Christ in our midst. They had mentioned in their letter that they recited the Lord's Prayer in Latin at eleven o'clock each night. In order to cooperate and build bridges, I told them I had been to consult Father Ninian at Pluscarden Priory near Elgin, so that we could learn the correct Latin pronunciation of the prayer and recite it ourselves at eleven.

On the same day as I posted that letter, the latest book from the Recorder of The One arrived. I read it at once. It did not bode well: it proclaimed that those who saw visions of the Christ and other such beings were receiving from the 'plane of illusion', and the forces of darkness were deluding them.

Sure enough, we soon had a long letter back from the Recorder of The One accusing us of receiving messages from the devil. It went on to say that we had obviously been guided to Father Ninian so that he could exorcise us, and we had missed the opportunity of asking him to do so! I thought 'fair enough' and returned to Pluscarden with all the correspondence as well as some of Eileen's guidance, which I put to Father Ninian so that he could be the judge.

He believed that the proof of the pudding was in the eating. For the many years we had been at Cluny Hill Hotel we had frequently visited the Priory, and Father Ninian said he'd known by the light in our eyes that we had a source of spiritual power and assistance. He said that the Glen Rossal group's stumbling block seemed to be that we received from God; but people had been receiving from God all through the ages, and there was nothing unusual about that. Father Ninian suggested that if we invited them to meet us and see the fruits of our guidance, then any differences would surely dissolve.

I followed his advice but they refused the invitation. The Recorder of The One maintained, with all her authority, that we were hopelessly trapped on the plane of illusion. We continued to say the paternoster at 11 pm, however, and to send them Love. I secretly suspected that pride and jealousy might be at the heart of the Recorder's censure — that in *her* eyes she was only receiving from the Archangel Michael, while we claimed we were receiving from God Himself.

Part III

The Universe Responds to Action

Chapter 21

Opening Doors Without

*I am power. That power manifests in me,
is directed by my thought to nothing but good*

IN THE SUMMER of 1965, my father wrote to say that the doctor had advised him to move from his large, three-storeyed house with its steeply sloped garden, to a small bungalow — both my parents were getting on in age and found it difficult to cope with their present home. Father offered to pay my expenses if I would come down in August and help them with the moving. This seemed a wonderful opportunity to take Naomi and Dorothy to Glastonbury, where they could stay while I went on to my parents in Devon; it would also enable me to meet various spiritual people in Britain and tell them what we were doing at Findhorn. After months of making inner connections, we were told that the time had come to start making outer contact with like-minded people, and that many would be drawn to Findhorn 'like steel to a magnet'.

I wrote to about twenty people to tell them of my journey south and my desire to link up with them. However, much to my dismay, I had not received a single reply before we set off. This was very puzzling; I felt sure that these contacts were the real reason for the trip. Therefore I arranged to telephone Eileen each evening that we were away, at the public phone box in the caravan park, to find out if there were any late replies.

The three of us set out over the August Bank Holiday weekend, the worst possible time as far as road traffic and accommodation were concerned. But we knew that all would be well. Eileen received,

> *As a group you have no fixed pattern to follow. Therefore let My spirit guide you. Freedom of the spirit — this is what I have given Peter, to take with him as his motto, and so with each of you.*

Our first stop was in Edinburgh to take a basket of compost-grown fruit and vegetables to the Countess of Mayo. She continued to be a legendary worker for the Light, and many years ahead of her time. Lady Mayo had written to say that there was a 'most highly evolved soul' staying with her, whom she hoped I'd be able to meet: her name was Eileen Keck, and she was helping Lady Mayo to organize an international ecumenical conference in Edinburgh. On hearing that we'd not booked accommodation, Lady Mayo invited us to stay the night in an unoccupied flat on the floor above.

Eileen Keck was leaving on the following day to visit a group in St Annes-on-Sea, at Blackpool in Lancashire, so I offered to take her there. The group was the Universal Link, founded by Liebie Pugh and inspired by a series of prophetic messages received from a spiritual being known as the All-Knowing One (sometimes called 'Limitless Love and Truth').

We arrived at St Annes late the next day and took Eileen Keck to visit Liebie Pugh at her home in St George's Square. We intended to leave Eileen there, but at the last moment decided to stay and meet Liebie also. First, however, we had to confront a guardian on the gate: Joan Hartnell-Beavis, Liebie's secretary and treasurer, who lived in the flat next door and was obviously devoted to Liebie. When we arrived she said that Liebie was quite tired and that it was long past her meal time; we could only have an appointment the next day. I replied that we had to go to Glastonbury in the morning and Joanie, as we came to know her, relented. We later discovered that Liebie rarely saw anyone without an appointment, for she was in great demand: people came from all over the world to see her.

Liebie Pugh was a remarkable woman. She had an unusual face, like a Tibetan's, and her features seemed neither male nor female, neither oriental nor occidental, but had elements of all; her skin was slightly yellow with the most wrinkles I have ever seen in a single face. She took my hands, and the first words she said were, 'St. Germain' — she recognized that I had a strong link with the Master of the Seventh Ray. I realized that we were in the presence of somebody who had an extraordinary effect on people — when she took Naomi's hands, for example, Naomi immediately went into a trance!

Although Liebie Pugh had been a member of the Catholic Church for two years and had written several Catholic booklets on religious matters, she had travelled along or knew of most spiritual paths and seemed to me to embody 'Limitless Love and Truth'. She looked only for the best in everybody and everything and drew it forth. With Liebie everything had to be done perfectly, effortlessly and with love. Her ability to see the truth was disconcerting. The name of her group, the Universal Link, was apt: her approach to spirituality was universal, embracing the truths of all religions, and she knew more spiritually inclined groups and individuals than anybody I had met, linking many of them with a regular newsletter.

We left St Annes on the following day, knowing that we would see Liebie and Joanie again. (In fact St Annes was to become a regular staging post on my journeys to and from England.) On the way to my parents I dropped Dorothy and Naomi off at Glastonbury to stay at the Chalice Well Guest House, run by the Chalice Well Trust. This had been founded by Major Wellesley Tudor Pole, known as 'TP', to safeguard the ancient holy well at Glastonbury; we had visited Glastonbury many times before and had frequent inner contact with this centre. Tudor Pole was founder of 'the Silent Minute' during the dark days of the Second World War, a time of praying for peace, as people throughout Britain observed a minute's silence when the BBC broadcast Big Ben striking 9.00 each night.[1]

After five days in Devon helping my parents move into their new home I returned to Glastonbury. We had been told that we could not spend our last night at the guest-house, since the annual meeting of the Companions of Chalice Well was scheduled for the next day and Major Tudor Pole wanted the house to himself for the night before. At the last moment, however, the housekeeper relented, and the three of us spent the whole evening with TP. This was indeed an honour, as he was an extremely busy man who was difficult to see — one normally had to make an appointment far in advance — and we had the opportunity of getting to know him in a relaxed atmosphere.

At dinner TP recounted some marvellous stories. One of them concerned a mysterious meeting on a train journey while he was crossing Europe on his way to an archaeological expedition in Turkey. TP had noticed a man, dressed in a cloak, who had passed his compartment several times and looked at him with piercing eyes. The stranger eventually entered and sat opposite TP and they began a fascinating conversation. TP asked many questions about spiritual matters and received enlightening answers, but the strange thing he noticed was that the man was not moving up and down on his seat

---

1 When the BBC decided to close down the Silent Minute after the war, TP was guided to replace it with the lighting of ever-burning amber lamps in upper rooms. Sir George Trevelyan took up this suggestion and the first lamp was lit in an upper window of Attingham Park, the Shropshire Adult College, in 1964; the idea caught on and the Lamplighter Movement was founded as a result.

with the motion of the train. When TP asked him to join him for dinner in the restaurant car, the stranger replied, 'I don't eat', and by the time TP returned to the compartment he had gone.

In Istanbul, organizing the transfer of his luggage to a local train, TP caught sight of the man in the distance. He hurried after him but by the time he crossed the platform the man had disappeared, and when TP returned to board his train he found that it had already left. Later he learned that the train had crashed and all the passengers had been killed. TP felt that his life had been saved by this mysterious stranger. When I asked him who he thought the stranger was, TP replied without hesitation, 'St Germain'.

After the women had retired I spent some time alone with TP. To my surprise a tremendous energy possessed me. I told him about the warnings we'd been given from higher levels about the disturbances in the world, and of the vital importance of Magnetic Centres like Findhorn and Glastonbury preparing for the thousands of people, particularly the youth, who would be drawn to these centres. I even suggested that the adjoining Tor School for boys, of which he was director, might be used for the purpose of providing dormitory accommodation. I paced back and forth in front of him, emphatically stating that he was the guardian of Glastonbury. Dorothy and Naomi had visited several spiritual groups in the area and found them at loggerheads with each other — what was he, Tudor Pole, doing about it? He was flabbergasted. I don't think anybody had ever talked to him like that. Whatever the source of the energy that inspired me, I was as surprised as he by the content and forcefulness of my words.

Dorothy, Naomi and I hastened back to Edinburgh to catch the last day of Lady Mayo's conference, since we had heard that Dan Fry and his wife, friends of Naomi, had arrived there. (Naomi had cabled an invitation to them in the States on behalf of Lady Mayo, before we had left Scotland.) Dr Daniel Fry was the American space scientist who became famous when he wrote a book titled *The White Sands Incident*, describing the landing of a spacecraft within a few feet of him in New Mexico. According to this account, Dan was asked to enter the craft and was taken on a trip of 3000 miles to New York and back in a few minutes; it was three years before he could bring himself to write about it. Dan now spent his time touring the world and sharing his experiences, to bring home to mankind the existence of life on other planets and the desire of our space brothers to help humankind through a time of crisis.

The Edinburgh Ecumenical and International Convention 1965, to give Lady Mayo's conference its full title, was a curious gathering of church ministers, vegetarians, ufologists and healers brought together to rise above their petty differences and help 'to render null and void Atomic Warfare'. Unfortunately, without a strong and united team behind her, Lady Mayo's forceful personality tended to exacerbate the very divisions and resentments the convention was supposed to solve. We arrived for the closing sessions and found a lot of people feeling hurt, bruised, trampled upon or ignored, with more disunity and disharmony than when they had started. The lesson I took from all this was that success could only come through a united group force, everybody contributing his or her unique gifts and thus balancing each other.

One amusing feature of the convention was that hand clapping after speeches, performances, etc. was forbidden lest it disperse the energy that had been built up. Instead, we were instructed, appreciation was 'to be shown in the Tibetan way by the waving of hands, as one does when spotting a friend on boat or train on arrival'. It is a practice that has spread widely since, often to the bafflement of uninitiated performers.

When we returned to Findhorn, I found that not one of the twenty 'spiritual' people I had written to before our trip had replied — but we had met well over thirty others, including many who were to play a vital role in the days ahead. Dan Fry, his wife and a friend came back to Findhorn with us: they were our first residential visitors and we managed to squeeze them into Naomi's caravan. Eileen received guidance that many more would follow and we would need to provide accommodation for them, but that this and all our other needs would be perfectly met. Just as well, I thought, since the guidance went on to say *the path which Peter is pioneering will be followed by thousands and thousands of souls.*

Shortly after the Frys left we had two more visitors, Eileen Keck and Meg Emerson, who came to us from Glastonbury. They both wanted to visit Iona, as did Naomi and I; we had heard that the St Columba Hotel on the island had recently been bought by a man, John Walters, who planned to make it a stopping place for pilgrims. It seemed important to forge a link with him and offer any help he might need, so I agreed to take these three elderly ladies on the journey, provided they agreed to flow with me as I was guided in the moment: there would be no hanging about over cups of coffee if I had an inner urge to move.

There is something unique in the atmosphere of Iona, a quality that sets it apart as a spiritual oasis, just as geologically it is separated by tens of thousands of years from neighbouring islands of the Inner Hebrides. There is a sparkling clarity to its light, for the sky seems to open directly to heaven; not only does the sun go down in incomparable splendour, but on most days when lowering clouds hang over Mull and the mainland, it miraculously breaks through to bathe Iona in light, seeming even brighter against the sombre unlit hills on the opposite shore. Thousands of people are drawn to this place of pilgrimage each summer. According to Eileen's guidance, however, our trip was to be more than just a pilgrimage:

> *It is a linking up with a very strong Centre of Light. This is a triangle, Glastonbury, Iona, Findhorn. You may not see the significance of this now, but you will do in the days to come. Peter is to be open to every contact, and there will be several very important ones. They will be drawn to him. My blessings are on this journey. Many important events will spring from it.*

Eileen then had a vision of a great Angel of Light, with wings spread out, hovering over the whole of the island, as if guarding and protecting it from the forces of darkness. It reminded her of a mother bird just about to land on its nest, whose eggs were ready to hatch.

I set off with the three ladies and we had a glorious drive to Oban, from where we took the car by ferry to Mull. On Mull we passed through a valley by an empty road that climbed up the forbidding mountains clouded with mist — 'the valley of the shadow of death' that I had first walked almost ten years earlier, when Sheena had sent Douglas and me on our pilgrimage. We left the car at Fionnphort and crossed the narrow windswept Sound of Iona in a tiny boat, to be met by John Walters on the other side. He took us to the St. Columba Hotel in one of the only two cars on the island.

John Walters was a tall man who had been an army officer and then served with the Palestine Police. There he had met a sensitive, John Morris, who later formed a group in Glastonbury. Years later Walters went to see Morris, who received a message indicating that John Walters should go to Iona, which he did, making the acquaintance of a woman there who was also a sensitive. Her guidance suggested that John should buy the St Columba Hotel and have sole control over it — and that it shouldn't be licensed to sell alcohol, because Iona was a place of spiritual power and a license would spoil the special atmosphere of the island.

John had never run a hotel before and, just as we had found at Cluny Hill, he knew that it could only be done with God's help. First of all he had to obtain the hotel. It did come on the market and he was able to raise the money to buy it, but he learned that the hotel had first to be offered to the Duke of Argyll, who as the island's owner had an automatic option to buy any property that came up for sale. On this occasion the Duke wanted to have the hotel to accommodate his guests and applied to obtain a liquor license for it. Pondering the message that he'd been given, John set about petitioning the islanders to oppose the granting of the license, but his solicitors told him that he hadn't much hope of success because most members of the Licensing Court were tenants of the Duke's estate.

The petition was successful, however, and the Duke did not get his license. He invited John Walters to his castle to stay with him and offered John the joint managing directorship of a company to run the hotel. Again John remembered the message, which had said that he was to have sole control, so he turned the offer down. He was later invited back to the castle and this time was offered managership of the hotel, with a large salary, but again he politely refused. Finally the Duke gave in and John bought the hotel outright; he had been running it for six months when we arrived. The story showed me John Walter's calibre and strength of character, which would be needed in the years ahead to keep the light burning brightly on Iona.

During our two days on the island we had several interesting talks with John about Iona and his future role there, which seemed to be that of a guardian and one who could bring unity among the various spiritual groups and factions drawn to the place. Naomi received a lot of inner information for John, including a message that he should control the bulk of the accommodation on the island, which would mean purchasing the only other hotel, the Argyll.

John gave me the names of a few people to meet, including a remarkable healing mystic, Ellen Hilton, and her companion, Miss Bamber, whom we visited in a large white house, Grianon, on the north side of the island. We also went to Traigh Bhan nearby, a house whose powerful sanctuary (meditation room) — to judge by the visitor's book — attracted people from all over the world. Throughout our journey across this tiny island, including visits to the restored abbey and several ancient spiritual sites, I felt a growing sense of the importance of its connection with our work at Findhorn.

My musing on this, as we motored homeward across Mull early the next morning, was interrupted by Meg Emerson asking me the time of the next ferry to Oban in case we missed the one we were aiming for. I replied that it was immaterial — we would be there in perfect timing. Meg disagreed. She had been a school teacher, and in her life she always had to have an alternative plan, which more often than not would have to be put into operation. This was a red rag to a bull as far as I was concerned: a classic example of bringing about what you think. 'Of course if you project an alternative plan, the perfect won't work out,' I told her, 'because your energy is more concentrated on the *alternative*.' She caught my drift and we caught the ferry.

On our return, Eileen's guidance confirmed the importance of our pilgrimage and said that I was to be prepared to go over and help John Walters, and to tell him so. John and I had discussed the possibility of starting a garden for the hotel, and demonstrating that vegetables could be grown on Iona — up until now, all of the vegetables had to be imported — so I wrote and offered him my services as gardener, to work in the background and support him in every way I could (including sharing my experience of running Cluny Hill Hotel). As it happened, God had other plans for me, but the offer served to cement our link; and when John later wrote to say that the way had opened up for him to buy the Argyll, Naomi's message that it was vital that he run both hotels, to accommodate conferences on spiritual themes, became real.

* * *

When I returned from Iona there was a pile of letters waiting for me. Although the weather was fine and I was tempted to work outside, I felt it important to read and answer them at once. At the bottom of the pile was a letter from Sheila Walker, the Secretary of the Scottish UFO Society, to whom Lady Mayo had introduced me in Edinburgh. Sheila wrote of a conference of 'New Age group leaders' to be held at the Adult Education College at Attingham Park, Shropshire, whose Principal was Sir George Trevelyan; Sheila had been invited to attend but couldn't, so she suggested that I go instead.

My immediate intuition was to agree. Several sound reasons then came to mind and I asked Eileen to confirm my decision in meditation, but all she received was, *I do not say go or not to go, Peter will know himself what is the right action.* I was in the car and on the road within half an hour. Eileen was most perturbed about this, as I'd just been away for a week and there was a lot of work to be done in the garden, but her guidance told her,

My child, let go and relax, Peter had to make his own decision and he has done so. Now leave him in My safe hands. Think positively about this trip of his, so that there is no pullback and all goes smoothly. It is so right for him to be guided in action.

I stayed the night in Edinburgh with Sheila Walker and her mother, Molly. Sheila explained that she would not be able to get time off from her job (she was a headmaster's secretary) to attend the conference with me, but I pressed her to try, particularly as she had a great desire to visit Liebie Pugh, whom I was planning to see at St Annes on the way. Sheila asked and, to her surprise, was given permission to go. The next day, when we met her in the park at St. Annes, Liebie was even more surprised that we were going to Attingham without checking first: the conference was an invitation-only affair and a friend of hers, Merta Mary Parkinson, an energetic woman who travelled extensively linking up spiritual people, had come all the way from the USA to attend, only to be refused.

I straight away telephoned Ruth Bell, Sir George Trevelyan's secretary at Attingham. Ruth explained that it was all right for Sheila, as Secretary of the Scottish UFO Society, to attend, but she hadn't heard of me. She stressed that the conference was not open to the public, it had been planned over an entire year and was only for the leaders of the various spiritual groups and movements in Britain. Who was I, and why did I think I needed to be there? I rather haltingly began to explain, when a patrician voice came on the phone and said, 'My dear fellow, of course you must come!' Apparently, a sensitive had been standing with Sir George near the telephone and had told him how important it was that I be there.

Sheila and I arrived at Attingham, a stately country mansion, in the early afternoon. We were shown into the library, where I met Anthony Brooke and his partner Monica Parish. To my surprise and delight, Anthony greeted me by throwing his arms around me and saying, 'Here's Peter. We've known each other for millions of years!' Both John Walters on Iona and Liebie Pugh had told me a lot about Anthony, and Liebie in particular had been most anxious that we meet.

Anthony Brooke is a delightful man of great charm. He comes from a colourful background, having been the last ruler of Sarawak, a country larger than Scotland, adjoining Borneo. He was the second head of state to declare war on Germany. When the British Government deposed the Brooke family after the Second World War, Anthony was so popular with his former subjects in Sarawak that he was banned from the country, for fear they would demand his reinstatement! He has often said that he lost one kingdom but had gained a greater one, the Kingdom of God. He became a sort of ambassador of the Light, visiting most of the countries in the world; he was invited to communist Moscow, met both Mao Tse-tung and Chou En-lai in China, and knew U Thant, then Secretary-General of the United Nations, very well. He and Monica Parrish were the founders of the Universal Foundation, closely connected with the work of the Universal Link and Liebie Pugh. This meeting at Attingham was the beginning of a long and happy association in the work with Anthony; there was an immediate rapport between us as if we had indeed met before.

The conference's first speaker, Christopher Hills, invited us all to pool ideas so we could formulate a charter for the founding of a New Age Community. The ensuing suggestions and discussion puzzled me and then began to try my patience, so I got up and said that we were already doing at Findhorn what they were all talking about. We had been guided in the moment by God, step by step, I explained, and only in retrospect had we been able to look back and see a pattern and plan. It was nonsense to draw up 'charters' or 'blueprints'! I resumed my seat; the room was suddenly silent.

Sir George relished such 'fighting talk' and later invited me to speak about our work at Findhorn and its development. Of course, at that time it was only in its early stages, and I had little idea of where it was going, but remembering Sheena's advice to 'stand up and let God speak through you', I did the best I could. At the end of my talk there was an even more profound silence; then Air Marshall Sir Victor Goddard got up and asked me if I'd tell them something about our financial policy. *Financial policy?* We didn't have one — we were still living on National Assistance! Sir Victor had me for a moment, but then I found myself saying, firmly, 'It's quite simple. One gives up everything to put God and His Will first, then all one's needs are met perfectly from His abundant supply.'

I wondered, in the hush that followed this, whether some were now writing us off as hopeless idealists. But I had said nothing less than the truth — all our needs *were* being perfectly met — and I was glad Sir Victor had forced me to stick out my neck. In the tea break that followed, a woman came up to me and said that in olden times I would have been burned at the stake for saying some of the things I'd said. 'Then aren't we lucky to be alive today?' I replied sweetly, thinking she would have been one of the first to reach for the matches.

As it turned out, within a few years nearly everyone at that conference would come to visit us at Findhorn, and the contacts and deep links that were formed at Attingham proved essential for the future unfoldment of our work.

But that was not the end of the contacts made on this memorable journey. At the conference I renewed my acquaintance with Kathleen Fleming, a delightful woman whom I'd first met at St. Annes, and since she had just been to Iona and Glastonbury, I suggested that she also visit Findhorn to complete the triangle. Kathleen was a sensitive, so I made it clear to her that Sheila and I would be happy to go along with any inner promptings she might receive on the journey. Sure enough, after we had visited Liebie at St Annes and were heading for Edinburgh, Kathleen felt strongly that we should make a detour to the Lake District and meet Jessica Ferreira, who owned Traigh Bhan — the house on Iona whose sanctuary I had found so powerful. It was to prove an important connection.

We spent the night in Edinburgh, where we left Sheila, and the next morning I sent a telegram to Eileen telling her that Kathleen and I would be back at Findhorn by lunchtime. Kathleen's guidance had other ideas! First we went to Strathmiglo to meet Major Bruce MacManaway, one of the finest healers in Britain; he was due to see a patient but his car mysteriously refused to start that morning until we had completed our visit. A little further along the road, Kathleen said that she felt we should see some spiritual people in Abernethy. When we'd finished there, we were diverted again to a Colonel Mathieson at his home in Aviemore.

It was late at night by the time we got back to Findhorn. Eileen was not pleased and gave us a frosty reception — in turn she had prepared lunch, afternoon tea and dinner for us and was less than impressed by my enthusiasm for the contacts I had made which had delayed our return. I vowed, to myself, never again to plan or announce my movements ahead of time.

Chapter 22

Road-Works Ahead

Be always and in all places a good ship, a mariner, a compass and an untier of knots.
Keep calm in troubled seas.
Think of your port and objective

ALMOST THREE YEARS after we had moved to Findhorn Bay Caravan Park our time of isolation was over. While the inner work of aligning ourselves and listening to the God within continued on a daily basis, and the outer work in the garden went on producing phenomenal results, I was drawn increasingly to continue travelling and forging links with individuals and groups up and down Britain — just as they, in turn, were drawn to visit us to see with their own eyes what we were up to. I have always chuckled at the thought that here we were, apparently defying the biblical injunction not to build one's foundations on sand! But, of course, the true foundations were built on rock-like faith.

A part of that faith now was trusting that as God had told us to expect an increasing numbers of visitors, so He would provide for their shelter. A letter from Sir George Trevelyan after my trip to Attingham echoed the promise of visitors:

> *Let me say how deeply I enjoyed your visit and value the contact with you. We have just finished a conference with the Soil Association, and I spoke to them about you and the work you are doing in plant growth. This is to warn you that some of them may approach you to know more about it.*

It also came to me with considerable force that Liebie Pugh and those at St Annes with her should move to Findhorn in the near future, if that were part of the Plan; I wrote to tell her so, adding that thanks to the garden we would be able to sustain a community without outside supplies 'in case of emergency'. (We continued to believe at that stage that the world was heading towards disaster.) Liebie was also overtaxed and drawn upon too much by many visitors, some of whom came from curiosity only, and Findhorn's relative inaccessibility would ensure that only the right people would reach her.

While Kathleen Fleming was still with us on her first visit to Findhorn in October 1965, she had a vision of us having several cedarwood bungalows. I told her that this was unlikely, as special planning permission would be needed to build bungalows on a caravan park. Then it occurred to me that there already *was* a cedarwood bungalow on the caravan park, a mobile home called a 'Sun Cottage' which was assembled in two parts. Because of its 'technical' mobility — an undercarriage with wheels — it fell within the existing regulations. I obtained the sales brochures and details and within six months Molly Walker, Sheila's mother from Edinburgh, had bought and sited one near us.

Before then, however, we also manifested our first guest caravan. When Meg Emerson had visited us from Glastonbury, she became convinced that she should join us and had negotiated with the owner of the park to buy a caravan, adjoining the shop, for £700; but during our time on Iona it became very clear to her that her place was to remain in Glastonbury. I therefore approached the caravan park owner and said that we would buy it instead, provided we could move it to a site adjoining ours (even though I had no idea where the money would come from!). He agreed. Then out of the blue, Dorothy received a cheque for £750 — her share of her mother's will — and I went down triumphantly to close the deal.

The caravan park owner was in fact on his way up to see me, to say that he had decided after all not to sell the caravan: he needed it for office space and to heat the water for the shop. I was dumbfounded. The caravan was perfect for our guests' needs and we had the money! The owner promised to find a similar model, but there were very few of that type in the district and I was told that the chances of one coming up for sale were highly unlikely.

When I arrived back from a trip to Glastonbury the park owner *had* found another caravan of exactly the same make, recently refurnished and in far better condition than the original. The asking price was £750 — but Dorothy meanwhile had bought a radio set, so only had £700 left from her inheritance. We offered the seller that amount, cash down, and he accepted it because he was anxious to sell the caravan before he travelled south for Christmas. This, our first 'official' guest accommodation, was moved into its position the next morning just in time for our latest visitor, John Shelly, a friend and well-known potter in Glastonbury, who bought one or two things that were needed for it. Subsequent visitors did likewise, as each person saw a need and met it, and before very long it was equipped perfectly. Miss Bamber — 'Bambi' — from Iona also decided to buy a small caravan around this time and had it moved up from the lower caravan park to be sited beside the garden.

Kathleen Fleming left us after ten wonderful days, during which our conversation often turned again to the triangle of Findhorn, Iona and Glastonbury, which we continued to link in our morning meditations. For me they were the three brightest places on the map of Britain just then. My intuition, confirmed by Eileen's guidance, suggested that I had a role to play in all three centres; as it worked out, the auditions for those roles followed in swift succession.

My strong feeling of connection with John Walters and his work on Iona prompted me to pay him another visit, this time with Eileen, which would be her first trip away from Findhorn in the three years since we'd been there. We went across for only two days, to find that John had already opened negotiations to buy the second hotel on the island, the Argyll. I reaffirmed my willingness to come over during the following Easter to help him run the hotels and cultivate a vegetable garden. Although the Argyll was really too small to justify Eileen, Dorothy and myself taking it on fulltime, I suggested that one strategy might be to manage the St Columba and the Argyll Hotels together, only opening the latter when the St Columba was full in the summer. I was also keen to demonstrate that the island could be self-sufficient in producing its own vegetables, by applying the same practices as we had at Findhorn.

Eileen loved the island and shared my enthusiasm for cementing a connection between Iona and Findhorn, finding an agreeable relationship with John Walters and having many powerful visions while she was there. After this memorable (and whirlwind) pilgrimage, I wrote to John to confirm my offer, adding:

> *The National Assistance Board is aware that there is something strange going on in the way I am prevented from obtaining employment, but they have now said that I must be prepared to leave Findhorn and seek employment further afield. Up to now I could not see myself working in any other hotel than Cluny Hill because I could only work for a*

spiritual motive, but now the possibility of helping to create a centre of Light on Iona and working with you attracts me enormously.

Eileen had received the following:

> *My child, the full significance of that pilgrimage to Iona has not dawned on each one yet. It was all done so quickly they are still in a daze, but things will clarify and great will be the outcome. It has meant more to Peter than anyone. The link he has made with that great soul* [John Walters] *was something that had to happen.*

I was already wondering whether John Havelock Davies, a horticulturalist whom I had met in Glastonbury and who was due to join us soon, could take over the operation at Findhorn to enable us to be on Iona for a time. I had no idea what arrangements we'd make for the boys, who were happily established in school, but as I also wrote to John Walters, 'we are simply to know that when something is right and blessed by God, it will be right all the way round'.

Hallowe'en came — a traditional folkloric occasion which is far more celebrated by the Scots than the English — so as a treat for the boys we decided to have a big party. We spent days preparing for it (which is most fun of all), making horrible black spiders, witches, cats, witches' brews, signs, hollowed-out turnips and toffee apples. Seventeen children came to the party on our little patio. Christopher had carved and painted a magnificent scimitar to go with his pirate costume, and David was in drag as Mother Hubbard, but Jonathan — who was normally untidy at that age and couldn't give a hoot what he looked like — was so taken by the elegance of his Cavalier's costume, from feather tip to buckled shoe, that he quite fell for himself and insisted on dressing the same next day so that his photograph could be taken! Although on looking back I wish that I had taken more time to spend with the boys as they were growing up, on occasions like this I could share their happiness and know that all was well with them. I remember that Christopher at this time had fallen under the spell of joss sticks! Every lunchtime for a period of months he would come all the way home from school just to light a stick of incense and bask in its scent.[1]

* * *

[1] Curiously, my youngest son Daniel (born in 1982) developed the same fascination with incense at around the same age

The next call of the road came from Glastonbury. I received a letter from my potter friend, John Shelly, who wrote to say that the Tor School (next to Chalice Well, and about which I had so strongly spoken to Tudor Pole earlier in the year) was in danger of being sold and made into a brewery. A group in the town wished to turn this boy's school into a spiritual and healing centre instead, but first they needed to raise the money to buy it and to convince both the trustees of the school and those of Chalice Well (which owned the land it was built upon) that their credentials and plans were sound. Would I agree to be the director of this project?

I felt that I could not do so. Apart from my destiny at Findhorn, I had already agreed to help John Walters on Iona next summer. I suggested that John Shelly take on the job himself, but I would come south to assist; Sir George Trevelyan had anyway invited me to a second conference at Attingham in November, this time on 'The Education of Specially Gifted Children'. While on the road, I could include in the journey visits to all those healers and other spiritual people that I had met, to discuss means of raising the money that would be needed and invite them to a meeting about the project.

About fifty of us came together in the south west of England at the end of November 1965 to draw up plans for the Glastonbury Foundation, the name we gave to the proposed charity to acquire the Tor School, and to find a suitable chairman who combined spiritual awareness with experience of working charities. To my delight Ronald Heaver was chosen, a crippled but doughty man who had served both as treasurer and secretary to the Garden Tomb Association in Jerusalem (the Garden Tomb that had impressed me so much on my visit to Jerusalem thirteen years earlier); he maintained the Sanctuary of Avalon just outside Glastonbury and seemed the ideal choice. To my surprise, I was asked to be the first warden of the Foundation for six months and heard myself agreeing.

Anthony Brooke had just returned from a world tour the day before the meeting and, on hearing about it, immediately came all the way from London to join us. He said that the only person that he knew who had the £30,000 plus needed to buy the school was a businessman, Andrew Wilson, who lived near Glasgow: he was also a healer, and the founder chairman of The Truth Research Foundation, a trust that supported healing projects. Anthony went on to say that he felt that Andrew Wilson would not release his money without first consulting the medium to whom he went for advice about such matters. Since I was to pass through Glasgow on my way home, I invited

Anthony to accompany me so we might have a chance of meeting him. Anthony anyway wanted to visit Findhorn.

I was very interested in how God was going to get me back to Scotland — on this particular journey I had been as far as Cornwall, at the southernmost tip of Britain; I was now well over 500 miles from home and, after filling the car with petrol, had only two shillings and sixpence left in my pocket. I laughed at the apparent precariousness of my situation but now I had to go and tell Anthony how little money I had. He burst out laughing too. 'Don't bother about that,' he said, 'I can cover our expenses. It's all the Lord's money anyway!'

Anthony and I set out like a couple of schoolboys on a great adventure, despite the fact that we were both middle-aged: the sense of rightness and urgency in our work, which was confirmed by the guidance received by Eileen as well as those we met along the way, left us no time to rationalize our behaviour. En route north from Warminster on the edge of Salisbury Plain we even set out in search of the Holy Grail — the physical cup! — but after battering through snowstorms decided that the road would be blocked. Instead we turned the car to Attingham Park, where the following morning we had a delightful breakfast with Sir George and his secretary Ruth, and concluded that finding the inner Grail was all that mattered. Liebie Pugh confirmed this later that day, with a twinkle in her eye, when we reached St Anne's in the north of England. Kathleen Fleming was also there. She told us that she was aware of a being who manifested great power — the Archangel Michael, who stood before her with outstretched hands and was apparently guiding our work. I was startled, because it reminded me of a vision Eileen had received a couple of months earlier on St Michael's day, September 29: *I saw the Archangel Michael. He had a foot in Glastonbury and a foot in Findhorn and a sword pointing to Iona, as if uniting the three* . Now, through Kathleen, apparently the same being was telling me that Glastonbury was the melting pot, and in answer to my specific question about the Tor School, told me 'The school will become the property of Chalice Well. You may be sure that all will go according to plan'. This truly puzzled me, as we were on our way to see Andrew Wilson to seek material assistance to buy Tor School for the Glastonbury Foundation, not the Chalice Well Trust (which anyway owned the land and would need to approve any potential purchaser of the buildings on it). Also, my intuition told me that he was going to agree to our request. But I had learned from long experience to accept apparent paradoxes and contradictions in the inner messages people received for me: sometimes they were tests, and often their full meaning would only become apparent with hindsight.

In all, we had a miraculous journey, as if the biblical pillar of fire had gone before us to prepare the way: even the snow which had closed the notorious pass at Shap Fell in northern England for seven days melted enough to let us through. We arrived on time in Glasgow to meet Andrew Wilson, whose appointments diary was so full it would not have permitted a later meeting; he told us about some remarkable 'psychic surgery' he had just witnessed but refused to discuss the Glastonbury plans at all until after a session with his medium and us on the next day. I found Andrew Wilson to be a curious mixture of spiritual seeker and pragmatic businessman. His house had recently burnt down, he said, and through it he had discovered that material things after all didn't really mean anything to him; but like many of us, he complained that while he was able to pass life's *big* tests easily, it was the little things in life that got him down.

When we met Andrew Wilson again the next day we found that his medium was a very quiet, humble man who preferred to stay in the background. In the trance state he channelled a North African who called himself 'Ali' and immediately started talking about Glastonbury: how it had been a place of healing and Light down the ages but was now slumbering and needed to be brought to life again. Ali went on to say that each of us had a part to play in this — Anthony, myself and Andrew. Ali gave a slight chuckle when Andrew asked what his part was to be. 'Financial, of course!' replied Ali. Andrew Wilson laughed and agreed to make the money available for the school.

We drove on to Edinburgh, where Monica Parish (Anthony's partner) flew up from England to join us for a meeting at Sheila Walker's home. A whole group of us spent a happy time talking about the saga of Glastonbury until four o'clock in the morning. When we spent the next night at Strathmiglo with Bruce and Patricia MacManaway, Bruce (who had been guided to make the long journey to join us for that meeting in Devonshire) noticed that two of the tyres on my car were worn very thin, and with Monica's connivance took the car and had two snow-grip tyres fitted instead, without me knowing about it. We were thus enabled to get back through heavy snows in the Cairngorm mountains to Findhorn safely.

Altogether I went on eight journeys around Britain in connection with Glastonbury, filled with the tremendous zest and energy that comes when one 'knows' that what one is doing is right. The universe seemed to confirm this by assuring that all my needs were met, and met perfectly. Every time I left Findhorn I had very little money, but on almost every occasion I returned with more than I'd started with. Once I set out without a penny in my pocket, planning to stop en route at the Labour Exchange in Forres to collect my £9 and 10s National Assistance.[2] But by the time I got there I already had £30 — I had met the postman on the way, and he had two letters for me, one with a £10 note and in the other a cheque for £20.

On another occasion, when I was in the south of England, somebody called me on my faith, remarking that living that way didn't really work: the battery of my car was flat and I had to start the engine every time by using the crank. Driving up north on my return journey, that remark really niggled me. I stopped by the side of the road and found that I had £12 and 15 shillings in my pocket — not quite enough, I thought, for a new battery. However, I soon passed a garage that was advertising batteries for £12, 12 shillings and sixpence; as I drove past, a little voice in my head seemed to say to me 'Where is your faith?'. I immediately reversed the car and bought the battery.

This left me with only 2 shillings and sixpence, and I was still a long way from home. My next stop was to have lunch with Ellen Hilton and Bambi; they persuaded me to stay for tea, and then the night, as they were having a meeting and service in their chapel. I enjoyed it very much. In the morning Ellen Hilton said, 'Now I'm going to show you how Pilgrim House works'. First she gave me some flowers from the altar and asked me to take them to Liebie Pugh at my next stop, with her love. Then I was given a candle from their altar for our meditations at Findhorn. Finally Ellen emptied the box where people put donations for healing and gave the contents to me. I was taken aback by this generosity and thanked her heartily. Soon after leaving the house I stopped the car and counted out the money. It came to £12, 12 shillings and sixpence — the exact price of the car battery.

* * *

By December 1965 I had still not heard from John Walters about my offer to come over and help run the two hotels on Iona the next summer, so I wrote

---

[2] Having to 'sign on' for Social Security every week usually dictated the time I could be away from Findhorn

and told him that since the money to buy the Tor School in Glastonbury was now promised, I had instead decided to accept the warden's job there — but only for six months, as I felt my real centre was at Findhorn. John understood perfectly and we continued to enjoy strong and close links with him thereafter.

All was not well in Glastonbury, however. For some reason there was a spiritual rivalry between Tudor Pole at Chalice Well and Ronald Heaver, chairman of our committee, that had been going on for 40 years. When TP heard of the Glastonbury Foundation's plans to buy Tor School, he stepped in and raised the money himself so that the Chalice Well Trust could buy it instead: just to keep it out of his rival's hands. Eileen had several visions relating to the battle between these spiritual giants, and guidance that I was to bring them together, but the result of my efforts to do so was that both of them turned on me, each thinking I was in the other's camp!

The Tor School thus became amalgamated into the Chalice Well Trust, true to Kathleen's prediction from St Michael, and the Glastonbury Foundation was disbanded. The whole adventure had taken six months and thousands of miles on the road, often leading me to people and places that I had never met before. Not only had the original goal been achieved — to turn the school over to spiritual rather than brewing purposes — but also, and more importantly, I had visited most of the key people and centres in Britain that were seeking or already expressing a spiritual vision for the New Age, and played my part in making them aware of each other. William Blake's 'new Jerusalem' is often associated with Glastonbury, but for me the awareness was dawning that all these different people and places throughout Britain were together forming the temple of the true 'new Jerusalem' — and my job was to be one of its building inspectors.

Home at Findhorn came further hints from Eileen's guidance about our future, although this talked of a tent rather than a temple: on 26 December 1965 she received:

> *Try to see this whole site occupied by a community very committed to Me and My work. See the limitlessness of this whole thing. What started in a very small way will grow beyond recognition. It has only just begun. It is in but its embryo stage. The tent of Abraham will be immovable, and great will be the multitude, all singing My praises and doing My work.*

Chapter 23

Beyond Belief

The Master is willing to comfort and guide you, so long as you are willing to learn

ON MY TRAVELS to England and back in 1965, I would usually stay in Edinburgh with Sheila Walker and her mother Molly, and through Sheila's connections as secretary of the Scottish UFO Society I came to know an extraordinary man whose contribution to our work would be invaluable. I first noticed him when the society's chairman, Colonel Henderson, began bringing him to the gatherings in which I shared the latest developments at Glastonbury.

Robert Ogilvie Crombie (known to some of his friends as 'Roc') was an older, softly-spoken Scottish gentleman who stayed in the background, listening much and saying very little. He carried an air of wisdom and quiet authority about him, with a twinkle in his eye as if to say that nothing should be taken too seriously; I became very interested in him and enquired into his background. Roc was a man with many talents. He had been a radio operator on a boat in the English Channel during World War I, had studied music at university and was an accomplished pianist and an actor. He was also trained as a scientist, but a congenital heart defect prevented him from full-time employment; although born and raised in Edinburgh, he was advised by his doctors during World War II to live in the country, which he did, spending ten years in an isolated cottage 9 miles from Perth. He was supported by an invalid's pension from the State and developed a close rapport with nature, as well as devoting himself to studying a wide range of scientific, philosophical and spiritual subjects. He now lived frugally in an immaculate Edinburgh flat whose walls were lined with thousands of books, and despite his heart condition regularly swam in the icy sea. In all, he was an extraordinary man with whom I soon developed a close rapport.

I wondered about Roc's connection with Colonel Henderson and the UFO Society. Until recently, he told me, he had wanted nothing to do with UFOs or space beings — as a scientist he 'knew' that such things could not exist. Then one day as he was sitting reading in his flat, he became aware of a being in what looked like a spacesuit, sitting in the chair opposite him. He thought he must be going out of his mind, but decided to keep quiet and see what happened. The being disappeared. Later that evening, after Roc had retired, he was astonished to find the same being standing at the foot of his bed. It said to him, 'I'm from Venus — and what are you going to do about it?' Roc laughed and replied, 'What do you mean?' The being said, 'You don't believe that I exist, do you?' Roc said, 'No, I don't. If you say that you are in a physical body like ours, then I don't believe it'. He was quietly amazed to find himself in this conversation in the first place — it *must* be a hallucination, he told himself, but it looked and felt so normal. 'You're quite right,' the being said, in answer to his earlier point, 'because beings from the other planets, from space, have higher vibrating bodies that cannot be seen by your physical eyes. But when we come to this planet, we lower our vibration, lower our spin, so that we become solid. And if we were analysed, you would find that there is no difference between our matter and yours. We do have a tendency to raise our vibrations and disappear to your eyes.' That at least made sense to Roc, who knew from his reading that there were many reports of spaceships just vanishing. Now, with this 'space being' standing before him, he was open-minded enough to accept the evidence of his senses; and from then on he brought fresh eyes to his study of the subject.

This was only one among several encounters with various other-worldly beings that Roc began having at this time, as if a curtain had been drawn open into other dimensions. They were not visions, such as Eileen and other sensitives perceived, but for Roc actual experiences of an alternative reality that overlaid, yet seemed as natural as, the world around us. The most exciting of these, as far as our work at Findhorn was concerned, occurred in March 1966, shortly before Roc paid us his first visit. He was sitting with his back to a tree one sunny afternoon in Edinburgh's beautiful Royal Botanic Gardens when, to his astonishment, he saw dancing before him a little faun straight out of Greek mythology; it seemed as real and solid as the other people in the gardens. The faun was as amazed that Roc could see him, and the two were soon in conversation.[1]

[1] 'I cannot be certain whether I was speaking to him mentally or aloud,' wrote Roc in *The Findhorn Garden* (and says in the audio-tape *Conversations with Pan*), in which he gives the full story of this encounter

Kurmos (as the faun was called) was a nature spirit, one of the elemental beings responsible for helping individual plants grow to the overall blueprint held by the deva of their species, just as builders work to an architect's plans; Kurmos himself was concerned with helping the growth of trees in the park. (Roc later explained to me that these elemental beings are actually whirls or vortices of energy that can appear to human eyes — at least to his — in the archetypal forms of fauns, elves, sprites, etc., as that is the easiest way for our brains to interpret the sensory information. Some people see them only as little bursts of light or colour.)

Kurmos and Roc had several meetings after that, either in the gardens or in Roc's flat, and Roc learned much about the relationship between the human and nature kingdoms, particularly the danger of humans continuing to abuse, pollute and exploit the natural world. If the nature spirits 'withdrew' their energy as a result, it would have a disastrous effect on all life. This warning was sounded even more clearly a month later when Roc had the awesome experience of meeting the great being and overlord of all the nature spirits — Pan, the traditional god of woodlands and the countryside.

I was tremendously excited when Roc came to Findhorn at Easter on his first visit and shared this news with us: it was to add a new dimension to our work in the garden. We had known of the existence of the nature spirits, of course, but had never opened direct communication with them (Dorothy's work was almost entirely with the devas: the higher, angelic realm). In turn, Roc's exposure to what we were doing seemed to increase his experience and strengthen his understanding of the inner worlds to which he had recently gained access; he really started blossoming. In a letter to Eileen, he wrote

> *It is impossible to tell you what a wonderful experience my first visit to Findhorn has been. I cannot find words to do so. There is a wonderful feeling of harmony and peace in your community, something I have never felt to such an extent anywhere before. I am sure you have many worries and difficulties to face from time to time — there always are in life — but the overall feeling is that you all rise above them. There is such a sense of being close to the presence of God which is very wonderful, and I thank you all for a wonderful experience.*

Although self-effacing and quiet, Roc was one of the most powerful men I had ever met. Molly and Sheila Walker brought him up to Findhorn nearly every other weekend and he also always seemed to appear at the right time to deal with any problems. While he is best known for his contact with the nature spirits (of which more later), Roc's great knowledge and increasing experiences of other aspects of the inner worlds were his major contribution to our work in the early years. He was responsible for our protection, building up an inner fortress of light against the forces of darkness and black magic that sometimes attacked us.

At first Eileen had a hard time understanding the apparent duality of 'light' and 'dark' forces, and the need for Roc to 'do battle' against the latter — surely, she reasoned, that if everything were simply held in the Light of God then darkness would naturally disappear. But her own guidance pointed out that Roc's and her work were simply polar opposites, equally important and both necessary:

> *Tell Peter to follow out with great care all that Ogilvie* [Roc] *passes on to him, and all will be very very well. Ogilvie's work is to spotlight the evil, the darkness and to vanquish it.* [He and Peter] *are a very powerful force and must work closer and closer together.*

Though it was one of my responsibilities to spot people who weren't right for the community, sometimes someone would slip through and it was Roc who would 'catch' them. Once, for example, a woman had flown up from the Isle of Man to visit us, and Roc and I went to pick her up at Inverness Airport. In the car she talked incessantly about her time in Kenya and her experiences there with magic and medicine men. It was quite late by the time I had seen her to a caravan, but Roc said, 'That woman is a witch, and either she goes before the morning, or I go'. We wanted Roc there the next day to meet with two key visitors, so as usual I had to do the dirty work. I explained to the woman that our centre wasn't for everybody, and as it appeared that she was in the wrong place she would have to leave on the first plane at 6 am. She graciously accepted the situation and seemed to understand.

Eileen had guidance that as leader of the community I need only consult one person about situations and events at the time, and that was Roc. While I anyway valued his experience and wisdom, it was his connection with St Germain, the Master of the Seventh Ray, that I esteemed most highly. At a public talk I'd given in Edinburgh about Glastonbury and how I felt that the whole operation was being guided by St Germain, Roc had suddenly seen a figure appear behind me at the mention of the name, grinning, nodding and pointing to himself. Some months later I was again in Edinburgh on a return trip from Glastonbury, this time with a sensitive called Kathy Sparks, a bubbly, loving woman in her early forties whose husband Eric, a Rosicrucian, had trained her in esoterics and spiritual matters. Before we had set out from Glastonbury, Kathy had been told from within that we would 'meet' St Germain on our journey, so we were on the lookout everywhere we went but with no luck. As we came to the door of Roc's flat, however, she excitedly said, 'He's in here!'.

Roc quietly accepted her story and said that it had been coming from all directions; in fact, he had just been given a copy of St Germain's *Trinosophia* and found the symbols and experiences in it strangely familiar. He did not claim, however, to 'be' St Germain. It was rather that he felt the essence of St Germain 'overlighting' him, sometimes becoming at one with him in consciousness, and he spoke from this consciousness to hazard an explanation from St Germain:

> *I can so completely take you over that we become one, as we were in the past. There is mystery here which you cannot understand. I am not reincarnated in you, as you understand reincarnation, and yet it is as if I were. We are one, you are me, and I am you. In the same way I become Peter, and Peter becomes me. You and Peter are one. In the both of you are me, and yet you are each individual human beings. Simply accept this mysterious fact. Do not worry about it, and offer no resistance. You have both much work to do: some of it as your individual selves, some of it as me. Often this will be together, working as one, and yet in different aspects, but sometimes it will be alone. Through you* [Roc] *as channel I will help and direct, as much as I'm able.*

We were later told that it was almost impossible from a human point of view to understand the concept of 'three souls in one': the closest image given was of a large lump of mercury that could divide into three separate blobs and then become one again. Furthermore, St Germain explained that he was only able to offer suggestions and advice rather than telling us what to do, for it was essential that we have free choice and take the personal responsibility that comes with exercising it.

Roc was at first as bewildered as we were about the import of this communication, but he reasoned that so long as no harm came from it then he may as well accept it. The fact that it was independently confirmed in messages received by many others at the time, including Eileen, Naomi and Liebie, strengthened my own conviction that here we had a powerful and benevolent source of wisdom to draw upon.

At the beginning of May that year (1966) Roc, Kathy and I set out in all innocence from Findhorn to return Kathy to her home in Devon in the south of England. We then wanted to collect a couple we knew, Wilfred and Violet South, and take them to Glastonbury for a four-day holiday, and to call on various power points en route. What followed was an extraordinary adventure, utterly unexpected, that made a nonsense of all our plans and even today seems too fantastic to commit to paper.[2]

We began this 'unpremeditated journey' by going to Iona and ended it back at Findhorn after two exhausting weeks of travel in Scotland and England, with Kathy still on board. It appeared that the main purpose of our trip was to discover and 'cleanse' the ancient network of power centres that are dotted throughout Britain, and I had never before experienced so many punctured tyres, people's changed plans, blocked roads and bridges up for repair to ensure that we found them all! The journey became such a lesson in living in the moment that often, on approaching a T-junction on the road, I would only know which way to turn when I arrived at it. Inevitably it would lead in the opposite direction to that which we had intended to go but would take us to yet another power point, confirmed by both Kathy and Roc. Their inner experiences of the place would always match, and the 'cleansing' would happen by Roc anchoring through his body into the ground what he experienced as a magenta ray of light.

This puzzled all of us until we arrived at Attingham Park, where Sir George showed us a book on Goethe's 'Theory of Colour' and took a prism between two dark surfaces to demonstrate. If the spectrum is bent back on itself, so that its first and last colours (akin to the First and Seventh Rays) blend, the colour magenta results: this, we were told, had a cleansing and purifying effect on those places whose power had been abused or neglected in the past. Of course, I had to take it on faith that what we were doing was having an effect, but the agreement of both Roc's and Kathy's separate accounts, and the incredible number of 'coincidences' that attended our journey, left me in no doubt about some method in our apparent madness. On our

---

2 Although at the time I did write a 150 page account of it for private circulation

return to our centre at Findhorn, where this 'new' ray was also anchored, Eileen received in meditation:

> *This ray can be very dangerous, because it is a destroyer of anything that is of the dark in any soul, and where there is any resistance to it the darkness will be destroyed...from now on only the right people will be able to remain here. Those who are not of the light will feel so uncomfortable that they will have to depart.*

Eileen herself felt somewhat uncomfortable about the unreal nature of some of the experiences we described from our 'unpremeditated journey' but her guidance reassured her:

> *When you are actually listening to the story of this amazing mission, on which those three have just been, your consciousness is raised. Then you see everything so clearly. Step by step you see exactly what has been happening. Then when you go away by yourself, consciousness is lowered and the whole thing becomes so fantastic and unreal. It becomes a thing of fantasy. Be not disturbed or distressed, but try and keep your consciousness raised no matter what you are doing or where you are. Accept that these are indeed extraordinary days, and that the things that are happening are truly amazing.*

Two weeks later it was Whitsun[3] and a group of about sixteen carefully selected people (plus a few gatecrashers!) gathered with us at Findhorn. We had been told to expect an attempted landing by our space brothers, so we all assembled on the beach at the landing site that we had prepared and built up in our meditations over the years. Those with inner sight actually described a spacecraft as it came in and hovered overhead; I saw nothing as usual, of course, but when Roc was told to stand in the centre, where a beam of light would be focussed on him to 'raise his vibrations', even *I* saw him disappear briefly! It gave me quite a shock. Yet while nothing else seemed to happen afterwards — according to the sensitives, the spacecraft flew off again — all of us there were filled with a tremendous feeling of upliftment, as if something very profound had changed and things would never be the same again. Eileen's guidance later confirmed it:

[3] The seventh Sunday after Easter, commemorating the descent of the Holy Spirit at Pentecost

> *Let none of you have any feeling of disappointment regarding last night (the landing of our space brothers). All was in preparation for something far, far greater than any of you have ever contemplated. Raise your thinking and you will raise your living on to an entirely new level. Do it this instant, going your various ways, knowing that this is actually happening to all of you. Rise together.*

The guidance went on to indicate that sufficient Light had been anchored on the planet so that destruction was now not inevitable. All that had been prophesied in the early years was no longer true. There was no need for an extraterrestrial 'rescue mission' to evacuate some of the population from this planet — the spacecraft that had come, as we thought, to arrange one such evacuation had in fact 'popped in' to tell us that everything was all right.

We were all very inspired by this reassurance and the corroborating messages received by others. Several of us — Kathy Sparks, Roc, Molly Thompson (Liebie Pugh's deputy) and I — left a few days later for a conference at Attingham on 'The Darkness and The Light'. We called at St Anne's on the way and were further inspired by Liebie, who had always refused to see the dark. She said that if you think 'gloom and doom' then you will attract them; instead she stressed the importance of positivity, 'Risen Thinking' and 'Risen Being'. By the time we arrived at Attingham we were in a high state and asked to see Sir George immediately.

We shared with him the messages that Eileen and others had received, and urged that the conference should not consider the darkness but only the light: Sir George should therefore rewrite the address that he was going to give. I think he thought that we'd all taken leave of our senses! We came so charged up that we realized we all needed to calm down — each of us individually had to harmonize with the others attending the course. Sir George also had to walk on a tightrope because he was, after all, the Principal of a respectable adult college, but now he was faced with a position where he had to step one way or the other and go with the old or the new.

On the Sunday morning, after a long inward struggle, he gave the most magnificent talk he'd ever given, lifting everyone to a higher state of 'Risen Thinking'. He even ended with the playing of the 'Hallelujah Chorus'.

The whole episode seemed to me to be a turning point in human history, because up to then we'd been preparing for the worst. Now the tide had turned and we were united. Key people from the various Light Centres in Britain pledged to work as one, to establish the New Heaven and the New Earth of the New Age; there would still be turmoil, we were told, but not complete destruction. There was hope — this was a time of resurrection. Many of the sensitives at that conference received the same messages as Eileen had, and we left reassured but acknowledging that the real work was only now beginning.

* * *

In October Eileen received,

> *The magnetism of this place is drawing more and more souls. You must be ready and prepared for anything at any time. Never hesitate to branch out and have more caravans to accommodate those who are drawn up here. Allow your vision and your heart to expand as rapidly as your consciousness. See this place filled with souls, working for the Light, living together in peace and harmony, doing My Will. This is a unique living, working group, so do not seek for a blueprint, but find it growing very naturally and very rapidly as each one comes.*

A fortnight beforehand, Aileen and Ross Stewart, two friends of Joan ('Joanie') Hartnell-Beavis (Liebie Pugh's secretary and treasurer) came to visit us during a holiday in Scotland. Aileen was a member of the Universal Link, and her husband was a retired naval captain, Deputy Lord Lieutenant of the County of Hampshire and a Justice of the Peace. Joanie was not at all sure about how Ross Stewart would react to such a community as Findhorn. We were shopping in town when they arrived, and on our return we found a note saying that they had found accommodation in a local inn in Findhorn village. We swiftly changed clothes and drove down to see them, arriving just as they were leaving to see us. Ross invited me for a drink and led me into the bar, where he asked what I would like. During my years in the RAF I'd learned that the favourite drink of the Royal Navy was pink gin, so that's what I asked for. His face lit up — I rather think he was expecting me to order carrot juice! — and we had a great talk and became firm friends. (People have sometimes asked me why so many senior members of the armed services seem to be drawn to spiritual groups and centres like ours. I believe the clue lies in the word *service*: serving one's country is just a step away from wanting to serve the world. The camaraderie, morale and discipline involved in working with others in a group effort may also have something to do with it, plus the surprising amount of attention given to spiritual matters at senior staff level.)

Another visitor that October was Joanie Hartnell-Beavis herself. There was such a surge of love between her, Eileen and myself that I was taken aback temporarily — it seemed that in the busyness of our days my heart had closed somewhat, and here it was suddenly opened again! Eileen received that our relationship was unique and that we three were united as one in Love, a triangle to balance the triangle of Light made up by Roc, Kathy Sparks and me.

Roc and I had just returned from another 'unpremeditated journey' around the power points of Scotland and England to anchor the Magenta Ray, ending up at St Anne's where eighteen people from all over the country had gathered. We all met in Liebie's room. Most of those attending were sensitives, and I was asked to conduct the proceedings. I was told that instructions would be given to me in the moment. The purpose of the meeting was twofold: to unite those who had been drawn to St Annes on that occasion, and for them to be used as channels for the anchoring of the new Magenta Ray there. Roc did not attend the meeting, as he'd had guidance to be in the public gardens in front of the building.

During the meeting, Kathleen Fleming became aware of a glowing, vivid green beam of light rising from the floor at her feet, spreading fan shaped to about 36 inches in width and moving upwards through the ceiling. It was the colour of grass at its most brilliant growth in the spring. Then, to her right, she said she saw objectively and in solid form the figure of Pan.

She told this being that she'd appreciated and honoured him from her earliest childhood, and her description of him was certainly graphic. He towered above her, and his massive yet beautiful haunches, rising to the height of her shoulders, were covered in luxuriant, fawn-coloured fur. His leg was delicately outlined in violet light, which was luminous and pulsating, being fringed with an edging of white light. He gave her these words, *You are to be my representative, to speak for me this afternoon.* Kathleen was deeply impressed by his dignity and the tremendous outpouring of power.

Pan said through Kathleen that humans had poisoned his kingdom with insecticide and spray, and broken it with our cruelties and callousness, but that now cooperation and understanding must be established so that all nature could be linked in unity with us. He too worked under the command of

God. We had distorted his function and the expression of his face, and made a mockery of his real beauty.[4]

I then called in Roc from the gardens so he could share with us his experiences. He said,

> *I was aware of the presence of Pan. Pan then took me over, as he had done on a previous occasion, and I became aware of the cloven hooves and the shaggy legs. There was a tremendous sense of power. Pan then called on all the nature forces and spirits to gather together and help in what was to take place. I was aware of all the plants and trees being alive with beings of many kinds, such as I'd seen before. I turned and walked around the pond to some high ground. Standing, looking towards Liebie's room, Pan, through me, called on the Green Ray of the nature forces to rise up through the house like sap rising in a tree, filling the room and those present there. I was aware of raising my hands and arms at this point, and I could see the Green Ray responding and rising up through the building. Pan went on calling the Ray up, and it gradually rose right up to the roof and emerged above it.*
>
> *At the same time the Magenta Ray descended. The two rays met and blended producing a band of blue-green colour. After about ten minutes Pan withdrew, and I knew that the objective had been achieved. Shortly afterwards Peter came out and rather startled me by saying that Pan had been in the room and had spoken to Kathleen.*

The two accounts, by Kathleen and Roc, dovetailed perfectly. It was evident that during the afternoon the Green Ray of Pan and the nature kingdom was blended with the Magenta Ray of spiritual power, which had been anchored in the morning session. Nearly all present were particularly conscious of these two colours.

In the evening Kathleen, Roc and I strolled in the gardens and Roc was aware of the Magenta Ray coming down and dividing into three and passing to each of us, while the Green Ray was coming up from the ground. As we walked, both Kathleen and Roc heard voices coming from trees, bushes,

---

[4] The early Christian Church transformed the image of Pan into that of the Devil, a horned, goat-like grotesque

from all sides, saying, 'Welcome, welcome, friends of Pan'. They felt that this confirmed the anchoring of the Magenta Ray and its blending with the nature forces.

Sometimes I feel blessed *not* to be directly experiencing these inner sights and sounds, because I can respond to the truth of the message and act on it and be spared the dazzling special effects. And there are other, side-effects I'm happy to be without. After these experiences, Kathleen and Roc felt that they had to keep away from human beings for a while, because they were seeing humans through the eyes of nature spirits. And in those eyes people seemed clumsy, awkward, lacking in understanding, ungraceful and unsympathetic.

* * *

Liebie Pugh was dying of cancer, but only two or three people knew. She was in physical agony but seemed able to rise above all the pain — a true demonstration of the 'Risen Thinking' she had so strongly proclaimed. On an inner level Eileen had been very aware of Liebie's condition for some months; as early as January, Liebie herself had dictated to Richard Graves a message from the 'All Knowing One' saying that 5 December 1966 would complete Liebie's 'Earth function'.

Liebie refused to have a doctor, to take any drugs to stop the pain, or to go to a hospital; she was looked after by Joanie, but it was a great strain, so arrangements were made to move her into a hospital on 5 December. There was a 'Propinquity meeting' — a gathering of those closest to the Universal Link — that had been already planned at St Annes for the day before, and Eileen received,

> *Nothing will be allowed to stop this meeting on the fourth. It is absolutely vital that it takes place. Only those who are very close and are completely dedicated will be able to attend.*

Dorothy, Roc and I travelled down two days before the meeting itself. When we arrived we learned that Liebie had spent her first day in bed and, much to my surprise, she wished to see me. She was very alive and mentally alert. On the same day, Merta Mary Parkinson arrived from the United States of America; having read about the previous session at St Annes, in which the Green and Magenta Rays were blended, she turned up wearing a green and magenta coat, a magenta dress, stole, shoes, and even huge magenta ear-rings. Roc shuddered but like me could see the humour in it.

At the meeting on the following day, Merta Mary was inspired to suggest that all thirty-two of those attending celebrate the occasion with a champagne dinner party. She was an even greater proponent of positive thinking than I — it seemed impossible to be able to organize such a banquet at a seaside resort in mid-winter on a Sunday afternoon. But I knew that if it was in the Plan, all would work out perfectly. We saw the manager of the Hotel Majestic and he agreed to close the cocktail bar for our party: Roc sat at the head of the table, Liebie was toasted with pink champagne, and we had a magnificent five-course dinner with sparkling, magenta-coloured burgundy. It was just the sort of experience that Liebie would thoroughly support, to celebrate her release from all the physical suffering of this Earth plane to the realms of Light.

Eileen, though still at Findhorn, was very much in touch with what was happening at St Annes. She received,

> *This meeting will be like turning over a page of the Book of Life. The page has been completed and now a new and glorious page will present itself. Tremendous changes are taking place here at this Magnetic Centre, Findhorn. A new power is being transferred here, and because of this the work will advance by leaps and bounds. And the whole nature of the work will change. Be ready for these changes.*

On 4 December, Eileen received,

> *Today is a day of days. There will be a tremendous release of power this day. So be ready to receive it and absorb it. Remember this, when outwardly things seem to be at their worst.*

At this time Eileen was experiencing, though, of course, to a lesser extent, the pain and suffering that Liebie was going through. She received,

> *Liebie's outer body is disintegrating at a great speed. Very soon there will be but a very small portion of it in existence. The less there is on the physical, the greater the spiritual ascent, until there is nothing of the physical left and all is spirit. This gathering at this time is to help hasten this. The greater the power which is gathered together, and which is realized, the quicker it will come about. Accept the fact that the personality is non-existent now. She is more out of the body than in it, and the time is at hand when she will no longer be able to*

> *return to this body, but will remain in the spirit. This will be a time of great rejoicing, for all those who are aware of what is happening.*

The day after the banquet everyone left, except for seven of us — true to a vision Eileen had seen earlier of seven people taking Liebie across dark and turbulent waters into glorious Light. *She was left in the Light, and the group came back rejoicing.* These were Anthony Brooke in the bow navigating, with me steering; Kathleen Fleming with Liebie's head on her lap, Roc at her feet, and Monica Parish, Molly Thompson, and Joanie singing songs of praise. With the exception of Dorothy — who appeared to be deputizing for Molly — these seven in the vision were those with Liebie at this time.

As Liebie was to go into the hospital the next day, Anthony suggested that we spend the night in vigil in Liebie's sitting room, adjoining her bedroom. She was delighted with this and saw each one of us for a final word: to me she confided the name of a wealthy benefactor of the Universal Link and suggested I get in touch with him.[5] She went into a deep sleep and passed away at 11.30 pm. The doctor, undertaker, nurse and ambulance quickly arrived, and she was out of the house by midnight.

There were many decisions to be made about the cremation service and notifying people, but we found that we all worked as one and that decisions were immediate and unanimous. Within 24 hours of Liebie's passing we'd conceived, written, printed and posted 500 copies of a brief account of what had happened. The funeral was very simple, with one white rose on her coffin. Afterwards we exchanged reminiscences of Liebie; I discovered that very few people had known of her illness and suffering, and that the top half of her body was eaten away by the cancer, because she'd risen above it by positivity and sheer will power. But that was Liebie!

---

[5] I later followed this advice and the benefactor subsequently made many donations to our community

Chapter 24

Factor X Marks the Spot

The world within is the practical world in which the man and woman of power generate courage, hope, enthusiasm, confidence, trust and faith by which they are given the fine intelligence and practical skill to see the vision and make the vision real

AS ONE DOOR closes, another opens: Liebie's death produced an immediate and remarkable shift of energy from St Annes to our group at Findhorn. People who had previously written to St Annes started writing to us instead. The shift was best exemplified by Joanie, who had served the Universal Link (and Liebie) with such pure love, and who now confirmed her decision to move up and join us once she'd tidied up affairs at St Annes. She wanted to buy her own bungalow, a physical symbol of more permanence than the existing caravans.

I was helped to erect Joanie's bungalow by a man named Willie, who was half blind and quite deaf and truly simple, but his passion in life was hard work and he was very strong. He couldn't be left unsupervised, so we altered our midday break from 12 to 12:30, as that was his lunch time. He also didn't like stopping for tea breaks, as that interfered with his work. Willie helped me lay the concrete for Joanie's bungalow on the base that I'd prepared (it had taken me over a month to lay the water and drain pipes and electricity). Then when the ready-mix concrete arrived in mid-winter, Willie kept tripping over the wires and pipes, pulling them out. In the meantime the concrete was solidifying! As darkness descended I had to turn my car lights onto the site to try to smooth the top of the concrete — it was a nightmare. When the bungalow finally arrived it had to be manoeuvred into position, and I said 'push' and we all pushed and it went beautifully. But when we went to the back we couldn't move it. I found that Willie hadn't heard, because he was deaf, and he was still pushing the other way! Finally we put one person in charge of watching Willie, who had such tremendous strength that he could out-push three or four people.

I had indeed put a lot of energy into the foundations and placing of Joanie's bungalow, and in erecting a wooden fence on top of a concrete wall to surround it. The garden around the bungalow was completed just a quarter of an hour before Joanie arrived in March: the whole operation seemed a miracle.

Around this time Roc received a message from St Germain, to the effect that our aim at Findhorn must be perfection, and that there must be nothing second-best, as we were doing God's work. Only the perfect was good enough. Joanie revelled in this, for with her bungalow we were able to achieve as near perfection as possible, and this air of perfection was to be gradually spread to the rest of the community. Roc received,

> *Plan for perfection. Perfection must be the aim, for here at Findhorn the Kingdom of Heaven is to be made manifest on earth. In the Kingdom of Heaven there is only the perfect. So in its earth counterpart, there must also be perfection. This is not easy to achieve at the moment, as mankind is far from perfect, but it is the end to strive for... there are those who have led lives of self-sacrifice, dedication to God, who have denied themselves things they might have had in the belief that this was pleasing to God. In order to follow this path of life, they have made do with the less good, the imperfect. This way of life is right for them. It has been a sincere way of life, and has great merit for those called to follow it. But here at Findhorn, such a way of life is not right, now... This does not mean luxurious living or extravagance. It is a question of need. If a true need exists, it must be met by the best, i.e. the most suitable in every way.*

This message made a great impression on me. It became very much part of me, and I knew it by heart; I recited it every week during our meditations and did my best to put it into practice.

In January 1967 we had been warned that many more people would come to visit us:

> *As more and more are drawn up to this centre, there will be many who will want to join you, and learn to live and work as a group. They will need no persuading, no encouraging, in any way, but when they've made their choice, then cooperation is to be given in every way. Much Love will be needed, deep understanding and tolerance. All will be different. All will need special handling and understanding. Never try to lump people together. Each one is an individual who needs very special care. Each one has specific problems, which need to be sorted out. Great patience will be called for. It will not always be easy, but keep very close to Me and let Me guide every word and every action.*

In 1967 Evelyn Sanford, whom I'd met the previous October at St Annes, came to join us. She wrote to us in January 1967 wanting to know if she could come and visit us. We thought this very strange, that someone in her sixties living in the extreme south of England, would want to come to the far north of Scotland in mid-winter. When she arrived, her first question was, 'Can I come and join you?' Apparently, some thirty years before, she had been told by a psychic that she would end her days in a community in the north of Scotland. After her visit, she returned home, sold her house, and came and made Findhorn her home, and made a great contribution to the life of the community. Evelyn was like everybody's aunt, and people went to her and she had the time to listen when everyone else was too busy. She also made an important contribution to the inner work.

A delightful and dedicated young couple, John and Janet Willoner, also came to join us at this time. John was a quiet man, spiritual and intuitive, with much inner strength. He resigned his post as a prep school teacher to come to Findhorn. In fact, it had been Janet who introduced John, who in turn introduced Dennis Orme (a young psychology student at Hull University) to spiritual things. Dennis told me that he was looking for some hard physical work — and there was no shortage of that!

John, Janet, Dennis and a young Scot named Andrew made up a team of hard-working young people, starting work at eight o'clock in the morning and often not finishing until eleven at night. They worked in the office putting on stamps, then in the garden, on construction, and later they led outdoor activities. I shall always be eternally grateful to John and Janet for doing so much with our three boys, like rock climbing, camping, walking, exploration in the Cairngorms, that I was unable to do because of my work at Findhorn. They were in a way surrogate parents to our boys.

The early workers at Findhorn were nearly all young, not elderly ladies with tinted hair, as some people have implied. At one time a friend of Dennis took me aside and said that it was time that Dennis had a home and wanted to buy him a caravan, and of course the right one was just available: it provided a home for Dennis, John and Janet. Andrew was a keen photographer, who loved taking photos of the beautiful sunsets over Findhorn Bay and the Moray Firth, but he never got around to taking any of the work we were doing, or the splendour of the gardens. (This is why we don't have any of the early days of the community — to the frustration of many who subsequently sought to document the history).

As our numbers grew there was an increased strain on our domestic arrangements, but everyone pitched in happily and it seemed the work was always done. Eileen did all the cooking in our caravan, sometimes for as many as sixteen. She still used our two-burner stove, and sometimes when we had many visitors, we'd have a buffet. People would come in one door of the caravan, pick up their meal in the kitchen, and file out through the sitting room to the patio. The patio was also the focal point for our meditations, which were held outside. We continued to enjoy wonderful salads, made up from the various vegetables and herbs in the garden. Joanie gave Eileen the gift of a washing machine, and what a change that brought in her life! She no longer had to kneel and wash the laundry in the tiny bathroom tub.

Up until September 1967 I used our caravan as an office and had a filing cabinet there. We only received about a dozen letters a week at that time, but we also kept typed copies of various messages from sensitives, and all of Eileen's, Dorothy's and Lena's guidance. One day Eileen said that we should have a separate caravan for an office. I felt that we should have a building, and Eileen received confirmation in guidance that this was so and we would be shown exactly what was needed. Immediately I went down to the Sectional Builders' Office and said that we needed a garage two feet longer and two feet wider than Joanie's (which they'd supplied), because that was what the guidance had directed. I asked for windows to be put in, and for the inside walls to be lined. Of course we had no money, but I'd taken immediate action because I knew that it was a need and that our needs would be met. I therefore ordered this garage, as we were told that much speed was needed in getting the office ready, and nothing was to hold it up (we did not know the reason for the hurry at the time). It was to have the best equipment that was available, so I ordered the best typewriter I could buy, an Olivetti for £350; we were also told that we were to have enough equipment to allow six people to work there. That didn't make sense to the mind, as we had so little correspondence — but we had learned obedience, so went ahead in faith.

The office was quickly erected and painted, and on the day it was finished the furniture arrived — four desks, six chairs and various bits and pieces. Three thousand copies of the first printed edition of *God Spoke to Me* also arrived! Earlier, our friend Iris Ratsey had been very impressed by Eileen's messages and said that they should be sent out to the world; she had offered to edit them. She had also given us a duplicating machine. At this time Eileen had received,

> *My Word is ready now to go out... Let it go out in hundreds and thousands. The need is very very great, withhold nothing. Cast your bread upon the waters, and the nets will be filled to overflowing... You will be truly amazed at the response.*

The first six to seven thousand copies of the booklet *God Spoke to Me* were sent free to those on the Universal Link mailing list; another benefactor later enabled us to publish *God Spoke to Me* in book form. (In the early days there was no charge for our literature, because the words had been freely given by God. After thousands of copies had been distributed, however, people wanted to buy them from bookshops — these wouldn't distribute the books unless there was a price and hence a profit margin. So we were compelled to charge for our literature.)

Dorothy had been working as a secretary locally, and had given a month's notice, but a week later, on the day our office was completed, she was given a month's pay and told that she could leave immediately. So four wonderful things happened on that same day — but how was the office paid for? Well, a few days later, we received a cheque for a thousand pounds from an anonymous donor. The response to *God Spoke to Me* was tremendous, and this is what really started our expansion; Dorothy was kept busy from morning until night dealing with enquiries.

In September, Eileen also received,

> *Expect the most wonderful and unexpected things to happen... As your thinking expands, as you begin to think 'big*

> *thoughts' so you bring them about one by one. The whole of the work here is to expand and grow in power and strength. The few will become the many... There is much work to be done, but there will be many hands to do the work, and it will become light and joyous. All needs will be met... This place will become world renowned.*

At the time there was quite a lot of publicity in the press about layabouts on National Assistance, not doing enough to get themselves a job, so I was repeatedly asked to come before a special committee to find out why I still hadn't found employment! They knew from my record that I'd been manager of Cluny Hill Hotel and that I had a good reputation, and that I was fit and healthy. Why was I without a job? In each case, when a vacancy had come up, I had done as guided and gone for interviews; but something would always crop up to prevent me filling it. Finally, a representative from Head Office of the National Assistance Board came to see me, carrying a thick file on my failed efforts to find work. After he had gone through it, questioning me closely, he looked up and said, 'Would you say that God is preventing you from getting a job?' I was amazed, and said, 'Yes, indeed'. 'Well, then, presumably if we cut off your money, God will also provide for you'. Hoist with my own petard! I stammered, 'Yes, I — I expect He would'. So that is what they did: and just at that time, donations started arriving in response to the first edition of *God Spoke to Me*, and these supported our family and the community.

* * *

As more and more people came, I would let them get their own inner direction about how to do a particular task, but it was vital in those early days that I retain overall leadership and direction. Sometimes people came up with their own ideas about what Findhorn should be like and how it should be run — then someone else would come along and say something totally different. For example two very strong women, regular visitors, said that we should charge a fixed amount for a person's stay, whereas our policy was for people to give a donation, as they felt guided. I had to explain to them that Findhorn was run under guidance and our guidance said *not* to charge. One of the women persisted, saying that we could work out how much it cost, taking into account their food, electricity, etc. I said we wouldn't do this, and they replied that they wouldn't come again unless there was a set price. And they never did come again. We could not have people coming from the outside telling us how we were to run this pioneer centre, because there were no blueprints. During this time Eileen received the following guidance:

> *I told you a short while ago that the time would come when each one would become so sensitive, you would all know exactly what to do, and will not have to be detailed to do certain jobs. But until this time comes, it is very important there is one who holds the reins, and that one is Peter. If any of you cannot accept his leadership, it will be best to just drop quite quietly out of the community, because until the time comes when there is perfect love, understanding and sensitivity in each one of you, when I guide and direct your lives from within, Peter will have to be My hands and feet and voice, and I will work through him... I tell you the time will come when you will each one be completely guided by Me, by that still voice from within. But until that time comes, do not fight and struggle against Peter's leadership. For I have chosen him to do this work and he will not fail Me, even if it means being seemingly ruthless. It takes tremendous strength to carry out this task I've given him to do. So each must choose, either to go along with him and his leadership, or just fade out of the picture. I tell you all opposition will be brushed away. So if you are opposed to his leadership be prepared to be brushed away. This is the way it must be. The task is too great for it to be otherwise.*

Time and again we were tested by those whose inner direction seemed at variance with the needs of the whole community. When Naomi's work at Findhorn had been completed and she returned to the United States, we used her small caravan as a sanctuary for our meditations, but by the end of 1967 it had become too crowded. Eileen was given a vision of a cedarwood building to replace it, and Naomi's caravan was moved to another site (where Roc would subsequently stay on his visits). At the time a young couple was with us; the man was a healer and a medium, and he began getting messages that the Sanctuary was to be for healing. He said that it should be blue, with a healing couch in the centre, and two annexes, one for herbs and one for massage. Around the walls were to be symbols of different religions. I thought this was marvellous, and that Eileen had received the vision of the overall outside structure, while the details would come through others. The only trouble was that we had eight mediums visit us in quick succession, and each had a different idea for the Sanctuary! One was a builder, who thought it should be made of stone (and not cedarwood); another, who was Jewish, saw it like Solomon's temple with an inner and outer court. Yet a third person said it should have no windows, but a light over the centre altar. There was a vision of an urn over the place of power, that would stand on the open ground, through an opening in the floor. Of course in the midst of this confusion, absolutely nothing was being done about actually *building* the Sanctuary.

Then one morning I realized what was happening. About 80 per cent of what the mediums were receiving appeared to be true, but 20 per cent was causing division in our group. I then remembered the warning received through Roc that as 1967 drew to a close, all Centres of Light would be under attack from the 'forces of darkness' and that we should be prepared for this. I said to Roc that we were fully protected, and he replied that we were from the *outside*, but not from within. He cautioned that it could happen subtly through mediums, as they open themselves to astral energy[1] and the negative forces can reach them through their own jealousy, pride or anything else that was in negative in them. They thus can be used to cause division and chaos in the community.

One person with a large ego, when the Light was shone on him, demonstrated a resentment and pride that caused considerable disruption. From then on we realized that we must get our direction from God, in the clear, concise Light of elevated awareness, and not through mediums. All trance-medium work was immediately stopped and I realized that mediums receiving from the lower astral levels have no place in this New Age. When I told Roc this over the phone, he was delighted that I had at last realized the situation. I thought, 'How could I have been so blind?' But other, younger members of the community had to see the truth as well.

Eileen then again received a vision of the Sanctuary as a simple structure without *any* symbols or pictures on the wall, and with no altar: people coming from different spiritual paths or religions would thus all feel equally comfortable and at one when they gathered there. She also said that it should be a perfect Sanctuary, and that I would be guided in action; in fact I designed the building just five minutes later! I went down to see the Sectional Builder and said, 'I want a building 24 feet by 24 feet,' as that was the first number that came into my head. It was to have windows and an annex. Dennis,

1 often comprised of unresolved emotions or thought-forms

John, and myself dug the foundations, which involved moving tons of sand and gravel. We mixed the concrete with shovels by hand, so that we could add our vibrations into the very foundations and into the ground.

The money for the building and furnishings came in amazing ways, including a generous gift from an anonymous donor. An army major and his family came and helped with the electrical work, installed the heaters and even put up the curtains. The major was a very meticulous person who fitted in perfectly. A friend, Geoff Everett, who had a furnishing business came and laid the green carpet that we had chosen, and would not let us pay for it. We had fifty chairs, but Eileen had guidance that we needed more. Although we had no money, I ordered another twenty, at a cost of ten pounds each. At that time we received a cheque from a Canadian lady whom we'd never met or heard of, for £200, so they were paid for. The curtains were to be magenta and the chairs gold, but gold material was difficult to find. Eventually we discovered some material made in Germany that could be scrubbed a hundred thousand times without wearing out. We asked Geoff to use this material to cover the chairs, but he wrote back that it was too good to be used on chairs; we eventually found some thin material and sent that off instead, but weeks later Geoff responded that the company refused to make them up, because it was not thick enough. We had forgotten that God had said, *Count not the cost*, and we had the chairs covered in the original gold material from Germany. Over twenty-five years later, these chairs still look as good as new. We had learned an important lesson.

Three days before the Sanctuary was due to open, we had a phone call to come and collect a parcel at the Forres railway station. It was a beautiful weaving, a panel depicting a sunrise, designed and woven especially for us as a gift from the Donavourd weavers at Pitlochry in central Scotland. It consisted of many colours or rays leading to its centre, a wonderful focal point for our meditations in the Sanctuary and a visual reminder that all paths lead to the one Truth of God.[2]

In January 1968, Eileen came to me and said that she had been given a vision of seven mobile cedarwood bungalows to be placed on an area next door to our caravans and surrounded by beautiful gardens and banks of flowers. But it was no more than a dumping ground; I didn't see how we could fit

---

2 Patrick Liddington of the Donavourd weavers passed on the loom, pattern and method of weaving sunrise panels to members of the studio at Findhorn, which continues today to produce them

seven bungalows in that space, and there were four other caravans, a greenhouse and sheds already there. Within four days, however, by 'chance' all those caravans were removed. Another community member and I immediately spent the day measuring the area to see if seven bungalows *could* fit on the site. To our surprise we found that it was possible, and planned it so that each bungalow could see Cluny Hill out of their front windows.

On the site where these bungalows were to go was a hollow, sixteen to twenty feet below the rest of the ground, that had been used as a rubbish dump for the caravan park, as landfill to make room for more caravans. Gradually, soil was also being tipped there. I knew that we would need concrete bases and a lot of rubble. One day a lorry arrived to dump garbage, but someone told him that we didn't want it there; but as the lorry driver began to leave I told him that what we *did* need was rubble and broken concrete, and asked him if he could dump a load there. I was away the next day, and when I returned I discovered that a continual fleet of eight-wheeled trucks had come and covered the whole area with mounds of rubble, bricks and concrete. We had certainly manifested abundance.

The sites needed to be prepared first. Dennis Orme, who had come to Findhorn thinking it was only a stopping place on his way to America where they would be more receptive to his ideas about psychology, was put in charge of completing the concrete bases for the bungalows: he had said, after all, that he was looking for 'hard physical work'! It was a tremendous task to break up all this material with sledge hammers. Dennis and I did this, with Willie's help. When I asked God whom the bungalows were for, I was told that the right people would arrive at the right time. All seven bungalows arrived, and had to be paid for within seven days; and still there was no sign of whom they were for. However, when I inspected the bungalows, I found that they were in poor shape and more work needed to be done on them. I told the company that I would not pay for them until the poor workmanship had been rectified, The result was they sent a team of five workman, a joiner, an electrician, a plumber, an engineer and a supervisor. Again I asked God whom the bungalows were for, and again I was told that the right people would come at the right time. This was indeed what happened. The Ross Stewarts soon decided that they should have one. I told him of a Betty McPherson who was going to come and visit us and it turned out she was their next door neighbour, in a small village in Hampshire. Ross mentioned that she was quite a wealthy woman. Betty was a healer and came to visit the next week. She planned to come up once a month to do some healing, and wanted to buy a caravan. I showed her one of the bungalows, and she said it would do fine, and bought it straight away. Her method of healing was acupressure and she used her powerful thumbs. It was amazing that people who had complained about their aches and pains got better as soon as she arrived — her thumbs were often more painful than the ailment, as I discovered by personal experience!

Anthony Brooke bought one of the bungalows to be the headquarters of the Universal Foundation. He would spend three months with us, three months in Scandinavia, and six months travelling in the United States. God had said that the right people would come for the bungalows at the right time, and indeed they did. The wealthy benefactor to the Universal Link whom Liebie had recommended to me bought one of the seven bungalows, hoping that Eileen and I would live in it, but we felt that the time was not right so used his gift as our guest bungalow.

All seven bungalows had to be completed before we allowed their new owners to move in — everything must be perfect. The whole area around the new bungalows needed to be levelled, dug, the weeds and couch grass removed, and the garden planted with trees and shrubs and banks of flowers. This would complete Eileen's vision.

More and more people were coming all the time — and every kind of person. One woman named Mary Coulman arrived and proved to be the most negative person that I'd ever met. She found fault with everything. She said that she would never come to live in a place like Findhorn, but that she'd only come to see what it was like. But she said that if she *did* come she would only live in a particular make of caravan that she had seen, and only if it was placed on a particular site — then occupied by an RAF family who had been posted nearby for the next three-and-a-half years. Fortunately, Captain Gibson was unable to locate such a caravan and I thought, thank God for that. With a sigh of relief, I took Mary to the train to return to London. Sometime later Captain Gibson told me that he'd written to Miss Coleman and told her that he'd been able to obtain the caravan that she wanted, after all. I thought, oh no! Soon the RAF family was posted elsewhere as well, so Mary Coleman came, and for many years she continued to find fault with everybody and everything. She was our tester, because if we could love her we could love anybody. However, she did love plants, cats and children. They couldn't answer her back!

I received a letter from Martha Woeger, aged 82, from San Diego in southern California. She said that the Lord had given her the green light to come to Findhorn. I thought, how can such an elderly woman want to come from sunny California to the north of Scotland in winter? So I wrote, putting her off, but she wasn't going to be put off. She wrote again saying the Lord had told her to come and she was coming. She sent a list of things and enquired if she should bring them, and the last item was an electric fan. I replied that we weren't far from the Arctic Circle and the winds blew all year round, and that she certainly wouldn't need an electric fan — I thought that this information would stop her. But she said no, the good Lord wanted her to come, and He knew what the climate was like, so she guessed it would be all right. And of course it was all right. It was perfect. There was just the right caravan available, with central heating and double glazing. It was on the site next to ours: but it was presently occupied by a couple who were against what we were doing, and so objectionable, that Eileen had said, 'Oh well they'll have to go and find a better site'. As at Mary Coleman's site, the man had just been posted to the RAF base next door, but then Captain Gibson's assistant told me that they had decided to leave in October; in fact they moved out just a week before Martha arrived. Martha was with us for two years, and was an example to us all, with her positive enthusiasm, vitality, faith and dedication.

I was concerned that antagonism and jealousy toward Findhorn might prevent people from visiting us, particularly as two of those who were negative about us were people of considerable standing. However, St Germain through Roc reassured me that this could be put to good use, as it would separate the sheep from the goats, preventing the wrong people from coming and ensuring that the right people would visit us at the right time. Sir George Trevelyan was one of those who had been put off, but he finally came in April 1968. The timing of his visit was perfect in every way, for there was sufficient development in the garden for him to see the results of what I'd been speaking about in theory; he was also able to see that our 'financial policy' worked.

Sir George was thrilled with what he saw. He remarked that we were in a position to be able to 'go the whole hog', for we were in the world, but not of it, and we were completely free to devote ourselves to God's Will. His visit was a great tonic for all of us, particularly Dorothy, as it brought home to her the significance of her contact with the devic world. Sir George was very interested in her experience, and that Dorothy had stressed that the devas do not want to plan the garden, but cooperate with us in carrying out our designs. (This does *not* mean giving every species free rein. I once asked a young man why he had planted willowherb in one of the beds, and he replied that he had tuned in to the deva and it 'wanted' willowherb there. I replied that man creates the garden and decides what should go where, and if left to grow, willowherb will take over any place it can.)

After his visit Sir George wrote to me:

> *I am immeasurably pleased to have been to you. So many mixed comments filtered through, that one simply must see for oneself. You will have realized that I was thrilled. What is happening is important beyond all words. I realize that in the general pattern of a God-guided group, you are in a position to show us a prototype pattern. People are rarely in a position to 'go it' as completely as you do, but all of us can be inspired by the example, and many will in the coming times find, with joy, that this is the way. Then the gardening — the picture goes on surging in my mind. Factor X, the Deva/elemental conscious contact, is the most tremendous step forward, is indeed the step which mankind must take. Obviously, some tremendous individuals have already demonstrated it, Steiner for example. But for ordinary folk, to show that your little group, starting from scratch can get this help and coaching is of quite tremendous importance. You are blessed in being a team with Dorothy and Ogilvie and Eileen who make the contact consciously... conscious cooperation and communication, which makes the leap forward at Findhorn so outstanding. I shall speak about it whenever possible, since Soil Association circles should know of it where they can understand. I appreciate the continued and now heightened link with you and your daily projection of Light to us, which is reciprocated.*

From then on it seemed as if Sir George talked about the exciting things that were happening at Findhorn in almost every lecture that he gave. The result was that many people came to Findhorn to see what was happening for themselves. After his visit to Findhorn, he also wrote a memorandum to Lady Eve Balfour, the Founder and President of the influential Soil Association:

> *I write about a phenomenon of which you should be aware. At Easter I stayed with Peter Caddy, who lives with a small group of friends on the caravan site on Findhorn Bay in Morayshire. There caravans are surrounded by a lovely garden. There were daffodils and narcissi, as beautiful and large as I have ever seen, growing in beds crowded with other flowers. I was fed on the best vegetables I have ever tasted. A young chestnut tree, 8 feet high, stood as a central feature, bursting with astonishing power and vigour. Fruit trees of all sorts were in blossom - in short one of the most vigorous and productive of small gardens I have ever seen, with a quality of taste and colour unsurpassed. Many species of broad leaved trees and shrubs are planted and thriving, yet the caravan site is on the landward slope of the dunes. The soil is simply sand and gravel on which grows spiky grass. Exactly opposite them is Culbin Sands where after 50 years of growing, conifers have rooted and held the dunes so that tough grass can begin now to root. Other folk on the caravan site, seeing the lovely burgeoning around their neighbours' caravans, put in cabbages and daffodils which come up as miserable specimens. Caddy claims to have grown a 42 lb. cabbage. He brings in straw and other ingredients and makes compost. Some beds are liberally mulched and composted, though some seem to strive with only a modest amount mixed into the sand.*

Soon Sir George called a conference of the leading associations of those connected with the soil, like the Biodynamic Association, and the Soil Association, to consider 'Factor X', as he called it — cooperation with the devas and the nature spirits.

Another important visitor to Findhorn was Richard St Barbe-Baker, conservationist, forester, founder of Men of the Trees, and an author. He worked with President Franklin Roosevelt to establish the Civilian Conservation Corps, which involved six million youths. He also started the Save the Redwoods campaign in California, and was instrumental in the planting of over 26 trillion trees internationally, by organizations he founded or helped. St Barbe-Baker spent his whole life encouraging people to care for the trees, as if they were our elder brothers, for when we fell trees we sow the seeds of future deserts. I first met him at a conference at Attingham, where he was being honoured for *Sahara Conquest*, just acclaimed as the Book of the Month. At the time I thought that he was only interested in trees, not spiritual matters. However, sometime later I wrote to him in New Zealand with a copy of *God Spoke to Me*, and shared news of our experiments in the garden. To my delight, I discovered that he also put the spiritual life first — in fact he was a Baha'i[3] — and he came to visit Findhorn soon after my letter.

St Barbe-Baker had long been aware of the forces of nature and the help he received from them. On his first visit Dorothy received a message from one of the tree devas,

> *There is high rejoicing in our kingdoms, as the Man of the Trees, so beloved of us, links with you here. Is it not an example in your world, that it is one work, one cause under God being expressed through different channels. You understand better now why we've gone on and on about the need for trees on the surface of the earth. Great forests must flourish and man must see to this, if he wishes to continue to live on this planet. The knowledge of this necessity must become part of his consciousness, as much accepted as he needs water with which to live. He needs trees just as much. The two are linked. We are indeed the skin of the earth, and the skin not only covers and protects, but passes through it the forces of life. Nothing could be more vital to life as a whole than trees, trees and more trees.*

After his visit, St Barbe-Baker gave us the full support of himself and the Men of the Trees. He was a remarkable man. One was struck not only by his single-mindedness, but also by his seemingly endless energy. St Barbe-Baker visited the community many times, and inspired us in our work and imbued us with his unique warmth.[4] He gave us a great deal of practical advice on the planting of trees, and designed shelter belts that worked to protect us from the strong Scottish winds. At one point he suggested that we move the entire community to the Sahara, and establish ourselves there in caravans to help reclaim the desert. He even wrote to the Director-General of the FAO, Baron Porcelli, asking him to provide suitable caravans for us!

---

3 Follower of an Eastern religion founded last century and working for the peace and unification of mankind

4 Findhorn Press later published his autobiography, *My Life My Trees* (see bibliography)

He was disappointed when I respectfully declined, saying that our work was to remain based at Findhorn.

Thanks to the support of these and other worthies who came at the time — and in particular to the enthusiastic endorsement of Sir George — our little caravan park community was indeed developing the 'world renown' that Eileen's guidance had promised.

Chapter 25

Many Hands Make Light Work

When each and every one realizes unity, he will not ask who is standing on the right or left, but welcome all, and give a helping hand to his fellow brothers

WE FELT THAT IT WAS TIME that we became a non-profit foundation. Bob Copley, an English solicitor with a spiritual background, undertook to launch us as a trust; he had been astonished to find that we didn't own the land upon which we had already built our Sanctuary, office and other buildings, not to mention the garden itself! He was most disturbed that we had no security, but when I told him that our security was in God, he replied, 'Oh that's not good enough'. As a solicitor he had seen others lose everything in similar circumstances. Bearing in mind Wellington's dictum to 'trust God but keep your powder dry', I asked him to proceed, but told him that I felt Captain Gibson, owner of the caravan park, would never agree to a lease. One evening Bob was not at dinner: he had gone to see the Gibsons, where he used his considerable charm (including kissing Mrs Gibson's hand) to obtain their agreement to a 21-year lease. When the agreement was signed, Bob said, 'I'm going to pay your legal fees — it was worth it to prove you wrong!'

We were also receiving so many enquiries about the garden that, with Sir George's encouragement and active assistance, we began the writing and production of three little books detailing the roles that humans, the devas and the nature spirits were playing in our 'experiment in cooperation between the three kingdoms'. Collectively we published these as *The Findhorn Garden,* with a foreword by Sir George and testaments from several of the soil and gardening experts who had come and proved the results for themselves. Eventually a much-expanded version of the book, with photographs, was published by Harper and Row.

We were scarcely prepared for the next strange and exotic appearance and growth in the garden, however: 'the flower people'. In 1968 I received a letter from a Neil Oram, and it had no return address: he had purposely omitted to give an address, because he said that he was coming to Findhorn with his wife and daughter and did not want me to tell him not to come. They arrived some days later at 10 o'clock at night, bubbling with excitement — but to my dismay, they were dirty and dishevelled hippies. Neil had long matted hair, and they all smelt, since they had been living rough with gypsies. They wanted immediately to go and meditate in the Sanctuary, while their little girl ran all over our beautiful golden chairs. Joanie would not allow them into a caravan until they had bathed, which they eventually did, though Neil would not wash his hair until after a battle of wills with Joanie (that he naturally lost). Living with this family was a test that helped us all to learn many lessons. On our part, we had to learn tolerance and understanding, and an appreciation of the childlike, loving simplicity of the flower people. They had to learn that dirty, torn and slovenly clothes were not acceptable at Findhorn, particularly in the Sanctuary.

Some months earlier, Roc had enjoyed a long discussion with another young hippie who had arrived at Findhorn, and it became apparent to him that the hippies felt that they *were* the New Age, and that anybody else, over the age of twenty-five, who dressed normally or had short hair were of the old and couldn't move into the new. It seemed that they had rejected the older generation, its values and way of life, and therefore had avoided contact with the various spiritual movements and Centres of Light; but having dropped out of one society, they hadn't yet found anything with which to replace it and tended to live a negative life in rather squalid conditions.

After this conversation, Roc received guidance from higher realms that it was important that *both* sides reach for understanding and tolerance. He said that the hippies must eventually merge with those who were older or seemed more traditional, and that this would happen at Findhorn. My heart sank as we were told that where these two streams merged, there would be a certain amount of turbulence, but eventually there would be harmony.

Joanie in particular was concerned, as we were expecting the Ross Stewarts to arrive for a visit and she felt that we should ask Neil and his family to leave beforehand. Eileen sought guidance on this and was assured that all was well, and to leave the mixing of people in God's hands. All was indeed well: for when Ross, the retired naval captain, met shaggy Neil, they smiled at each other and got into deep conversation about the things that really matter — and became firm friends in the process.

I did not fare so well with Neil. He was quite a well-known poet amongst his friends and he loved talking all day; he was also a leader and didn't agree with the way that I was running the community. Finally I had to very lovingly but directly explain to him that if he really thought that he knew how to run a group, he should go off and start his own. He was not to start doing it at Findhorn, but he could go elsewhere and put his ideas into practice there. There can only be one leader in a group, I explained, and I was the leader at Findhorn. I told him that he was creating dissension, and pointed out that he was pulling some people off beam by talking too much. Well he didn't go, and finally Eileen put all their possessions in a pram, put it in the back of the car, and drove them to the outskirts of Forres. There she pointed the pram in the direction of Inverness and sent them on their way. Eventually they found near Loch Ness a derelict house which they turned into a centre.

A short time later, a girl named Sabina arrived. Sabina was in her early twenties and had been running her grandmother's farm in Ireland with a half dozen hippie friends. Their group-living experience failed and she had returned to London, but she'd felt an impulse to come to Findhorn to learn about group living. She hitchhiked to Findhorn from London with her three-and-a-half-year-old son. There was a snowstorm and it took them two days, but when I contacted her friend in London to tell him of her safe arrival, having assumed she'd be returning their shortly, he said it would be better if she remained at Findhorn: 'For as long as you can stick her, and she can put up with you'. She was at Findhorn for several years and learned many lessons, as our ways were strange to her, and hers were to us. But under God's guidance and with the great love that grew up between us all, necessary compromises were made so that we had harmony and oneness.

Shortly after her arrival Sabina discovered that she was pregnant. She and her son were living in a one-bedroom caravan, with a toilet but no separate bathroom. She had heard of the 'laws of manifestation' and decided to visualize a caravan with another bedroom and a bathroom, and we agreed that it was a very good thing to do. She made her needs known, and to her overwhelming joy, within a few days she received a cheque for £200. Just at that time, a person who'd bought a caravan decided not to come. Joanie, our generous and loving treasurer, said that she would buy it for Sabina and told Sabina that she could repay her as she manifested the rest of the money. She moved in but it was clear that she did not appreciate her new caravan. In no time it became a pigsty — it was dirty and chaotic. Two days after she moved in, the cheque was unexpectedly cancelled.

Sabina was very upset over this. Some months later, there were several messages, through Eileen and Dorothy and others, about the importance of expressing gratitude. The laws of manifestation, as I have learnt them, include giving thanks to the donor and to God, the giver of all good and perfect gifts. Also, as an expression of this gratitude, it is important to love and cherish and look after what one has been given. It dawned on me why Sabina had not manifested any more money: she had never thanked Joanie for the caravan, nor did she look after it. I therefore took the caravan away from Sabina, and she had to return to the old one and make do with that. She put posters all around the caravan, which said ***I must express gratitude***. She had learnt her lesson, that if one does not express gratitude, the supply is cut off.[1]

John Michell, author of *The View Over Atlantis* and other books, was an inspiration to many youth, with his accounts of the mystical traditions and earth mysteries of Britain and elsewhere. He had been educated at Eton and Cambridge and was highly intelligent — but he had also adopted the dress and style of a hippie. I felt that the time had come for him to meet some of the older leaders of the New Age movement. Roc and I were to meet Sir George Trevelyan on a visit to Major Bruce MacManaway, who was giving Sir George healing, so I invited John Michell to join us. Roc and I met him at the railway station, and took him to the MacManaways — whereupon Bruce met us at his front door, looked John up and down and said, 'Would you like a bath?' John replied, politely enough, that he was fine. Before long Sir George and John both recognized in each other a scholarly approach to spiritual truths, and got along very well. Eventually Bruce also warmed to John, and even invited him to give a lecture to a number of highly respected people at the Dowsers Association's annual conference. Many of his group had been drawn together because they had received healing from Bruce, including the general commanding the army in Scotland; after his talk, John received many more invitations to speak. He wrote to me saying, 'As our numbers increase, misunderstanding can easily arise among those who approach the same goal from quite different directions, using ways that seem good to them, but not to others'.

---

[1] For several years, every autumn we seemed to experience a financial crisis in the community — causing the membership to examine itself to see how well we were applying the laws of manifestation. For example, were we expressing gratitude? Were we looking after what we'd been given? Have the tools been well cleaned and put away?

I shared with Sir George a vision that Eileen had had of him on a white horse, clad in armour with a sword in his hand. It came to me that he was the perfect one to relate with the hippies at an upcoming course at Attingham, 'The Allegorical Journey', covering everything from Homer's *Odyssey* to Tolkien's *The Lord of the Rings* — the latter being especially popular with the hippies. Indeed a troupe of them, in full regalia, did appear and sit at the back. After the lecture they approached Sir George and told him that his talk was just what they were looking for, and they hadn't known that anyone in the older generation spoke their language. When the idea was raised of holding a similar course for them, they were very enthusiastic and offered to fill the house with their friends. This was agreed, and sixty-five of them later gathered at Attingham; those attending found that Sir George crystallized their hopes and ideas in words they could understand, and he also inspired and uplifted them. It was apparent to Sir George that the youth, because of their rejection of society, had not had the opportunity to learn of the various activities taking place on the spiritual front in the world, and particularly in Britain. (For example, none of them had visited Chalice Well in Glastonbury, because to them it was middle-aged, middle-class and respectable, and thus to be avoided at all costs!) But more and more of those who dropped out of society were drawn to Findhorn, and we worked to bring understanding between the two generations. Ross Stewart, now our Chairman of Trustees, was of invaluable help, because of his vast store of experience and his love for young people.

As like attract likes, we found that we had a stream of hippies, hitchhiking to Findhorn from the South: the word had gone around that Findhorn was a place where they could find accommodation and everything would be supplied. We still had numerous problems to solve, as we were a working group and all had to contribute, both financially and with skills and gifts. We needed dedicated people, capable of making a useful contribution, whether it be in the office, the garden, cooking, plumbing, electrical work, etc. Because they'd dropped out of society before their educational training was completed, most of our 'flower children' were usually unqualified and had no experience or skills to contribute. They wanted to live in communities, but didn't have the practical experience to be able to do so. They could not all remain with us, and had difficulty starting their own centres. When one young man arrived, I asked him if he could dig the garden, and he replied, 'Yeah, I can dig anything', so I handed him a spade and pointed to the ground that needed digging — but that had not been his interpretation of the word 'dig', and he soon tired and left.

It was not by chance that another young man arrived at Findhorn. He too had 'dropped out'. One night he'd been lying in bed, in terrible confusion about the way to lead himself and other young people out of the chaos manifesting all over the world, when he finally heard a voice say, 'Come to Findhorn'. But he did not come immediately, for he did not believe that inner voice; instead he tried to analyse the experience logically. In the weeks that followed, everything collapsed around him and he was left without any money and nowhere to live; his prospects, and those of his friends, seemed quite grim. He travelled around and visited many communities, and found many who seemed to be suffering in their battle for survival and sanity. What he didn't realize was that this suffering was of great importance, as it helped strip away everything.

Eventually he found himself at Findhorn, the place to which his inner voice had guided him. 'I know now,' he said, 'That I ought to have obeyed immediately. Had I done so, I should not have had to spend those weeks struggling under the illusion that we are the only children of the New Age.' What he found at Findhorn amazed him: a group of spiritually attuned people, of *all* ages, working under the direct influence of God. We had learned to manifest the visions that had been given us onto the material level. He grasped the fact that work is Love made manifest. He also discovered that Findhorn was only one centre in a vast global Network of Light, composed of individuals and groups who were working to raise the level of human consciousness to the highest to bring in the New Age. By dropping out of straight society, he recognized that hippies had often lost contact with their true spiritual development, also rejecting the very people who had worked so hard in building the early foundations of the New Age. He saw that our discipline had given us the experience and strength to carry out, in the face of formidable negative forces, the vast work ahead. He said, 'We must learn to see through the various masks of personality that great souls have adopted, in order to work on Earth, and not brand all 'straight' people as negative. So many of us, although aspiring to a spiritual life, live in conditions of squalor and have become lethargic'. He went on to say that so many of his generation, after receiving a vision (through the use of LSD or other drugs) of what has to be done in the future, had merely 'sat back, viewing the surrounding chaos and upheaval, echoing the words "impossible, impossible". He continued by saying that we must not only reject — because rejection results in being without anything. We must also realize that all is in the hands of the infinite, but it is up to the free will of each human being, whether or not he plays a part in building the New Age. The New Age needs hippies and dropouts, who have received a vision of a truly harmonious world, based upon the laws of love and wisdom. But it also needs those of every age, who are going to use their various gifts and develop them to the utmost, and applies the skills of actually building.'

He concluded that now the New Age had dawned, it was time for all involved to forget about personality differences — *all* old ways may have to go. He believed that 'straight' society would have to give up its materialism and outworn traditions, and hippies would have to forget about drugs and all-night living. His visit gave us all food for thought: the implication was that it was no longer a question of the old and young, but that the real division was between those of the old and those of the new. This understanding was one of the most valuable insights I have had into the so-called generation gap.

* * *

Early in 1969, I had a telephone call from the BBC, wanting to include us in a television documentary about alternative ways of life; I declined, because I felt that we were not ready for publicity on such a mass scale. Later that day Eileen had guidance that we were no longer to hide our light under a bushel. I then had a telephone call from a Shirley Fisher, who was doing the research for the BBC programme, and she said that she 'happened' to be coming to Scotland and wanted to meet us anyway. Eileen's guidance went on to promise us that 'great good' would come out of the interview, and that our prototype of group living would be followed by 'thousands upon thousands'.

Shirley Fisher spent a whole day with us, and explained that many people felt that the answers to today's problems lay in group living, but did not know how to go about it. Several weeks previously she had set out with a list of dozens of groups that had been given to her, but to her frustration she had found that the majority of them were all talk, had ceased to exist or had moved. She was surprised to find us so well established in contrast to others. A group in Wales, for example, had been written up as having 300 members. She went expecting to find thirty, but in fact there were only three, and she felt that two of them were fit for a mental home. Then at the eleventh hour she'd discovered our community.

I pointed out that it was a pity to film Findhorn in the winter, but she explained that she wanted to show groups as they really are, under the most adverse conditions. Many groups sprung up in the summer when everything looked lovely and people camped out in tents, and this is how 'flash-in-the pan' groups flourished, only to die when the winter came. I reversed my earlier decision and agreed for the production to go ahead.

On 2 February, two days before the team was due to arrive, we were in the middle of a blizzard which had raged for two days. In several bungalows the water pipes were frozen, and it seemed that the visit by the BBC would best be postponed. The garden, in particular — one of the most important features of Findhorn — was covered with snow. Eileen had guidance that I was to telephone the producer, tell him the conditions, and let the BBC make their own decision, which we would abide by. The BBC delayed their decision until the following morning, the time of their proposed departure from London; when they telephoned me I told them that it was still snowing and we were frozen up. In fact, it was more like a freezing hell on Earth than heaven! Their decision was to come, as there were no guarantees that it would be better the following week. Just before the telephone call Eileen had guidance to the effect that things weren't always what they seemed: *My ways are not always man's ways. But remember My ways are perfect. Put all in My Hands and all will work out perfectly.* We therefore left everything in God's Hands. That evening the weather turned warm, and by the time the BBC team arrived, on the morning of 4 February, the snow had gone, and the sun was shining — it was a perfect day. We agreed with the producer that community life would carry on as usual, and let them film what they wanted. This included the morning session in our Sanctuary. We were slightly apprehensive about this, but Eileen received, *Rest assured, all is going perfectly. Those who are in charge of this operation are very sensitive, so be at peace.* The experience was simply tremendous, and we were able to rise above the television lights and whirring cameras.

The next day they wanted to interview me in the greenhouse, but Eileen resisted: she had guidance that she should do it, that God needed vocal cords to speak through. The interview went so well that Harold Williamson, the interviewer, was quite overcome. He told us that he'd never experienced anything similar: there was a radiance that shone from Eileen, and he said she appeared to speak without thinking what she was going to say. And afterwards Eileen could not remember anything she *had* said. On the final morning of filming we went down to Findhorn Bay to take photos of the brilliant blue sea and sky, and there was another interview with me. No sooner had they finished than the sky darkened and we had another blizzard. God's timing had indeed been perfect; we'd had three warm, sunny days in between weeks of snow and frost.

Shortly before the programme was shown on television, Harold Williamson phoned me to say that all the barbed questions had been cut out, because our answers were so charming that it showed them (the BBC) in an unfavourable light. Such an experience was almost unprecedented, he explained, as normally they strove to present both sides; but in this case the film was almost entirely sympathetic to Findhorn.

There was a wonderful response to the BBC show, with hardly a negative letter. Our correspondence and guest numbers grew ever larger, and people were requesting news of Findhorn, so we decided to publish a regular periodical, *Findhorn News*. The press were also hungry for information, so I wrote *The Findhorn Story*, and made it available. In this way I hoped to avoid sensationalism and inaccuracies.

Although we were only about ten permanent members of the community at that time, we had guest accommodation for over thirty others and it was no longer practical for us all to dine in Joanie's bungalow as we had been. After the 'hippie invasion' began, St Germain through Roc insisted that we dine in a civilized manner, that we wash and change beforehand, that the table appointments were of the best, and that we ate in beautiful surroundings. Of course, Joanie was able to offer all these — except the space for us all — and even when we spilled over into Betty McPherson's bungalow there was still not room for everyone.

After lunch one day, Betty said that she wanted a word with me. For some time she'd been thinking that the time was fast approaching when we'd need a central kitchen and dining room for the community, and she was prepared to help financially. This was confirmed for her at lunchtime, when there had been thirty for the meal, which we'd had outside in the sunshine — what would have happened had it rained? I agreed, so we immediately looked for a suitable site and decided that the empty space on the other side of the road from the driveway to the Sanctuary would be ideal. We found that we could fit a building, 30 feet by 40 feet, into that area. I sought and received the approval of the owner of the site. Later that day Eileen received,

> *This community centre had to come. See it as a place of beauty, as well as utility. Do not be satisfied with just anything. Everything is being done for me, and therefore must be of the best. So be not satisfied with anything shoddy. I will provide all your needs, and the hands to build it and run it.*

I contacted the Planning Officer at once, and we discovered that the complete plans would have to be in by the following day for the next Planning Committee meeting — otherwise, we would have to wait for three months. He said that if I went round to his office he would tell me what was required. I drove to Elgin, about 15 miles away, and was told that they needed six copies of our plan. Plan? I said, 'How am I to get six copies of the plan in by tomorrow?' I was told that if I brought the plans in they would photograph them on their machine. I then enquired if they knew an architect who could draw up the plans by the next day. The staff looked at each other in bemusement — I think they considered me a nut case. (Since then, I've discovered that an architect would normally take about nine months to get the plans through for a building like the one we wanted!) So they smiled at me indulgently and said that they didn't know of such an architect.

I returned to Findhorn and asked Eileen to get some guidance on all this. We were told that now was the time for us to have a community centre, and it was to be one of the very best, and no expense was to be spared to make it so. Also, that God would meet our needs from His limitless supply. I asked what architect I was to get to design the community centre and draw up the plans. I was told, *Peter is to design it himself, and not get outside help. He knows what is needed more than anyone. Therefore, he is to design it.* I was also told that the kitchen was to cater for 200 and the dining room designed and constructed so that it could be extended later. I designed it in one evening, and it is interesting that if I had to do it over I wouldn't change anything. Some of the details were not put down, but we worked them out as we went along.

Later that evening I took the rough plans to a girl in the Sectional Builders Office, and asked her if she could redraw and improve it for the next day's meeting of the Planning Committee. She did, and I took them to the Planning Officer — only to be told that we needed building permission as well, and *that* committee wasn't meeting for another six weeks. I therefore phoned the official Building Inspector and asked him to come over straight away. I presented the plans to him and asked him to write on them what specifications the committee would require — for example, how thick should the concrete be, where the drains should go, and if we needed a septic tank. In fact, the building had already been erected by the time we had permission to build it! But we'd known that all would be well, since the Building Inspector himself had told us what we would need and would hardly be expected to reject his own recommendations.

One day around this time I overheard two new members of our community talking about the laws of manifestation and expressing doubt about them. I explained how everything at Findhorn had been manifested. First we were given a vision or guidance, and then we would go ahead in faith, knowing that God would meet our needs. Never did we have the money first. One of them looked at me doubtfully and said, 'Well, if the money comes for the community centre, which will cost thousands of pounds, *then* I will believe it'. Later that morning, when we were offered a sum of money that we thought would be sufficient to cover the cost of the building, our doubting ones were speechless. But we too were dumbstruck when we received the estimate for the construction of the building alone, as it was for £3800, far more than we had anticipated. This didn't take into account the expense of kitchen equipment, dining room furnishings, painting, heating, lighting, etc. We wondered whether we should rethink the whole project, and possibly have it constructed in a less expensive material than cedarwood, like concrete blocks or stone. But everything seemed to be right and all had gone smoothly. Eileen sought guidance:

> *Fear not, little flock, for it is My good pleasure to give you the Kingdom, and when the Kingdom includes a community centre, a community centre of the very best will be forthcoming. Go ahead in absolute faith and confidence and order it. Step by step all the needs for the community centre will be met. Never limit Me in any way. I want only the very best. What is being done will have very far reaching results. So feel yourself expand with all that is taking place. It is definitely to be a cedarwood building, the dining hall should be carpeted and really comfortable. For it will be used for many different occasions, not just for feeding. All is very well, so give eternal thanks, and see it come about.*

A few weeks later, our friend said that she had sold some jewellery and would increase her contribution from £3,000 to £5,000. This still did not cover the final entire cost of £10,000, but we knew that God would meet our needs, through His channels, one way or another. Kitchen equipment was ordered. We started off with a minimum, but the best. Carpeting and curtains were chosen, but we were still concerned about the cost. We again received reassurance, *I tell you your every need will be wonderfully met regarding the community centre. Do not skimp in any way, over anything. Draw from My limitless abundant supply, and expect the very very best. All is being done to My honour and glory. So you all may see My hand in everything.* One day Joanie, our treasurer, came to me and said that she had two big bills of great expense to pay, and we had no money. I was spending the money and had the faith that there would be more, but Joanie had to pay the bills. She said, 'We've got these big bills coming in. There are only ten members in the community. We really don't need the great big potato peeler, or a large Hobart Mixer, and we certainly don't need a hot plate. We can serve from the stove. Should we not get these later?' I considered the matter and said, 'No, Joanie, we've been given detailed guidance about this community centre, and the promise that all our needs would be met. So we go ahead in faith.' Her face fell and she left shaking her head. I think her heart sank. The very next day she received a letter from a lady whom we'd never heard of, who said that she'd just received a copy of a Findhorn publication and was so impressed by it. By the same post she'd been given a gift of 3000 shares, and said that obviously they were meant for us. Joanie sold them for £650, the exact amount of money of the outstanding bills.

One has to be very careful what one says and thinks, particularly in a Centre of Light, for through the power of thought whatever one thinks is speedily brought about. For example, we jokingly said that if we went on expanding, we would have coach parties arriving — and sure enough we had a letter from a society in Aberdeen, saying that after Sir George and Bruce MacManaway had both given lectures and talked to them about the Findhorn Community, they wanted to bring a party of forty-seven to visit on 15 June. Joanie, who always provided tea for visitors, visualized the party in her bungalow for tea, and demanded that the community centre be finished by that date. We had only six weeks time, and it didn't seem humanly possible but with God, all things are possible. Just the right people and materials became available at the right time. For example, we had a heating engineer, who was a trained electrician and plumber, join the community for six months; but his wife had a dreadful laugh, and she was encouraged to have her meals in her own bungalow. I wondered what we were going to do about that laugh when we all moved into the new dining room. Then I remembered the dining room at Attingham Park Adult Education College, where one had to shout to be heard, so at great expense I decided to put in a sound-absorbent ceiling. The lady with the laugh left two days after the ceiling was completed! I felt that the good Lord had even used a laugh to ensure that we had the perfect: I certainly wouldn't have thought of the sound-proofing otherwise.

It was a wonderful experience going out and buying only the best of everything, like all stainless steel for the kitchen. (It had to be the most suitable, though not necessarily the most expensive.) Geoff Everett obtained the best tables for us at cost price but they went missing during shipment. At the same time Geoff had a visit from the head of a furniture manufacturing company, and asked him if he could make ten tables like the ones that we had ordered, and deliver them to the north of Scotland in two weeks. He said that he would deliver them himself, if we could give him accommodation overnight, as his wife hadn't had a holiday for four years. So we got our tables at the right time.

The community centre was finished on the evening of 14 June, ready to serve dinner for thirty-two, and prepared for the coach party the next day. It seemed a miracle, but we had been taught to expect (and then accept) miracles.

A large patio, with a lawn and garden, was constructed just outside for use in the warm weather. The whole was enclosed by an interwoven fence. We sowed the lawn in November, the wrong season, particularly in that climate. It did grow though, and the right man came to help with it: by profession a greenkeeper, he had just lost his only son, and had come to Findhorn for three weeks to bury himself in work. He taught the whole community how to maintain a lawn, and for the next three weeks he had us think only of lawns.

About five days before he left, another great enthusiast came, Donald Wilson, Founder-Secretary of the Soil Association, and a compost fanatic. When Donald came no one was allowed to think about anything except compost. For him, it was the be-all and end-all of gardening. Donald was surprised that we had so many young women with us, as he'd expected men to make the compost; when Martha, our 82-year-old member, heard of this, she said, 'Lord, we need young men, to make this compost. Send them.' That night they started to arrive from all over the place, and by the next day we had seven young men to do the heavy work of making the compost. One of these men was an architect, and I remember seeing him up to his knees in pig manure, sewage sludge and seaweed, and I thought, I wonder what he'll think of this place. Two months later he wrote that the time he'd spent at Findhorn making compost was the happiest time of his life.

There was one more happy manifestation that year, for Eileen, the boys and myself. Merta Mary Parkinson had visited us and on her return home she wrote that she felt that I was not applying the laws of manifestation to myself and family in connection with our accommodation. She felt that it was of vital importance to the community and to the work that we have a bungalow, as the work hinged on Eileen and myself. She felt that we should have accommodation at least equal to the best, instead of being crammed into the worst — it was wrong for six of us to live in the only caravan without a flush toilet. I wrote back that we were doing fine.

Eileen, however, had also been saying that the boys had grown much bigger and needed more room, and that it was time for us to move into a bungalow. I felt that we could continue as we were. But the next day I had to lie down on one of the boy's beds, as I had gallstone trouble, and I saw for myself how small the space was. Then I moved to my own bed in the sitting room, and Ross Stewart visited me there. He had never seen our cramped conditions, and was appalled. The next morning his wife Aileen came to say that she'd had guidance in the Sanctuary that she was to help provide us with another caravan, alongside, to give us more accommodation; we expressed our appreciation, but I pointed out that this wasn't feasible, as there was not any room for another caravan. That day, while lying in bed, I pondered on the question of a bungalow. Then I realized that there was a spare site opposite the Universal bungalow, beside the road, in the centre of the community; but we could not find the perfect bungalow to put there, with an additional room to allow sufficient space for the three boys.

Then Mrs Gibson, the joint owner of the caravan park, who knew of our need, came over in an excited state with a letter from a manufacturer who had written to say that they had one special model left, which would accommodate all of us, and it could be delivered right away. In the meantime, Joanie had written a letter to all those on the mailing list, saying that she felt that we needed better accommodation than the little caravan we'd been living in; so we went ahead in faith, and I gathered about twenty people to clear the site and lay the concrete, just in time for the bungalow's arrival.

Many people contributed to both the buying and furnishing of the bungalow. We had a housewarming party on 5 November, Guy Fawkes night, and finally moved in on New Year's Eve.

A Unity minister from the United States, had visited us a short time before. And one of his sayings was, 'When you put your hand in the Lord's, hold on to your hat with the other hand!'. Over and over again we had found this saying to be true.

Chapter 26

Revelation

I plant only on prepared ground.
I will sow thought seeds freely, and they will sprout where there is depth of soil

DURING 1970 the group expanded from 17 members into a community of 42 adults and 9 children, and we had over 500 visitors spending a night or longer. Whereas in previous years the accent had been on material expansion of the garden, caravans and community buildings, this year it was definitely on people. *There is a tremendous feeling of expansion in the air*, said Eileen's guidance. *As your consciousness expands so does your horizon, until you realize there is just no limitation to what can and will come about.* We had proved what could be achieved in growing plants; our work was now to concentrate on growing people.

I am often asked why the garden at Findhorn stopped producing the extraordinary specimens (like 42-pound cabbages) that had first secured its fame. Some people suppose that they were just the freak products of a single season; others suggest that as I withdrew my primary attention from the garden to concentrate on organizing and running the community, those who succeeded me in the garden lacked the same relationship with it. Both suggestions are wrong. Quite aside from the fact that our astonishing specimens were not limited to a single season, I feel that the devas and nature spirits had proven their point about the need for cooperation, and it was no longer necessary to produce outsize advertisements for it. The garden reverted to growing healthy, normal-sized vegetables, just as vital, nourishing and delicious as ever, and although after years of compost we were gradually building up the soil, it was still a remarkable (if more understated) achievement. Besides, if people came all the way to us just to gawp at fat cabbages or hope for a fleeting view of pixies among the pansies they would be missing the whole point of our work, which was to demonstrate in *all* aspects of life what is possible when God is put first.

Looking back, it is remarkable to see how quickly the Findhorn Community assembled itself, so to speak, guided only by my intuition, Eileen's messages and Dorothy's clarity — as if God had given us a paint-by-numbers picture and it was simply our job to ensure that the right colours were applied in the right places. This required faith, obedience and discipline — and of course a lot of hard work, but when one is in the right place at the right time doing the right thing, with the right attitude, the reserves of energy available are tremendous, and hard work seems more like fun. The 'big picture' sketched out in Eileen's guidance was breathtaking — *It has started as a family group, is now a community, will grow into a village, then into a town and finally into a vast City of Light* — when even the immediate view seemed way beyond our resources.

For example, around this time Eileen received a vision that the large and chiefly neglected area of the caravan park called Pineridge, which was to the north east of the central area and reached by a spur road that ran between a farm and a plantation of firs, was to house four craft studios and yet more bungalows. This excited me, of course, but it also puzzled me. Where were these artists and craftsmen supposed to come from?

In the event, they were drawn to us very quickly. Shortly after Eileen's vision, I received a letter in August 1969 from a man who had read about us in (of all places) *The News of the World*[1]. He explained that he was one of a group of seven people who had been receiving guidance that they should form a community somewhere in the wilds of the Cairngorm mountains, not too far from Forres. He went on to write that they were nearly all artists and craftsmen...

The group then started getting guidance that they should come to Findhorn instead, but none of them wanted to do so. The guidance persisted, as did their resistance, until the group itself faced self-destruction. Finally Ken resigned his teaching job in the north of England and applied for another one in Nairnshire, close to Findhorn, although he and his wife Kate still had no intention of joining our community. When he drove up for the job interview, however, his car broke down a few miles outside Forres and he rang me to ask if he could spend the night: in fact it took a week for the car to be repaired, and during that time Ken had a powerful realization that he and his group belonged with us.

---

1 A racy Sunday tabloid newspaper usually more interested in naughty vicars and women's breasts

Two others in the group, Jonathan and Dorothy Snell, quickly followed. A third, Brian Nobbs — an experienced printer, potter, and arts teacher (and an excellent cook!) — had deeper doubts: he had been a Benedictine monk for five years and wondered whether his Roman Catholicism would permit him to join our spiritual work. Despite reassurances from the prior at his former abbey on the Isle of Wight that we did seem to be divinely guided, Brian's soul-searching continued. He longed to talk it over with Canon Andrew Glazewski, whom he respected greatly, but came up to Findhorn anyway to check us out. As he arrived on a Sunday, Brian's first thoughts were where he was going to attend Mass: imagine his surprise and delight to find Canon Glazewski about to say his daily Mass in our Sanctuary! Brian's remaining doubts quickly fled during their talk afterwards.

The sudden influx of artists and craftsmen continued to surprise me, and they often arrived in the most unexpected ways. One fine spring day, a team of ten people had been digging away a ten-foot high sand bank to make room for the new printing office. The builder was coming the next morning to lay the concrete base, so after teatime I made a final measurement and found to my dismay that the space was still two feet short — and by this time, members of the team had gone home to their caravans and were anyway too exhausted to continue. Sadly, I got into the car and drove off to Forres to postpone the builder.

On the road, I spied a colourful character headed for Findhorn — in those days the hippies stood out like birds of paradise against the soft hues of the Moray landscape, and they would almost invariably be coming to us to roost — so I immediately pressed him into service with a spade to complete the job. It was obvious that Ian knew what he was doing (he had been working in the Parks Department in Lancashire), so when he had finished the printing office site, I put him to work helping plant several hundred trees, a job that I couldn't manage alone. Then I discovered that he had hitchhiked and walked all the way from the south of England, arriving tired, hungry and thirsty, and I hadn't even offered him a cup of tea! Nevertheless he decided to join us with his new wife, Carol, a trained typist (which we also needed), and after several months of working in the garden, Ian surprised us all by revealing that he was a professional pianist and budding composer.

With regards to our many visitors and new members Eileen received,

> *Many will come here, will see what is being done, and will want to contribute their specific gifts to the whole. There are*

many fields which have not yet been explored. The experts will come and will give and will give willingly. There is as yet an untapped source of wisdom and knowledge waiting to be drawn upon. Every aspect of the work is still in its infancy.

Expert help and advice continued to arrive for the studios. Elizabeth Grindley, an architect and Radionics[2] practitioner was coming for Easter; I wondered if she would be the right one to design a pottery for us. I wrote to two experienced potters whom I knew from my travels, John Shelley and Mary Jackson, asking for their suggestions which arrived on Good Friday, a day ahead of Elizabeth. When she arrived, I asked her if she knew anything about potteries; to my delight she told me that she came from a long line of potters, lived in the pottery country of England and had designed many potteries. She was perfect for the job and spent most of her holiday weekend with us drawing out the plans. When Monday came, however, and it was time for her to leave, she was still not happy with the results, because she lacked the necessary measurements of the equipment to be installed.

It seemed doubtful that the plans could be completed in time for the Planning Committee's deadline the next day. But half an hour after Elizabeth left, Pat Johnson, a skilled potter from Glasgow arrived, and 'by chance' had brought the measurements of her own equipment and some catalogues of pottery equipment. So during the rest of the day Pat completed the plans.

Two visiting architects planned the layout and landscaping of the arts and crafts centre and its surrounds, so that I was able to apply for planning permission for both that and the pottery, and in principle for the weaving studio and a building for music and drama. Much to my surprise, planning permission was refused on the grounds that a caravan site is licensed for caravans only. Eileen received,

There are many vitally important lessons, which have to be learnt, and principles to be put into practice, in order to enable the seemingly impossible to become possible. Without patience, persistence and perseverance you will get nowhere. You must never take no for an answer. Never accept second best when the best is there being held out to you. Ask and ye shall receive.

---

2 A form of energy (or vibrational medicine) in which a practitioner uses the radiesthesic faculty and instrumentation to discover the energy imbalances in the patient and to 'broadcast' corrective energy patterns

Spurred on by this message I went to see the Planning Officer. 'I know that you and your committee have to abide by the regulations,' I told him, 'but we need to have an arts and crafts centre on this site, a pottery, other studios, and bungalows for the people to live in. So, how do we get around the regulations?' 'That's the problem, Mr Caddy', he replied, 'We can't.' I beamed at him. '*Can't* isn't a word in my vocabulary, and I don't believe in problems. So, how do we get around the regulations?' He cleared his throat nervously and began listing possible alternatives, all of which — remembering Eileen's guidance — I turned down, because they were second best. Finally, to put the poor chap out of his misery, I proposed that the Findhorn Trust lease the land from the owner of the site and *then* his committee could license it for the studios, caravans and bungalows. Of course I had no idea whether the owner would be amenable to this, what it would cost or how the community would respond: but I was determined. The Planning Officer could see this, and also a way out of our impasse, so he accepted the proposal.

In the car on the way home, it occurred to me that if I invited the caravan park owner to be joint managing director of the studios he might be more open to granting the lease, and so he was. In spite of some local opposition, formal planning permission was granted at a subsequent meeting between the Planning Officer, the site owner and myself.

It was quite clear that we were to do the building ourselves, so we prepared the site with new roads, drains, electricity and water. The various artists and craftsmen, including four potters, were drawn into the group, so that their own energy went into the construction of the studios they would later be using — and, by working together, they would learn to adapt their individuality to the needs of the whole. I felt it was very important that they blend into the community before resuming work in their particular fields of excellence and, if the energies of the New Age were to find expression in their art or craft, it would only be when they had learned to put God first.

The performing arts also began to flourish. In addition to classical concerts, a choir was formed, and I also organized 'Fun Nights' — evenings of music with song, dance and skits, which were held regularly in the Community Centre. I constantly sought out new talent and encouraged members to perform, and when some of them formed a 'skit gang', I was usually the butt of their jokes (which I enjoyed more than anyone!). We even staged a one-act opera, written, composed and performed by members of the community.

* * *

Essentially we were a *working* community, and if people wanted to spend time in discussion or meditation then they could do it at night or go some place else where the emphasis was on such things. It certainly wasn't at Findhorn: *Work is love in action* was our primary ethos; 'By their fruits shall ye know them'. It was quite clear to me — and confirmed by Eileen's guidance — that we were to be a centre of demonstration, and that could only be done in action.

Because of our growing numbers we needed to establish a rhythm for the day so that newcomers — as members or guests — would know what was expected of them. Therefore I established the following daily programme and posted it for all to see:

	Breakfast in your own caravan or bungalow, and housework completed before 9am
9.00	Sanctuary
9.30	Work
12.15	Swimming (weather permitting)
1.00	Lunch
2.15	Work
4.15	Tea in your own caravan or bungalow
5.00	Work, lecture, rehearsals, choir practice, yoga, swimming, etc.
7.00	Dinner
8.15	Sanctuary
8.30	Music
9.00	Evening programme — announced daily

For the efficient running of the community, punctuality is essential.

While I drew on my catering, RAF and hotel management experience in organizing the Community's rhythms, perhaps the greatest single influence on the direction I wished to give us came from my memory of how Dr Sullivan had organized the Crotona Fellowship. The arts, outdoor activities, education, hard work, meditation and fun had all found their rightful place and balanced each other in his 'ashram', and so I wished them to do at Findhorn, although I had no intention of putting us forward as a 'Rosicrucian community'. Quite apart from the oath[3] I had taken, there was so much new

3 The so-called oath of the four esses: Silence, Secrecy, Sincerity and Service

material being received in meditation by Eileen, Dorothy, Roc and others that I realized we were on the cusp of something new and should not be limited or bound by the old ways, forms and traditions. Even Liebie's apocalyptic messages received through Richard Graves from the intelligence known as 'Limitless Love and Truth' seemed to have passed their shelf life, although Anthony Brooke and others still warned that the Earth was in danger and we should maintain our preparations for the worst scenario, 'just in case'. But there was a new spirit in the community, pregnant with the promise and possibilities of a peaceful and joyful transition into something completely new and different. Eileen's guidance hinted strongly at it; my own intuition was sure of it. It could almost be seen shining in the brightness of people's eyes and heard in their laughter as they went about their work. Nobody had yet named it, however, so we simply got on with our busyness.

Also in 1967, Anthony had met a remarkable young man in San Francisco, David Spangler, and he brought back a book by David called *The Christ Experience and the New Age*. This book had a great impact on all of us, and was all the more remarkable for David Spangler being in his early twenties when he wrote it: such wisdom would have been rare in a person twice his age. The book seemed to express what we were experiencing. Both Eileen and I felt that one day we were sure to meet David, but despite the fact that his name came up in conversation from time to time we made no attempt to contact him, feeling that when the time was ripe we would come together.

Therefore we were thrilled to receive a letter from David in June 1970 saying that he and his partner Myrtle Glines were in London and would like to come up and visit us.[4] The moment they arrived we found an immediate bond. On his first night I asked David to give a talk in the sanctuary — an invitation unheard of before — and I was very impressed by his clarity, the flow of his words and his wisdom. Very soon I realized that he needed to be in a heightened state of consciousness to give his talk, and that we certainly had to raise our consciousness to understand what he was talking about!

Although the community was buzzing with summer visitors, I drove David and Myrtle down to Edinburgh to meet Roc. Since David and Roc

[4] In fact, David told me much later that in the summer of 1969 he had planned to visit us and had come all the way to Inverness with Myrtle; but over breakfast on the morning they were going to drive across to us, he had a strong intuition that the timing was not right, so they passed the Findhorn turnoff from the highway and continued their travels. As usual, he was right: we would not have been prepared for him then, all our energy going into building the Community Centre and other projects at the time

were both naturally shy and reserved, I felt I needed to be there to draw them out; otherwise the pair of them would probably have just sat there looking at each other. There was an immediate rapport among the four of us, and we were told that the meeting heralded the beginning of a new phase for all of us.

Myrtle was considerably older than David and neatly complemented his ability to attune with higher streams of intelligence by bringing her own natural wisdom, maturity and psychological tools into play — she was expert at dealing with and counselling people, and together they were a perfect team. Although they had only planned to stay with us for a week or so and to return to the United States in early July, it quickly became clear to both of them that their place was to be with us. Years later, David gave this account:

> *When I was in the US in 1969 and 1970 I was told inwardly that the next step in my own work was to travel to Europe and find a centre that was carrying on the Rosicrucian tradition (or more accurately, the inner spirit of the Rosicrucian Order) in a new way. I though I would be looking for a place in Switzerland or Germany, and half expected it would be at Steiner's headquarters. Yet when I arrived at Findhorn, I knew immediately that it was the place I had been told about, because I recognized the inner signs that I had been told to look for. So, for me, I always saw, and continue to see, Findhorn as a new centre of that particular Spirit that also gave birth to the Rosicrucian Order and its tradition...*

I was seized by the unshakeable conviction that David and Myrtle had come to us in perfect timing to play a pivotal role in our development, so within days of their arrival I invited both of them to become co-directors with me of the Community. Sir George Trevelyan was also excited about David's being with us, and the two were soon engaged in a lively correspondence; Sir George invited David to speak at Attingham at the end of July and again in October.

Just before leaving on a short visit to England, David told the community:

> *We know that we are moving into a New Age. One of the concepts of our future is that each one of us is the Word made flesh. We are each the Voice of God, seeking to express itself. In ages past man walked and talked with God, because he was one with himself. With the development of mind, oneness has*

become lost or misplaced. But as man learns to lift his mind into higher faculties and to listen and attune, he will again walk and talk with God, and hear that Voice... hear the Voice, blend with it, and in this way you are pioneering the next two thousand years.

Many people, however, both in our community and abroad were still prophesying doom and gloom — violent Earth changes, nuclear holocaust, industrial pollution and other horrors that hovered over the cradle of the New Age waiting to devour the child; I received many letters on the subject every week. One day, such a letter came from Australia and I took it in for David's feedback. Did he agree with its contents? Definitely not, he replied. His idea of what we were doing at Findhorn had nothing to do with maintaining 'a kind of survival centre, waiting for the coming of space brothers, waiting for apocalypse, and waiting for the New Age'. Instead we should be proclaiming that the New Age had already arrived, and we were there to build the models that would demonstrate it. He felt very strongly about this.

As a result of this and other promptings, a small group of us came together in one of the bungalows to explore this theme of 'the New Age now', leading to David channelling information from a higher stream of intelligence previously associated with the being whom Liebie Pugh had known as 'Limitless Love and Truth'. This was the first in a series of revelations through David, culminating in an open session before the whole community on 15 August, and they certainly set the spiritual cat among the apocalyptic pigeons! Their basic message was that the New Age *is* here, it is constantly revealing itself to you in and around yourself, so you may as well get on with it and leave the doomsayers to their own devices.

Well, some of the doomsayers fought back, claiming that David had been possessed by some evil entity through whom the community would be taken off its true path (whatever that was). David's transmissions went out first in the form of several short booklets to our private mailing list, much of which we had inherited from Liebie: it brought an angry response from almost half our subscribers, many of whom dropped away. Needless to say, David and I greatly enjoyed the resultant rumpus, but underneath the fun there was a parting of the old and the new ways that would leave our own way forward uncluttered. As the Chinese say, *It is better to light a single candle than to curse the darkness*. We later published the material, with additional commentary, in a book, *Revelation: The Birth of a New Age*, one of the first off our fledgling Findhorn Press and highly successful in the market for which it was intended.

* * *

David's first visit also helped me face the changes that *I* was required to go through. That year (1970), on my fifty-third birthday, Eileen had received that while I was still to hold the reins in the community, I must now hold them far more loosely if I wished to draw the best out of others:

> *A good leader must plan his work and work his plan. He must be willing to do anything that he asks anyone else to do. Tell Peter that he will have to find a new depth of love and understanding with those he leads, so he has their full cooperation and help in all that has to be done. He must treat them as human beings, not as machines.*

About two years earlier, after occasional bouts of pain, I had been diagnosed as having gallstones, confirmed by X-ray, and no amount of spiritual or other complementary forms of healing could be found to heal them. Several healers told me that gallstones were an occupational hazard caused by overactivity and urged me to slow down, but I felt this almost impossible to do. My doctor recommended a surgeon and arranged for me to go into hospital, which — after one last try to seek an alternative cure — I reluctantly agreed to. At least the operation would give me time on my own to digest fully what had been given to me and the community in various messages through Eileen and David.

In May, Eileen received, *Tell Peter to be at peace. He will have to have these gallstones removed, but it will be done at just the right time, and everything will go smoothly.* The timing did indeed work out. I went into hospital on 9 November, at the end of a period of intense activity. It was around the time David and Myrtle returned to the United States to pack their things: they were planning on returning to Findhorn during mid-March of the following year, this time to stay. Meanwhile, we'd been intentionally discouraging visitors, as we sought to use the winter months as a period of quiet, during which the group might draw closer together.

With me in hospital was a load of various kinds of literature that I had not found time to read before, and a number of David Spangler's tapes — I thought that this would be a splendid opportunity to get up to date. To my consternation, it was nearly two weeks before I could even look at a tabloid paper. I had had no idea what such an operation involved. I couldn't move, and the pain was unlike anything I'd ever experienced. I disliked the feeling of being absolutely exhausted and weak and felt that every nurse should have a similar operation, so that they'd be more aware and understanding; for example, I was only allowed a teaspoonful of water at a time and suffered from raging thirst, but to attract a nurse's attention to get me that water seemed to take forever.

The day before I was due to be discharged from the hospital, it was discovered that I had a blood clot in my leg. This meant that I was confined to bed, and my departure was thus delayed for two more weeks. Then I was utterly frustrated, as I couldn't even put my feet on the floor. It came to me that this was all part of God's Plan, to render me immobile as long as possible, so that I would have time to reflect on my life and the growth of Findhorn and the changes required of both the community and myself.

But I do not say that I learned this lesson gracefully or, at the time, with much gratitude. I would have much preferred to enjoy a complete rest abroad, where I'd been invited for a holiday. Before coming out of hospital there was yet another delay: it was found that my liver was not functioning properly, and I had to remain for further tests. Eileen received, *He needs this time to be still; a thing he has never found easy. Rest assured that he will be released from hospital at exactly the right time.* And indeed I was, on a weekend when most of the young people were attending a course at Attingham, so things were quiet in the community.

My recovery was slow, and further rest was needed. All the energy had been withdrawn from me to keep me quiet. But I still found it difficult to remain sitting in the bungalow and watching people at work. One day I got impatient at the slow way in which some gardeners were digging and adding compost on a piece of ground near our bungalow. So I got up, took a spade, announced 'I'll dig!' and sent the others to get compost. As a result I burst my stitches and had to go back into hospital for a time, to be restitched and for the wound to heal. 'Obedience to spirit' is a lesson that must be constantly relearned. Most people need the merest tap on the shoulder to draw their attention to this; sometimes with me it took a sledgehammer!

Chapter 27

One Incredible Family

A myth is a veiled truth or symbol,
containing a great cosmic truth

MANY OF THE YOUNG PEOPLE who were coming to Findhorn had little or no prior knowledge of esoteric concepts or New Age ideas, beyond their use of vague expressions like 'Can you feel the energies?' or 'Must be your karma!'. Others, who had been well-trained in one spiritual school or another, were amazed to find us proving things that they had only before known as intellectual theory. With David's and Myrtle's arrival in 1970, and their inspired work and lectures, we realized the importance of Findhorn not only as a demonstration of work as 'love in action' but also as a training centre where theory and study could also be made available.

But where? It was hard enough finding bed space for everyone, let alone classrooms, offices and a library. Eileen's guidance had for some time indicated that The Park building — the house and grounds adjoining us, and belonging to Captain and Mrs Gibson, owners of the caravan site — would one day be part of the whole community; so, as the needs for a 'college' building became obvious I was not surprised when the Gibsons put the house up for sale in Spring 1971. They had bought a larger one, Cullerne, closer to the village. The asking price for The Park was £12,500 — another large, seemingly 'impossible' sum for us to manifest.

Just at that time, a visitor who had been staying in the community for a few days came to me and said that she would like to join us: could I find her a suitable site for a bungalow? I did, and also took her to see The Park . She was not herself interested in the building but told me that her late husband had left £12,000 to be given to a worthy, forward-looking cause that they both would have shared interest in. She felt she had finally found such a project in ours, and offered to buy us The Park building if she could build a bungalow next door to it and use the house's large annex as her painting studio. I was thrilled by the offer and went straight to David to share the good news.

David would have none of it, declaring that since the entire house was under St Germain's protection, whoever bought it for us would have to release it to the community with no strings attached. Somewhat dispirited, I wondered whether she was not the right person after all; but that night, David had a vision of St Germain enfolding the house and grounds in his robe and assuring him that it was all under his protection (St Germain or the Master R, as you may recall, is in charge of fostering new culture and civilization). The next morning, the visitor came again to me and said she had woken with the clear feeling that she should buy The Park building and its grounds and give them to the community entirely and without conditions — she would buy a bungalow for herself down the road at Pineridge and build her studio there.

Thus our college now had a physical location in which to take birth. David and Myrtle were appointed joint Principals, and an ambitious schedule of seventeen classes was drawn up to prepare lecturers, teachers or leaders in New Age projects in skills and subjects ranging from esoteric wisdom to outdoor leadership, from public speaking to communication with angels.

The performing arts continued to flourish, with drama, folksong, classical recitals and dance — there seemed no end to the astonishing diversity of talents that we attracted at this time. The Community Centre was extended to twice its original size, with much of the tableware (candles, pottery) coming from our own craft studios, and an old shop in the caravan park was rebuilt into an excellent seventy-seat theatre where sometimes as many as three shows a week were performed for the general public.

At the four solar festivals (the summer and winter solstices, the vernal and autumn equinoxes) David led us in celebrations of our ongoing links and cooperation with nature, and around those dates we took a week off all but essential work to enjoy outdoor activities, prayer, meditation, dance, picnics and parties. 'It was a good excuse for a holiday!', he told community members many years later, only half-jokingly. We *were* a very hard-working group of people, but you could almost reach out and touch the joy, and I felt sure that Dr Sullivan would have been proud of the balance we brought to our many activities.

* * *

For years it had been my practice to read aloud Eileen's guidance — collectively known as *God's Word* — every morning in the sanctuary, fresh from her having received it during the night, and while it was an inspiration for the day and the centre point of community life, it was creating a dependency. *God's Word* also went out in monthly booklets to thousands around the world, allowing them to keep in spiritual communion with us; but it was disquieting to see closer to home a tendency to regard Eileen's words as the *only* source, the 'official' spiritual guide — rather than for people to see that each of us has our own access to the same source of inner truth. Eileen herself had been told in 1968 that the greatest help we could give any soul was to encourage him or her to seek directly within, where there was no need for an outside interpreter of any kind.

On 20 October 1971, Eileen received the following message that dealt directly with consciousness and responsibility:

> *My beloved, now is the perfect time for a complete change of rhythm for you. It is no longer necessary for you to receive a message from Me each day for the community and for the many. For a very long time I have gone on day after day repeating Myself. It is now time My word was lived and demonstrated. For those who have failed to take it to heart, it is there for all who need to be reminded, printed in black and white. Now is the time for living it, and the sooner this is done, the more quickly will changes come.*

More than any other event that year, this change was the most significant, for it dealt with attunement [1] within the community as a whole. Eileen no longer had to sleep most of the day to make up for her nightly meditations, and she was freed to move into closer personal work with members. I hasten to add that this does not mean she stopped meditating or hearing God's voice at that time — indeed she continued to get personal guidance for me — but it signified a major shift for her personally and for the whole community. It was as if God had put His foot down firmly on the idea that

---

[1] 'Attunement' is a word used at Findhorn either to mean an individual coming into harmony with God, and hence sensitive to receiving divine guidance; or an individual or group coming into harmony with the indwelling divinity of themselves, each other, or any other thing, be it animal, vegetable or mineral: it is a sympathetic vibration with the universal mind that has created and thus exists in everything. Just as a note struck on a piano will cause the strings of the same note in other octaves and even on another piano beside it to resonate in sympathy, so attunement with the divine produces a corresponding sensitivity

people should look outside of themselves, instead of inside, for the ultimate source of wisdom and truth. I believe that one of the main reasons for the Findhorn Community outliving so many others is that there was no guru or, once we were established, other external spiritual authority telling everybody else what to think, how to act or what to do.

Eileen's guidance was still read out every morning at the beginning of the meditation in the Sanctuary, but these were 'staple' messages taken from the thousands she had already received, and chosen according to the taste and sensitivity of whoever was leading the meditation. Instead of being received as God's fresh instructions from the night before, they were evergreen reminders of the ABCs of a spiritual life and simply served as key thoughts to be taken into the silence that followed.

* * *

In 1972 we legally became the Findhorn Foundation, a religious, educational, charitable trust, giving us income tax and rating benefits. The Trustees were Captain Ross Stewart, RN DL JP, Chairman; Joan Hartnell-Beavis; Pauline Tawse; John Hilton and Sir George Trevelyan, Bt MA (I mention their various titles because it used to tickle me how we were still regarded by many as a hippy commune!). The overall policy of spiritual direction still rested with Eileen and myself, in consultation with David Spangler, and I retained final authority on all matters affecting the whole community. The day to day running of the community increasingly became the responsibility of the heads of departments.

I had to learn to delegate more and more to others, even though I was responsible overall; but first I had to let go, and allow others not only to do the work, but also to be responsible for their own area. For example, when I handed the garden to a team, it was not easy to see things done differently, even though they were being done with love and to perfection. If there was anything done that I did not approve of, I would say so, but I always endeavoured to see the best in people and what they were doing. I tried to draw out the gifts that individuals had come to give. Those who were not in harmony with the whole would leave, even without my asking them to do so.

At the same time we formed a management committee, with me as its chairman. This had the responsibility to see that the spiritual direction of the community was implemented; it also insured that the legal and financial directives of the Trustees were fulfilled. In the spirit, perhaps, but not always to the letter! Eileen had received:

> *It is absolutely right for Peter to feel free to go ahead on the crest of the wave, without any restraint or pullback from the trustees or the executive and finance committees, when he is inspired to do so. What is being done here cannot be judged by the methods of the world... Those around Peter must realize that he is not doing what is being done in his own strength, but in My strength. His methods may appear to be very strange and even ruthless at times, but it is essential that they are carried through without any fear or negativity on the part of those around him. When timing and speed is necessary to get something done, those around him will have to learn to trust him implicitly. So he can go ahead without even consulting them, when he is inspired to do so.*

This was a red rag to a bull for the Chairman of the Trustees, all of whom are held legally responsible, under Scottish Law, for the financial affairs of the community. Eileen was told from within that we were to go with Joanie and Ross and Aileen Stewart to Traigh Bhan, the community retreat house on Iona, for a week.[2] I wondered why we were being sent there when I had so much work to do in the community, but soon discovered that Ross and I were to discuss the relationship between myself and the Trustees. I told him that I must act on my intuition and Eileen's guidance immediately, without conferring with the Trustees, but knowing that our needs would be met by God whether we had the money in the bank or not. Ross hit the roof: this was outrageous, he said, and contrary to any sound business or administration practices! Ross was the former captain of a battleship, a Justice of the Peace, a Hampshire County Councillor and on a number of county committees, and he was used to giving orders and having them obeyed; but I was implacable. For several days the tiny house on Iona was like a pressure-cooker, until Ross came to terms with the situation.

One decision of which Ross *did* approve was when guidance had come that it was time to charge for guest accommodation, on a sliding scale. Previously we had allowed guests to contribute whatever they could give, but this policy had been abused by some.[3] The vast expansion, shortage of ac-

2 Traigh Bhan, towards the north-east end of Iona, was given to the Findhorn Trust in 1972 by Jessica Ferriera through her friendship with community member Katherine Collis

3 To be fair, many were misled by mischievous information in some 'alternative' guides and publications in London that we were a free, friendly place to stay after 'burning out' on drugs

commodation, and the large number of young people the community was carrying necessitated a change. Part of our vision was that anyone *anywhere* can lead a New Age life, if one is willing to turn within, attune to God and obey that inner voice or intuition — there was no need to come to us for it. We were inundated by letters from people who wanted to come and join us, but Findhorn is not for everyone. Many people found community life and the constant interaction with other individuals difficult to take; some found the work programme a challenge, as their consciousness of spirituality did not recognize the necessity of 'earthing' energies and demonstrating the inner life through outer service. Others found it difficult to adjust, as the community demanded that people change and grow within themselves.

Personal problems could be healed in the community, but it was not a place for people to come to with that objective. Findhorn is a place for people who are willing to sacrifice self in dedication to building a new culture, a group consciousness, and a new vision. Those with emotional problems usually would find them intensified and brought to the surface, and this made their life even more difficult. Many of the psychological skills and natural wisdom possessed by older members, particularly Myrtle, again proved invaluable in helping the greener ones find their feet (even if that meant pointing them towards the front gate!).

Service was also a key requirement from anybody there, no matter who they were or what they were doing. For a time, the art and craft studios flourished, run as a separate business but in every other sense considered as part of the whole. Unfortunately we found that members of this group were gradually drifting away from the whole and putting themselves and their own needs first, often neglecting their own spiritual unfoldment. They were using the community to serve art, rather than art to serve the whole community. Ken and Kate in the weaving studios, for example — two of the hardest working members of the community — were so determined to make a financial success of the studios that they even took their meals down there to eat, rather than in the Community Centre. They didn't want to take any time from their weaving. Other members of the studios were no longer coming to meditate in the Sanctuary or attend community meetings. I told Ken and Kate that they would either have to change or leave; they chose to leave, and emigrated to New Zealand. It was sad to see our hardest working couple go, but we knew it was right. Finally, we decided to close down the studios altogether, until they could be properly incorporated into the training aspects of the whole community. David, Myrtle, Eileen and I interviewed each member of the group and explained the situation to them: they were all told that they would have to leave, with the exception of Craig Gibsone, the only one who was fully integrated into the community. He was a potter, an actor, singer, dancer, and was involved in education — a whole and balanced person. He coordinated the studios when they later re-opened as part of the College.

The performing arts, however, continued to flourish. The New Troubadors, a group of singers (including David) from various countries who had met at Findhorn and stayed, began making professional recordings of their original songs, which expressed perfectly the spirit of the day. Dance, drama and classical recitals continued to break down barriers with our suspicious neighbours; even if they still considered us odd, they could appreciate the time and care put into mounting a professional-looking production.

The Station Commander at RAF Kinloss, one of the largest Royal Air Force stations in Britain and our nearest neighbour, had felt that there was considerable misunderstanding about the Findhorn Foundation. He also thought that there was probably some misunderstanding in the Foundation about the role of the RAF at Kinloss. He therefore invited fourteen members of the community to meet a similar number of officers in their Mess on the station. The evening programme included a talk by the Station Commander, illustrated by slides on the role of RAF Kinloss, followed by a talk by myself and David Spangler with slides of our community. After a tour around parts of the station we got together over coffee and had a most interesting discussion until late in the evening. We arrived at the conclusion that we were all seeking the same goal — peace on earth — but by different routes. We felt that peace could only come to the world first by achieving peace within, and then by living at peace within a group or community; afterwards, those groups and communities all over the world could be linked. The Group Captain agreed with our spiritual aims and principles, and felt that he and his community and like-communities throughout Britain representing the RAF, Army and Navy, were helping to stabilize the political and military situation in the world so that humanity would have time in which to experience an inner and more lasting change of consciousness. As he spoke, it occurred to me that but for certain twists on the road, I could have been the Group Captain sitting there addressing the happy flock of 'flower children' from over the base's fence!

This was the beginning of many exchange social and cultural visits between the two neighbouring centres. Certain individuals on our side of the fence, both young and old — but mostly visitors, I'm happy to report — were privately critical of our community forming connections with what they considered to be a military establishment, which they regarded as dedicated to killing people; they felt that if we were truly a spiritual centre, we should be *picketing* the air base. However, our philosophy was that the route to peace lay through the understanding of others and through building bridges of communication, through which greater forms of communion could arise. If an individual came to our community and said 'Well, I'm against the arms race, I'm against poverty, I'm against pollution, I'm against ripping the planet off: I want to join the work you're doing here', I would reply 'That's fine — but come back when you're not just *against* everything, but have something positive to offer.' Eileen's guidance often echoed the question 'Are you part of the problem, or part of the solution?'

Dick Barton, who was a Flight Lieutenant at RAF Kinloss and later became a community member at Findhorn, arranged for the Station Commander to visit us with three senior Wing Commanders and their wives. After a tour of the community they joined us for dinner and then a time of further discussion. The Station Commander asked me about the future of Findhorn in the next thirty-five years. One of the wives cut in and said, 'Oh, I suppose you'll be taking over RAF Kinloss'. I replied, 'Well as a matter of fact we will!' remembering Eileen's guidance about how we would evolve into a 'City of Light'. Another wife said 'I thought so!' My remark brought forth much laughter, but I believed it to be true and still do. In the meantime the RAF have created a centre for over 5,000 staff and their families, with a theatre, gymnasium, swimming pool, hospital, library, and lots of housing.[4]

* * *

Our growing community at Findhorn quite often attracted fanatics with regard to food, and as an ex-catering officer and hotel manager I knew how vital it was to keep them well away from the kitchens (to which those with some bee in their bonnet about diet were invariably drawn). In fact, if we

---

4 With the end of the Cold War and massive contractions in Britain's Armed Forces, at the time this is written, personnel numbers have been greatly reduced at RAF Kinloss and there has been regular local suspicion about whether the base would be entirely decommissioned by the end of this century. At the same time, speculation is growing that Eileen's phrase 'vast City of Light' refers not to a geographical settlement but the rapid spread of the computer-based Internet, the global information 'superhighway' that people in the New Age movement were among the first to join.

The New Troubadours: first flourishing of the arts in the Community

Peter and Eileen dressed for dinner in the early 70s

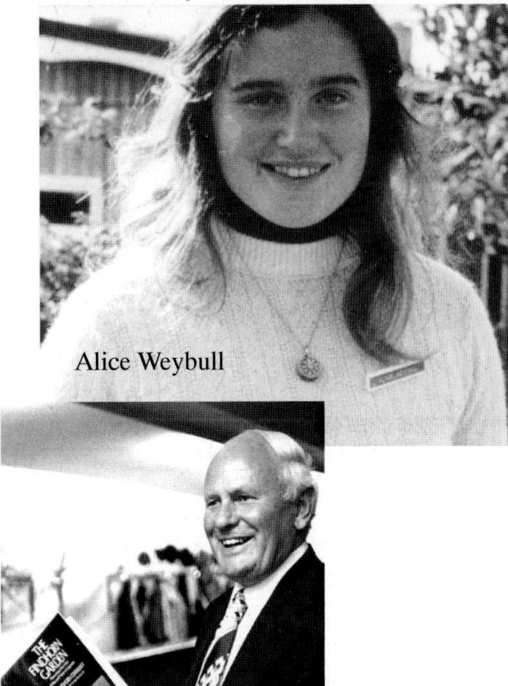

Alice Weybull

The Findhorn Garden spreads news of the work

Inside the sanctuary at The Park

Peter cuts the Findhorn Community 30th birthday cake; on his left, Eileen and Dorothy; on his right, François Duquesne

The Universal Hall at Findhorn

The Findhorn Community on its 30th birthday
(17 November 1992) outside the extended Community Centre.
In the centre of the third row, Dorothy, Peter, Eileen (with grandchild Arran) and Joanie

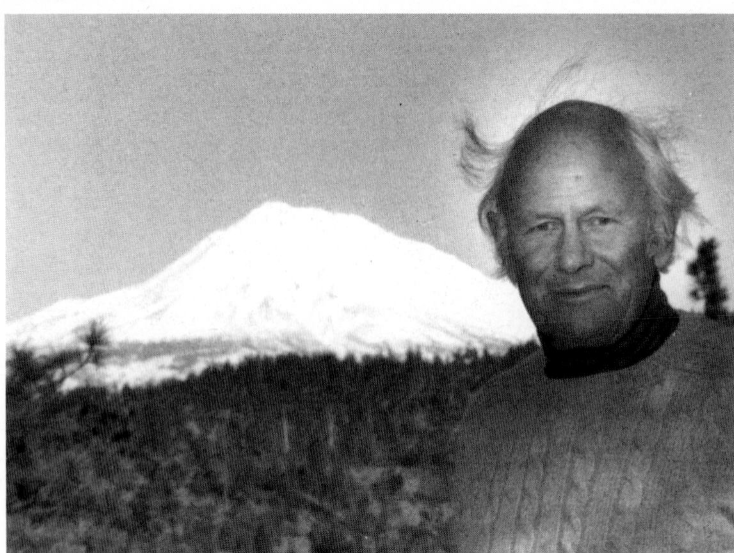
Mt Shasta on a windy day

Paula, Peter and Shari

Peter and Paula married in 1982...

... and had a son, Daniel

Kailash marriage —
Renata and Peter

Haidakan Ashram
with the 108 steps down
to the Gautam-Ganga River

Peter at work in the 'Paradise Garden' by the Lake of Constance

Sir George Trevelyan, Peter and Renata, outside the Universal Hall at Findhorn

Peter and Swamiji Ganapati Satchidananda (the 'fire-swamiji')

With close friend Peter Dawkins

Peter and Jeremy Slocombe

The news about the seeming miracles at Findhorn spread far and wide, and while my energy was needed in the community to cope with the increasing numbers of visitors, guests and would-be members, I still managed to journey south from time to time. On one occasion, I was invited by the Reverend Vere Hodge to give a talk on 'the Laws of Manifestation and Faith in God', to the clergy composing the Synod of Glastonbury. I was very amused to be invited to talk to clergymen on faith in God!

Our little party stayed at Moorlinch near Glastonbury, in the Victorian Rectory, which probably hadn't changed much since the days of Queen Victoria (except, thank God, for central heating). Vere Hodge was very precise: everything for the conference had to be worked out beforehand to the last second — something more New Age organizers could learn from. In fact, when planning the next day, he wanted us back for high tea at 5.29 pm not 5.30 pm.

There were about eighty in the audience composed of most of the ministers in the district, their counsels and the press. Vere Hodge opened with a very beautiful prayer, asking people to open their hearts and minds to new ideas. Then in his introductory remarks he told a little about our work at Findhorn and what had been achieved there, and how we had really put into practice the adage to 'seek ye first the Kingdom of Heaven and all else will be added unto you': and how this really does work when one puts God's Will first. I then gave an off-the-cuff address, based on some slides of Findhorn that I intuited might shed light on the success of our faith in God and the laws of manifestation. I gave many examples to show we were actually *doing* what others were preaching and teaching, but so often failed to do.

Vere Hodge kept fussing about the time. I was to finish at 8.45. I finished, not to the nearest minute, but to the nearest second (and cheekily showed him my watch from the platform to point it out). It was an example of attunement rather than planning, since my address had been unscripted and there was no physical clock to refer to. Half an hour of lively but never antagonistic questions followed.

In his closing remarks, Vere Hodge said that he hadn't asked me what my expenses would be, because he didn't think that I would tell him, but he had found out himself that it would cost about £38 to come down by car, and a rail ticket was £37. He therefore asked for a collection to be made to cover my travelling expenses; this would be done while we sang a hymn. At the end of that hymn, the organist would still be playing while the money was counted, because he felt sure that the audience would like to know just how much had been collected. In other words, he was putting this whole question of manifestation to the test.

Earlier he had asked me, what would I do in their circumstances if I had to raise £5,000 from their Chapter for their annual contribution to the Bishop's fund for overall expenses? They always had lots of arguments, he explained, so what would I do? I had laughed and said, 'At Findhorn we would not do it that way. We would make the need known and then let God open the hearts and minds of people so that they would give and, I would be sure, when they counted what had been given, that it would be exactly the right money.' So now he was putting me and the whole thing to the test. When finally the money was counted, the vicar of the church came out and announced that it was £37.50. We were just 50 pence short, which was soon given. He later told me that such a large sum had never been collected at a single session in this church before.

Faith is the vital factor in manifestation. I remember listening at another time to a talk on the laws of manifestation by Canon Andrew Glazewski. He made an interesting statement: 'If you keep on praying for a thing you'll not manifest it, for you put into operation the reverse laws.' I did not understand him at the time, so when I met him again some months later I asked him what he had meant. 'It's quite simple' he said. 'If you keep on praying for a thing it shows you've not the faith. You need to ask only once and then go ahead in faith.'

* * *

Internationally we were becoming known in the mainstream media. In November 1972 an article appeared in Harper's magazine, entitled 'Love amongst the Cabbages' by Peter Tompkins, author of *Secrets of the Great Pyramid,* and Christopher Bird, a biologist and anthropologist. It began,

> *'The most far reaching revolution of the twentieth century may come from the least expected quarter, the bottom of your garden. Scientists everywhere in the world, amazed by the results of careful laboratory experiments, find themselves coming to the conclusion that plants have emotions similar to those of human beings, that they respond to affection, and that they can be adapted to the service of mankind.'*

The article ended with an account of our garden at Findhorn. A few days after receiving this article, the BBC phoned us up to say that by linking Findhorn with other scientific experiments in the field of trans-sensitivity, the authors had effectively given 'official' recognition to our work, and I was again invited for interview. Peter Tompkins came to visit us and spent an intensive thirty-six hours investigating and taking photographs to include in his best-selling book *The Secret Life of Plants* (most editions of which include a whole chapter about our work). He also was interviewed by the BBC, in London, for a programme repeated in *Pick of the Week.* These two programmes resulted in a positive response from the public.

* * *

There is not the scope in this chapter to offer more than some tasty samples from the rich feast that was the Findhorn Community during the three years David and Myrtle were with us (1970 — 73). However voluminous and sometimes specific Eileen's guidance had been, nothing prepared us for the explosion of growth and talent of that time, which deserves a whole book to itself: not only for the insights and delights it would recall, but for the enduring spiritual lessons it would preserve, in simple stories, and also the unique social record it would represent.[5]

In the spring of 1973, David and Myrtle and a small number of their new-found friends and working colleagues here decided the time had come to leave the community and return to the States, to set up their own, non-community-based educational programmes. (They called themselves the Lorians, and Dorothy Maclean was to join them later in the year.) The College at Findhorn was up and running, meanwhile, with able hands to take it over from them. We had almost more than enough study papers and other transmissions from David's higher sources to see us well into the next century, and, of course, we were all to continue working together closely in the future despite our geographical distance.

Eileen had always seen David as a happy troubadour, and I think that with his own very clear inner direction and vision we could not have kept him if it no longer served his higher purpose. Already he was feeling the strain of being put on a pedestal as a 'new Christ' by some people, and his ideas for more focussed, formally-applied education may have been diffused

5 [Jeremy Slocombe writes:] Peter Caddy was himself planning at least one further book along these lines

by the hurly-burly of community life had he taken them further here. Besides, he had been only twenty-five when he joined us and had a whole life and family of his own ahead.

Though David and I initiated many projects we often found that those who continued after us gradually lost the original enthusiasm and energy. We therefore found it was best to support those people who had a clear vision of their *own* projects, and were prepared to take responsibility for them — and then watch them go! In that way we were often the perfect team.

But despite the fact that there would be many more adventures to come for me and David, I still think of his departure from Findhorn as the end of a certain era so that a new one could follow; and in case I get caught up in relating the next chapter too quickly, let me pause here and thank David for all that he gave — as a way-shower, prophet, pioneer, friend — and brother.

As this period ended, Eileen received,

> *Findhorn is no longer a slender sapling tossed about by every wind of change. It is now a sturdy oak with its roots sunk deep within the soil, firmly rooted and grounded. Its trunk is strong and sturdy, and every bough and branch is perfect in every line, shape and detail. See each new aspect of the work as a new branch growing out of that sturdy trunk. I am the sap, the very life force flowing in that tree. I am the very power and strength of it. The wind may ruffle its leaves, storms may even make the boughs creak and bend, but nothing now can effect the true beauty, perfection and power of My work, for I AM the I Am within all that is being done.*

Chapter 28

The Heart has its Reasons

The greatest law is to live by love

ABOUT SIX MONTHS before he left, David Spangler had remarked to me that I had developed the qualities of a powerful male leader over many lifetimes, and my training had been in developing my will, faith, ability to take action, and to administrate. In partnership with Eileen, and balanced by her feminine qualities, these are what it had taken to be at the spearhead of a new age.

But now, David went on, the community no longer needed those qualities to the same degree: therefore I needed to become more balanced, more whole, and to develop the so-called feminine part of myself, my heart, love, imagination, being. I found that difficult to be told, having worked so hard developing the masculine qualities. Soon after these words of David's I'd been in hospital for a hernia operation and had so many problems with it — everything seemed to go wrong. Yet Eileen had continued to receive guidance that all was very very well; David told me that all was going according to plan. This 'plan' was apparently that nothing else would have stopped me for long enough to be still, to turn within and understand that what David had said was indeed right. I did need to develop my heart more and to be more loving.

I returned to the community, full of will and purpose, saying, 'I must be more loving!'. Well, it didn't work that way. As I was convalescing in my front room I was disturbed to find that the community seemed to be falling apart without my enforcing discipline. Members weren't getting up in the morning and were taking an hour for coffee breaks, two hours for lunch. The lights weren't being turned off at night. Finally, my middle son Jonathan, who is very wise said, 'You know Dad, you won't be able to be more loving, until the community takes on more responsibilities and embodies more light'.

How right he was. I'd had difficulty relating to people while I continued to be aware of all that needed doing, and I was also aware of all the things that had been left undone. So I invoked love, but little did I know what was going to happen next.

I fell in love with Alice Weybull! She had come from Sweden to visit Findhorn when she was nineteen, in the summer of 1972. She only intended to stay for a week, but her stay kept getting extended, until finally she told me that she was going back to Sweden to collect her things to join the community. I said, 'Oh no, you must finish what you have started and complete your education at university'. For it had become our policy only to accept those who had finished their education. I explained to her that if she didn't get her degree now, it would be very difficult to return later. But Alice insisted and there were floods of tears. She was determined to come back, and in the end I relented for I recognized that her soul knew the right way forward for her.

When she returned a few weeks later, I made her responsible for cleaning the lounge, the entrance and the toilets of the Community Centre. This work was a wonderful training ground for future leaders, for it was necessary to be very aware: to make sure that the tables were lined up, the salt and pepper pots were full, the window sills dusted, and that the tables were laid in time for each meal. It involved real discipline and attention to detail, and was where the founding principles of Findhorn could be put into practice — to love where you are, to love whom you're with, and to love what you're doing. When that was so, it was reflected in the work.

After about three months Alice came to me and asked me if she could be transferred to more creative work in another department. I said, 'Let me see your toilets'. I went to see them, but they did not reflect a consciousness of love. I told Alice that only when she could demonstrate to me that she was working with love, would I allow her to move on. I reminded her that the floors had to be polished every day until they shone. Another three months passed, and Alice came to me again, and said, 'Now can I move on?' Once again I headed for the toilets, but I looked and told her that they did not yet reflect a consciousness of love. Several months later she came to me with shining eyes and said, 'Peter, come and see *my* toilets', and with pride she showed them to me. The floor was shining, the seats were highly polished, there was a vase of flowers in the room, and the whole place gleamed.

I said to her, 'Right Alice, now you can move on, as you've really demonstrated that you love these toilets'. She had learned her lesson — and so could pass it on to others.

As this was the period in which David Spangler and other 'key' Americans left the community, Alice took on many responsibilities. I placed her in charge of the daily tours around the community, as well as of our fledgling guest programme. She soon found that this was too much for one person so formed a group, which was the beginning of the Guest Department at Findhorn. The community was expanding at this time, and we needed to move beyond having one person being responsible for different areas, to a group or department holding that responsibility.

After a busy summer season, Alice started working with me in Personnel. This involved deciding who joined the community, where they worked, what they were able to love and where the greatest balance between their own growth and contribution to the whole could be found.

To begin with Alice consulted with me about everything, and I found that she had a remarkable awareness and ability: with an inner knowing that guided her in decisions as to who should join the community and where they should work — which wasn't always their preference or ego desire. At that time a large number of people wanted to join the community, for the word was beginning to spread around the world about what we were doing at Findhorn. When people told their story about how they'd heard about Findhorn and how they'd been led to join us, we would watch to see if we could see God's hand in their coming; and Alice had an acute inner knowing and perception about people. We sometimes studied people at lunch in the Community Centre, to observe whether a prospective member helped with kitchen clean-up or sat down instead to read a newspaper. The former was definitely a good sign, the latter raised doubts in my mind.

Findhorn could be seen as a community, as a spiritual community, as a University of Light, as a Mystery School. It was often a mystery how it worked! but it did. I feel that above all it was a graveyard of egos. Sometimes, an experienced worldly middle-aged man would come, thinking he was God's gift to Findhorn, but he'd be turned down by Alice who saw straight through him. It was a great blow to his ego to be turned down by a girl in her early twenties, who couldn't even speak English properly! I came to trust Alice's inner knowing and perceptions completely, and after a time she was solely responsible for who joined the community and where they worked. When this became too much for one person, Alice gathered a group and formed a Personnel Department.

As the numbers of people joining the community grew, we formed an Orientation Programme to integrate them properly. It was important to share the vision of Findhorn with those joining, to unite them with a common vision. They also learned how the community was organized, how it functioned and what was expected of them. Alice took on more and more responsibility.

At this time Eileen was not involved in the organization and administration of the community, whereas Alice played an ever increasing role. In the beginning she always checked with me before taking action, but after about a year and a half I completely trusted her intuition and gave her full responsibility in the areas in which she worked. We were working very closely together, as we had many matters to discuss. Alice was working extremely hard from early in the morning until late at night; she had not realized that she'd have to put part of her life on one side to do the work.

On occasions during the summer, when the weather was particularly good, the entire community would take a break and have a picnic on the beach on the shores of the Moray Firth. On one such day we went to Primrose Bay. Alice and I were sitting on the beach discussing some community matters, as we often did, and on this occasion it brought us closer together. Alice had beautiful eyes, and as we started talking that day a flow of love began through our eyes, which are indeed mirrors of the soul. I really did not know what to do about these feelings of love, and I felt completely out of balance. I didn't tell Eileen about what was happening, because I didn't know what to tell her.

Shortly afterwards Alice and I decided to go on another picnic, this time just the two of us, and when I dashed into our bungalow to grab a blanket, that aroused Eileen's suspicions that something was going on. Eileen intuitively found out what was happening and was extremely angry. The three of us had many talks, sometimes together with other people whom we consulted about this situation. It shed light on the imbalances in our marriage, which was not a normal one — to say the least.

For some time, Eileen had had a room in Joanie's bungalow where she spent most of the night in meditation and prayer. She went to bed very early, and not until 5 am did she come back to our bed in the bungalow. For me this was not satisfactory from a human point of view: I felt that things were dangerously out of balance. There had come a day when David and Myrtle had asked to see Eileen and shared with her that they felt that unless Eileen came back into my bed our marriage would not survive. Eileen told Myrtle that she was putting God first, to which Myrtle replied, 'What about the God in Peter?' Eileen along with Joanie and Anthony Brooke believed that in the New Age children would no longer be conceived through sex, but instead would be conceived on a higher level — through the power of enlightened thought and spirit. Therefore sexual expression should be raised on to that higher level.

I thought that this may be so in a few thousand years time, but not yet! My approach was that love should be brought down on to all levels, including the physical, and without that physical expression love was not complete. My entire vision of Findhorn was to 'bring down the Kingdom of Heaven to Earth', into matter; whereas Eileen was more concerned with raising the physical to the spiritual. She did take heed of what David and Myrtle had said, but I feel she returned to our bed more out of a sense of duty than with a sense of joy and wanting to express love on the physical plain.

I had been completely faithful to Eileen the whole time we lived together at Findhorn, and before that at the Trossachs and at Cluny Hill. When Eileen and I first came together, love was indeed physically expressed, and it was a very happy and satisfactory relationship. It was only with time that this changed. I told Eileen that I would accept everything that she received in guidance, except on matters of sex, as I felt that her words were coloured by her experience with her former husband, and her strong beliefs. My relationship with Alice, which was *not* a sexual one, started big changes in me. I felt like my heart had been opened and I developed more feminine qualities to balance my powerful masculine energies.

It is impossible to keep anything quiet in a community like Findhorn. People knew that *something* was going on, but they weren't quite sure what. We had a community meeting, and Alice and I shared what was happening. Alice said that the part she was playing in the opening of my heart would benefit the whole community in the long run. She added that the whole situation was very hard on her: some members thought that she was trying to break up a 'divine' marriage.

On 18 July, Eileen received:

Release, relax, everything is working out according to My Divine Plan. What is happening to Peter is that he is moving into the universal Love pattern, and you expect it to happen overnight. Think of a rosebud, how it unfolds, imperceptibly, revealing its full wonder, beauty and perfection. Peter is unfolding. At the moment he does not really know how to handle the Love energy. Be very loving, very patient, and know all is very very well. This relationship with Alice will level out. She can help him, and balance him. Trust her completely. She is no threat to your relationship with Peter, or to your marriage. When Peter was away, your heart was open to Universal Love. When you had that vision of the door of your heart being flung wide open, I told you to take the door off its hinges, and fling it away and let my Divine Love flow freely. And this is what happened to you. You experienced such freedom and such Love for everyone. This is what Peter is moving into. Hold back, do not try to push anything away, not to react negatively, but simply know the time is near at hand when you'll both be functioning the same way. And My Universal Love will pour forth from both of you. This is the Cosmic Christ energy which has been released here. Now it is a question of learning how to handle this tremendous Love energy with great wisdom and understanding. It is all happening, but imperceptibly, like a rosebud.

Be ever aware of this truly wondrous transformation which is taking place within and around all of you. Love as you've never loved before. This is My Universal Love. It is affecting every soul here in the community, and some have been knocked completely off balance. Some are bewildered and wonder what has happened, what has hit them. Others do not know how to handle these energies, and are floundering around. When there is such a tremendous change of energies, there is bound to be a time of adjustment, of sorting and sifting. This is what is happening now. Be not disturbed or distressed. To be forewarned is to be forearmed. Be a help. Let me guide you. Truly wonderful things are taking place, revolutionary things, flow with it all. This is not for the few, but for the many. Rejoice, rejoice. My Will is being done.

I certainly was bewildered by the flow of Love that had been awakened in my heart. I did not understand or know how to cope with Eileen's anger — fury, really — at what was happening with me. She seemed to think that I was just having a sexual affair with Alice, in spite of the guidance that she was receiving, and our protests to the contrary. From this time on Eileen seemed to be very suspicious of any affection or interest I expressed towards anyone of the opposite sex.

Our home life had seemed very strained for years, and honestly I felt like I was living with a volcano about to explode. I know our changes were hard on Eileen, but both of us seemed to lose the ability to be spontaneously affectionate and considerate of each other. After attending meetings all day, I would relax in front of the television at night, and Eileen went to bed early and got up early. Our bungalow was always open, and people would constantly visit — any hour of the day or evening — so there was no real privacy. I was so focussed on the running of our community at Findhorn that my personal relationship with Eileen just did not get enough time or energy to flourish, and we seemed to move further and further apart.

Our spiritual relationship was also changing. Just as Eileen had been told a few years earlier that she was no longer to get guidance for the community, so too she surprised me one day — when I went to her, as I often did, with a question to put to God — by saying that the time had come for me to stop relying on her guidance. Of course, all along, my turning to Eileen for answers had been not so much to receive 'instructions' from God, but to confirm and expound my own intuitions; nevertheless, Eileen was told from within that even this was now limiting my own spiritual evolution. It took a while for me to accept this, and it certainly didn't stop me asking questions! With hindsight, however, it *was* an important part of the changes I was required to make at that time, and indeed the whole community could be seen to benefit — for it only strengthened the individual self-reliance and responsibility its members were required to take.

* * *

The withdrawal of Eileen's guidance for me was not an overnight affair but a gradual process, and from time to time personal messages would still come through. In 1974 Eileen received:

> *Peter's work in the days ahead will be universal, but in the meantime, this place, this Centre of Light, needs to be*

really sound and running smoothly, for this is a centre of demonstration and a University of Light. Peter's work has been to establish this centre. The time will come when he will be free to move into the universal work. Tell him to let go of the reins more and more, and to allow the community to learn and make mistakes if necessary, but learn they must. He must be free.

We had cancelled a planned tour of Europe that year, for it was thought to be more important to visit the USA first. David Spangler also felt that we should visit the Lorian Association in the States before he made a return trip to Findhorn; then Eileen had guidance that she was needed more at Findhorn, so that I should go alone. I wondered how I was going to finance the trip — there was no money in the community's coffers for it — but Eileen refused to get any further message on the subject. That evening a phone call came from William Irwin Thompson[1] and David Spangler inviting me to give a lecture at a conference at Expo '74 in Seattle, Washington, on 21 and 22 May, with the promise of other speaking engagements elsewhere — with all expenses paid.

I spent a month touring six cities, visiting friends and talking to many groups and centres. Everywhere I went I was welcomed with warm hospitality and an eagerness to know more about Findhorn; in turn, I discovered the so-called American way of life, which both attracted and sometimes appalled me. 'Never again!' I said, after having a hamburger on a soft white bun with greasy French fries and synthetic ice cream in downtown Manhattan — now I understood better why so many Americans visiting Findhorn were such health food fanatics.

In New York, at David Spangler's suggestion, I met Donald Keys[2] of the Association of World Federalists at the United Nations, who gave me a behind-the-scenes tour of the building and lunch with many of the delegates; it was thrilling to be among so many workers for world unity, and seemed a far cry from a little caravan park in the north of Scotland. Yet at Expo '74 in

---

1 William Irwin Thompson is a cultural historian, author and philosopher who has been a good friend of the Findhorn Community over the years

2 Founder of *Planetary Citizens*, an organisation affiliated with the United Nations Economic and Social Council and Department of Public Information, and Unesco; *Planetary Citizens* works at both the grass-roots and international diplomatic levels to promote the awareness that we are all members of the same human family, regardless of national, political or spiritual identity, and share equal responsibility for good stewardship of the planet we inhabit

San Francisco, where the theme of our symposium was 'The Dilemma Facing Man', when William Thompson described Findhorn as a tangible, fully functioning approach to solving world problems through a change in consciousness, I began to see that it was more a question of scale than substance that appeared to separate us. Later, a meeting with Medicine Story at the Rainbow Tribe campsite in the Spokane countryside marked the beginning of many years of meeting with American Indian leaders, and had a great impact on me. I had been shocked at the physical evidence of man's vast exploitation of this great and beautiful land, and felt that its native peoples held a vital key to renewing respect for it.

Perhaps it was because of spiritual rootlessness and a sense of disconnection with the land that my lectures, audio-visuals and interviews about Findhorn found such favour with so many Americans, particularly the younger ones. They were thrilled in particular by the tales of Dorothy and the devas, and Roc and the nature spirits; I was surprised to find that counsellors were advising people to visit Findhorn, until I realized that there was so little to hang on to in modern American urban culture.

Thus my first transatlantic tour was a success on all levels, and I felt that it was guided throughout. The range, diversity and popularity of so-called New Age activities impressed me greatly, and I began to see why the 'mythological' aspects of our story had such appeal — while at the same time, the simplicity and openness of our message allowed me to be used to bring together people from totally different spiritual paths who might otherwise not have known of each other's existence, or kept their distance. I knew that my 'universal work' had begun, although as yet I had no idea where it would lead me.

* * *

While I was away on this US tour in 1974, George Ripley and a group of architects had prepared plans for us to build a hall at Findhorn, to be used for meetings, meditations, plays, music, audio-visuals, films, etc. At the same time, during my absence Eileen had received:

> *Many changes are taking place, and that means changes in Peter as well. Tell him to really open his eyes and see the wonderful changes that have taken place in the community, to recognize how much people have grown and want to take on responsibilities. Tell him to help and encourage them. He needs*

to give them far more freedom, so they can grow, as they take initiative. This may mean blending into the background, to enable them to do it. It is essential that what is developed is allowed to grow. This 'group consciousness' in the New Age is the 'new look' for community living. It is not democracy, but something beyond and above that. Tell Peter to be patient and see how it works, and to allow it to work and develop. Everyone is learning and is learning very quickly. It would be very beneficial for everyone if Peter could become an observer, as adviser or consultant when necessary; but to take his hands off the internal departmental workings of the community.

He needs to realize that individuals are unable to grow as long as they have to rely on him for everything. He must be willing for some to make mistakes, for they will grow very quickly from their mistakes. He needs to be willing to open his eyes and be able to recognize what is happening in the community. The community is moving into adulthood, and is no longer irresponsible as with an adolescent. But this needs to be recognized and accepted by Peter, who can be likened to the parent. All he needs to do is stop and look back at his own growth: how he had to be really strong to break away from his parents and to find his maturity. The community needs to find its maturity, and it can be done painlessly without any struggle, if Peter can accept fully what is happening. Tell him to relax, release, and let go, so that all can grow in strength, beauty and oneness. The time has come for this to take place.

In other words, this construction of the hall was to be a truly *group* project, with me more in the background showing interest, encouraging but never directing it. Not an easy thing for me to do! George Ripley, for example, as leader of the architects, had drawn up two or three alternative plans, which were made into models; the group chose model 'A', which Eileen also felt was the model that should be built — but while a place of beauty, it was to be seen as a utility building from where the energies generated could flow up and out.

Unfortunately, Eileen felt that the word 'utility' implied something that was useful, cheap and easy to make — a hangover description left over from the war years — whereas I and others preferred the Oxford Dictionary definition of 'utility' as being something used for many purposes. Above all, I wanted it to be our latest expression of something built to the glory of God and hence with perfection, a demonstration of the talent and spirit of those then in the community.

The model we finally agreed to proceed with was one of a large, handsome, five-sided building that would take much energy and time to complete. Our plans obtained Building Permission, to many people's amazement, as the site was on sand dunes on the land immediately adjoining the Park Building. This permission was achieved by forming a good relationship with the planning authorities and especially the local Master of Works, whom I'd gone to see with George. We sought his advice on a number of points, including him in the design process, and I think he was won over when I particularly praised his ideas for a cesspit, of which he was proud!

Lyle Schnadt — the master builder who had overseen the construction of the Community Centre — had returned to America but offered to come back to focalize the group in charge of the hall's construction, with one condition: he insisted that the foundations be laid before he arrived. We ordered the cement but there was some trade union strike which prevented it from coming. Then I recalled that there had been guidance — I forget from whom — that the building would be delayed, and that the reason for this would become apparent.

We waited expectantly. In June we had a visit from Wayne Guthrie and Bella Karish, leaders of a spiritual group I'd met in May in Los Angeles during my tour. I was prompted to show them the plans of the hall, and a model that George had constructed, and they were excited about the whole project — but said that one thing was not yet right. Bella explained that the axis of the building's five-pointed foundation was just a few degrees out of alignment with the cosmic power point on Cluny Hill, about 5 miles away, and Ben Malvern, a mountain to the north.[3] This slight misalignment was corrected — which required more than a slight degree of physical effort — and immediately that was done, the strike was over and the cement was delivered. The foundations were laid, Lyle arrived and the building got underway.

I visited the construction site every day, but — mindful of Eileen's guidance that this was to be a group endeavour — tried only to stay in the

[3] For those interested in ley lines, this is the one which extends from here south to Glastonbury in south west England

background, supporting and encouraging. It was sometimes difficult not to step forward when I saw what to my eyes appeared slovenly or slapdash but when I managed to hold myself in check, marvelously the group itself corrected these things. This was a wonderful lesson, to see that 'group consciousness' and 'love in action' were proving themselves without my needing to resume the role of authoritarian 'father'. Although I was busy enough with other new initiatives in the community, I felt freer than ever before to open up to the next steps for myself and the 'universal work' that I knew lay before me.

* * *

That autumn we held a conference at Findhorn on 'Cooperation with Nature', and among those attending was a beautiful, part-Hawaiian spiritual teacher called Ann Franklin, who brought a party of five with her from Hawaii. Ann ran a metaphysical bookshop in Honolulu and was apparently a 'sensitive'. On the last day of the conference, however, when she told me that I would visit Hawaii many times — the first time being before the end of that year (it was already November, and I had no intention of going to Hawaii, although Eileen and I were planning a six-week tour of the States) — I thought her a pretty poor seer. Ann went on to say that she saw Findhorn as being the present 'head centre' of the planet, whereas Hawaii was its 'heart centre', and that the heart should always rule the head. My doubts remained, although I am always open to surprise.

Eileen then surprised me! She wanted a fortnight alone with David Spangler to seek his advice about the traumatic time she still seemed to be going through concerning my relationship with Alice, and the future of her (Eileen's) and my marriage. Remembering Ann's invitation, I then wrote to her and suggested that she contact me once I was in the States to see if anything could be arranged for two spare weeks — could she arrange some lectures to cover my costs of going to Hawaii? It was a bewildering time for me. On my way through London en route to the States, a reliable and sensitive friend of the community told me that I would eventually leave the community and go to America to establish a centre on the West Coast but with a much younger partner, while Eileen's 'mother energies' would require her to stay at Findhorn.

This was too perplexing: I put the whole business on the back burner until I arrived in the States. When I met with Eileen after her visit with

David and Myrtle she was very upset. David had received a message from higher levels that Alice was playing her part in the plan, in helping to open my heart and should be honoured for the part she had played — but her sometimes queen-like behaviour was not appropriate, and it was important that she and Eileen establish a closer relationship and help each other. Moreover, when I later saw David and asked why I should be going to Hawaii, he replied from his inner sources:

> *Your visit to Hawaii has significance to you as a personal being. There is an attachment between yourself and the energy field of that environment and the earth elementals, which are very strongly concentrated in that environment. At some time in the future there will be a work pattern to unfold in the Islands, which you will be connected to... there is an act of energy of purification for you, Peter, which is taking you to this island. I cannot explain this more fully.*

The message did go on to say in general, however — very clearly (as usual with David) — that the Pacific Basin would become more and more important, in the years to come, for the influx and expression of those energies with which the New Age is associated.

In light of this, and as I had already committed myself, I chose to go to Hawaii. When I arrived in Honolulu I was struck by the luxuriant growth and the warm soft tropical air. I was met and garlanded with a lei of frangipani flowers by Ann Franklin and her two children. Ann took me to her beautiful home 1,500 feet above Honolulu, where there was evidence of her connection with Findhorn everywhere, from the weavings to the candles; she had all the Findhorn books, a whole set of David Spangler's tapes, as well as a wonderful library of other spiritual and mystical books. Ann had recently separated from her husband and said that I could stay in her guest bedroom.

After a candlelight dinner on the terrace, we watched the sun setting and the moon rise above the twinkling lights of the city far below. We went into the lounge and she played the grand piano beautifully and then put on some music for us to dance to. Ann also rented a house on the beach on the other side of Oahu so that we could swim in the early morning and watch the sunrise. We went to a luau that was for native Hawaiians only — as she spoke Hawaiian, Ann obtained permission for us to join in the ceremonies and the singing and dancing. When an Hawaiian kahuna[4] opened the ceremony, I felt deeply moved in my heart. I had never felt so deeply touched by any experience. I felt in tune with the sea, the people, the elementals and my own primal being, to a greater degree than ever before; I could not hold back the tears.

The whole atmosphere of Hawaii, the beauty of the island, the power of nature, had a profound effect upon me. As we toured the sacred sites, waterfalls and pools on both Oahu and the Big Island of Hawaii, Ann told me that she was in communication with the devas and nature spirits, and with the goddess of fire, known as Madam Pele. She said that she received from them that I was to help her establish a centre on the Big Island, where she owned land. But I remembered a message that David had received:

> *It becomes the responsibility of yours to carry back to Findhorn your own wholeness, the fires of your love, the illumination of your wisdom, that which nourishes and supports the growth of communion through relationship, and which can assist your partner in achieving her breakthrough at this time.*

I told Ann that I was returning to Eileen and the community, but she seemed not to hear me. She laid on all her charms until I felt that she was out to catch me: I was taken to the best French restaurants, and Ann was a superb dancer — which I have always appreciated and enjoyed, throughout my life. I had one of the best times of my life in Hawaii, enjoying the music, the Hawaiian people with their aloha spirit, the clear blue warm waters for swimming, the brilliant fish when we went snorkelling. Ann exposed me to everything that Hawaii could offer, and I took the bait, hook, line and sinker: but I also made it clear that our relationship was not to be permanent — and that my destiny was to return to Findhorn.

[3] An indigenous shaman, or holy man

Chapter 29

Balancing Act

Release, release, release: for only then can you relax into God

ON MY WAY HOME to Findhorn from Hawaii, I spent time once again with David and Myrtle and shared news of my recent experiences. At my invitation, David received a long message from a higher source about what was unfolding for me, the choices offered to me and how the community was likely to be affected by my choice. The gist of this message was that the elemental forces I had encountered in Hawaii represented a particular aspect of heart energy — 'the energizing passionate aspects of fire' — that would quicken the opening of my own heart, whose concerns had been rather set aside during the effort of will and concentration needed to establish the community.

It went on to say:

> *Findhorn has been partially created by the impact of your elemental force, your will and that energy which you have termed Light, which you will now come to recognize as not truly Light, for Light is a blended energy, whole and serene, composed of love and will and wisdom and intelligently applied energy. It becomes a responsibility of yours to carry back to Findhorn your own wholeness, the fires of your love, the illumination of your wisdom, that which nourishes and supports the growth and communion through relationship and which can assist your partner in achieving her breakthroughs at this time.*

I gave careful consideration to this message through David, and interpreted the choices it suggested. One was to move out of the community to do planetary work, helping other centres to form and grow. Another was to return to Findhorn and move from what David called the 'Moses principle' to the 'Mary principle'. I could see that I could help Eileen to develop the masculine side of herself, and she could help me to develop the feminine qualities. Then we could work not as two halves of a whole, but as two whole and integrated individuals working together in love and harmony. It occurred to me that my relationship with Alice had served to split the 'old' combination of Eileen and me, and that at least for a while the three of us could work as a triangle as Eileen and I went through our changes. Therefore my decision to return to the community was confirmed by David's words of wisdom; and as it turned out, during my absence Alice and Eileen were already learning to work beautifully together with a sense of mutual support.

When I came back to Findhorn there seemed to be a completely new spirit in the community. I began learning to temper my authority with love and wisdom, and as I did so it appeared to draw out the potential of more and more members. They got to know Eileen and me better as we shifted our roles from playing strictly parental figures to becoming fellow travellers in the adventure of transformation. As a simple example of this, once a week Eileen and I would take over the community kitchen and prepare a variety of omelettes for everybody's evening meal.

The time had also come for a fundamental shift in the way the community was organized and managed. Eileen and I were preparing to go on another tour, this time of Europe. During our last tour I had put two people in charge of the community in our absence, Alice Weybull and John Hilton, the retired bank manager and vice chairman of our trustees. Although the three of us had worked harmoniously together, upon my return I found that their joint endeavour had not been entirely successful. John, who was wise and experienced in the ways of the world, found it hard to work with such a young, inexperienced woman. Alice, with her highly developed intuition and inner sight, was frustrated by John's lack of awareness and understanding. It would be unfair to both of them, I thought — let alone to the whole community — to ask that they repeat the exercise without others to help them.

Therefore I decided to form a Core Group before Eileen and I left again. It would be the central, coordinating policy-making body for the community. Up to that time all major decisions had been made by me. As Eileen was no longer getting specific, regular guidance for the community or for me, I had to rely on my own inner knowing. It took about a year for me to gradually share with the Core Group all that I knew about the running of the community, since up to that time I was the only one who held all the reins and knew what was going on in all areas and departments.

About these changes, Eileen received:

> *You and Peter are responsible for this, My Centre of Light. You have invoked it and all you invoke you are responsible for. That is why it is important that the right Core Group is established to run the community, whenever he and you are away, and that that Core Group is essentially sound, grounded and dedicated. Unless this is so, and Peter is fully aware of it, he will not feel free to move out into the universal work. For I have much need of you both to be free to move around. You have much to give the world. You will always be responsible for this centre. Peter must be willing to let go, and really trust those who will form the Core Group and know that the community will be run under My direct guidance, and to My honour and glory. Unless this centre is really sound and united, it will be a waste of time going anywhere to talk about it. For this is a living demonstration of a way of life, and unless it reflects the way of life at the centre, it will be like an apple with a rotten centre, and would rot away and be useless. Therefore, the centre must be pure, sound and whole, and must be kept that way at all times.*

It took time for the Core Group to learn how to work as a group. On one occasion, for example, a particular problem was discussed and reflected upon totally from a mental standpoint, and no answer was found. The following day Eileen received:

> *Why waste time and energy discussing and arguing about a problem and how to handle it? Why not be still and in the silence go within, and let Me reveal the truth to you? Never try to work out a solution with the mind. Let the mind be your servant, never the master. When you attune to Me, you each reach the same solution, for I am the universal mind. No problem is too small to bring to me. See the group functioning from the universal mind, and then everything will run smoothly, and there will be perfect harmony and oneness.*

The Core Group was in charge of the overall policy of the community, but we soon found that it was handling too many detailed administrative matters. We then formed three branches: Administration, Education and Community, the latter composed of all the heads, or what we called 'focalisers' of all the departments. A community meeting was held every week. Policy would emerge from the Core Group, and be passed to the Administration Branch or the Education Branch, to see how that policy would work; next, feedback would be given to the Core Group. Then the matter would go to the focalisers, and finally brought to a community meeting for discussion. Thus decisions were made in groups in an hierarchical manner, and gradually came down until they were shared with the whole community.

To begin with I was the focaliser of the Core Group, the Administrative Branch, the Education Branch and the Community Group, because there was no one else with sufficient experience. Eventually I was able to release all these positions, as the right people were able to take over in these areas. I did remain overall Focaliser of the community.

Once this structure was up and running, Eileen received:

> *Now is the time for the Core Group to begin to stand on its own feet without Peter, so it is really strong by the time he goes away. Peter will have to let go and give them the opportunity to see exactly where they're at and how sound and united they are. This will not be easy for them, nor for Peter. Unless he really lets go of the reins, he will find that he will not be able to go away for any length of time. This time of training for the Core Group will reveal many things. Expect the best and see it come forth.*

As it happened, I handed over power too suddenly, and Eileen received that I should let go more gently, and that then they *could* find their own feet.[1]

* * *

This year — 1975 — was indeed a time of great transitions for all of us. After an illness of several weeks, Roc died at Loch Tay on 8 March. He was a dear friend, as well as the community's mentor, and on hearing news of his passing I felt shocked and a great sense of loss. I thought that we still had a great deal of work to do together.

[1] During this time, Eileen obviously continued to receive guidance on important issues affecting the whole community

That evening the entire community came together to mark his death and to appreciate all that he had given us. Alongside a natural grief that he would no longer be with us physically, we drank a toast to Roc in love and joy at his release from the confines of his earthly body: we knew that he would not forsake us, but would continue to watch over and guide us from a higher level of consciousness.

Three days later Eileen and I attended Roc's funeral in Edinburgh. Sir George Trevelyan conducted the ceremony superbly, with an appropriate balance between solemnity and joy. He referred to Roc as one of 'the great pioneers of the New Age' and added, 'To many of his friends he was counsellor and guide, bringing a depth of wisdom and love and helping them on the path towards widening of consciousness and awareness. . . . Roc, as an advanced sensitive, made the breakthrough into direct vision of the world of the nature spirits. The importance of the bridge between man and the elemental world at this time cannot be exaggerated. The great initiates and adepts of the twentieth century, such as Rudolf Steiner and Tudor Pole, had direct contact with these invisible beings and have spoken of them. Roc, however, had a special mission: to bring the reality of these worlds into public knowledge. His association with Findhorn has given this opportunity... The redemption of our polluted planet clearly involves man's cooperation with the invisible world of the devas and the nature spirits. The work in the Findhorn garden and the achievement of Ogilvie's link is of paramount importance. The bridge once established, a wider knowledge and energy and cleansing for the planet will result. Ogilvie was indeed a beautiful soul. The radiance of joy, wisdom and love shone from his face... Truly he was the Merlin of our age... in the very best sense a white magician.' My eyes were pricked by tears.

After the funeral, Roc's friends went back to his flat for a few hours and we enjoyed a spread of food and drink. The assemblage there reflected the many different facets of Roc's extraordinary life, which for the first time I realized he kept in watertight compartments, each separate from the other, thus maintaining the 'cover' that magicians require to be most effective in their work. As an example of this, Colonel Henderson — who had known Roc for seventy years and was one of his closest friends — had no idea of the side of Roc that we knew at Findhorn. For me, Roc's passing marked the end of an era: but more importantly heralded, triumphantly, the beginning of a new one.

* * *

Also that year, the publication of Paul Hawken's *The Magic of Findhorn* — an extension into book length of an article earlier commissioned for *East-West Journal* by its editor, Robert Hargrove — created a sensation. Paul had been the highly successful general manager of Erewhon, then the largest health-food distributors in the world; although he had heard of us on the grapevine in California, he was frankly sceptical when he accepted Robert's commission. He was even more sceptical when he first visited us and Eileen shared with him her guidance that his magazine article would 'sweep across the United States like a bushfire'. But that is exactly what happened. Paul later wrote to me:

> *More and more reactions to the article are coming in, so I guess part of that bush fire has been lit. There seems to be in so many people an empty space, which the story and message of Findhorn fills and makes whole again. I really do not know where to begin to express to you and Eileen and everyone, the overwhelming sense of gratitude and joy I feel towards you all. It is really quite indescribable, but so utterly tangible and real. I feel that in some way, not yet fully understood, that Findhorn is a crossroads in my life, and that my experiences there will not fade in my memory, but will rather grow within and become greater throughout my life. It is a testament to Findhorn, that even within the rather barren soil of myself, that you all have been able to plant a seed which is growing and nourished. Did you not learn first to plant a garden, and so I feel that this world is your garden, and that people who come to Findhorn are like seeds that come to life, within the love and nourishment of the community. And that these people are then like seed pods drifting across the planet, sowing the new seeds of a new age, and making them grow. How perfect is the symbol of the garden for Findhorn, and how marvellous was the fact that you started in sand. For is not the world very much like those dunes and hillocks, waiting for the love and consciousness of new beings to transform it into life and beauty?*

His wife added, in a separate letter, that Paul was a transformed person after his time with us; but after the publication of *The Magic of Findhorn*, the boot was on the other foot, because the Findhorn Community was transformed by it.

Paul's simple but lyrical narrative really caught the 'magic' that was at Findhorn at the time, and as a result a flood of people wanted to visit us. We simply could not accommodate them all and had to turn so many away. The success of *The Magic of Findhorn* may have been the chief cause of this upsurge in our popularity, but it was not the only one: *The Findhorn Garden*, *The Findhorn Cookbook*, a number of Eileen's and David's books (published by our own press), as well as innumerable newspaper, magazine, radio and television features had suddenly made us the 'hot spot' to be. A film about us was shortly to be released. When he learned about this, a visiting high-powered public relations man from the States pointed out that we were about to be inundated, and that 'nothing short of barbed wire or machine guns' could keep the people out. What were we going to do about it?

I immediately knew the answer: Cluny Hill Hotel. Hadn't Eileen's guidance, all those years ago, promised that we were to return there, after we had built up the centre at Findhorn and when the timing was right? Without pausing for permission or approval from any of the various community groups that would want to be consulted, I went to the telephone and rang Phimister Brown[2]. I suggested that he *could* buy Cluny Hill Hotel and run it, and we would provide the guests. He said that he would contact Gammak Clark, the Managing Director of the chain that owned the hotel. A couple of days later, Phimister rang me back with an interesting story: when he had phoned Mr Clark, shortly after my call, he was told that either he had a spy among the hotel chain's directors, or he must be psychic: that very day, the directors had decided to sell Cluny Hill Hotel.

This was my cue. I took the subject of purchasing Cluny Hill Hotel to the Core Group and the Administrative Branch, and arranged for us to visit it: we liked what we saw. Four of us then met with Phimister — whose firm had over 200 hotels on its books, so was hardly lacking in experience — and invited him to put forward his proposals. Instead he surprised us by making a counter-proposal: why should we not buy it ourselves, run it as part of the Findhorn Foundation and only admit members and guests of the community? His profit/loss estimates of running the hotel *as* a regular hotel matched ours, and appeared equally pessimistic: much work needed to be done on the building, which — true to Eileen's guidance thirteen years earlier — had been allowed to run down. Phimister suggested that if we did proceed to buy

---

2 The solicitor who in 1962 had offered me the management of a hotel in Aberdeen — see page 196

it, we might consider advertising to our guests 'the therapeutic value work might have for them'. I couldn't suppress a chuckle as I explained to him that we were anyway a working community, and that our guests in fact paid to be allowed to work with us! Before leaving, Phimister said that we couldn't possibly fail.

The building was valued and insured for £1,390,000 and would be able to accommodate about 150 guests, with 20–30 staff. Phimister told us that there should be no difficulty in raising a bank loan and that he himself was prepared to guarantee £10,000; but I could foresee that the proposal would meet some pretty stiff opposition from many quarters of the community. Some members thought that the money — if we could raise it — would be better spent on buying a farm, so that we could become self-sufficient in our food production. Others thought that if the money were available, we should upgrade the existing members' accommodation in the caravan park. (Bungalows were mainly reserved for guests: most members still lived in caravans.) A few muttered that we should be like the Franciscans, taking a humble vow of poverty and giving whatever extra money we earned or attracted to other worthy (and more deserving) causes.

In order to reach unanimity, I took the community members in parties of twelve — which was all our bus could hold — across to the power point overlooking the hotel and invited each group to spend time in silent attunement. Afterwards, they were encouraged to share any personal insights or feelings they had. Then I called a meeting of the entire community, at which I showed slides of the hotel and its grounds, and the financial and personnel details were discussed. Michael Shaw, who focalized the Administrative Branch at the time, ended the meeting by saying, 'I think I've thrown every possibility of a practical nature against Peter, over the last three weeks, and the solution for every one of them has fallen into place. I have gradually come to the conclusion that despite the apparent illogical nature of this decision, it might be the will of God that we acquire the hotel'.

This certainly seemed to be the case. Despite its valuation of over a million pounds, we bought the building — which included all the furniture, two grand pianos, teaspoons, linen, five and a half acres of grounds, a large garage, a cottage, tennis courts, a swimming pool and sports pavilion — for just £60,000. It was a superb example of group manifestation.

* * *

Over the next few years the community continued to grow and we acquired several more properties in the local area. Eileen and I spent more and more time on tour, often with other community members, in Britain, Europe, the United States, Australia and New Zealand; everywhere we went there was evidence that the 'Network of Light' we had for so long visualized was coming into form as communities, groups and centres.

The Findhorn Community was not only growing in size, but also growing up — as more and more members took on responsibility for their work departments, so I was able to loosen and finally let go of the reins. A new Core Group was formed towards the end of 1978, with François Duquesne as its (and thence the community's) Focaliser — he had a shrewd sense of business, and in the rapid physical expansion of the late 1970s the Findhorn Foundation had need of his expertise. Our permanent membership had grown to around 300 people, with about 4000 residential guests — who stayed with us for at least a week — and 10,000 visitors a year. A new book, *Faces of Findhorn,* had been commissioned by the publishers Harper & Row in the States following the success of *The Findhorn Garden.*

In January 1979, I attended the Rainbow Rose Festival in Pasadena, California, a huge gathering of about 120 speakers and workshops leaders. I was to be introduced by Shari Secof, the Findhorn 'contact person' in the Los Angeles area, whom I had forgotten I had met at Findhorn in 1976. Neither Shari nor I had any idea just how much the festival would change our lives.

On the first day, Shari heard a divine command from within to 'Get closer to Peter'. She wondered how to do that, but thought that if the instruction did come from the 'God within' then the way would open up. As it happened, that evening I asked Shari if she would like to join a few people from Findhorn who were going to Hollywood to hear a community member's sister sing at a nightclub; it seemed a friendly gesture, as she was the contact person there.

We set out as a party of four: me, Shari, François Duquesne and Linda Morris from Findhorn. However, before getting on to the freeway for Hollywood, François and Linda asked to be dropped at their hotel, as they were feeling exhausted both from travel and the festival. Shari took this as as a sign that her message had been correct: she certainly had the opportunity to get closer to me. We became acquainted that evening at the nightclub and returned to her hotel, only to find it closed and locked. The result was that she spent the night with me in my hotel.

After the festival I had a few free days, before my return flight to Britain, because a Canadian engagement had been cancelled. I'd had a letter from Helen Rubin, an ex-community member, saying that she thought it a good idea if I could visit a group of five adults and four children from Findhorn, who were now living together on the Hawaiian island of Maui; so I managed to spend two wonderful days in the sunshine there. I returned to Findhorn feeling fit and clear, touched again by the extraordinary loving energy of Hawaii.

My relationship with Eileen had been growing steadily rockier in the past few years, and on my return I was resolved to try and work things out with her. I therefore rang Shari to tell her that anything between us was off: I was going to reunite with Eileen, and do everything possible to save our marriage. Shari was outraged, shocked and hurt, but accepted my decision, never expecting to hear from me again.

I was intending to tell Eileen about Shari, but my fear of Eileen's anger prevented me from confessing to our one-night stand in Los Angeles. It was a tricky situation: I knew that Shari was planning to visit Findhorn in the near future with the group with whom she had been working in Los Angeles for several years. David Spangler and others had intimated that Eileen and I might separate and that I would have another partner, but I really wanted to try and work the marriage out. We did not seem to be having much success, however, despite counselling from several good and trusted friends.

Eileen was still suffering with the splitting apart of our relationship that had taken place since Alice, and she felt that we should separate for a time, though we had planned to tour the United States together. David and Myrtle thought that it was right for us to separate, but I thought that this would only be for a few months. We were told that the situation was foggy, but that each would be minutely guided over the next period, until the time of a major decision.

At the last moment, Eileen decided not to tour with me so I went on alone. My first stop was with Bill and Louise Trigg, the Coordinators for Findhorn on the East Coast, where I was to give a series of talks. Bill told me that he'd been unable to get the Findhorn books that I'd requested, but that all would be well: he had solved the apparent problem by calling on the West

Coast Findhorn Coordinator — Shari Secof! So I then phoned Shari, and she said that she'd packed up the books, put them in her car and asked her daughter to send them on a plane, as Shari was off to a conference; but when she'd returned she discovered that they hadn't been sent. I suggested that she meditate and seek inner direction as to whether she should bring the books over herself, because they were needed the next day.[3] Shari phoned back to say she would come.

I told Shari that Eileen and I were separating, probably until September or October. When Shari arrived she told me that she was angry at my having only a temporary separation — she was not interested in having a relationship with a married man. I admired her candour and we agreed to leave matters in God's hands.

Shari decided to go with Bill Trigg and me to the Koinonia Community, about two hours away from the Triggs, where I was giving a talk; Shari would then leave afterwards. Once we arrived, however, the people at Koinonia asked that I stay on, as they were having a number of problems and would appreciate my counsel. Bill Trigg said that a friend could drive him back; Shari also was preparing to leave, but at the last moment changed her mind as she wanted to hear the discussion. This went on until quite late, so we decided to stay overnight. There were plenty of single rooms in the community, but to our surprise we were shown into an apartment above that of the community's leader, a minister. The room had just one double bed. It seemed inevitable that Shari and I were meant to be together.

Shari, for me, was the embodiment of the feminine principle, with a highly developed intuition and hardly a left-hand side to her brain[5]. Somehow she knew how to draw the feminine side out of me. I shared that my goal was to become androgynous in this lifetime; that we were both individuals, and I was not looking for a woman as much as I wished to complete the expression of the 'woman' in myself. I was already discovering that Shari could help me get in touch with my emotions and express them more easily than I had been able to before. We talked about a partnership, both knowing that it would not be forever — at that time I still felt that I would return to Eileen.

---

3 The sale of books and tapes at workshops and lectures was an important source of income on every tour

4 This is not as uncomplimentary as it may sound! My understanding at the time was that studies had suggested that the left-hand side of the brain was primarily concerned with cold logic and rational thinking, whereas the right-hand side has more to do with intuition, imagination and feelings

We left Koinonia together to go to a large conference at Paul Solomon's new centre in Virginia, where Sir George Trevelyan and I were to be the main speakers. Paul Solomon contacted his own inner guides and confirmed that it was the right step for us to embark on this relationship, though the form would change. He said it would also be right for Eileen and her growth, as it would help her to develop the masculine side of herself and to stand on her own feet, and likewise for the community. I was beginning to feel that my next step was to go to Maui, since I had found it a place of such powerful heart energy.

Paul Solomon arranged for Shari and me to be accommodated at a nearby hotel — Sir George was a little surprised when I removed my things from the room that we were to have shared! When we woke up at 6 am Shari was told in meditation that we should go and visit some caves. I told her that there was no time with my full programme, but she said that we could go before breakfast. Now I don't particularly like getting up early or going out before breakfast, but we left and went to the caves — only to find them closed. So much for the right-hand side of the brain! Shari told me that everything was all right and led me up the hill, through long grass, stinging nettles and poison oak — and I was only wearing shorts. I was fed up with having started out so early in the morning and missing my breakfast. Shari kept leading first to the right and then to the left and so on. I meekly followed behind.

After about an hour and a half we started going downhill again and came to a clearing. There was a van with some people cooking breakfast, and delicious smells wafted towards us. I recognized the people as being close friends of mine from the Renaissance Community, and could imagine their surprise at seeing me with a woman emerging out of the bushes in the early hours of the morning! After much laughter at this unexpected reunion we had a wonderful breakfast, and through this experience I gained a new respect for the working of the right-hand side of Shari's brain. Furthermore, the people from Renaissance had made friends with the owners of the cave and arranged for us to have a special, private tour of them that evening. Sir George was really quite envious when he learned of our exploits, as he'd heard about the caves and had wanted to visit them but was unable to do so.

At the end of this US tour I spent ten days with Shari, going through all kinds of exercises, meditations, drawing, art work, to develop the right side of my brain. We had breakfast one morning with Dr Brugh Joy, who also tuned into my situation, and said that it was absolutely right for Eileen, for Shari and me and for the community. He said that it was important that the 'etheric umbilical cord' that linked Eileen and me was cut, and he undertook to do this. (Barbara Carpenter, whom he had instructed, later came to Findhorn to help Eileen do the same.) We also met with Wayne Guthrie and Bella Karish, two dear and very wise friends, and shared with them what was happening: Bella once again confirmed the rightness of what we were doing.

From then on I allowed Shari to lead me around wherever she felt prompted we should go. It was a delightful time together — we held hands, ate ice creams, giggled over the silliest things — and I felt that I was enjoying the adolescence that almost sixty years earlier I seemed to have missed out on. When Shari came to see me off at the airport I asked her to be my partner, but not in marriage. I felt that it was still possible that Eileen and I would reunite. Shari accepted this, to her credit and my lasting gratitude.

I returned from the United States in time for our eldest son Christopher's graduation from Medical School in Edinburgh. Instead of touring the United States with me, Eileen had gone to Hawaii to rest and reflect on her life; while there, she had taken an opportunity to meet with Ann Franklin, with whom she related well. She returned to Scotland relaxed, suntanned and determined that we could work things out between us. When we met in Edinburgh, Eileen suggested that we could both go to Hawaii together in September. I was dumbfounded: I thought we had already made the decision to separate for a time.

It is only now, setting down these memoirs, that I realize that I had earlier mentioned to Eileen that I would be moving to Drumduan House[6], and also had in mind spending time away from the community; but Eileen must have interpreted our separation as a time for me to remain at Drumduan and for us to continue working on our relationship. Today I understand and can empathize with her shock and hurt, but at the time I gently replied to Eileen that we couldn't go to Hawaii together, because I had already planned to go with a woman named Shari Secof, who would help me go through my changes there: I had already bought the tickets. I reminded Eileen that several years earlier David had prophesied that the Hawaiian Islands would be a base for my future work.

---

5 A large and handsome house on the other side of Cluny Hill, acquired by the Foundation in 1978

Eileen exploded with anger and threw her wedding ring at me, immediately demanding a divorce. I was shattered as I realized how hurt and abandoned she felt, and how I had spoiled her vision of us being together in Hawaii. Christopher was a great help to his mother, as well as to me: when I explained what was happening, he said he completely understood and supported both of us. After the graduation Eileen went off to the south of England to help her daughter who was having a baby, and I returned to Findhorn to wind up my affairs.

Chapter 30

Love Will Find a Way

The ship must often tack to go against the wind, that is, go off its course to get on to its course again in a safe though roundabout way.

ALL MY LIFE I've been an inspector, I realize now — from Lyons tea shops in my early twenties; then in enormous catering outfits in the Royal Air Force; at Cluny Hill Hotel; through the gardens, buildings, workshops, programmes (and the state of Alice Weybull's toilets!) in the Findhorn Community; to those people and places around the world who claim to be creating or working with the forms of a new age. Just as responsibility brings awareness — 'eyes of light' — to the tiniest corner, so too should awareness bring responsibility: for example, if you are walking by the Community Centre at Findhorn and notice a piece of litter on the road, you don't wonder where the maintenance crew is, you pick it up yourself.

One keen young man at Findhorn in the 1970s was so taken by the poetry of this concept that he prayed to have 'eyes of light' like mine. His prayer was granted; but within a few days he was praying for the gift to be taken back again! For he had seen so much that needed doing and yet he was unable to take personal responsibility for setting it *all* right: the light was dazzling him. As a result, he had a new appreciation of one of my roles in the community at the time.

Those 'eyes of light' have never left me: I suppose I will always be an inspector, whether it's to people's liking or not. Self-inspection, on the other hand, came late to me, as my primary attention always seemed to be on other people and activities.

Soon after handing over focalization of the community to François Duquesne, I drove with him and three of our trustees to Erraid.[1] François

---

[1] In 1979, two Dutch brothers, Henk and Arend Van der Sluis gave the Community custodianship of this tidal island near Iona for eleven months of each year. The small group living

was driving. He comes from France and appears to many people as a reckless driver; I'm also known for my fast driving and going around blind corners at speed, relying on my intuition to 'take' the corners. On this occasion François was driving very fast along the narrow winding road beside Loch Ness. I was in the front passenger seat beside him and kept on putting my foot on an imaginary brake, saying, 'François, you're going too fast! Supposing something was coming around the corner?' By mistake my foot slipped on to the car's accelerator, which further alarmed me until I thought how ridiculous I was being: this was just how I drive!

Then I realized that what was happening in the car was happening in the community. François was now in the driver's seat, and intuitively he knew what to do and when. Nobody sitting beside him knew the situation as he did, and the same was also true of him as the Focaliser of the Findhorn Community. While I was the Focaliser I had the overall picture, and that intuitive knowing which meant that the major steps to be taken usually came to me first. Only the one in the driver's seat has the complete picture, the intuition that springs from that and the responsibility for acting on that information.

I also realized that the Findhorn Community had grown like a human being. The first seven years were primarily focussed on the development of its physical body. The next seven, leading up to the acquisition of Cluny Hill Hotel, dealt increasingly with the emotional body, and people worked on their emotions using various psychological tools like rebirthing, co-counselling and similar techniques. The third seven years involved the development of mental clarity. François was the ideal person for this stage of the community's evolution, as he had a clear and logical mind and had been trained in finance and business management. For some years he had been in the background in the community, developing his emotional body, and many newer members did not know that he had already focalized Accounts, Education Branch, Publications and the Core Group. I also knew that the community would not work at the time of my departure unless there was one person who had final responsibility and therefore final authority to cut through the confusion when groups could not agree.

The sociologists are happy to point out that most intentional communities fail after the death or removal of their original, charismatic leader.

---

there maintains vegetable gardens, welcomes guests and practices cottage crafts such as weaving and candlemaking

I think that in the case of the Findhorn Community, with me as the strong leader withdrawing and handing over control, that pattern was broken — even though the community did go through some challenging times.

After the shock of Eileen's fury in Edinburgh and her departure south to be with her daughter I moved my belongings to Drumduan House and called a special community meeting. François and the new Core Group were now firmly the centre of power in the community and I needed everybody to know what was happening. Before a packed hall I said that now that the Findhorn Community was about to enter its eighteenth year — the age of majority — it was growing up and needed to take on full responsibility for its affairs. I was going to leave. Furthermore, Eileen and I were going to separate and pursue our own spiritual growth to become balanced individuals. I said that just as our three boys were now out in the world and no longer needed us, so the community we had created no longer needed us as 'parents'. I needed time away to continue developing my feminine side, and Eileen needed to develop her masculine side. Our marriage had worked really well when we complemented each other, but now it didn't. I felt that as Dr Brugh Joy had indicated, it would be too difficult for me to make my changes within the community and so I had to leave.

I then asked the community for its response. There was a strange pause in the Universal Hall as people were wrestling with the import of what I had just shared. Most of the 'old hands' knew already, of course, but for newer members and long-term guests who had either tried to dismiss the rumours, or hadn't heard them in the first place, my announcement came as a shock, and for many there was an unspoken fear that my separation from Eileen and departure from Findhorn would mean the death of the community. Some of our canny local suppliers had already caught wind of the changes and were reducing our lines of credit.

Ross Stewart, the Chairman of the Trustees, was first to his feet. Describing me as 'a man of destiny' for whom 'the so-called conventions of ordinary life' didn't come into my makeup, he expressed the whole community's love and support, and wished me well in my next steps. It was a sincere, heartwarming and often witty speech in which Ross recalled his early struggles for me to be 'reasonable' in conducting the affairs of the community but had come to see that my 'fierce determination' to put God first had always won the day. He finished by asking François to convey the whole community's deep love to Eileen, too, who was still in England helping one of her daughters who was expecting a baby. In thanking Ross for his words, I told the meeting that although Eileen felt that the community no longer needed her, she still had a big part to play there, and that she and I may yet have work to do together but not in a marriage relationship.

François then wanted to share a few words:

> *In a meditation all I could tune into was a tremendous sense of flowering, both for Eileen and for Peter and for the community, and that was the paramount theme, even though the news greatly saddened me personally. That is because of my close association with those two people, whom I love and respect; and perhaps because in each one of us there is a deep longing for security, for stability, for home, for that kind of relationship which will not change and will remain there as a stable foundation — always looking for that particular marriage that says 'those that God has put together no man can put asunder'. But those God has put together,* God *can put asunder. For me that brought home that the only security that I have is the security each one of us has, which is indeed in God — not in any kind of marriage, in any kind of stability. If we're asked to be stable points in the world of transition, then the kind of training which each one is put through somehow requires that our stability and our security be completely in God: and that to me is the inspiration which this process brought home.*

Vance Martin, a former Focaliser of the Core Group who had been (and remained) a close friend and counsellor for both Eileen and me, added:

> *I feel [this] means something really good. Not only will people learn not to put anybody on pedestals and get their own images in the way, but I feel that in a certain sense Findhorn is being freed. Peter and Eileen have put themselves forward at this time in their relationship to cause people to really test Findhorn, in the sense that we've already been getting feedback from people who knew that they were going to separate a month ago: 'Well, that means that Findhorn is finished!'. This is the image that's going to come up in the world, because there is cleavage in the centre. I breathed a big sigh of relief, because to me that's freeing us*

— to the maximum — of the old images of Findhorn, and allowing us to start to move in a new direction. Throughout this the main thing is to come together within ourselves; and know the love and trust that we have for these two individuals, to work out their particular patterns, and for us to move ahead into our pattern.

After this community meeting, in which many others also spoke from their hearts and offered nothing but encouragement, I immediately wrote to Eileen and sent her a tape of all that had been said. After a flurry of meetings with the Trustees, Core Group, Administration Branch, and the Education Branch, to discuss the running of the community after I'd gone, I left Findhorn to spend three days in London.

I had been very impressed at our latest conference by a South African healer named Andrew Watson. I knew that he was a healer who dealt with energies in the body, and I felt that I should see him about an acute pain that I had in my back. When we met in London, Andrew told me that there was a complete blockage in the flow of energy in my spine, and that the block was in the area associated with my solar plexus. He said that unless this was unblocked, not only would my spine become rigid, but that I would become bent double — and remain so. He said that the blockage was caused by a deep hurt.

Other sensitives had told me this in the past, but I could never find out what or where this deep hurt was. Then, one day in the Sanctuary at Findhorn, I had suddenly become overwhelmed by deep sorrow, and convulsed with sobbing, for I realized the source of the hurt: it was that my relationship with Eileen had not been fully expressed on the physical level. When I told this to Andrew Watson, he stressed that I should do something about unblocking my sexual energies, and not take on feelings of any guilt about doing so. With this and much else on my mind, I left London for San Francisco and then on to Hawaii, where I was joined by Shari.

We went to Maui together and lived on various parts of the island, linking up with many friends from Findhorn who lived there, and experiencing its astonishing and diverse energies. We explored most of the island, from rainforest to grassland, forests to scrubland and desert. We especially enjoyed the beaches and swimming in the warm waters of the Pacific, which was for me like a baptism from one life into another.

It was difficult to leave the island but consoling to know that we would be back. Shari and I flew to New York, where I played a leading part in the Festival of Mind, Body and Spirit, and then on to Findhorn for the annual One Earth Gathering in October and a special meeting among members of the Lorian and Lindisfarne Associations and Chinook Community, who with the Findhorn Foundation were exploring the establishment of a 'global university' whose campus might incorporate these and other forward-looking places. I lived in Drumduan House while Shari stayed at Cluny Hill College, where she took part in the Findhorn Experience Week programme. Shari and Eileen, meanwhile, had started to get to know each other — they had talked on the phone and corresponded and had met in person in Toronto — but I remained wary and unsure of how things stood between Eileen and me.

The community's seventeenth birthday on 17 November that year seemed to me to mark the turning point in Eileen's and my relationship with this our most unwieldy child. I felt that it had at last learnt the fundamental lessons that we had tried to teach, above all to put God first in all things and to realize that in doing so one would find true security — something that would be needed to pull the community through the times ahead. It would be important that Eileen and I as parents stand back and not criticize or condemn but allow it a graceful freedom.

My 'final' leave-taking — by which I mean that I had packed my belongings to move permanently (or so I thought at the time) to the States — took place ten days later, on 27 November 1979. Once again the Universal Hall was filled to capacity, and the appreciation, sentiments and best wishes for the future given to me were overwhelming. Tears pricked at my eyes as I looked around the shining faces, took up my hat and coat and began making my exit up the gangway. The Tibetan hand-wave turned into solid clapping, and then a loud, stomping, whistling standing ovation. I turned at the door for a last look at the uproarious crowd and then motioned for silence by raising my hand. There was an instant hush. Barely able to project my voice over the lump in my throat, I said 'What a memory to take back with me!' Then the wild applause resumed and I quickly turned and left the building, the tears now flowing unchecked.

* * *

After Findhorn, the next phase of my life was to be rest, relaxation and recuperation of my health. I felt depleted from continuous activity over a long period of time. I had left the community with travel tickets to Hawaii and only about £100 in my pocket; so when Shari and I were invited by Dr Brugh Joy to stay at the Intercontinental Hotel on Maui as his guests for nine days from the end of November, I felt that this was indeed a gift from God. Brugh was leading a spiritual tour group who were delightful company in this four-star hotel set in luxurious surroundings. I wondered where we would go after the Intercontinental, but I had complete faith that all our needs would be perfectly met.

I then remembered that a wealthy woman had once invited me to stay at her beautiful home, next time I visited Maui — she often invited visiting spiritual leaders to lodge in the guest house. As it happened, Brugh Joy's group planned to spend a day with her; but as her son was in the intensive care unit in the hospital, and she had also recently been burgled, the group was only invited for an evening. I took the opportunity to remind her of her invitation and asked if Shari and I could stay in her guest house, but she politely refused, explaining that she was about to rent it out. I said that I would need it only until December 27, when we were going to a seminar on the mainland with David Spangler and Brugh. It turned out that she was going to the seminar also, and in light of this she told me we could stay after all.

We were thrilled and moved into a beautiful home, with a superb view overlooking the blue seas. We were beside the swimming pool and everything seemed just perfect: we gave thanks to God and expressed our appreciation to our hostess. We went shopping and filled up the fridge. In the morning, after we'd had a swim in the pool, our hostess invited us to go north to a bay for an ocean swim. We had a delightful time, and in the car on the way back she played a tape by Joel Goldsmith, who would visit her when he came to Hawaii. The tape was about his journey to South Africa and losing his luggage en route, which upset him until he reflected upon the fact that it comprised only material things, whereas it was spiritual affairs that really mattered to him. When he had that realization, the baggage was found.

As we got out of the car, Shari asked our hostess how she felt about her antiques being stolen and said that surely they were only just like the baggage. The woman froze and refused to discuss the matter. I realized that Shari had really blown it. A few hours later our hostess phoned me and said, 'I'm sorry to have to tell you this, but I need to be alone, and I must ask you to leave by twelve noon tomorrow'. I was shattered, as I felt that the guest house was the right place for my recovery. Shari calmly said that if *this* wasn't the place, then God had somewhere even better. I replied, rather sharply, 'There's nothing! There is nowhere on this island more perfect than this house!' That evening we had a meeting with some of the key people on the island and told them what had happened; they smiled knowingly, and told us that they'd all been through similar experiences.

The next morning Shari woke up and said that we should do the Pritikin Program. I didn't really know what the Pritikin Program was, except that it was a diet and exercise regime held at the Mana Kai Maui Hotel in Kihei, and that Helen Rubin from Findhorn was its present director. Helen had been on many tours with Eileen and me; I immediately phoned her and told her what Shari had received, and she responded that she'd known all along that I should do it. I told her that I hadn't any money, and asked about a bursary for Shari and me to do the programme. She said that she would speak to the hotel's director, James Christman. A little while later Helen rang back to say that we *could* have a bursary; the program started the very next day and was the last one of the year. I realized that Shari's seeming *faux pas* was absolutely right: if we hadn't been asked to leave our 'ideal' accommodation, this even more ideal plan would not have been set before us. 'When one door closes, another one opens'.

We took part in the Pritikin Better Health Program for one week. This involved having my blood pressure monitored each day and having a full blood test at the beginning and end of the week. We also had seven daily snacks or small meals at a special table in the hotel restaurant overlooking the ocean, and three lectures a day on health subjects. If I'd known what the Pritikin Program was I probably wouldn't have done it in the first place, because it involved eliminating everything from my diet that I enjoyed, like salt, fat, and sugar. The diet is based upon Nathan Pritikin's studies of the eating habits of native peoples who don't suffer from degenerative diseases, so there were lots of brown rice and other whole grains, vegetables, fruit, salads (without oil dressings), low-fat dairy products and herbal teas. It was an example of God meeting my needs and not my wants!

As I was on Maui to rejuvenate and become healthy, this was a perfect opportunity. There was ample time for swimming in the hotel pool or the ocean, and we walked miles along the sandy beachfront every day. Shari watched over my diet, and I supervised her exercise. During the week I held a slide show and told the story of the Findhorn Community to the participants, and programme director James Christman was so impressed that he rang one of the staff at the Pritikin Headquarters in California. She asked

James how he had convinced me to join the programme and told him that if I toured around the world looking slimmer, younger and healthier, it would be a wonderful advertisement for them! As a result, Shari and I were invited to stay on at the hotel and to eat at the Pritikin table, in exchange for Shari doing two hours work in the office each day and for my general help, advice and attracting people to the hotel. This was perfect, particularly as we didn't have the money to go elsewhere.

We spent the days walking and running along the beach, swimming in the sea and eating a healthy diet, and we both quickly lost ten pounds in weight. After a time, more and more people were coming to stay at the hotel, because they knew I was there. This was great for the hotel but it wasn't what I needed, because soon too many were making demands on my time. Help arrived in the form of a party of nine from the Madre Grande Community near San Diego. Three of them, including Perry Vickers and Diana Soash, had followed an inner voice to come to Maui to see me. They then decided to move to the island, and offered to share a home with Shari and me.

We found just the right house in one of the island's loveliest residential areas, Maui Meadows on the lower slopes of the 10,000-foot Haleakala Crater. It was about 1,000 feet above the Mana Kai Hotel. The house was spacious and airy, with four bedrooms, a swimming pool and a wonderful view of the Pacific shores below. Our friends rented it for six months and Perry, Diana, Shari and I moved in at once. Shari and I had a private bedroom and bathroom; we had no furniture but I soon discovered garage sales, and had great fun buying everything for our new home. We had a housewarming the day after we moved in, and among the fifty or so people at the celebration were many ex-members of the Findhorn Community.

Maui seemed to be a magnet for ex-Findhornians — there were twenty living there at the time, including children, and they all loved the climate, playing on the beaches and swimming. But when I asked them which they preferred, Findhorn or Maui, every single one said that they would rather be at Findhorn. I found this hard to understand but supposed it must have something to do with the freedom, companionship and spiritual atmosphere that they had enjoyed in the community.

The party was so successful that we decided to hold a pot-luck dinner every Sunday, and thus the house quickly became a point of synthesis and beauty, where people of like mind and spirit could gather. The day after we moved in, Anthony and Gita Brooke arrived to visit, the first of a stream of guests from all over the world. I was also kept in touch with the latest news from Findhorn: Eileen wrote some long letters, describing the wonderful changes she was going through, and François sent regular tapes.

Shari and I tried to maintain a perfect balance of work, exercise, relaxation and sunshine. Each morning we would rise before dawn, go for a swim and have a run along the beach, watch the sunrise over the water, and then meditate before breakfast and the start of the day's activities. Previously I'd neglected my body; now I was living on a wholesome diet, receiving advice from two health experts, treatments from two chiropractors, and daily massages from Shari, a professional masseuse. Sensitives were at hand to advise on the deeper causes of any physical imbalances (I even had an 'aura-balancing' haircut!) but above all my greatest rejuvenation came from the loving care that Shari showered upon me.

Around that time, Shari wrote:

> *Peter has been drawn here to discover a golden balance, between his mind and his heart, his masculine and his feminine sides, between giving and receiving. Many do not realize that Peter has been relentlessly giving to Findhorn and the world for eighteen years, without sufficient relaxation. Maui lulls him to be more laid back, and yet she calls out to him to be a synthesizer, to pull her many parts together, but in gracefully slow Maui time. The house provides an excellent interim phase for Peter, for it is a place to be action orientated, yet allow for play as well... Our differences are becoming more apparent, and although we do not need each other we choose to stay together to discover the other parts of ourselves. Because of our awareness of the process of relating, a good sense of humour, gratefulness for this time together in this house on Maui, and the accent on unconditional love, we're rapidly growing and touching each other and those around us very deeply.*

From the distance that this new life afforded me, I began to understand the nature of my future relationship with the Findhorn Community, one which Eileen had long held in her vision but whose timing had not come around until now. I was to be more of a friend and counsellor, no longer concerned with the day-to-day administrative affairs of the place. True to what many had said, it had been necessary for me to leave Findhorn completely before the changes I was now going through could take place.

* * *

In May 1980 Shari and I went on a six week tour of the west and east coasts of the United States, giving many lectures and workshops and visiting a number of centres. During the tour, it occurred to me that the One Earth Gathering held at Findhorn each year could also take place in different countries, and that the first of these should be on Maui.

We formed a group to organize the event. At first one strong person wanted a gathering without any organization or format, with casual dress and behaviour and free use of marijuana[2]; fortunately he withdrew after some meetings. Jay and Joan Jerman became the focalisers of the event, with a very strong team and much support from all the ex-Findhorn members on the island. It was good that I was able to delegate the running of the Gathering to others, knowing that they would do an excellent job.

The One Earth Gathering was held at the Mana Kai Maui Hotel, with me as the MC and coordinator of the event. The speakers included Lionel Fifield of the Relaxation Centre in Brisbane, Australia, a well-known lecturer on prosperity consciousness; Patricia Sun; Bill Mollison, the founder of Permaculture; and Robert Whiteside, the founder of Personology[3]. Eileen came from Findhorn. We held the main lectures in a big hall at the InterContinental Hotel in Wailea, while the guests stayed at the Mana Kai Maui Hotel, where we also held workshops and served meals. During the day we had bus trips to places of spiritual power, so that people could experience the energies of the island. As was my practice on such occasions I asked a kahuna to give the opening blessing and talk. One of my main contributions had been to publicize this gathering when I'd been on tour, so we attracted 250 people from the States, Australia, New Zealand, the Philippines, Canada and England. Shari had had inner direction that she should not play a part in the One Earth Gathering, so she wasn't on the committee and didn't take part in the event.

During the Gathering I had some good talks with Eileen and we both received counselling, which helped us to work things out so that the way was open for us possibly to travel and lecture together in future years. The event ended with a superb luau with Hawaiian music, song and dance and

---

2 There is a particularly strong variety of marijuana available on the island, called 'Maui Wowee': I believe that its abundant use was a major factor in the failure of many young people to bring their dreams of building a community into physical reality. Another factor, of course, is the equable climate — why bother working when the sun is hot, the beer's cool and the surf's up?

3 Myrtle Glines — David Spangler's spiritual partner at the time — had introduced Personology to Findhorn during their time with us in the early seventies

wonderful food: it definitely recreated the atmosphere of Hawaii, in all its beauty and warmth. People commented on how much fitter and relaxed I looked, and I did feel full of energy and vitality. At that time I realized how much I had changed, as I was much more aware of and focussed on people, rather than on things that needed to be done. Maui had indeed been a place of change and restoration for me.

* * *

When Shari and I visited David Spangler that year I was in for a big surprise. Through David's insights, it became clear to me that Maui would no longer be my home, that my next base would be in the mainland United States and that Shari would no longer be my partner for future work, although we would continue to be friends. I was told she had been part of the cycle of change in my life, and that it was now time for us to go our separate ways. Shari took this news with remarkable ease and understanding, which was so typical of her openness and bigness of heart, and I greatly appreciate and honour the role that she played in my life at that time.

As usual I had no idea of what God had in store for me next, so I continued to take things one step at a time. Tours and workshops continued to keep me busy. At the beginning of 1981 I went on a three-month tour of the United States and Canada, with Helen Rubin and another ex-member of the community; Shari joined us at the beginning. The tour culminated with a networking conference that I organized for groups and communities on the West Coast, at Stewart Mineral Springs near Mt Shasta in northern California. Later that year — towards what would turn out to be the end of my stay on Maui — I went on an extensive world tour, from Honolulu to San Francisco, London, Findhorn, India, Nepal, Ceylon, Singapore, Hong Kong, and then back to Honolulu.

* * *

Shortly after returning to Maui from my US tour, and before embarking on the world one, I received a letter from a Paula McLaughlin, a young, tall, forthright woman I had met at the networking conference at Stewart Mineral Springs. Apparently she had found two cheques made out to my name in a book she had purchased there after a workshop, so she was sending them on to me. I wrote back to thank her, and mentioned that I was coming to San Francisco for two days in May. Soon after my letter, Paula — who lived in that area — contacted me and we arranged a meeting.

When we met in San Francisco, Paula suggested that we go and meditate. I agreed. During the meditation I received what was to my mind probably the most ridiculous inner prompting I had ever had: to ask Paula to marry me. This was absurd! I did not know her, she was half my age, I was not in love with her, and besides, at that time I had no intention of ever getting married again. But my inner 'voice' persisted. After the meditation, there was an awkward silence between us; Paula seemed as reluctant as I was to share what she had 'received'. When I finally coaxed it out of her, the information was even more staggering than mine: not only had she had been told that we were to marry, but also that I was to be the father of her child, who had been appearing to her in her meditations.[4]

This was stunning news, and it caught me unprepared. I was approaching sixty-five, after all — hardly an age to be starting another family. Yet somehow I felt the hand of St Germain in it all, and I had also learned so many times in life not to ignore such clear inner instruction, however baffling it might seem to the logical mind.

During lunch afterwards Paula and I discussed the situation. She agreed with me about the total unsuitability of our match — on Paula's side, I was certainly not the age or type of man that she wanted to marry. But we were both dedicated to God and His plan, and as the message had come through so strongly to both of us, we agreed there and then to go through with it. I flipped through my diary and said, 'I'm booked up for the next few months. However, I do have two free days later when I could pop up to Mt Shasta and do the deed.' Bizarre though it sounds, we were both very clear at the time. Paula later contacted me to let me know that she had even bought a tent so that we could conceive the baby on the mountain itself.[5]

As could be expected, the news of our extraordinary partnership created considerable consternation and resistance from Eileen, David Spangler, François Duquesne, the Findhorn Community and others. Had I taken leave of my senses? Comments in a letter I wrote to François summed up my reaction to the hue and cry:

> *As to the disturbance people feel as to my present course, I think we should realize that we've seen this effect before, and*

[4] So strongly, in fact, that she had already begun attending prenatal classes, despite the fact that she wasn't pregnant!

[5] Mt Shasta is one of the most powerful power points on the Pacific coast of North America, and a magnet for all sorts of spiritual types and activities

may well see it again. For example, when I announced to my friend that I was going to marry Nora on seeing her for the first time, if I had not followed that intuition I would not have received my early training and initiation into the Rosicrucian Order by Aureolis... When I left Nora, my children, and the Rosicrucian Order, there was indeed an uproar from Nora's family, my parents, Sheena's family, our friends, and the Rosicrucian Order. When I was prompted to move in with Sheena — who was [eventually] Eileen's, Dorothy's and my spiritual teacher — after only our second meeting, where would we all have been if I'd not followed that impulse and heeded the resulting outcry? When I received from within that Eileen was my other half and that God would bring us together, although she was already married and had five children, there was again an outcry from her family, my family and our friends. Where would Findhorn have been, if I had listened to others and not followed my own inner direction? Looking at this pattern it is clear what my course has been and must be. Each major change in direction is accompanied by a change in partner, which in turn is accompanied by an outcry. Please do not mistake my meaning. I am very sympathetic to the distress which these changes bring to people who have been concerned about me and are dear to me, and I wish I could do something to mitigate their distress, but I cannot.

Paula and I were married in the town of Mt Shasta on 5 June 1982, by a North American Indian and a Roman Catholic priest, who became the President of our new Foundation, which we called Gathering of the Ways. It was our intention to start a spiritual community there.[6] To begin with, our headquarters were at nearby Stewart Mineral Springs, an ancient place of healing power, where we held workshops for the many spiritual leaders that I had come to know in different fields.

I felt, at the time, that one of the purposes of Paula and my being brought together was, as two individuals whose masculine and feminine energies were seemingly balanced within themselves, to co-create a foundation and a family. With the Gathering of the Ways, Paula did the organizing and handled the finances, while I looked after people at the workshops in a car-

6 For various reasons — too complicated and of too little general interest to relate — this was not to be

ing, more sharing way. This was a big change for me — not since my time with Sheena over thirty years earlier had I played such a role to that extent. At home Paula and I equally divided the housework, cooking and washing up; and while I'd never had much to do with the upbringing of my other children, I took care of our son Daniel Elijah (who was born in December 1982) for at least half of the time.

One day I received a phone call from Eileen at Findhorn. She was very excited: she had just returned from a gathering in India, where she'd given a talk to over 3,000 people. I congratulated her and remarked on how great were the changes both of us had gone through since we were together at Findhorn. There she was, 'feeding the multitudes', and here I was, feeding Daniel and changing his nappies!

* * *

The Findhorn Community had become legendary in California — home to some of the best and worst expressions of the New Age — in the fifteen or so years since Paul Hawken and others had first written about it. Therefore as one of its founders, I was assured of a warm welcome wherever I went, and there was never a shortage of lecture and workshop opportunities. I had a new family in Paula and Daniel; a larger 'family' of many, many friends, old and new; and a comfortable, spacious home, in a superb and sunny climate which encouraged people to spend more of their time outdoors than inside, and seemed to make them friendlier and less inhibited. But try as I might I could never really feel truly at home in California. While the Americans and I shared a common language (most of the time!) there was a cultural gap that I simply could not bridge. It was hard enough to find a decent cup of tea!

Perhaps the problem is best illustrated by recollections of my first tour of the United States in 1974, which included a visit to David Spangler and the Lorians. David had always enthused about Disneyland and one of his dreams was to take me there, so during my stay a large party of us set out in three cars to drive to Los Angeles. We spent the day at Disneyland, and I was appalled. For the first time I saw tourists en masse in their summer clothes which revealed their gross bodies and bulging bellies. I realized why the people were so obese when I searched for something to eat: it was the first time I had been exposed to such a plethora of junk food, and the only refreshment I could find was wonderful fresh orange juice. The rest was white bread, hot dogs, donuts, candy, etc. — everything to eat seemed to be man-made and artificial.

The birds and animals on display were all mechanical, though I did catch a sight of one live sparrow somewhere. I took a trip in a bogus submarine and saw artificial seaweed and plastic tropical fish, which was quite boring after having seen the real thing when diving in the Red Sea and the Great Barrier Reef off Australia. I could not understand why people came in their thousands to see all the artificiality, but then when I looked at the suburbs of California, everything seemed artificial. At the end of the day David came up to me with bright eyes and said, 'Well, what did you think of it?'. I remarked that I did enjoy the one live bird that I'd seen. Although I had been taught to see only the positive, that was the only positive thing I could find.[7]

The longer I lived in California, however, the more I *was* able to find its 'sunny side', the positive and often delightful aspects of its outgoing lifestyle, and I expected that I would spend the rest of my life based there; yet the doubts remained about whether I would ever truly fit in. In Mt Shasta there was a 'genuine' English pub, 'The Spinners Arms', run by two expatriate Britons whose excellent menu offered such fare as steak-and-kidney puddings and Lancashire hotpots, and I must admit that it was more often than not my first choice when inviting visitors out to dinner.

The cultural difference — and no doubt the age difference — also created misunderstandings and miscommunication in my relationship with Paula, which began to develop storm clouds. After about three years of marriage Paula announced that she had inner direction that we were to separate, and that she was going to start a business in San Francisco. I was shattered. I went to the Esalen Institute[8] for a week to grieve, literally crying out my feelings until I came to accept the rightness of her decision.

For the next year I lived in an apartment in Mill Valley, near to Paula and Daniel, and came to enjoy being on my own, taking care of myself and doing some travelling and lecturing. I picked Daniel up from school each

7 But let me hasten to revise that jaundiced view of Disneyland itself. Some years later, Sir George Trevelyan and I were the keynote speakers at the Whole Life Expo in Florida, and we were accommodated in a large hotel next door to Disney World. Sir George opened the events for the day with morning meditation, but one morning he was missing and couldn't be found. At lunchtime he appeared, enthusing about his visit to Disney World and I was amazed. Sir George invited me to go again with him in the afternoon, which I did, and we had a wonderful time! I saw Disney World through his eyes, as if through the eyes of a child, and so entered into the spirit of the place. I felt that I'd learnt an important lesson: 'Except ye be as a little child, ye can no wise enter the Kingdom of Heaven.'

8 The Esalen Institute, at Big Sur, California, was and remains a pioneering centre for the exploration and development of human potential and personal growth; over the years, it has enjoyed an ongoing friendship with the Findhorn Foundation

day and took him swimming or hiking, and he spent several nights of the week with me.

Later I moved to Ashland, Oregon, where Lawrence and Sylvia[9] Schechter had formed a group called Alcyone; Paula and Daniel also resettled in the Mt Shasta area, just over the state line, so that we could maintain contact. My work remained educational, as well as bringing like-minded, like-hearted and like-spirited people together — even if they didn't always know it beforehand! I feel that two of my more important contributions during these years were to pass on to others the Rosicrucian teachings that I had received when young; and to counter the pessimistic prophecies and predictions that 'Earth changes' were about to plunge us all into Apocalypse. In California particularly, rumours of an imminent great earthquake had seriously frightened many people into selling their homes and migrating east. Whenever I had the opportunity, I would explain that *we* are responsible for creating our own reality, which affects the whole world, and to feed fuel to fears is a dangerous and foolish operation.

* * *

In 1987, the year of the Findhorn Community's twenty-fifth birthday (and my seventieth), Eileen invited me to join her to do a three-week tour of Europe, with Loren Stewart, a long-term and redoubtable community member. It would be the first time that Eileen and I had toured together in almost ten years, and I was intrigued by her invitation. Was this an exploratory attempt on her part to see if we could be reunited as a couple, or a genuine calling from spirit for us to continue the work that had brought us together in the first place? I chose to see it as the latter. We had each, it seemed, successfully gone through those changes for which we had separated and I had left Findhorn: both of us were now strong and balanced within ourselves, and the community itself was thriving, long after the shift from its original leadership.

In fact 1983, four years earlier — significantly the year the community turned 21 — had seen a remarkable upswing in its fortunes. A successful fundraising campaign had enabled it to buy the whole caravan park, where plans were underway to build a permanent 'planetary village'; the community hosted, that same year, the 3rd World Wilderness Congress, attracting

---

9 This is the same Sylvia whose angry mother, Elsie Moss, had set off 'the Nameless Ones' hue and cry (described in Chapter 12) when Sylvia's then-husband Fred Astell had left Sylvia to follow Sheena at the end of 1956

cabinet ministers and other prominent figures in the mainstream of society, whose attendance established a certain respectability in the eyes of the world, thus paving the way for further conferences in future years to deal with business, politics, spirituality and the arts; and after several rocky years 'in the red', the Foundation's finances became stabilized. The Findhorn Community looked fair set to sail into the next century as a flagship of innovation made possible by the demonstration of its founding spiritual principles. Now in 1987, Eileen's and my tour appeared to offer an ideal opportunity for us to share the same platform and declare the good news.

I should have known from the outset to expect the unexpected. I was not prepared for the 'new' Eileen and her new-found assertiveness, nor was I expecting to find in myself the degree of emotional vulnerability that I was now experiencing. Addressing an audience or giving an answer to some question, I was sometimes hurt and embarrassed when Eileen interrupted me or sharply pulled me up and gave *her* — quite different — version of the same event (whether I felt it to be accurate or not). At other times I was annoyed by the thought that she was using the opportunity simply to niggle or to get at me personally. Occasionally I even felt she was using me as a stooge for her own self-assertion, and I didn't like the feeling.

Yet people were principally drawn to these meetings because of their interest in the latest news of the Findhorn Community, and Eileen had the rightful claim to be living there still; whereas I had based myself elsewhere years earlier, although returning to the community regularly. Loren was a smooth diplomat and moderator, and helped fill the breach between Eileen's and my picture of the community, but it was an uncomfortable realization for me that we could not turn back the clock.

On one occasion, in front of a large gathering somewhere in France, Eileen was relating the story of how she used to go down to the toilet block to meditate for four or five hours during the night, every night, for so many years — I had told the story myself often enough before, for it was the messages she received at these times that helped lay the true foundations of the community. But on this occasion, as she retold the story all these years later, I felt as if I had been punched in the stomach and the wind taken out of me. Suddenly I was overwhelmed by unexpected, unsuspected and long-buried feelings of anger, jealousy, hurt and *unfairness* that the God I served seemed to have taken from me in those days the woman I loved.

Loren, who had noticed my distress, later asked me to tell him what was going on, so I did. 'Of course it had to be that way,' I added, 'for everything else to happen. But tonight was the first time it hit home, how much it hurt me personally.'

The tour continued and was a success — in terms of interest, audiences and income — and I think and hope that few people who came to hear our talks and presentations noticed or were unsettled by any personal friction between Eileen and me. I was too weary from meeting the demands of our busy schedule to have things out with her properly, behind the scenes, and I was also wary that she might still be carrying secret hopes of our eventual reconciliation as a partnership. If so, I couldn't reciprocate that feeling. What was plainly obvious to me from the tour was that the time for our working together again had not yet come — if it ever would.

At the same time, however, at a deeper level I was full of admiration and appreciation for just how far both of us had come, and grateful for the years of selfless service Eileen had given and continues to give to the Findhorn Community; and for her love for me, after all we had gone through together.

* * *

While we had been planning this tour I had received a letter from Renata Zürn, whom I had met several times previously both at Findhorn and on the Continent and with whom I had maintained a correspondence. She had written inviting Eileen and me to give a workshop at her centre by the Lake of Constance in Southern Germany during the tour, but our itinerary would not allow it. Undeterred, Renata invited me anyway to spend a few days in the healing atmosphere of the place to recover from the tour before my return to America. This offer I gratefully accepted. Since our first meeting, years before, I had realised that Renata and I had a deep personal link and a work to do together — something she'd known all along. Her centre was called Quell des Heilens, 'Source of Healing'. At the time, after this punishing tour, I felt in need of some.

Intermission

by Peter Dawkins

PETER CADDY was killed in a car accident on 18 February 1994, the day after he had completed his work on the chapter you have just read. He had gone with Jeremy Slocombe, his ghost-writer on the book, to Frankfurt airport to pick up his eleven-year-old son Daniel for the holidays. Within miles of their reaching home after the four-hour journey, a van suddenly pulled illegally across their lane of the highway and a crash was unavoidable. Peter died almost immediately; Jeremy escaped with a smashed elbow, and Daniel suffered concussion and minor bruising.

At the time of his death Peter was in the process of concluding his memoirs by narrating the story of how he and Renata Zürn came together and subsequently married, and of the eventful and stimulating years they enjoyed together.

My first meeting with Peter Caddy was in Edinburgh, in the early 1970s, at an illustrated lecture given by Peter and Eileen about the Findhorn Foundation. By this time the Findhorn Community was well established and world famous, and the lecture hall was filled with several hundred very interested people. By contrast I was still a young(ish!) architect, newly-married, who had recently moved to Edinburgh where my wife was a student of Edinburgh University. At the end of the lecture Peter leapt off the stage and, with Eileen close behind, ploughed straight through the audience and up to Sarah and myself at the back of the lecture hall. There, with only the briefest of formalities, he enthusiastically invited us both to go and live at Findhorn as part of the Community. Although circumstances were to prevent us doing so, Peter and I became friends and — much later in his life — we began working together closely.

The incident provides an example of how Peter lived and worked: how he would often immediately act on a strong hunch or intuition, without necessarily knowing why. One of Peter's special gifts was his uncanny ability for being in the right place at the right time, and acting as a kind of lightning conductor for cosmic (or spiritual) energy to enter the Earth. Many times I was able to watch this occur. Like the lightning spear of the Archangel Michael, the spiritual energy 'awoke' the energies of the Earth and began a process of healing and transmutation, and release of a light in the world. He did not often know why, or indeed see what happened himself, but he was aware of having completed whatever he was supposed to do. Of course, he liked it confirmed when possible.

From the sun-drenched balcony of Peter's well-equipped study-bedroom, beyond the garden and beyond the glistening Lake of Constance, can be seen the Swiss Alps— for Peter a dream world, with the mountains reminiscent of the Himalayan peaks. Although he didn't know it then, this was the place where his soul had chosen to round off his full and eventful life, to write his autobiography and finally to die.

Yet the last seven years of that life were missing from his memoirs: Peter was awaiting Renata's return from India so that they could work on these chapters together. Tragically this was not to be; but thanks to Renata's own diary and clear memory of their time together, the story need not end here.

One of the lesser known things about Peter Caddy is that except for the last few years of his life spent with Renata, he was a scrupulously careful man when it came to keeping records. Since his late teens he kept all letters written to him that he considered important (which is virtually all of them), and likewise copies of all correspondence he ever sent in reply. This also applied to all diary notes, reports of meetings, messages, advice and transcripts of tape-recordings, concerning all manner of things with which he was connected during his lifetime. For most of his life he was given secretarial assistance by friends working mainly voluntarily out of love and respect for him and the work he was doing, which made this mammoth task possible.

All these records are carefully preserved and filed— much of the detailed filing and referencing having been painstakingly done during the last few years of his life by Peter himself, and in the final year with the expert help of his friend Jeremy Slocombe, whom Peter engaged to be the editor and ghost-writer of his autobiography. In a sense this habit and foresight of Peter's has provided a historian's paradise, and has enabled almost every story to be checked and cross-checked for detail and veracity.

Full honours go to Jeremy for the major part he has played in giving birth to this book, and to Renata for the difficult task of completing on her own, and in her own words, the last section of the book concerning her seven years of marriage with Peter. But her patience, persistence and perseverance has resulted in an ending which I hope you will find as absorbing and inspiring as I do.

Part IV

The Crowning of a Life

by Renata Caddy

Originally it was Peter's intention that we would co-write the following chapters about our initial meetings and the years of our life and work together. However, his sudden and unexpected death prevented this.

I have written these chapters in my own words to complete the book of Peter's life.

Chapter 31

Heart-Meeting

The One without colour appears
by the manifold application of his power
with many colours of his hidden purpose

May the Being of Splendour
in whom the world dissolves
and from whom it rises
grant us a clear understanding

– Swetavatava Upanishad IV, (1-4)

PETER AND I first met at the beginning of June 1975 at Castle Schöneck, the family seat of a friend of mine, Wiwi Woeller-Paquet, in a beautiful mountain setting near Koblenz in the German Rhineland.

There Peter, accompanied by Eileen, their son David, and François Duquesne, told the Findhorn story for the first time in Germany. I arrived at the end of their slide show, bringing with me friends who had just come back from Auroville.[1] The inspiring songs of the New Troubadors were being played, and they gave me such a feeling of 'coming home' that my heart jumped with joy. After the lunch break, I felt so light that I found myself jumping down the stairs, taking many at a time, and with a big jump I landed right in front of somebody who was just coming out of the conference room. It was Peter.

After an amazed 'hello!' he gave me a welcoming hug and we went out into the garden together. We sat under a large tree to talk: Peter spoke about

---

[1] Auroville is an international community near Pondicherry in Southern India, inspired by the teachings of Shri Aurobindo and his French spiritual partner known as 'The Mother', who had the vision of Auroville

the origins of Findhorn, and I about the origins of Auroville. I had been there a few years before and still felt strongly connected. As we talked, I gradually came to understand that Auroville was a real sister-impulse to Findhorn.

Peter's radiance touched me. I found that here was a man with enthusiasm, simplicity and humour, and a very pure heart. On the next day, Wiwi asked me to translate for him; I sat side by side with Peter, and I saw in his profile enormous concentration, determination and will-power. At the end of the weekend, he gave me an embrace which I shall never forget: he held me a long time in his arms, silently. It was not an embrace from man to woman, but from being to being, completely still — a moment of eternity.

I next met Peter at Findhorn in May 1978 during my first visit to the Community. What an adventure it was, to go through the Findhorn Experience Week[2] and to touch into the powerful living Christ consciousness which is anchored there! It amazed me how, as a group of newcomers who had met each other for the first time there, coming from very different parts of the world, being of very different ages, spiritual backgrounds and inner development, we all came to feel that each one of us was a part of the whole. This happened mainly through the regular, short 'attunements' we held. Before any action was taken, we attuned to the divine source and asked for help; then, linking hands, we attuned to each other and to the work that had to be done — for example to a tree that needed replanting. We gave it our love and asked for its cooperation. The digging out then became surprisingly easy.

To know God within you, above you, below you, around you — to have God as your best friend at your side, to see God and the good in each other and in all things, to call it forth, to work with the Divine hand in hand, be it in the form of nature spirits, of angels, archangels, master souls, or the divine spark in each fellow human being — this was such an inspiration: what a healing balm Findhorn provides for each one of us and for our troubled world! I remember the focaliser of Cluny Hill College telling me that without meditation and attunement, morning, noon and night, they could never hold it all together; but with God as their centre, everything was possible.

In my second week, I chose to join a workshop called 'Creating a Centre of Light' and to my great joy Peter led several sessions. 'How bright you are —you are just radiating!' he greeted me, and I could have said the same of him. I greatly enjoyed Peter's talks in the workshop, and learned a lot

2 The introductory programme for all newcomers

from them. Afterwards I shared with him an intense and meaningful dream I had about him during this period. At that time, however, both of us were preoccupied with solving our own inner problems. Mine involved allowing the transformation of my whole life and of the relationship with the beloved friend with whom I lived, and I was being stretched to the limit in doing so; Peter — as I only learned later — was coping with the challenges which he faced in his own relationships.

Two years later, in October 1980, we met for the third time, at the One Earth Conference at the Findhorn Foundation. Peter had just come back from Hawaii, fresh, rejuvenated, his skin brown and his eyes shining. It was then that I heard of his separation from Eileen and of his having left the community a year before. Once again there was a great, spontaneous flow of love and joy between us. One evening in the ballroom at Cluny Hill College towards the end of this conference, Peter asked me for our first dance, a waltz — the most beautiful waltz of my life. Without a word, his eyes met my eyes and would not move away as we turned and turned in this seemingly eternal, swirling dance.

Much later I learned that Peter had completely forgotten this and other spontaneous expressions of love between us, but when I reminded him he remembered immediately. 'Obviously the time was not yet ripe for our coming together,' he explained, and of course he was right.

Peter and I maintained contact through letters over the years. I had heard from him at the start of 1981 that he was no longer with Shari and spent most of his time on tour and giving lectures. His work seemed to take him all over the world. He wrote to me in 1983 that he would be going to Findhorn that November with Paula and their nine-month-old son Daniel, and hoped that I would be there too: there was a lot he wanted to share with me.

Thus our fourth meeting was to celebrate the Findhorn Community's twenty-first birthday. So many former members returned for the occasion from all over the world that Peter's short visit was packed with meeting people: his own family, the larger community family and others gathered for the reunion. One evening when we were sitting together in the lounge at Cluny Hill, I began to share with him about a being who was very meaningful to me: Mahavatar Babaji and how I came to meet him. Peter listened with full attention and very openheartedly.

I had first heard of Babaji in 1975 through a friend, but while there had been an instant spark at the mention of his name, I was not interested at the time in finding yet another spiritual teacher. My inner path seemed clear to me. At the beginning of 1978, however, in a time of great inner emergency and prayers, Babaji became very present to me and in my heart clearly called me to come to him. Since circumstances allowed it, I immediately booked myself on a flight to India. During the night at home, after I had received my tickets, I had an intense experience of Babaji taking me up to the realm of Infinite Light, of merging in the All-Oneness of Divine Love and Light which was his substance, his being and reality. Since this experience, once and for all I have known who he really is.

Babaji is considered to be a mahavatar— a descent and a manifestation of pure divinity into time and human form — who down the ages has come to help mankind at critical times.[3] Paramahansa Yogananda, in his *Autobiography of a Yogi*, described Babaji in his former appearance as the 'Yogi-Christ of Modern India'. In our time, when Babaji appeared publicly in 1970, it was in the form of a radiant youth in a cave at the foot of Kurmanchal Mt Kailash opposite Haidakhan in the foothills of the Himalayas. He came to bring unity and peace to the world, and to take upon himself our human problems and suffering. Babaji gave his message, trained disciples, and left his body in 1984.

When asked for his purpose, he said 'My concern is the suffering of the whole world. I am not here for the curious, I am there for the seekers only. You can recognize me only through love — through loving God.'

When I met Babaji physically for the first time at Haidakhan, his welcome to me was 'I met you in Germany!' A few days later he began painting in an empty book that I had brought to him: these paintings included Germany, the Lake of Constance, our house, a Garden of the Lord, Tibet and a vision of the New World. He called this book *Omkareshwar*[4] These paintings made it clear to me that the place where I lived — at that time as part of a group of four, including my friend Marcel[5] — should be built up as a spiritual centre.

It was Babaji who in my heart inspired me to visit Findhorn, and to my

---

3 'Babaji' means 'dear father'; 'avatar' is the descent of divinity into a human body, while 'mahavatar' means literally 'great avatar'— the great descent of divinity into a human form, usually not born through a woman. The Babaji of whom I write here is known by many names: Mahavatar Babaji, Shri 1008 Haidakhan Wale Baba, or Haidakhan Baba; he is simply called Babaji

4 'Om Kareshwar' means 'the seat of the Lord whose name is Om'

amazement, I experienced at Cluny Hill the same light that I had experienced through him so many times. When I told Peter about Babaji, I felt his presence there; Peter and I were both highly inspired, forgetting time and space completely — which is not something that often happened to Peter.

* * *

The Lake of Constance— known in German as *Bodensee*— is a large beautiful lake in the heart of Europe, where three countries meet: Germany, Switzerland and Austria. My home is in a lovely little village above the lake.

At the end of May 1987 — twelve years after we had first met — Peter came to visit me there for three days. My life together with my friends in the house had come to an end and they had moved to the other side of the lake, so my place was in complete transformation.

I had invited Peter and Eileen to give a workshop and lecture during their tour of Europe but their schedule was already full. After the tour Peter had been invited to a conference in Yugoslavia, which was cancelled at the last moment: so it became possible for him to come and spend a few days with me before his return to America.

As I had mislaid my driving licence the day before his arrival, I had to fetch him by train from Zürich airport; when I met him there, he was holding under both arms luggage with handles that had just broken. There was such an irrepressible joy between us: it was such a gift to be finally together, to have time together! 'Let's make the best of it!' said Peter. Throughout the train journey home, Peter held his arm firmly around me, not letting me move to the opposite seat.

We crossed the lake by ferry boat and soon arrived at my home. 'What an atmosphere — how still it is here,' were Peter's first words when he entered the house; he was standing at the top of the stairs, looking down to the big white room with its fireplace and chimney, large enough for meetings and seminars to be held with up to fifty people or more. 'This is the cozy room,' I told him. 'But where can one sit?' asked Peter, puzzled, as it was empty of chairs. 'Oh you can sit wherever you like, there is so much space on the floor and I have many pillows,' I replied. 'It's the sense of space and

---

[5] Oscar Marcel Hinze is the founder of the Academy of Phenomenology and Integral Science; he gives lectures throughout Germany and Europe and is a spiritual teacher and friend for many. After leaving my first husband, I lived and worked with Marcel for twelve years, giving many different workshops on self-discovery, unfoldment and transformation

stillness in this room that makes me feel so at home here.' 'My goodness!' said Peter, 'My idea of cosiness is quite another one. Don't you have a comfortable chair?' We both laughed and I found him a rocking chair. We were just beginning to discover our polarity...

Peter gazed with amazement at my paintings on the walls. I am an artist, painting under the name of *Nila*. My work expresses in free forms and colours my experience of the inner worlds, and they seemed to mystify Peter: all he could say then was 'I don't understand a thing about them, but they touch my heart'. Later, looking down from the outside balcony, he saw a large, wild and romantic garden. 'The garden is the most important thing here,' I explained.

After a candlelit supper Peter — to my surprise — stood up to dance with me, out of pure joy. Three very blessed days followed — a festival for our hearts!

We also had deep sharings. It seemed to Peter that both our spiritual paths, as well as our very natures, were totally different. Peter's spiritual traditions were firmly rooted in the West, while I had also — besides my obviously western connections — deep links with India. As Peter had recently been told that the time had come to learn spiritual paths other than the one he had been on, it now felt right for him to go to Haidakhan... and for us to go together. So we made tentative plans to visit India at the end of the year.

In those three days, Peter and I realized the depth of our soul-connection, and we were both shining with that knowledge. But when he had to leave and we were on our way to the airport he became very silent; and just before his flight home to the States was due to depart, he looked extremely bewildered. 'Oh my goodness —now I'm going back to marry Virginia!' His face darkened considerably.

This was not news to me. Soon after his arrival he had told me how on his seventieth birthday, which had been celebrated in San Francisco with 250 people, and then later in Los Angeles, he had been brought together with a woman first introduced to him as a potential business manager who would organize his lectures and workshops. She had also turned out to be a good networker, and she got along well with his son Daniel (Peter and Paula had by then been separated for four years); and, as it had been prophesied that in his seventieth year Peter would meet his future partner, it looked as if Virginia were the one. Although he had met her only a couple of weeks before leaving for the European tour he had just completed, she seemed to fit perfectly into his life in America, where he was convinced that he would spend the rest of his life.

And now here we were, having just experienced this great flow of love and joy between us... It was at the airport that Peter said, with a heavy heart and mind, 'If I had known that it would be like this, I would have thought twice before coming to see you.' We had a farewell embrace. 'Now we must give it all into God's hands.'

* * *

I felt a pain in my heart like never before, as if it had been hit, physically. I asked God, 'What shall I do?' 'Bear the pain,' came the answer. 'I showed you through this love — Peter's and your love — how much I love you.' And I heard Him say, 'Express my heart in a painting, then you will know the New Heaven'. So I relaxed into God's love as much as I could.

Part of me was wondering if Peter would cut off that flower of our love which had now begun to surface so happily again. Would he simply put it in the background of his memory, as he had done so unconsciously earlier? Peter was always first married to his work, to his service to God. I understood that I did not fit at all into Peter's life and work, as he was convinced that this lay in America... and it was just as obvious that my task was in Germany to build up this centre.

So when he returned to America, despite feeling a deep heart connection with me, Peter still believed that this American woman was to be his partner. They moved into a fully-furnished house that Virginia had found on the slopes of Mt Tamalpais outside San Francisco, which seemed perfect for their purpose. Then Peter discovered that the workshops that she had arranged for him on the East Coast were not set up for him alone but for her as well: doing them together with her did not work for him at all. Returning to their new home Peter fell very sick with a serious bout of bronchitis and a touch of pneumonia; while lying in bed over the next two weeks, he wondered why. It dawned on him (and this was confirmed by 'sensitive' friends) that he had met with this woman to clear a strong karma from the past. Peter told me by phone that it had become clear to him that he should see me again before our planned trip to India.

So we arranged for him to fly over and give a lecture and workshop in the middle of August that year (1987) in my home — the only time available to both of us. Against his doctor's advice, Peter rose from his sick-bed and flew to Germany, where he arrived at my place to find the terrace full of easels and people painting happily at the end of one of my workshops. He was coughing so badly that I took him immediately to his bed.

This second stay — for twelve days around the Harmonic Convergence[6] on 16 and 17 August, which also marked the tenth anniversary of my move into the house — was to be a turning point in both our lives. Whatever the impact of this global Harmonic Convergence, Peter and I certainly experienced our *own* 'harmonic convergence' at the time.

As Peter gave his slide presentation about Findhorn to the many friends who had gathered, I was amazed to see the power he had regained in just a few days. Later, full of oomph and laughter, as he gave his workshop in the garden on 'The Challenge of Change', during the Harmonic Convergence itself, hundreds of white birds suddenly came from all directions circling over us. They circled again and again, until finally flying off together. It was unforgettable and we all took it as a sign of great blessing.

The next day Peter saw an excellent doctor, an old friend of mine, who said that Peter had worked too hard for too long, and prescribed him a course of homoeopathic injections and complete rest. For the following ten days Peter just rested — and in the great peace that surrounded him our love could manifest deeper and deeper. We both felt it as a pure gift from God — a gift of grace. Peter said 'I have experienced a love I had not experienced in my life before'.

One Sunday morning, a week after the Harmonic Convergence, I was sitting on Peter's bed just holding his hand and feeling in a very relaxed and contemplative state. Then something extraordinary happened. All of a sudden I saw very clearly, in my mind's eye, a being dressed in violet robes standing behind Peter's head, smiling and emanating an awe-inspiring dignity and majesty. I could see and feel how much this Violet One loved Peter — and then I saw how he handed Peter over to a being of White Light in the middle, above us. I recognized this presence as Babaji. Much more followed. The vision ended with me seeing Peter standing next to me, clothed in deep red velvet with gold, his feet reaching down into the earth, being grounded far more than I ever could be. In this moment I knew that this was why God could anchor so much light through him on Earth.

---

6 A time of key planetary change, according to the Mayan calendar and other ancient prophecies, and marked by thousands of people linking in meditation from sacred sites throughout the world

I had never seen this violet being before, whom Peter and others in the Western Mystery tradition called St Germain or the Master R and with whom Peter had worked as a friend all his life. Peter (who also felt his presence) was very moved by the fact that he was now handed over by him to the being of the white light from whom all colours stream and in whom they are all contained.

Peter related to the Divine Being — the infinite being of Light, Love and Power — in its expression as the Christ; he saw the Christ as the One to whom we, as parts of the whole, can learn to open ourselves so that he can express through us ever more. Peter knew the Christ as a universal principle, a divine consciousness and energy without limit or form. I used to see it the same way and then I *experienced* the infinite reality through Babaji. So we realized that the Divine is one, the Divine is the same; it is only the gateways through which we come and the names which we give that are different.

Peter had great respect for Babaji as a Christ-filled being. To him, my vision made perfect sense; he had been told earlier in the year that now was the time for him to be working with the White Light. He also began to realize in what a state of complete and utter confusion he had been during the past few months, working out his karma with Virginia in America. We were now free at last to come together.

Peter became lighter with every passing hour.

Next morning we drove to Lake Zürich to meet a very special friend called Swamiji Ganapati Satchidananda, from Mysore in India. He is one of those beings born with powers that most human beings have not yet developed.

Our fire-Swamiji, as we call him, is in obvious relation with all the elements. For instance, on certain holy days he goes among the flames in a deep fire pit, wearing all his clothes, and stands there in profound concentration and prayers. The fire does not hurt him. He then leaves the fire pit, usually by levitation. He has also been found meditating for hours under water. Through him, all kinds of things are manifested for the blessing of others — sacred healing ash, malas (prayer beads), amulets, statuettes and other things. Many people have seen and experienced this, including myself.[7]

[7] I had come to know him in 1975 when he 'appeared' in a golden column of light at two o'clock in the morning in our house. We were sleeping in Marcel's room, and suddenly awoke to see him in front of the bookcase; he stood there silently for quite a while, just looking to us, smiling, and finally vanishing. A few days later, two friends came back from

Swamiji was delighted to meet Peter in Zürich and, like so many who could see Peter clearly, he expressed great love and appreciation for his being. He struck his hands together and materialized a crystal for Peter and told him that he should put this in water and place it in the sun, then drink the water for inner healing. Much was revealed and confirmed through him. He said that Peter's future work would now be mainly in Europe and that Peter and I were to work together, and with a big smile he concluded, 'Blessings on you both'. What a truly joyous meeting this was!

Next day the light-hearted Peter who left Europe was utterly unlike the bewildered Peter who had left after his first visit to return to months of complete confusion. Now he was clear. Now he knew.

When he told me on the phone, shortly afterwards, that he was packing up everything in America in order to come to me, I was overwhelmed by the speed with which he acted on his inner knowing. Once he was clear that we were to be together he took immediate action, no matter what others would think or say. What a step, to move so speedily from his firmly-rooted life in America over to Germany, when, for example, he didn't speak a word of German! Obviously he did not let the outer mind with all its pros and cons interfere with this big decision at all. As he was now clear, he just followed the truth of his spirit, the truth of his heart — in absolute faith and confidence. I realized that only his lifelong training in immediate obedience to his inner truth made such a speedy action possible. Later Peter told me that every major step in his life had been based on his own inner perception of what 'felt right' by God, and this he did, no matter what others — including 'channelling' friends — might say. With Peter there was never any pussy-footing around, once he knew something was right.

He wrote at the time:

> *I knew then, beyond a shadow of doubt, that my real partner for the future was Renata and that Virginia and I had been brought together so strongly to complete past karma... So my*

India and brought Marcel a book about a fire swami, and he recognized the face immediately. When Marcel later visited his ashram in India, he asked him 'Did you appear in my room at two o'clock at the beginning of April?' and the reply was, 'Yes, it's true'

When Swamiji first came to Germany (physically this time!) at Marcel's invitation, and entered our house, he went on his own straight up to Marcel's room and looked smilingly to the place where he had appeared. His stay in our house was a most amazing time, to say the least, not to mention travelling with him through Germany and then to Switzerland, where we introduced him to many people *next steps became clear. I had just two weeks before the three-week tour of the spiritual power centres of Britain in September, to return to the United States to clear up my affairs. I first broke the news to Virginia. Although she was shocked to begin with, our relationship now is one of love, friendship and mutual support. I then shared with Paula... There is love and trust between us and we are both concerned with Daniel's welfare and upbringing, although much of the burden and joy falls upon her. We also finalized our divorce to our mutual satisfaction.*

I had to sort out and pack up everything: my office with the accumulation of years in filing cabinets, etc., all my clothes and things, my library and books and magazines, pay bills, wind up my affairs and transport my possessions to the Findhorn Retreat Center in Mendocino in northern California. Finally I took Daniel on a farewell trip to Mt Shasta with Shari and John McCombe and to visit my son David and his wife Kacie.

After leading a wonderful tour of Britain and attending the conference at Findhorn 'From Organisation to Organism' in October I came back to what I knew would now be my home. It is one of the most perfect I have been to, a place of peace, harmony and beauty. It is inspired by Babaji who gave Renata her inner training. She is an artist, a painter, poet, therapist, teacher and workshop leader. The sanctuary has the same power and stillness as the one at Findhorn. For many years (since 1980) there have been weekly gatherings and [daily] meditations as well as lectures and workshops at the centre. I have a delightful room with a sunny balcony and a view over the lake to the snow mountains of Switzerland. There is a large and very special garden, full of peace and full of nature spirits.

The first evening after his arrival Peter asked me: 'Would you like to marry me?' I could only look at him — I could not say a word.

In the night I had a powerful revelation about both of us, a clear answer to his question; and in the morning I said, 'Yes, I'd love to marry you'.

Chapter 32

Kailash Marriage

I will burn fire and water together
and will be in the middle of the fire and water
and I will remain there whatever happens

– Babaji 1980

FOR OUR FIRST heart-to-heart meeting, we had been given three days; the second one — our 'Harmonic Convergence time' which made everything clear to us — lasted twelve days. Then our third and final uniting happened over twenty-one days, also in my home in Germany. This was the start of our great honeymoon, when we were able to give love with all the time and space needed to unite us step by step on every level. It was a time of love-as-meditation: surely a most wondrous time for both of us. So much happened...

Touch was important; touch sparked off revelations. So many mysteries are hidden in the body — the whole of our being, including the past, seems to be sealed within it — but love can reveal them, and touch can set them free! This happened for us, again and again, to our amazement.

A wise friend of mine, Dina Rees, once told me, 'When man and woman become one, they become God'. Indeed, grace is one of the gifts of love, and we both received much healing of our respective pasts.

We also began to realise our fundamental polarity, which seemed to stem from a spiritual origin: Peter's absolute interest in and his 'yes' to Creation, my deep and primary 'yes' to the Eternal beyond Creation; I loved the Eternal, the white light beyond the colours, while Peter loved it through its manifestation *in* the colours.

When I compared myself to Peter, I felt, from my core, like a meditating monk in a cave, saying, 'The world is, anyway, transient; the only important thing is the Eternal'; while Peter, from his core, would rather say,

'The Eternal is, anyhow, there; let us enjoy and celebrate the Creation'. We both met in seeing the Eternal within the transient, and in loving and serving God in His Creation.

The key to this, which had always been Peter's key to life, then became my key as well: 'Love wherever you are, whoever you are with and whatever you are doing'.

At the beginning we sometimes felt our different ways very strongly. In a drawing, one could show it as Peter — through his being — expressing more a horizontal line, and me, more a vertical one, when each one of us was travelling on our own ways; but when we touched, when his horizontal met my vertical, we formed a cross. This sparked fire, and the rose of love blossoms from the centre of this cross, which so becomes a rose-cross. This is why oneness meant so much to us and was guiding us so deeply.

Peter came out of these 21 days bright, fresh, and looking as young as anything. Standing in front of a group of my friends, he remarked about his transformation:

The ritual has not changed me.
The mantra has not changed me.
Meditation has not changed me.
Tofu[1] *has not changed me.*
But love has changed and transformed me.
Love is the power of transformation.

* * *

Peter then returned to Findhorn for two weeks to attend the momentous gathering held to celebrate the community's twenty-fifth anniversary. Immediately afterwards he left for India and I rejoined him en route at London Heathrow. It was a thrill for both of us to be together again and to embark on our first journey together — there are no words to describe our joy.

We landed in India at the end of November 1987, straight into the bubbling dust and dirt of Delhi, with the utter poverty and pain of India on the one hand, and the grandeur and flair of its ancient glories on the other — with all the levels and secrets in between, which give a glimpse from the lowest to the highest of all that life can be. After I introduced Peter to some special Indian friends, we had a

---

1 A soya product used as a meat substitute and said to be very healthy, which Peter was not keen on (to say the least!)

peaceful cup of tea on the lawn of the Imperial Hotel in the middle of Delhi, with the tiny treasure-filled shops, the loud and busy market life, the crowds and all the begging hands and eyes just a few metres away behind some trees and bushes. It brought back Peter's memories of his time in India 45 years before, when it was still part of the British Empire.

We set off north-east to Haidakhan — first to see Shri Muniraji, a wise friend and great teacher who lived in Haldwani, the little Indian town in Nainital District of Uttar Pradesh from where further transport to Haidakhan would be arranged. Our driver travelled at breathtaking speed along the extremely crowded Indian roads, full of bicycles, rickshaws, pedestrians, cows, pigs, ox carts and endless buses decorated with gold and glitter like the elephants of old. I was amazed to experience the world through Peter's heart and eyes on this journey... It was as if I were travelling with a king who was responsible for each and every detail of the well-being of his people: how this could be improved; how that could be done more efficiently; how drainpipes should be laid here. 'What needs to be done?' seemed to be his constant concern and his ideas were always very practical and down to earth, while I looked more at the atmosphere, the colours and forms, the spirit of the landscape and villages, and the eyes and beings of the people...

We reached Haldwani after a six-to-seven-hour drive only to learn that Shri Muniraji had gone up into the mountains to Chilliyanaula, where on his own land he had built an ashram for Babaji. So before going on to join him there we decided to stop overnight in Haldwani, where an Indian wedding with all its trumpets and noise, seemingly right in front of our little hotel, kept us awake for half the night! The next morning we left by car on the serpentine mountain roads, so different from the straight roads of the plains; and after a beautiful three-and-a-half hour journey higher and higher into the Himalayan foothills we reached Chilliyanaula.

Everybody at the ashram was taking their midday nap, except Shri Muniraji himself, who stood in the doorway obviously expecting us. Lovingly he welcomed us. What a light there was in his eyes when he saw Peter for the first time! And what a joy in Peter's eyes when we went up through this flourishing ashram and garden with its great marble temple, and he found a superb view of the Himalayas! It brought tears to his eyes, as it had done over forty years before when he had trekked over 2500 miles in these mountains. When he asked Muniraji why this particular sight had such an effect upon him, Muniraji replied that Peter had been a yogi there in a previous life.

'Muniraj' means 'King of Silence', the name given to him by Babaji.[2] Long before Babaji left his body he had made it clear that Muniraji himself was a high being, a master, and would be responsible for carrying on the work. Peter experienced Shri Muniraji as a very humble, loving friend. To me he is one of the most beautiful and shining human beings that I have ever met. We asked Muniraji if we could be married spiritually. He said, 'Yes, you can marry on Christmas Day in Haidakhan'.

After a few days stay with Shri Muniraji in Chilliyanaula, our hearts and spirits being filled with the light of the Himalayas, we went with him in his car back to Haldwani, where he arranged for a car to take us towards Haidakhan, and gave us his blessings. The road went over sticks and stones and came to an end at Damsite, a tiny village with some huts and 'chai' (tea) shops, from where we went on by foot, finding our way into the valley of the Gautam Ganga River. Happily for us, our luggage was carried by porters.

This valley is something magical, with stones of all colours, from shining white to purple, all round and washed by the Gautam Ganga which in the July–August monsoon season becomes a torrential river, filling the whole large valley with its rapids. This river with its clear, sparkling waters, springs from the Mansarovea Lake in Tibet and travels many miles underground until it emerges above ground near Haidakhan, filling the valley with freshness and life.

This visit with Peter was my twelfth to the valley and to Haidakhan, and I felt at home there, in a very deep way. The further we walked, the more Peter was touched, in his turn, by the wild beauty of nature in this valley, its surrounding hills and mountains, and Mt Kailash rising in the distance.

Mythology tells us that the Kailash that lay ahead of us — the Kurmanchal Kailash — is the original Mt Kailash, considered as the seat of Lord Shiva, the highest aspect of godhead in Eastern terms, ever since the beginning of Creation.[3] It was in the cave at the foot of the Kurmanchal Mt Kailash that Babaji had appeared to the public in 1970.

We first had to cross the river at a unique, natural rock-face, and there the waters looked quite deep, so Peter rolled up his trousers and tied his tennis shoes more securely. As I waited for him, three local women came

---

2 Shri Muniraji's Indian name is Shri Trilok Singh

3 The tradition maintains that when civilisation unfolded, Shiva moved northwards and established his seat on the unreachable heights of Mt Kailash in Tibet. Babaji is considered to be a Shiva-Avatar

walking graciously through the river with large grass bundles on their heads, passing us silently; immediately after them came a very upright, shining young man so unusual in appearance that we immediately wondered who he was. He looked like the messenger of a king. Where did he come from in this wild and lonely mountain area? I had never before seen somebody like this during my many times in Haidakhan. He wore a heaven-blue hat — not a self-bound turban but perfectly round, as if crafted by a professional hatter. Silk of the same shade of blue was wrapped round his waist; a cord crossed the upper part of his body diagonally, and he held a long staff in his right hand. His appearance was breathtakingly beautiful. His golden-brown eyes shone like the sun as he held us both in his view, looking at us and yet through us as if into a far distance. I shall never forget that look. Then he passed us at the rock-face where we were, and was off.

Throughout our river walk and on into the night, we continued to feel the power of those eyes, and kept wondering about the unusual appearance of this young man and who he might be.

During the two-and-a-half hour walk up the river, we had to cross the swift-flowing waters about sixteen times — each time feeling more purified, refreshed and vitalised —before we reached Haidakhan, the ashram created by Babaji.

We saw on our right the 108 steps leading up to the ashram and, opposite on the left, the nine temples built into the foot of Mt Kailash. These temples had been built by hand with only very simple tools and in a very short time, under the direct guidance and instructions of Babaji, and with his help. At the ashram itself we were heartily welcomed by those (mainly Western) people who were now responsible for running it.

Almost everybody there had heard about Findhorn, with its emphasis on putting God first and having work and service as its keynotes — indeed, an expression and living example of what Babaji taught: *Truth*, *Simplicity* and *Love*, with his emphasis on *karma yoga*, or work without attachment to the result. Babaji had said, 'In our time, *karma yoga* is the highest yoga... In this Age it is not possible to renounce the world. The way of renunciation nowadays is to dedicate all work, all deeds to God.' He also recommended the constant repetition of the name of God — any name of God, especially through the mantram 'Om Namaha Shivaya'[4].

4 *Om Namaha Shivaya*: this is the great original mantra. It is at one with the sound of Creation; it means 'I take refuge in God' or 'Thy will be done'. Babaji explained that this mantram can be given to everyone, and everything can be reached by it

Peter and I were given a special room with bath and toilet for ourselves and two big wooden beds, which we tried to soften for Peter with some blankets. In Haidakhan the daily routine inspired by Babaji is to rise at 4 am[5] to take a bath in the river (although there are now showers installed upstairs in the ashram) and get ready for the day; at 5 am 'chandan' is given — chandan is a blessing sign on the forehead for the clearing and peace of one's mind — followed by meditation or whatever feels good (but not sleep!) An hour's worship of God in songs starts at 6.30 am.

Of his experiences there, Peter wrote to friends, 'I enjoyed the sheer beauty and power of the place, situated at the foot of Mt Kailash: the clear air, sparkling sunshine and swimming in the crystal clear waters of the Gautam Ganga River where one can drink and swim at the same time'. His letter continued:

> *I was impressed by the high standard of the buildings. We had daily meetings with the leading members of the [ashram] to help solve some of their problems that had arisen after Babaji's sudden departure. They were deeply interested in Findhorn. Renata had brought to them all the Findhorn books over the years and they had been reading a message from* God Spoke to Me *each morning, along with one of Babaji's messages.*
>
> *However, during my stay I was certainly tested on 'Only those who are prepared to change their lives, their mode of living when required can be in the forefront of this energy flow'. The following are some of the changes I was required to make:*
>
> *1.To get up at 4.30 am instead of 7.30 am after only four or five hours sleep instead of my usual eight hours.*
>
> *2. Sitting cross-legged on a hard marble floor for three hours a day, trying to sing — when I can't sing — words that I did not understand.*
>
> *3. Twice a day, sitting cross-legged on the ground to eat the food that I dislike the most: white rice, beans and lentils — no eggs, fish, poultry or meat allowed.*

---

5 4.30 in winter

4. Eating with my right hand when I am left-handed — no knives, forks or spoons.

5. No toilet paper — squatting and splashing my behind with cold water with my left hand.

6. Sleeping alone in a sleeping bag on a hard bed with only a very thin covering underneath, so that all night long I had to turn from one sore hip to the other.

As always with Peter, however, rather than complain of his circumstances, he adjusted them to suit his needs. A little chair was found for him so that he no longer had to sit cross-legged on the floor; he bought himself a spoon to eat with. A friend, out of love and respect for Peter, brought a bucket of hot water at five o'clock every morning and gave a little knock at our door. After some initial attempts, Peter stopped trying to get up at that time, while by then I had already taken my bath in the Gautam Ganga River. One of the most beautiful experiences I know is to bathe in this river under a star-filled sky, with everything around so secretly alive. At first I did my best to wake Peter up with hot tea and gentle kisses, but he definitely preferred to get up at his own time, even if Karkhu's water bucket and my tea were only lukewarm or even cold by then. Peter was not convinced that he was nearer to God when he slept less, nor that his work for God had to do with long morning meditations, but he found that it was his responsibility to care for a healthy body, which in his view implied work done with love, good exercise, enough sleep, tasty food — and, of course, having fun in the process!

It was beautiful to see how everybody in the ashram, old and young, just loved Peter, with his warmth, his radiance, natural authority, tremendous experience, and his ever-amazing humour. He was well looked after during his stay!

The climax of our first stay in Haidakhan was our climb on Mt Kailash — Peter's first, and my ninth, time. It is said that climbing Kailash is a journey to Lord Shiva, the Eternal Being, so a journey up the mountain also means an inner journey to one's self. It is also said, 'On Kailash everything is possible'.

On the day of the climb, the sky was clear, the morning nicely fresh and a sense of excitement was in the air. Peter walked ahead to set the pace, which we would keep to carefully — he was already seventy but showed the vigour of a man half that age.

We soon gained the top of the first rise which already afforded an amazing view into unexpected valleys and further mountain chains. There was something magical about the wild beauty and loneliness of the place: one could well imagine the gods walking there. We moved on, holding to our quiet and steady pace, feeling lighter with every step, and as we climbed higher a white eagle appeared, followed by another one, and then several more. Altogether we counted ten eagles, two of them white, I had never seen so many on Mt Kailash before —and for both of us it seemed like a sign. I remembered someone once telling me that in Christian tradition it is said, 'Where the white eagles meet, there I am, the Christ'.

After a climb of about four hours, with a final effort we reached the summit, bare of trees and bushes, and we stood in the bright sunshine, marvelling at the sweep of the view and the vastness of sky, hearing only the beating of our hearts and that special sound that only utter stillness can produce. There was only sun and silence. The place was of immense peace and majesty, and we stayed there as long as we could.

Filled with the power of this realm of stillness, we made our way down. The descent was difficult and demanded pinpointed concentration. We had been to the seat of the god in the heights and were now returning to the river valley below.

Coming down again, we saw a large number of beautiful and well-cared-for black bulls, drinking from a spring near the bottom of Mt Kailash. The bull is honored as the animal Lord Shiva rode upon.

On my first climb up Kailash I had had a vision at the top of many souls floating up to the mountain top, one by one, as if they were leaving Earth via this place and passing here their Last Judgement (in Christian terminology). So for me it was no wonder that after his visit to the mountain, Peter saw his life as a whole and came down with the clear insight that the time had arrived to set down his life's story in a book.

* * *

The next day, to our joy, Shri Muniraji came to Haidakhan. He attended a sharing Peter had with a group of friends by the 'dhuni', the sacred fireplace dedicated to the Divine Mother. Shri Muniraji finalised our wedding date and gave me a red and golden shawl. He said that according to Indian tradition, women are eight times stronger than men!

When we asked Muniraji about the beautiful appearance of the young man we had encountered during our approach through the valley to Haidakhan, he confirmed what we had already felt. 'Yes, it was Babaji, who gave you both his darshan [6]', he said, adding that it was Babaji in the form of Bhairav Baba. When we visited Shri Shastriji — the great seer and priest of Babaji — he independently confirmed this when I also told him of the visitation. 'It was Babaji, in the form of Bhairav Baba. Later you will understand.'

Known as the chief 'man' of Shiva, Bhairav Baba is the guardian of the threshold and in charge of those forces that wield Shiva's powers. He is the great protector of those who live in truth and love, but he is feared by those who don't, as he burns away everything that is not truth, not love. This is why he is often described as Shiva's aspect of terror and transcendency. The heaven-blue colour is given to Bhairav Baba in his young and shining form. Bhairav Baba's day is Sunday, the day we met Babaji in this form.[7]

* * *

Together with Shri Muniraji, we left Haidakhan following the river, and after meditation and breakfast next morning in his house at Haldwani, departed for Delhi by car. Whilst in India, I wanted to introduce Peter to some other spiritual places and friends that were special for me. From Delhi we flew south to Madras and went straight to Pondicherry, the ashram of Shri Aurobindo and 'the Mother', with whom I have had deep links. We hired two bicycles in Pondi and headed off towards Auroville, Findhorn's sister community, about ten kilometres away.

The lovely atmosphere of the Indian dusk is unforgettable. The air was filled with all kinds of smells and fragrances, from incense to burning cow dung. Here and there were little oil-lights burning in the huts and shops. In spite of all the ongoing movements there was a sacred quiet in the air. Our cycle ride took us among other people, animals, bicycles and rickshaws until we reached the red earth of Auroville, shining like fire in the light of the setting sun. Then we were all alone. Night fell and there were no lamps along the way. As Peter's bicycle had the only light, he rode ahead on the pitted road — and then suddenly there was no light and no Peter! He had fallen into a ditch.

---

6 In India, the blessing that a saint gives by his presence

7 In January 1978, Babaji had painted a picture and given it to me; 'This is Bhairav Baba, he gives blessings also'. The picture shows a lovingly smiling face made out of flames

Despite bleeding and bruises (which we later discovered were more extensive than we thought) Peter remounted his bicycle and we rode on, this time with only the stars to give us light, and with the Matrimandir — the huge, sacred building at the core of Auroville — as our distant guide. When we finally reached the centre of the community with the help of a passing motorcycle that provided good light, an Aurovillian, who by chance knew Peter, and who then took us to our quarters for the night.

Word quickly spread that Peter Caddy was there, so the next morning we had a heart-warming exchange with a group of community members who afterwards took us to the Matrimandir. It is a masterpiece of art and architecture, with space at its centre for an immense glass sphere that will represent, according to 'the Mother', the soul of Auroville. We meditated there, and then continued on our bicycles to visit the different colonies that make up this community, spread out across the warm, red land. Peter felt that Auroville, besides all its other inner and outer work, was also making an important contribution to India and to the healing of the planet, with its organic methods of horticulture and farming, and by changing the soil, climate and watertable with the planting of thousands of trees.

From there we travelled on by car to Tiruvanamalai with its holy mountain Arunachala, the ashram of Ramana Marharshi — a most beautiful Indian saint who left in 1950. He was an embodiment of the eternal shining truth, teaching enlightenment through the constant remembrance of 'Who am I?' We went up the mountain to his cave. I had seen the ashram flourishing in 1973, 76 and 79, when a Swiss man was responsible for maintaining it, but the good man had since moved on to establish his own place nearby, and we found to our sadness that Ramana Marharshi's ashram at that time was run down. Peter took one look at the sleeping quarters, opened (and quickly closed again) the door to the toilets and announced that it would be impossible for us to spend the night there, so after a long bumpy drive into the night we went on to Bangalore.

Next midday found us at Sai Baba's ashram at Puttaparti, where there were crowds and crowds of people — very *organised* crowds, which seemed to leave no room for fun or laughter. As male and female, Peter and I had to sleep in separate rooms and eat in separate places; also when awaiting the appearance of Satya Sai Baba, we had to stand in separate areas, with no mixing of the sexes allowed. After two days of this, Peter decided that he'd had enough — everything was too serious for him, who always found joy as one of the fruits of the spirit — and in a deliberate act of defiance, under the very noses of the serious women who shepherded us, he embraced me and gave me a big kiss!

On the other hand, Peter was impressed by the great work that Sai Baba was doing in education. When Marcel and I had been there for ten days in 1972; we had two interviews with Satya Sai Baba, and everything had felt more open and free.

Back in Bangalore Peter and I discovered by chance that our friend the fire-Swamiji was also there, instead of at his ashram in Mysore (a four-hour train journey away), so we surprised him with a visit. Peter really liked him because he was surrounded by joy, humour and laughter. Swamiji blessed us again and gave us his gifts for our forthcoming marriage.

Peter later wrote, 'All these visits to different places made me appreciate Haidakhan with its whole magical atmosphere all the more. And there I had met real soul brothers and sisters. On our long journey back to Haidakhan for Christmas we stopped to visit Shri Shastriji, who lives in a small town in Rajasthan. He is 83. We enjoyed the experience of living with this great loving man and his large family. He had much to share about the past and the future.'

We found Shri Mishra Vishnu Dutt Shastriji full of vitality, wisdom and profound knowledge, living out of the fire of his heart and deep visions. Babaji, whose spokesman he was, once described him as 'the great seer and poet of all time'. In this life alone he has written 67 books. Shri Shastriji is also a wonderful ayurvedic healer and a well-known Sanskrit scholar.

We returned to Haidakhan on December 23. Christmas is one of the main festivals in the ashram, as Babaji honoured all religions and had declared that the Christ consciousness is the universal consciousness. On Christmas Eve, Peter gave a stirring rendition of his beloved 1 Corinthians 13 in front of the many people who had gathered there.

We were married on Christmas Day 1987, a Friday, in a ceremony around the sacred fire at the foot of Mt Kailash, conducted by Shri Shastriji and then blessed by Shri Muniraji, with around 400 people attending. 'Merry Christmas!' Muniraji kept saying to us, again and again through the day, while Shastriji said to both of us, 'Happy! This is the real marriage!' As it is customary, after the ceremony we gave a sumptuous 'bandara' (meal) for everybody there.

Actually Peter did not have a clue about what the different elements of the ceremony meant, but he performed them all graciously. One thing in particular puzzled him — bowing in reverence to the Divine, for whose presence a seat was placed. When we were later relaxing with Muniraji and some close friends, Peter wondered aloud 'How can I do *prasad* to an empty chair?' Everybody burst out laughing — 'prasad' means 'blessed food'. Peter had mixed up his words and had meant to say 'pranam' (which means 'bowing'). Our wedding day was filled with a lot of laughter and humour, a happy omen for our future life together.

We both felt our marriage there was a great blessing — also a challenge to grow beyond ourselves. We flew home to Germany just in time to celebrate the New Year with a spontaneous gathering of about seventy friends from the surrounding area, to share with them the news of our spiritual marriage (the legal one would follow later) and our love and great joy at being together.

Chapter 33

A Paradise Garden

As above — so below

– Hermes Trismegistus

SYNTHESIS was the great theme of our living and working together and of the place and the garden we built and we served. 'Let us together build one heart cell within the body of mankind'; when I had come together with Peter, these words continued to move me and became like a song within me. Later I came to understand a little more why.

In 1988 Peter wrote to friends:

> *Our life together is really full of wonder and surprise — full of challenges as well. As we are each other's soul polarity we seem to have the same intensity of living and joy, the same enthusiasm and dynamic action. We both have a love for perfection, beauty and harmony and above all a love for God...*
>
> *How this expresses through us is really polarised in many ways. She looks more within, I look more without (although I do act from intuition). For instance I like to read newspapers, watch the news on TV, and listen to programmes and music on the radio, as I am deeply interested in what is going on in the world. She loves the silence and to listen to that silence and to know everything from there... While I like to have a routine for the day, with regular meals and times for sleeping, she likes to live in the moment without a routine... I am a day bird, she is a night bird. Thank God we both have a great sense of humour and really laugh a lot, so there is always joy and lightness. Life together is always very fresh. We had a lot of occasions to discover overwhelmingly that the greater our differences, the deeper our love grows.*

'God would not have dared to bring us together earlier,' Peter often remarked when faced with these differences, 'Does He not have a sense of humour?'

Together we were like fire and water. Sometimes Peter was the fire, I was the water, but often it was the other way round. Fire can heat water, can even make it vaporise and become air, but water can extinguish fire... If it had not been love that had brought us together, that had married us, that kept us together, and that helped us all the time, how would we have managed our differences? But there was this thrill to be together, from the beginning till the end — seeing each other sparked light and joy, like a hundred dancing kisses per day, if not always expressed literally then through the eyes, the hands, the heart.

Time was Peter's friend. He had a strong sense of rhythm and brought a great regularity to mealtimes, walks or swims, and sleep in our life — a 'healthy rhythm' which, to begin with, the artist in me found almost fatal. But we learned to give each other space. Love is also space — to let each other be: not to want to change each other, or to make him the same as me, or vice versa; not to want to have the same spiritual practice, similar tastes in food, etc., but to allow our different ways to blossom. Indeed, only in this space of freedom was our continuously free and joyful 'dance' together possible.

Our polarity in action, however, sometimes also sparked 'thunder and lightning' between us, unconsciously provoked by Peter and expressed through me, mainly in connection with our garden — this powerful garden that brought up our differences most strongly. Within its large and secret grounds I had built a little sanctuary, a place where I loved to go to be still — sometimes with friends — a place dedicated to God. I knew that one day the whole garden would become like this.

When I showed Peter the garden for the very first time, he became very quiet. 'How do you like it?' I wondered, as people usually expressed their enthusiasm and amazement about the atmosphere of this garden immediately. But from Peter no word. When I asked, 'Don't you feel the atmosphere?' he finally said, 'Well, I see all that needs doing'. He saw all these plants that he would call weeds... and a large garden that he would call more or less a wild garden. Sure, it was full of life: full of evergreens, fruit trees and flourishing bushes of various kinds, with a meadow of wild flowers throughout, and few formal beds. Somewhere at the back stood an old caravan, a lovingly painted reminder of those at Findhorn. In the middle of the garden there was an open fire pit, solidly and safely built one metre into the earth and used on festive occasions. This was the garden Peter found, and it was not exactly right up his street, as I would soon come to understand.

It was his friend Peter Dawkins — who quickly became a very close friend of mine as well — who was the medium for the transformation of the garden. He came on the first of what was to become twice-yearly visits to our centre to give lectures and workshops, which I arrange for him and which people love to attend. Peter Dawkins is a man with clear perception of both the outer and the inner world, and wherever he focuses his attention he is able to see — be it the auras of living beings, or the Earth's ley lines and power points, and her different energies at different places. This ability has enabled him to set up his pilgrimage work throughout the world for the healing of Mother Earth. I must say that I am open to, but also critical of, all inner perceptions — my own as well as those of others — much more so than Peter[1] was. They can so easily become subjective and coloured, but with Peter Dawkins they rang a bell in both of us most of the time. I feel that it is through his humility and love that he is given this deep inner sight, including his awareness of the nature spirits, the angelic world and the divine realm.

So when Peter Dawkins came here in February 1988 for the first time, he saw this wonderful light in and over the garden — and he also saw that all the large trees in the middle of it were blocking the flow of energy. Therefore they should be removed. His vision convinced us, although it would mean a complete transformation of the whole garden, but as it felt true, Peter and I made a rough plan where the trees and bushes should go. We both had one thing in common: once the vision was there for something, we always took immediate action, knowing that then all energy and help would be given to realise it — and so it was on this occasion. All the trees and bushes were taken out, even in Peter's absence (he was then on his travels), with the help of some competent friends. They all thought it impossible that these tall trees could be replanted and grow again, but I felt sure they would — and with God's grace they did!

When the overall plan of the garden was clear, Peter's first decision was that the whole place had to be liberated from weeds, some of which I would have liked to keep because they were healing plants. But Peter found

1 Caddy, not Dawkins

they were in the wrong place and should be relegated to the back and sides of the garden; some species he banished entirely. He intended also to transform all the remaining meadow-like spaces into either beds or proper lawns.

So Peter began his work of taming and creating order in the garden: no weeds, no wild flowers, one pruning action after another... This was breathtaking for me! It was as if Roman soldiers were marching through the garden and to begin with, I was shocked. My beloved garden... and there he comes, the world-famous gardener, and takes out all the weeds and wild flowers, cuts off all the branches that get in his way (I *liked* their touch) and creates, first, human orderliness. Our garden, indeed, became 'civilised' through Peter.

For me, though, this was sometimes a very painful process. When it came to pruning in the garden, for example, we often had such deeply felt, entirely different viewpoints that sometimes there seemed to be no bridge between us. At the beginning, Peter — quiet but firm — would absolutely stick to his convictions. What was I to do when I was convinced of the opposite? It was like an irresistible force meeting an immovable object. The saving grace, however, was always the love that was simply there between us. Our hearts went out to each other, and then we always found a bridge. We discovered over and over again that love has nothing to do with mental or emotional agreements — not at all — but comes from another dimension. Love is the natural expression of the soul, streaming out through the heart.

A key to our relationship was complete openness with each other. It would have been unbearable to have a cloud to between us — to hide an anger or a hurt for a day, for even an hour! It needed clearing immediately so that the air would be always very fresh between us. So many marriages or close relationships suffer from the heaviness of all the uncleared material. Untruth, or not daring to speak the truth, is a killer for the flow of love and joy and also for any creativity: the air becomes leaden, because of all the poison in it, and everybody wonders why they get so tired in such an atmosphere.

Sharing and caring: truth liberates, love heals. Truth first, then love — and is not truth the other face of love?

So we shared immediately each and every little thing that could hang between us. For instance, when I discovered in the garden that Peter had again cut away the dancing arms of my favourite little tree, I felt very hurt for the tree, and stormed up to his room, making it clear to him what he had done and asking why, yet again, he had not considered at all how this would feel to me who was not only so deeply connected with this garden but also coming from such a different angle of awareness? Peter would usually just listen quietly and not say much. His focus on his goals, which enabled him to achieve so much, was so strong that he sometimes just could not entertain any different view. He would not easily change his pruning habits.

As I was always very straightforward and did not wrap my words in cotton wool, it could then sometimes happen that I felt I had hurt him. I would come back to him immediately and say, 'I did not want to hurt you. I am really sorry! But I had to tell you how this felt to me.' We would silently embrace each other and then share in peace our viewpoints. Most times, our clashes brought us even closer together.

I also came to see and understand Peter's profound care for nature and for this garden. Love was entering the earth, was flowing through his hands and spade into the heavy clay earth of the garden, the opposite of the sandy soil of Findhorn. When creating beds, Peter's spade always went not just one but *two* lengths deep into the ground, to let light into this very heavy soil. What a task! He did it all alone. Although there were friends to help, he found that none of them dug deeply enough.

So Peter anchored light within the ground. Whenever he fetched me to show me what he had done, I was really aware of it: the earth was filled with light where he had worked. What a difference to other places in the garden which he had not yet touched! 'One step at a time', he would say. 'You can only do one thing at a time, take one step at a time, live one day at a time — and have fun doing it.' Whatever he had decided to do, he did perfectly. He usually set himself or the group working with him a goal for the day and then went on to achieve it. 'Like this, one always feels content', said our friend Elisabeth, who often worked with us and whose dedication was superb. In this way, Peter showed us how not to be disheartened by the amount of work that still needed to be done.

His example was in many regards a great teaching to everyone here. Over the years, those who came to help in the garden just loved Peter, with his peaceful and humorous, free, warm way of being, his quiet yet dynamic actions, and found that not only his joy but also his discipline and concentration during the work were contagious. For instance a friend of mine, Susanne, after weeding together with Peter for many hours, came up with shining eyes and said, 'Weeding with Peter with such concentration, I feel I could weed with him for all eternity'.

Then there was our Herwin, a simple man from the area. Unique, with a big belly, an enormous capacity for work, and a lot of hidden wisdom — a bit like the shoemakers of old — Herwin came when we needed him for special work in the garden. 'No problem, no problem' would always be his comment, whatever the task. Watching Peter and Herwin converse was always very funny. Herwin spoke no English, while Peter's German was more or less confined to 'Auf Wiedersehn' (goodbye), 'Pfifferlingsuppe' (mushroom soup) and 'schlaf gut' (sleep well) — all of which he pronounced as if he were chopping wood. He managed to mix even these few German words, heartily saying, for example, 'schlaf gut!' to a doctor in the bright daylight when he meant to say goodbye. So while Herwin would happily rattle on in fluid German to express his ideas to Peter, Peter would just point with his finger and with one or two English words let his suggestion be known.

One day I agreed that a big pine tree should come down, since it stood in the middle of Peter's splendid rhododendron bed and was robbing the soil of too much moisture. First thing the next morning I found Peter at the top of this tree with a large saw, the long ladder on which he stood just leaning loosely against its trunk, beginning to saw off the branches with great gusto. Happily at my request Herwin soon turned up, and regarded the scene with horror. '*Peter, komm sofort herunter! Das ist gefährlich!*' ('Come down immediately. This is dangerous!') — and he pointed at himself to indicate he would do it instead. Well, Peter came down, and heavy Herwin went up with several ropes to fix the ladder firmly to the tree and then, carefully, one piece after another, he safely brought the whole tree down. Peter watched with amazement, remarking, 'He certainly knows the tricks of the trade'.

There was no work too heavy or too low that Peter would not take on himself in the garden, be it digging; turning the huge, threefold compost heaps; shredding, or helping to shred, the mountains of pruned branches for compost; or crawling on hand and knees to get the moss out of his precious lawn. He often used his bare hands to loosen the soil and mix compost into it in readiness for the planting of all the new flowers to come.

Peter usually wore no gloves for his gardening work, however heavy. He liked to touch the earth directly, and his hands always had the most ten-der and fine skin. It seemed to express the softness and sensitivity of his inner nature and his very gentle touch; I found that there was something magical about his hands.

I was always touched to see the love and care with which he ensured that each plant would have the right soil and conditions and be in the right place. (Does this plant want sun or shade? Which soil does it need? The companionship of which other plants does it like? How tall will it grow?) He also wanted to know what the other gardeners in the local area had discovered. He never threw out the traditional methods of gardening, explaining that the devas had been guiding mankind for ages.

Specially at the beginning, when my artist's vision — which would have liked certain plants, because of their colours, to be in certain places — clashed with his practical one, and Peter remained as immovable as a Scottish castle, we really 'suffered' from each other's different viewpoints in the garden. He would say, '*Man* is the creator of the garden, not the nature spirits, although they will help if we ask them, and do their best in a given situation', and I would think 'Well, in our case, "man" — the human being — consists of man *and* woman...' So we had to learn to understand and respect our very different approaches in order to gain a working synthesis. First the garden was only my way, then it went much more his way — and finally it became a synthesis. But what a challenge to let it become a garden of his way *and* my way! It was indeed 'heart work'.

Obviously God had put us together on this particular spot on Earth for this 'heart work' — an alchemical process, as it seemed to us. The ingredients were the differences in our natures and personalities, our hearts were the vessel in which the cooking took place, and the fire of our love kept the pot burning and brought the alchemy about — day by day. And thank God for the light touch, which made everything so much easier. Thus our love became fireproof.

'With God, all things are possible.' We had a striking example of this in the garden one very cold, snowy winter. We had been away for a few days and returned to find that the stalk of a white, weeping rosebush had been almost completely broken by the weight of snow on its already top-heavy crown; for three days it had stood frozen and exposed like this. 'Why did you do nothing about it?' I asked the friend who had been minding the place during our absence. 'Because I thought it was hopeless,' she replied, and

Peter agreed with her. As it was one of our favourite rosebushes, however, we tried to do *something*. I got all the Traumeel cream we had — a healing balm for human wounds — and applied it to the broken stalk, which we then splinted, covered with warm towels and bound firmly, asking for divine help and and giving the rosebush our love. The miracle happened: it not only survived but went on to blossom with the greatest abundance of flowers, and is today the most beautiful rosebush in the garden.

* * *

While we were not producing Findhorn-style phenomena such as forty-pound cabbages, the presence of the Divine and of the nature spirits can be felt everywhere in the garden if one is open to it. One time when Peter Dawkins was visiting, he again became aware not only of mighty angels and their vast light but also, among the myriad nature spirits, of a little gnome who told him that the roots of the trees required the application of a certain grey powder which we would find in a box at the back of the kitchen window-sill. Puzzled, we investigated and sure enough, there was the box — a preparation of minerals that somebody had given Peter to take, and that he had forgotten.

Peter's work was always meditation in action — very much so in this garden, where he gave the full force of his consciousness, his heart and his hands to Mother Earth. When I sometimes found that Peter was working too hard to maintain his very high standards in the garden all the time, his answer was simply, 'I want the garden to be as you want the house to be, an expression of beauty and harmony. This is a garden of God.'

Our place is a centre of synthesis. The theme and the teaching, for example, in the different kinds of workshops given here, has always been how to go beyond personality problems and live from the Divine Source. Synthesis for us means connecting above with below, spirit with matter, the inner with the outer, East with West, our love for God in the heavens with our service to Mother Earth and humanity.

* * *

The garden itself is a source of healing and light, of inner nourishment, a place of sheer enjoyment where, together with friends, we celebrate the year and its rhythms. It is a place where we work with God and talk with Him, where we communicate with the heavenly realms in the ways of our hearts. We call it our 'paradise garden'.

Chapter 34

Blending East and West

There comes a Sound, from neither within nor without,
From neither right nor left, from neither behind nor in front,
From neither below nor above, from neither East nor West...
...It is not given to us to describe such a blessed place

— Shams Y Tabriz

THE GARDEN PETER CARED FOR was not only the garden he lived in: his concern was also very much for the bigger garden, the garden of humanity. He was a planetary citizen, seeing the whole world as his home.

When asked about his spiritual path after leaving Findhorn, he often replied 'I seem to be a good excuse for a party, bringing people together from many different backgrounds and spiritual paths!'

Not belonging to any particular religion, Peter had a universal view and gave love, support and empowerment to all. At the beginning of our life together, he was more often away than at home. He specially felt he was working for God when he was on his travels, made possible through the support and help of many friends. His work was planetary, a work for peace and friendship.

Peter undertook to maintain and strengthen his links with the people and the communities that were inspired by Findhorn and by his own presentations and teaching, in Europe and, of course, in America. As I had introduced Peter to my friends and teachers in India, Peter was very keen for me to meet his friends and co-workers in the USA; he was also eager to introduce to me his young son Daniel and to show me his favourite places like Mt Shasta, Mt Tamalpais and Hawaii, especially Maui, the island which always remained very close to Peter's heart.

So after our official wedding, which was beautifully celebrated with many friends in our home, Peter took me on my first visit to the United

States. Wherever we went we could stay with friends, and friends gathered; with a number of them I felt a strong soul connection too. 'Of course,' Peter said, 'How could it be otherwise?' I could see how well-known and much-loved Peter was in the States. Through travelling with Peter in this way, I understood and experienced what he meant by the building and linking up of the 'network of light' around the world, on which he had been working since the early days at Findhorn.

When Peter was determined to accomplish something, he would overcome any obstacles. I experienced this when he wanted to show me the sunrise from Haleokala, the volcano on Maui. At 4 am (a most unusual time for Peter to get up), we were ready to set out for the volcano; but when we wanted to leave the Lemurian Centre where we stayed, we found our passage blocked by a large three-metre-high wooden door, sturdily built and firmly locked. Peter had never seen it before on his earlier stays at the centre.

I took this apparently impassable barrier as a sign that we should go back to bed, but Peter was determined to show me the sunrise. Gathering all the chairs he could find that were suitable for his purpose — mainly barstools — he stacked them up against this door and, while I held them, began to climb. Once at the top, and despite his 72 years, he climbed over with agility and somehow managed to drop safely to the ground on the other side. He called me to follow, which I did, but once I reached the top, the whole tower of chairs went crashing behind me. 'It doesn't matter', Peter said to me, helping me down the other side, as I marvelled at how he could have managed it alone. And we were off... 'You know, this is the zest of life!' was Peter's remark, as he drove speedily in the twilight up to Haleakala — which means 'the House of the Sun'. We arrived just in time to welcome the sun breaking through the clouds.

'Aloha' — the spirit of love which is said to be the spirit of Hawaii — was not only the spirit of our whole American journey, but something I found Peter carried and drew forth wherever we went.

* * *

Connecting East and West seemed to be a constant theme and task for both of us and between us. We returned to the Himalayas and their foothills. First we touched in with Haidakhan again, this unique place of universal pilgrimage. To get there this time we had to cross the then very swollen Gautam Ganga River several times, with the rushing waters up to our chests. We had to link arms with the locals in order not to be swept away. It was quite exciting, and just right for Peter's spirit of adventure, which carried him throughout our journeys, especially in India.

Then we went on to Chilliyanaula to experience the Navaratri celebrations[1] there and to meet Muniraji and Shastriji again. Together with Peter Dawkins, they were his greatest spiritual friends in the last part of his life. Although Vedic rituals remained foreign to him, the spiritual vibrations and atmosphere that were created there had a strong impact on Peter.

Peter was very drawn to see Badrinath again, the famous place of pilgrimage at over 10,000 feet in the 'Valley of the Gods' surrounded by high mountain peaks, where he had trekked on foot some 45 years earlier. Now there was a road — of sorts — and we went with a very fine driver and car that Shri Muniraji had provided us with for the occasion, travelling through spectacular scenery along this breathtaking and perilous road. Small signposts saying 'Inconvenience Regretted' were dotted along the way, as it often became so narrow that only one car could pass between a steep chasm on one side and the mountain on the other. The crazy thing was that Peter — who did not know fear — was always sitting on the mountain side of the car, while I faced the chasms; even when we swapped sides during the long, 22-hour drive to Badrinath, sure enough the road would turn around the mountain and our positions would be as before, Peter by the mountain and me by the chasm! It was obviously a test for me to be grounded in 'Om Namaha Shivaya' or the 'all is well' consciousness that had become part of Peter's nature.

It was in the same area that the young Peter had met a holy man in his nineties, of striking beauty and elegance, whose example was to have such an inner impact on his life: Shri Ram Sareek Singh, the Master of Badrinath. Thus a circle now completed itself.

It was strange, but again and again in India, Peter banged his very delicate head heavily on the top. As it usually bled, we would have to cover the wound with gauze or a plaster. He took it with humour, each time it happened again, even if it must have hurt a lot. We began to joke about God knocking at his crown chakra!

* * *

---

1 The festival for the Divine Mother that is celebrated all over India each spring and autumn; attending it is a great blessing on all levels

When the invitation reached us to attend the Kumbha Mela, the largest spiritual and religious gathering in the world, Peter was appalled at the prospect: around 15 million people were expected to attend, and the mere thought of the toilet facilities alone was enough to put him off. Only when I made it clear that I wanted to go, and when we heard that Peter Dawkins and two other friends would also go there with us, did an inner bell start ringing for Peter. Once there, however, he was most favourably impressed, as he later wrote to friends:

> *The whole Mela site was a vast city of tents and sand roads stretching as far as the eye could see, and further. The army had constructed a dozen pontoon bridges across the wide river Ganges connecting the many square miles of campsites. It was remarkably well-organised and policed. The roads were well-lit and swept twice a day. Water was laid on to every campsite. There were two dozen fire stations, several hospitals and many shops. Particular attention was paid to toilets and hygiene, to my great relief. I did not think that Indians were capable of this, but then they have been organising the Mela for well over 3,000 years.*
>
> *The Kumbha Mela attracts practically every yogi, swami, sadhu and guru in India and the greatest variety of colourful people that one could imagine. Gurus and spiritual teachers speaking through loudspeakers from their flower-decked marquees could be heard everywhere. The whole atmosphere was one of great devotion.*
>
> *We attended [fire] ceremonies and talks conducted by Muniraj and Shastriji... We also bathed in the Ganges.*

It is said that at the creation of Earth, a very important event took place which in Europe is connected with the Holy Grail, and in India with the 'Kumbha'. The Khumba is seen as a chalice or pot, containing the nectar of immortality. On its way back to paradise, some drops of this nectar are said to have fallen to Earth in four places.[2] Allahabad, at the confluence of the

[2]Allahabad and Hardwar on the river Ganges, Nasik on the River Godavari, and Ujjain on the River Sipra. A small Kumbha Mela is held in turn at one of these four holy places every three years, as is a larger one in a six-year cycle. The big Kumbha Mela that we attended takes place every twelve years, mainly in Allahabad

Ganges and Jumna Rivers (and the invisible, 'heavenly' river, Saraswati), is one of them; some of the nectar of immortality is said to be poured out from there on certain auspicious days during the Mela, which lasts a little over five weeks. Thus people come to the Kumbha Mela to bathe on these special days as much as for the spiritual contact with the myriad holy persons gathered for the festival. We went by boat to a sandbank in the middle of the Ganges/Jumna confluence and had our bath along with thousands of others. Any fears of bathing in the same water with so many people, many of whom could well have been carrying disease, were immediately washed away when we took the plunge into the water. It was a blissful experience. Some of us and our friends experienced the reality of the water being charged with golden light and life-force: one said it was like bathing in a glorious liquid fire.

We felt the Kumbha Mela was not only a great blessing for those who attended but also for India and the whole world.

When we were guided to travel on down the Ganges to Benares, and then to Haidakhan and Mt Kailash, we continued to experience a profound connection with the Kumbha Mela. The silver arms of the Ganges embrace the ancient city of Benares (Varanasi), traditionally seen as the first and holiest city of India and a great gateway to heaven; although we found it rather degenerated and almost dying, it remains a powerful 'city of the dead' where many believe it a blessing to die.

The five of us reached the valley of Haidakhan. We felt Babaji welcoming us, and when we spoke about it a large bird — a heron — came gliding down the valley just above and following the Gautam Ganga River, passing close by us. Was this a messenger sent from Babaji? It felt like that. The heron is called 'the king of fishers' and is seen in the Western tradition as a sign of the Grail King.

Two days later we set off to climb Lord Shiva's mountain again, Mt Kailash. It was raining slightly and the mountain was covered in clouds. Others warned us not to try the steep climb in the rain, but the inner call was imperative, and so we went. This was on a special day, February 5, and we had made a prayer for the right weather for the climb. Just as we came to the foot of the mountain and began to climb, we saw the heron again, this time gliding down the mountain towards us, following a stream that springs from somewhere on Kailash. In all my many visits and stays in Haidakhan, I have never seen a bird like that, before or afterwards.

Peter went ahead to set the pace; as usual when climbing Kailash, we were fasting. It was pleasantly cool during the climb with some gentle raindrops every now and then, but when we reached the summit, at exactly twelve noon, there was a tremendous downpour of rain, with masses of water in a very short time, so intense that it was even hailing. It was as if the whole mountain including ourselves were being baptised. Although we were thoroughly drenched, we felt it to be a most powerful blessing! From the mountain top, our prayers went out to God and the world for light, love and peace.

As I laid out the fruits and other things we had brought up, first to be blessed and then shared amongst us, to our surprise a priest came through the rain from a little hut not far from the top. He indicated that a fire ceremony was being prepared to take place that day at the havan kund (holy fireplace) on the summit. I immediately offered him some of our food for the ceremony, but — misunderstanding me — he took the lot! My friends were horrified to see our precious food disappearing like that, specially Peter, who had carried his share so carefully all the way up the mountain, in order to have a blessed picnic on the top — saving it all until then, even though he was very hungry.

The priest offered us shelter from the rain in the little hut. I would have loved to stay for the fire ceremony, but not so the others, as everybody was soaked to the skin. When we began the sharp descent, however, the rain stopped. Some deep revelations were given to each one of us on our way down as well as on the way up: we learnt a lot, and somehow the journey also seemed to make each of us conscious of our life's journey as a whole.

The Gautam Ganga River, receiving the energies of this powerful Kailash baptism, carried them down to the Ganges where the next day, February 6, the main bathing would take place at the Kumbha Mela, with millions taking their bath there. We took ours in the highly charged waters of the Gautam Ganga.

This whole trip was indeed a pilgrimage, 'a unique and wonderful spiritual experience for each one of us', as Peter wrote to friends. Each of our journeys was an inner as well as an outer one, but this one especially so.

Chapter 35

Peter, a Poet of Life

And now here is my secret, a very simple secret:
It is only with the heart that one can see rightly;
What is essential is invisible to the eye

— Antoine de Saint-Exupéry

THERE WAS SOMETHING MAGICAL about Peter: his heart was forever young; he was always daring, and open to the unexpected, whether at home or on his travels. Maybe this is why he did not appear to age. Friends who had not seen him for a while wondered at this.

One morning after our daily meditation in the sanctuary in our house, Peter disappeared. I found him sitting up a cherry tree in the garden, breakfasting on its ripe and delicious fruit. After I had spotted him, he came a little lower and began to feed me too, picking each cherry anew. Peter really knew how to enjoy life and to share his joy with others.

The trinity of the garden, the lake and the mountains beyond was very important to Peter — and all this in the heart of Europe, this ancient area of the Rosy Cross which turned out to be a real home for his heart and spirit.

The satin waters of the lake were an elixir of life to him. As soon as the days grew warmer we would go for a swim, Peter often twice a day, just a short dip into those lovely waters before lunch and dinner, usually after intense gardening or other work. 'How wonderfully it cleanses the aura!' he would comment, or — early or late in the year — call it merely 'invigorating' when the water was so cold that nobody else would dare swim in it. Peter did not mind, diving straight in every time.

As for his friends the mountains...

Peter loved mountains all his life. His focus had never been on the lower levels of the personality but always on God, on the heights. The mountains with their silent majesty expressed something of this — deep clear blue sky, bright sunshine and snowy mountain peaks. This somehow felt to me like an image of Peter himself, not only in the inner but also in the outer sense, with his radiant clear blue eyes, his ever fresh and suntanned face and his snow white hair. Often on Sundays Peter was off to the mountains, usually with his friend Dirk, who had travelled widely and with whom Peter could discuss politics and world affairs. This also gave me a break for my own creative work.

When they came back from their mountain strolls, there was sometimes the smell of turpentine rather than of a lovely meal to greet them. Peter would immediately go down to my studio and look very attentively at my paintings in their process of birth. To Peter it was more important that I paint than cook. Many times during the years, he would pop into my room and say, 'You know, your paintings are growing on me', with ever-new amazement in his face. 'They really touch my heart, especially this one, look!' And he would show me which one moved him most at the time.

The sun seemed to nourish Peter, on a very deep level, inside and out, like food. As soon as the sun appeared, if possible he would strip down to shorts and a little hat, so as to catch every ray on his body, and work like this, enjoying the sun to the full; it was as if he were opening all the cells of his being to its light. He even spent his lunchtime nap sunbathing on the balcony of his room. While I would fade away in summer's powerful midday sun, it was just right for Peter; no doctor or newspaper report about the dangers could convince him otherwise. Whenever people asked Peter on a given subject what would be right for them, he usually answered, 'This you must know from within; what is right for one person might be wrong for another', and for him the sun was right on every level. He also seemed to embody its qualities of light, warmth, and love of life.

Peter was always seeing with 'eyes of light', looking for the good in every body and every thing. While I, who had been trained to read the signatures in people through psychology, graphology, astrology and so forth would see both the lighter and the darker parts of a person, Peter — true to his Rosicrucian training — was determined to see only the light in people and to ignore the rest. 'That is how I built up Findhorn,' he would explain, 'by looking for a person's talents and strengths, not to what may be lacking. That which you focus on becomes real.' I experienced the powerful truth of this through Peter: by his giving energy only to the good, whether in people or situations, he would draw it out even more, and the 'not so good' would die from undernourishment. This was his way of supporting people in their unfoldment and in helping them to realise their true task and purpose. In this, he was a marvellous teacher.

So many people feel they lack the power to do what they want to do. Through his own example, Peter was empowering people to follow their visions, their intuitions, and giving them the confidence to do so.

One day I was outside on the patio, painting on some panes of glass, with Peter every now and again looking down from his balcony and seeing with wonder one creation after another come into existence on these panes. Then he noticed how the more I worked on each one, the more one after another rapidly lost its beauty until all of them had become dull. Finally the whole terrace looked like a graveyard of overpainted glass! I was completely exhausted and at the border of despair. Peter came to me as I lay down on a couch, peacefully putting his hands on my head for a while; then he said, 'You'll succeed with a new pane. It will be more beautiful than any you have done before. Now go and do it.'

And so I did. I had only one pane of glass left. It was a miracle: although there was only an hour remaining before sunset, he had given me the strength and concentration to paint the most beautiful glass window I had ever produced. I later hanged it in front of the window in Peter's room.

* * *

'The proof of the pudding is in the eating' was one of Peter's favourite sayings, and it was true of himself — he lived what he taught, and more. He encouraged and supported a number of other growing centres, for instance the Zegg community near Berlin. The central theme that ran like a golden thread through his talks and workshops in these last years, which he gave here and elsewhere in Germany and Europe, was always the empowerment of love — that Divine Love through which everything is possible.

In Germany he always had to be translated, which I did when I was with him. Some situations were surprising. Once, for instance, we were invited to Deggendorf in an out-of-the-way corner of Bavaria, and we couldn't believe our eyes when we saw the large room in which the lecture was to take place — about a hundred good-bellied Bavarians came to sit at long tables, drinking from large steins of beer which were constantly replenished throughout Peter's talk and Findhorn slide presentation. In spite of our mild apprehension, the presentation was well received and this was confirmed by later newspaper reports.

On another occasion, Peter had been invited to give an opening talk at the twentieth birthday celebrations of the Frankfurter Ring, one of the chief spiritual organisations in Germany. About 800 people were there, including many old friends and presenters like Baker Roshi, Sun Bear, Paul Horn and Al Huang. Here's how Peter himself described the occasion:

> *What we didn't know was that there were* two *opening speakers. Dr Peter Zürn, who was to talk about the early founding of the centre, said that he was first introduced to it nearly twenty years ago by his wife Renata Zürn, now Renata Caddy. The second opening speaker was me. I then introduced Renata, the remarkable woman who had been married to the two opening speakers! I shared that I felt that God must have a good sense of humour. There was much laughter, which got the celebrations off to a good start.*

Humour also played its part in the Rosicrucian training which Peter shared with friends in the area during his last years, the same teachings which had started Peter off on his own spiritual journey almost sixty years earlier. It felt very appropriate that he offer the teaching in our centre, and they indeed seemed to change the lives of many who took part.

'Eliminate all "ifs" and "can'ts" from your language' was part of Peter's Rosicrucian teaching, which I knew he had practised all his life. When I once proposed that he take part in one of my painting workshops, and he replied, 'No, because I can't paint', I said, 'Please, try it' and reminded him of his saying that every 'I can't' is really a hidden 'I don't want to...' So Peter agreed to join the workshop, which was called 'The Dance of Shiva'.

The theme was to re-experience, through painting it, how all of us have come from the All-Oneness (represented by a large sheet of blank white paper) but have veiled ourselves more and more as time passed by; this was done by applying layer after layer of a single colour (blue), watered down at first and then gradually thicker, to the paper, until we had developed a firm form — our individuality — which veiled the white, more or less. The whole exercise required concentration and patience.

Peter was doing very well indeed while he was painting with the lightness and density of one colour only, but on the next day, when the theme was to transfer this form to a new sheet, and then to bring this picture through a series of paintings in all the colours of the rainbow back to the original white, Peter had his own ideas. Instead of following the directions, he was inspired to express his own way back through the colours to the white, by drawing — with a compass! — seven circles and filling each one with one of the seven colours of the rainbow, not with watercolours but solid crayons, then giving during a break to the rest of the group a stirring explanation of the Masters of the Seven Rays, who were serving God in humanity, inspiring and guiding us, thus bringing us back to the White Light — to oneness with all.

* * *

Peter was very single-minded in his attention. For instance, if during a task I asked him what he was thinking, Peter would typically answer, 'Nothing, I'm driving' or whatever it was he was doing. He was fully focussed on what he was doing in the moment. He did not need to meditate in order to find his peace; there was a great stillness in him even in the midst of his actions, and thus he could be guided from within to do the right thing at the right time. In whatever work or actions he was doing, he had the same concentration and stillness of mind that others search for through meditation only, sitting with eyes closed to the world.

'I am guided by God in the moment,' Peter said. 'Before that moment comes, I haven't a clue what action should be taken.' His intuition was very strong, and in day-to-day life it often expressed in what he called his inner promptings. For instance, one morning we were having breakfast with some friends, when Peter jumped up — halfway through his boiled egg — and said, 'I have to make a phone call to Findhorn!' Minutes later he was back, radiant. 'Just in this moment,' he told us, 'I rang Cluny Hill and *all three* of the people I needed to talk to were there — and they all told me that later it would have been very difficult to catch even one of them'. He never lost his sense of wonder and gratitude for the rewards of instant obedience to his intuition.

Peter's pinpointed concentration was such that, when he was cooking and I came into the kitchen with some question, he would say 'I can't answer that now, I am peeling potatoes. One thing at a time!' While he was cooking, the kitchen became a meditation room. With gratitude, I left the cooking mainly to him. Like almost everything in his life he also did this with music (whether Joan Baez, Hawaiian paradise, the flute of the Indians or Russian choirs), and the loudness needed by the music in order to reach the kitchen meant that everybody in the house and garden knew that Peter was now preparing the salad for lunch, or cooking the evening meal. In spite of this pinpointed concentration, sometimes when I popped into the kitchen during his cooking sessions, Peter, inspired by the music and out of pure joy, would smilingly take me in his arms for some turns of a dance before continuing.

Our evening meals at the beginning consisted mainly of Brussels sprouts, potatoes and omelettes, all exquisitely done — and this every other day! Never in my life have I eaten so many Brussels sprouts, but they were really so delicious. This meal with omelettes was and remained Peter's favourite, when we had guests, even though, of course, he prepared many other dishes too. Timing was important, to have everything ready at the same time — and then everybody in the house had to come *immediately* for dinner when he called. That was a must!

Every now and then — even after a long day of work — Peter would take me, sometimes with friends, to a lovely restaurant by the lake, with an excellent band, and he would dance tirelessly late into the night. He was a light, swift and very gracious dancer, his gentle guiding almost imperceptible.

Music was such an inspiration to him, not only classical but also the folk music of the area. Whenever he heard 'oompah oompah', he would go in search of it. One time in February towards the end of carnival, while I was away, Peter even went *hemd-glonkern* with some friends, and was dancing in his pyjamas like everyone else on the streets of our little town.

* * *

Concerning the Findhorn Foundation, like the father who had released his child to its own growth, Peter nonetheless always remained connected with the Community and its further unfoldment. He tried to be there for its major events, like the annual conferences, where I was also sometimes invited to give workshops. Peter usually took his son Daniel there during his summer holidays. Daniel enjoyed his time with his father to the full, be it at Findhorn, in our German home or in the United States.

Although it sometimes frustrated Peter to see certain developments in the Findhorn Community when visiting, he wisely refrained from stepping in and interfering. One summer, however, Peter returned from Findhorn with a twinkle in his eye and looking very pleased with himself. The 'wild garden' there had grown *so* wild that he saw that drastic action was required, but he suspected that the present garden group would be either too timid or talk too much about taking the necessary action. After all, the 'wild garden' was supposed to be the exclusive preserve of the nature spirits, with no human intrusion allowed — but Peter, who had originally created it, saw that the overgrowth of certain species like gorse, brambles and willowherb was choking out the other wild flowers and plants. He recruited the one young gardener who could see the problem as clearly as he did, and without even telling the garden group they tore into this supposedly sacrosanct domain of the nature spirits, and before anyone could raise a protest the deed was done. Many Community members were horrified, but it was a *fait accompli* and Peter stuck by his guns; only after some time had passed did people appreciate the wisdom of his action.

* * *

A number of times, to our great joy, we had Shri Muniraji and Shri Shastriji as guests in our home when they came to Europe. It was always a wonderful celebration, with many friends. On occasion we accompanied the two of them with others on their European tours. Once we brought them to Findhorn with a party of thirty, and a Vedic fire ceremony was performed in the grounds of Cullerne House — for the blessing of the land and its people.

Worshipping the fire means worshipping the inner light.
Worshipping the fire burns karma, it is spiritual purification.
Worshipping the fire transforms into pure love all that is impure in the heart and mind.
The power of the holy fire,
The flame of love unfolds the qualities of a soul [1]

The fire ceremony is also given by Babaji and other great masters as one of the main ways of purifying and harmonising the elements in nature outside as well as within ourselves.

Peter showed the group all the various activities and properties that make up the Community. When we came to Cluny Hill, he was proud to present not only the power point, the sanctuary, and the kitchen — with its mounds of healthy, fresh salad ingredients waiting to be prepared — but also the former bar, the one place in the entire building where it was permissible

---

1 From *Babaji, Message from the Himalayas* (Maria-Gabriele Wosien, 1978)

to smoke. Muriel, our hostess, immediately took out her cigarettes and also offered one to Muniraji, who accepted it with a smile. A look of mischievous fun came into Peter's face and he too asked for a cigarette so that he could join Muniraji. It was his first (and last) cigarette in fifty years, and his pantomime performance as he produced puff after puff had us all in stitches.

* * *

Another time when we had Shri Muniraji and Shri Shastriji as guests in our home, with some close friends accompanying them, as usual on these occasions an evening of devotional song and meditation took place. Many friends came to meet these two holy men; food was served and there was a happy throng of people throughout the house and on the terrace. Suddenly, to my surprise, I saw Peter going down the spiral staircase of our large meeting room with his small Scottish tartan suitcase. 'Where on earth is he travelling to now?' I thought to myself. After a while I saw him returning up the stairs, making his way through the people, still carrying the suitcase. He came on to the balcony where I was with Muniraji, sitting and enjoying the evening with some close friends, including an Indian doctor. 'Ah, there you are!' Peter said to the doctor, 'I was looking for you in the garden caravan, where we had an appointment'. So saying, he laid his suitcase out on the table immediately in front of Muniraji, opened it and — to our astonishment — produced a bottle of whisky and two glasses.

It turned out that the good doctor, used to his home comforts in Delhi, had been missing his evening dram on this tour with Muniraji, and so had asked Peter for the whisky. To everybody's great amusement, Peter poured two generous glasses of whisky, one for the Indian doctor friend and the other of course for himself.

Chapter 36

A Planetary Citizen

From now on, always remember
that there are no enemies —
only friends and potential friends

– The Old Man

A GREAT FRIEND OF PETER'S, Donald Keys[1], who has given many lectures at Findhorn, writes:

> *For the spiritually trained person, travel or pilgrimage often has deeper importance than they may be aware of. They may be utilised by the energies of Spirit in the higher worlds to change something or initiate something for the future just by their being available in the areas through which they travel.*

This was very much so with Peter.

It was in July 1992 that we went on another pilgrimage[2], a trek through the heart of South America — Brazil — with Peter and Sarah Dawkins, our Brazilian friend May East and a group of twenty others. It was a very adventurous journey — through the Vale dos Somhos (the Valley of the Dreams), to the Roncador area, along the Rio das Mortes (River of Death) to the Chapada region of the Mato Grosso, culminating with a climb on Mt Sao Geronimo — but the highlight was our stay as guests of the Xavante Indians. We were the first large group of white people to be accepted into their village, which was in the Roncador area. When we arrived, Peter, courageously balancing our large rucksack, was one of the first to cross the bare tree trunk that served as a bridge high over the river between their hidden territory and the outside world.

---

1 See page 336

2 'Geomantic pilgrimage is analogous to working with acupressure on the meridians of the body— in this case the meridians of the planetary body— to bring about healing, balance and revitalisation.' — Peter Dawkins

Chief Ze Luiz, a strong and beautiful man who was the head of the tribe, had seen in a vision several years earlier an 'ancient ancestor', a great white figure of light who had told him 'that one day some white people would come whose hearts were good and who were not destructive or selfish-minded like other white people he knew. The Ancient One asked Ze Luiz and his people to open their hearts to these visitors, and to share with them their wisdom, ceremonies and sacred places. They were to build an "Affectionate Alliance" between the white and red races. Moreover, the white visitors were to be the recipients of the great energy stored in the caves, which they were to carry with them back to their countries, where it would be disseminated.'[3]

So this particular tribe of Xavante Indians[4], numbering around 80 people, thirty of them warriors and painted as such, not only lovingly offered us two of their eight maloccas[5] which they had made free for us — one for the men in our group, the other one for the women — where we slept in hammocks which we had brought with us, but they also let us bathe in their river, at different times for the men and for the women. They invited us to participate in a healing ceremony in which all the men of their tribe danced throughout the night, while chanting the same sounds all the time, like a mantra, calling on the spirits of their ancestors to heal a little girl who was very, very sick. The next morning, their medicine man was given the message that the little girl had been saved.

Then they brought us to their most sacred places, of which they were guardians: Lake UU, a lake of utter stillness and transcendent beauty hidden in the woods and which their traditions held so holy that none of them would ever dare touch its waters, and Cave UU, a huge cave reaching deep into the body of Mother Earth, charged with energy, feeling like a mighty womb. The Indians and some Brazilian friends maintained that this cave was one of the entrances to the Roncador underground world that reputedly consists of hundreds of miles of interconnected subterranean tunnels and caves.

When it was time to say goodbye, on the third day of our visit, Chief Ze Luiz gave a talk about the 'Affectionate Alliance' between us and our two

3 Quotation from Peter Dawkins. This trip was an example of the 'temple work' we did as planetary citizens

4 The Xavante Indians are a nation of many tribes, each one being a large family unit living in a village, just like the ancient Celts. The largest number a tribal unit normally reached was usually 120, governed by a chief; beyond this number the tribe would split in two, with a new village being established. We understood that Chief Ze Luiz was the chief of three villages

5 Round huts made from a kind of bamboo

races. Peter was moved to tears, inexplicably — although he didn't understand the language, the chief's words and the message they carried went straight to his heart. Later, when gifts were exchanged between our group and the Xavantes, Peter was the first to be honoured by the tribe and was given their greatest gift: a ceremonial headdress made up with seven large feathers. Our farewell embraces were firm and heartfelt.

Our adventures continued. Travelling in a bus called El Paradiso, and with a driver named Mr Cruz ('cross'), we felt that we would overcome any obstacle placed in our path, such as half-broken bridges over dangerous drops — and so we did. We touched into many remote and extraordinary places, like the Cruz de Pedra, a stone cross shaped by nature like an eagle; a cave called 'Dwelling of the Souls', in which there was a blue lagoon that we explored swimming; the Coxipo-Acu Valley surrounded by a mysterious mountain range resembling a crown; and Jamaca, which served as our base in the Chapada, a place from where we stepped off for yet more discoveries.

The day before we set off to climb Mt Sao Geronimo, Peter hurt a couple of his toes which then became so badly swollen that his mountain boots no longer fitted him, but he was so determined to make the climb with us that he did so in his Birkenstock sandals! It was a steep, perilous climb, sometimes with sheer rockfaces to be scaled, but in typical Peter fashion he not only managed it but had a wonderful time, as did all of us. The top of this mountain was like a huge pillow, very soft. This summit was difficult to reach, and then, from there, everything felt gentle, strong and light.

At the end of our journey we left the cool, clear, vibrant highlands and descended into the tropical press of the Pantanal and the abundant and luxuriant life that was teeming there. Plants, flowers, insects, innumerable birds and animals — everything seemed to be breeding profusely, from mosquitoes to crocodiles, but we all missed the magical, high atmosphere of the mountains and in a way felt out of our element. It was hot and humid, so Peter was the first to plunge into the large, slow-moving river we came to, innocently unaware of the crocodile that raised its head some distance away. He came back refreshed and safely. The next to go in, some young men from our group, soon realised that the crocodiles were moving towards them: they rushed to get out of the water and trod on some poisonous archer fish concealed in the mud.[6]

---

6 The fish shot poisoned darts into their feet, causing the agony. Eventually a local man took away the effect of the poison by burning a match under the place where the poison had entered the feet, the heat nullifying the poison.We later learned that the very place where Peter and the others had jumped in to bathe (regardless that after Peter's plunge our

This was the last stage of our Brazilian journey, which had been full of high adventures and deep experiences. But after almost three weeks of sleeping rough — in our sleeping bags, sometimes in little huts with cold winds whistling through them — somewhere in the wilderness, it was a celebration, as usual, to come back to our beautiful home and to its comfortable beds, the latter a special relief for Peter!

A few weeks later, however, I came down with a fever and felt strong, strange pains in my head and neck. Peter soon developed similar symptoms and then, oddly enough, so did Peter Dawkins, who was here for a few days giving lectures in our centre at the time. It turned out that all three of us had contracted malaria — the most dangerous strain of it, *malaria tropica*.[7] Fortunately, it was diagnosed at a very early stage by two excellent doctors, independently, through electro-acupuncture, thus it could be controlled very quickly with an immediate, highly potent remedy: otherwise this malaria might have killed us within a few days.

Peter rolled up in his bed like a sick animal, fasting for several days — as he always did when he was unwell — and sleeping as much as he could through the high fevers and pain. We were both very weak. Then one morning I awoke feeling reborn, and — full of joy and gratitude — I told Peter, who was also feeling much better. I shared with him that strangely, again and again in the night, I had been very aware of the Xavante Indian tribe, especially the men, and they were moving rhythmically. The same day Peter Dawkins contacted us from Britain to say that when May East, who was in Brazil at the time, had heard that the three of us were suffering from malaria, she was shocked. She somehow managed to get a message through to Chief Ze Luiz, and he had called his tribe together to do their healing ceremony throughout the night, this time for the three of us. Their dance took place on the same night that I saw them in the dream and woke afterwards feeling born anew.

Whatever the reason for our catching the malaria, it surely served to deepen the 'Affectionate Alliance' of the Xavante Indians with us in a most unexpected way.

* * *

Brazilian friend Mario had been warning them not to) was where the locals fed the crocodiles (in Portuguese 'jacaré) every day, and where the piranhas cleaned up the leftovers. The crocs and the piranhas thought it was mealtime— hence the panic to get out, once the others had realised what was happening. Peter was lucky to get out when he did, because he had a little cut whose blood might have attracted the piranhas

7 It had been unseasonably cold in the Brazilian highlands, therefore seemingly there were no mosquitoes, so we had stopped taking our preventative measures against malaria

It was not Peter's habit to give pain much attention, but one summer evening in 1993, when a pain that he had been feeling for several days in his left leg increased very much, he went to see his own 'traditional' doctor rather than waiting around any longer to be treated 'alternatively'. The doctor immediately sent him to hospital for a check-up. To all our surprise it was discovered he had a thrombosis, which had already travelled up the leg and almost reached his pelvis. Peter was given immediate medication to thin his blood. His condition was serious: five doctors gathered around him and debated whether he should be operated on immediately, as it could soon be fatal. The doctors explained that had he not come to the hospital when he did, he may well have been dead the next day.

Peter, suntanned and even in this situation full of peace, his blue eyes shining, was a picture of health in contrast to the pale appearance and worried demeanour of these doctors. As the medication worked sufficiently well, they dropped the idea of operating and instead insisted that he rest and keep up his leg for at least ten days. Peter was shocked and amazed at the idea that death could have found him so suddenly, and he was inwardly pleased that he had followed his intuition despite having been advised otherwise. This had saved his life.

What impressed him most in this hospital was the food, which he found excellent and clearly to his taste. One day he asked the nurse for a fly swatter — unheard of in this clean German hospital! 'There are no flies here,' said the nurse sternly. 'Oh yes there are,' Peter replied sweetly. No swatter was to be found in the whole hospital, so I brought him one.

After our visit to Brazil the idea had been born in Peter Dawkins and some friends during their stay with us, to organise a pilgrimage by boat from the Lake of Constance along the Rhine. This river flows through the lake, emerging near Constance into a much smaller lake around the island of Reichenau; it travels on to become the High Rhine through a landscape full of beauty and grace, passing ancient Rosicrucian places like Stein-am-Rhein, until it crashes as a mighty, thundering waterfall called the Rheinfall, at Schaffhausen. After a little while — at Basel — the river turns sharply north from its western course and becomes much larger, running through Germany like a spine, and then down to Holland and flowing into the North Sea.

The whole journey is rich in history and legend: the river carries the Rosicrucian mysteries of the High Rhine, and then, as the broader Rhine, its stories of the Ring of the Nibelungs and Siegfried's Rhinegold.

The pilgrimage started with a celebration in our garden — a fire ceremony, with the prayer that God would walk and act through our feet and hands during the pilgrimage and do the work that we on our own couldn't. Peter could only be there in heart and spirit, as he was still lying in hospital with the thrombosis. While I was wondering whether to stay with Peter rather than join the pilgrimage, he insisted that I go; but then he succeeded in discharging himself from hospital ahead of time, by successfully convincing the doctors, who did not want to release him so soon, that he had to be on this ship travelling along the Rhine. His wife was there to look after him, Peter explained, and there was also a doctor on board. And of course he would be able to keep his leg lying up when on the deck of the ship.

So another young doctor friend of ours agreed to bring Peter straight from hospital to meet us mid-voyage, where he was able to join our group of about thirty and complete the pilgrimage with us. Peter Dawkins, who led it, later wrote, 'This was something I found very moving indeed, and a sign of real friendship, courage and commitment to doing the right thing in service, whatever it required in terms of personal effort and self-sacrifice. I thought this act was an even greater feat than climbing any mountain, and one of enormous faith'.

On the pilgrimage, although he was supposed to have his leg up as long as possible, Peter also joined the group on land, not only exploring cathedrals like those at Speyer, Mainz and Koblenz but also climbing around crumbling castles. Our pilgrimage ended at Cologne, whose cathedral had always impressed Peter, especially its standing almost untouched during the last war when all around it the city had been flattened by bombs.

As on other pilgrimages, so on this Rhine pilgrimage we did our best as individuals and as a group to let love and light work through us and thus to give healing to the river, the land, its places and people — and of course we undertook to do the same for each other.. We felt specially that much love could manifest through such a diverse group of committed people.

Half a year later, in January 1994, we were on the road again, this time following the call of a peace initiative for the countries of former Yugoslavia. In spite of Peter's intense work on his book, he knew this call had priority. Peter drove all the way in a single, sixteen-hour journey from our home by the Lake of Constance to Samobor, a small town near Zagreb in Croatia. He was an excellent driver, and as on all our journeys, he never seemed to tire until we reached our goal. I had found this when he had driven us to Ste Marie de la Mer in the south of France — and thence to Montsegur, the secret and sacred hill of the Knights Templars and Cathars in the Pyrenees, which he was very keen to show me — or from Findhorn to Iona in a single stretch, then on to Glastonbury in the south of England. He fully enjoyed these long drives and cheerfully refused any offer by anyone else to take a turn at the wheel.

On this particular trip to Samobor, we travelled through the snow and ice of the Swiss Alps, into the mad traffic of the northern Italian motorways towards and past Venice, and then found our way via Slovenia to Croatia. Finally we arrived in Samobor around midnight, where we met up with Peter and Sarah Dawkins, and the five of us (Jeremy Slocombe had come with us from Germany) shared a large room in a small guesthouse in the central square of town, which was charming in the glistening snow.

Some of us — Peter Dawkins and another friend, Christine Bornschein, and myself — had been there two months earlier. We had responded to the call sent out by two women, Ema (Croatian) and Emsuda (a Bosnian Muslim refugee) to gather people of good heart and goodwill — especially women — in the common effort to bring peace to their countries. Inner bells had rung for us, particularly when we heard Emsuda's story. On her flight from the complete destruction of her home town near Banja Luka in May 1992, she had met an old man (a former neighbour) who had been warning people of this war long before it broke out. He seemed to know everything; so Emsuda asked him when the war would stop, if ever.

The old man's reply was to give Emsuda a mission: 'Bring the women of the world together. They should come to a certain place at a certain time.' He went on to say that a certain consciousness would be needed: 'From now on, always remember that there are no enemies — only friends and potential friends'. Emsuda thought she was dreaming. How could she bring all this about, how could she break through the barriers first? The old man predicted other events, which one by one came true, and gave her certain signs by which she would know the truth of his words; he also taught her a prayer, to be used like a mantra whenever she faced danger. Her experience was that it saved her life on several occasions.

So Emsuda came to realise that she had *not* been dreaming, and accepted that what she had heard was her mission. When she finally reached safety in Croatia, she met an older woman there, Ema, who had a similar vision. They formed a group and thus this peace initiative was born, called '*Srcem do Mira*', 'Through the Heart to Peace'.

We came to know all this through three fine and courageous women from Hazelwood House in southern England, who had supported the peace initiative from its outset a month earlier; like the three of us (Christine, Peter Dawkins and me), they came for a peace meeting in November, together with Noirin, an Irish folk singer. That meeting took place in a room at the local school in Samobor where Ema had been a teacher. Heavy snow kept the number down to around thirty.

Once they had shared their vision, it was not easy for Ema and Emsuda — both very dedicated women, full of heart — to work out a clear plan of action with those gathered, who were mostly Croatians and refugees from Bosnia-Herzegovina. There were so many different temperaments to contend with. As some of them shared their stories, it was quite easy to understand, given what they had gone through, that there was in the room a lot of grief, pain, bitterness and sadness. There was as well a tendency to put the blame on Western politicians for not doing more to stop the war. A list of demands was produced — maybe justifiable — but the general attitude was 'we must *fight* for peace'.

We were listening quietly; I was shocked, and expressed it to my friends: 'How can one *fight* for peace? Is this the way of a 'through the heart to peace' movement that aims to see "no enemies, but only friends and potential friends"?'

Finally it was music that brought us from the battling mind to the loving heart. Noirin stood up and walked around us, like a troubadour, playing her harmonium and singing in a powerful voice songs of the heart, songs of the love of God. At the end our friend Christine was inspired to lead us all into a simple, sacred dance and singing,which really brought our hearts together.

That was achieved even more on the following evening, when the core people of the group came together in Zagreb, and we laid out all the food we had brought with us for them, as a picnic for everyone. Real friendship could now be established amongst us; we could share more, and much more deeply.

After that first visit, we had driven back through heavy snow to Christine's house in Munich, where to our great joy Peter, who had taken a break from working on his book, arrived the next day so that we could all share our insights with him. We had a deep attunement and meditation together. It had become clear to us that the wound in the body of Europe caused through this war was like the wound of King Amfortas, the Grail King, which can only be healed through the compassionate action of all of us, who are Parzival.[8]

We all became very involved with this 'Through the Heart to Peace' initiative, and it required much clearing of communications between the few of us 'Westerners' and Ema and Emsuda before we had the concept settled. If a pilgrimage were to succeed, it had to be a prayer in action and not a protest against war. Love must be expressed through our hands and feet, not hatred. Compassion and forgiveness must replace bitterness and heal the wounds.

The invitation to a January meeting in Samobor and a subsequent peace pilgrimage was spread from heart to heart to as many as possible. So in January 1994, 350 people — mostly women, with a few men — from all corners of Europe descended upon Samobor.

Because of all these newcomers we found we were back to square one. Many of the Westerners imported their own issues and tried to impose solutions with little sensitivity for the local people or knowledge of the issues at stake. How could it be otherwise: to begin with, we seemed to contain within ourselves and between ourselves many of the elements that caused the war outside. All kinds of anger, envy, jealousy, glamour and other ego power trips that could separate us from each other came to the surface, and also gender issues through the question of whether there should only be women on the planned pilgrimage, or men also. Obviously, as work for peace, before further steps could become clear, we first had to identify and heal these things. A chain is only as strong as its weakest link.

Throughout all this Peter remained an ocean of peace. None of the dramas around us would shake him out of this; he embodied peace, which was like a tangible and wonderful substance, and he emanated it. He was loving and quiet, there for everybody — a strong and stable anchor of wisdom and light. God for Peter was not some distant heavenly being but an ever-present

8 As told in the book *Parzival* by Wolfram von Eschenbach: King Amfortas, the Grail King has a wound in his groin that gives him unbearable pains that cannot be healed, except when Parzival comes to the Grail Castle and is finally able to ask the compassionate question, 'What makes you suffer?' King Amfortas and Parzival can be seen not only as living individuals but also as archetypes, and the story may be read as a prophecy of what could take place in the world on a large scale

reality, God whom he loved and served, and on whom his absolute faith was based. He knew that God was guiding everything, so Peter was at peace. This surely is the true foundation for any successful peace work.[9]

9 [Jeremy Slocombe adds:] As it turned out, all the major differences at the meetings were resolved, and three courageous and successful pilgrimages to destroyed places in Croatia and Bosnia-Herzegovina were made subsequently. At the time of this writing, a peace seems to have been achieved

Chapter 37

Love Knows no Death

To him that overcometh I will give to eat of the hidden manna, and will give him a white stone, and in the stone a new name written, which no man knoweth saving he that receiveth it

— Revelation 2:17

ON 8 FEBRUARY 1994 Peter brought me and my friend Gisela to the airport, where she and I were to fly out to join a peace pilgrimage through India led by Peter and Sarah Dawkins. A special destination of this pilgrimage was the sacred island of Omkareshwar, the 'heart' of India which itself is seen in Vedic tradition as the heart of the world. Peter would have loved to be going too — and I would have loved him to come — but he needed to stay at home for his son Daniel's holiday visit and to continue working on his autobiography with Jeremy. A friend of ours was there to care for them all. Somehow I did not want to be leaving Peter at home this time, but we both knew that I had to go. It also made sense to us that by Peter staying at home and me going there, we could make a strong link between the 'heart of Europe' and the 'heart of the world'.

At Zürich Airport Peter waved and waved and waved — I had never seen him waving for so long — even from a far distance he still stood there waving. I phoned him from our pilgrimage whenever I had the possibility of doing so.

On February 16 I had a phone talk with Peter such as I had never had before. When I tried to convey to him my profound experience in Omkareshwar he seemed to know it all: it was as if we were one heart, one understanding, just *one*. It also showed how deeply Peter was connected with our pilgrimage — an active prayer for peace.

The story was this. From the 12th to the 14th we went on a boat on the holy river Narmada, first circumnavigating the island of Omkareshwar —

which indeed is shaped like a heart, with an ancient pilgrimage route laid out across it in the form of the Sanskrit letter 'Om' — and then sailing up the river's mighty flow, with the Rajah of Omkareshwar, who with much care had provided tents and meals for us during our two overnight stays on a quiet stretch of the riverbank. Elsewhere the banks were filled with the voices of the jungle, including tigers and panthers, which we had been peacefully observing from the safety of the boat. We continued upriver to the Narmada's light-filled waterfall, and there we bathed.

I was most impressed by the language of the high, powerful, dark chain of rock walls along the river there, which looked as if the whole destiny of mankind was inscribed in them.

Coming back downstream to Omkareshwar itself, we left our boat and explored the island on foot. In the light of the setting sun we reached the very high and simple temple on top of the island's hill, built around a huge black stone, a *Shiva-lingam*[1] that had originally been white but was blackened by fire; it is the biggest lingam I have ever seen, emanating majestic peace high up on this island of the heart. Then we had to find our way down through the dark to the main temple above the river, which contained one of the twelve miraculous lingams in India called *jyotir-lingam*, stone lingams that have materialised themselves at certain places.

When we were finally allowed, in little groups, to see this stone and sit around it while a *puja* [2] was done, I was horrified by what I saw and felt through the stone. I could clearly see a face in it, in utter pain, gazing upwards. How is it possible that so much pain is expressed here in this place? This was the evening of 14 February 1994, the same day ten years earlier that Babaji had left his physical body. He had said that there were 'a thousand knives in my heart, and I have only one heart to bear all the pain of the world'. I was there in Haidakhan with a few others when it happened. And

---

1 A Shiva-lingam symbolises the divine creative power and is represented by an elliptical stone. Eternal quiet or pure beingness can be expressed as a circle. When movement begins, the circle starts breathing: thus it becomes an ellipse. The ellipse is the expression of a living, breathing circle and shows the process of creation. All the planets, which move in ellipses around the sun, form a Shiva-lingam expressing the divine creative power. The Shiva-lingam often stands in a *yoni* (an inverted triangle), expressing the Divine Male— Shiva— in the Divine Female— Shakti, or, in another image, as a point in a circle, the infinite within the finite. Shiva is everywhere and nowhere; it is through his Shakti, the female— his power— that he becomes manifest

2 Religious worship using various forms of ritual

now — here on the very place of the heart of the world, again this pain? It felt like a cry from the depths of Mother Earth herself.

It struck me so profoundly that I needed quite a while to find my balance again. Then there was the unforgettable phone talk with Peter.

On Friday 18 February at four in the morning I left the group at Jaipur for a few days — or so I thought — in order to visit our great old friend Shri Shastriji at his home in Rajgarh. To my joy I arrived just in time to participate in his fire ceremony for the Divine Mother — Friday is the day dedicated to her. Afterwards, Shastriji and I had deep talks about Peter.

On Saturday morning to my amazement, Gisela stood in front of my door. 'How wonderful that you have come! What brings you here?' I asked her. She looked down silently. Then I also saw Peter Dawkins taking Shastriji aside. I went to greet him, who had travelled with Gisela five hours by car through the night to bring this message: 'There was a car crash in Germany — and Peter died.' 'Peter died? My beloved Peter died?' I absolutely could not grasp it.

Already a few hours after Peter Dawkin had heard about Peter's death, he had clear inner communication with Peter. 'He is very happy. He has gone into his greater power now. He is in the White Light. He is with Babaji in the [spiritual] Himalayas. He knows who Babaji is now, and that your Babaji and his Christ are One.'

In that moment all this did not console me much. There was only utter shock and pain in me — a pain for which there are no words. Were we not both convinced that he would live at least twenty more years, if not longer? And Peter and I had believed that —with God's grace — we would leave the Earth around the same time. Why did he leave already now?

I passed the news to Shri Muniraj by phone. I was weeping with the whole of my being. When I said goodbye to Shastriji, he told me that he would perform during the next twelve days the traditional rites for Peter, his beloved friend and brother.

From then on, everything happened as if carried on angels' wings. When we reached Delhi — Gisela having lovingly foregone the rest of her pilgrimage, including Haidakhan, to be with me — I phoned Indian friends and heard that they knew of Peter's death, were expecting us and had already booked new air tickets for us back to Germany that night. All this — as I later learned — had been arranged by Sarah Dawkins through many, many phone calls. There was loving help on every corner. In Delhi the message of Peter's death had already gone around. Other Indian friends came, they all loved and honoured Peter greatly, but I longed just to be still.

In the meantime I had heard that the accident happened on Peter's way back from Frankfurt Airport where he had gone with Jeremy to fetch his son Daniel. They had already reached the Lake of Constance and were not far away from home when they collided with a van driving the wrong way across the highway. Peter was entirely innocent, and he was dead within ten minutes —the impact of the crash burst his heart. This was at 4 pm on Friday 18 February 1994.

Seemingly the message of Peter's death went around the planet like a fire in a very short time — showing how much Peter *was* a 'planetary citizen'. It first reached our home, but at that time nobody was there. Then later, by chance our mayor was walking by the house just at the moment that a police car from the accident stopped there and — as I was not at home — the mayor was told of Peter's death; he kindly informed friends of mine immediately. The police had also found on Daniel's Californian address on his luggage, so that his mother Paula was phoned. The message went on to David Spangler in America and he phoned May East at Findhorn. She found out where the 'Heart of India' pilgrimage was at that time, and managed to reach Peter Dawkins by phone at a hotel near the Taj Mahal in Agra. Peter Dawkins then brought the news of Peter's death to me at the home of Shri Shastriji, who had married us.

In the following hours, days and weeks I was given enormous strength. I felt a most wonderful presence of light over my head. I knew this was Peter —what a blessing, what a grace! After landing in Zürich where we were fetched by Gisela's husband, I stopped briefly at home to drop my luggage and to take flowers and candles, and went straight to see Peter's body at the nearby hospital where they had brought him.

He was downstairs, while upstairs Jeremy Slocombe and Daniel were on their healing way. Peter's body was lying down there in a dark room — and I brought light with the candles and flowers. The shock of the accident was still visible: his face showed such an amazement. I felt love, nothing but love. This was my sole reality: 'I love you, I love you, I love you'. I had no other thought or feeling, it was my only prayer to him and to God. And, as if in answer to this, something miraculous occurred: his face relaxed more and more, and — very subtly —a smile began to sign itself in his face.

Meanwhile it turned out that my friend Marcel was waiting outside — he, to my surprise, was there in this moment. He later told me that when the news of Peter's death had reached him, deeply moved, he had gone to his piano and begun playing Bach's *Johannes Passion* with all his heart. Peter was so present to him; he saw his face so near, so clearly, in an intimate light, radiant, listening with close attention to Marcel's playing.

Now, as Marcel joined me in Peter's silent room, he too could see how in the presence of our love Peter's face took on more and more of a smile. He looked so beautiful with this fine smile around his eyes and mouth — and there was substantial peace around him.

First when I saw the vertical mark of blood (caused by the accident) going from his brow centre up his whole high forehead, I felt pain in my heart, as I did when I saw the deep bruise right in the middle of the back of his left hand (also caused by the accident); it was an even greater shock when I saw, two days later, another wound in the middle of the back of his right hand too, which I had not seen before. How is it possible that he who has been serving Mother Earth so much with his hands now has wounds on those hands, and both right in the centre? I really questioned God about this. And then I came to understand that all of this was a sign of God's blessing upon him, in the language of his blood, expressing the yogic triangle. The sign on Peter's forehead: the human will surrendered to the divine will, and the signs on the back of his hands: the radiant love of his heart emanating through his hands — his work as love in action, his karma yoga. And he had died from a burst heart.

I have always felt Peter as an archetype of a knight of the Holy Grail. As one can understand through the book *Parzival* by Wolfram von Eschenbach, the language of the Grail knight is the language of his actions. With one's vision directed to the Infinite, all deeds on Earth are done. Peter was a living example of this.

His body was then brought to a woodside chapel in our village where he lay in beauty and peace. Everybody who saw him then was deeply touched. There was not only the serenity of peace but also something very awe-inspiring about him, the dignity and depth of a life given to God, of a life signed by God. A mystery of the blood and the rose.

Epilogue

PETER LOOKED amazed in his death, and his death was as amazing as his life. It was like moving into a new birth, just as during his whole life he had always been moving on. In a sense his life was a constant birth and death process —called transformation — always daring and obviously in answer to the prayer in his youth that he would reach the highest.

In the meantime it has become clear to me that Peter's life was a complete life. He had reached his goal — the goal that was unfolding during his lifetime. When asked around Christmas, about seven weeks before his death, 'Have you reached your mountain top already?' his answer was, 'Not quite yet'. When, some time later, the same question was put to him by friends, he said to everybody's amazement, 'Yes, now I have reached the top of my mountain'. This was five days before his death. What a mystery of a man!

As old as his soul was, his heart was forever young, filled with the spirit of joy and absolute faith: he was always ready to take the next step into the unknown. His faith was inner love — love and knowledge of God — which then unfolded to outer love, expressed in work as love in action, then expanded even more widely in building up links of friendship in a network of light around the planet, and helping to heal the Earth in pilgrimages. So his work had become global — a global work for peace and universal brotherhood.

Peter would never stop — he was always moving further on. Beyond the mountains there are other mountains to climb, other valleys to pass. Peter was a man of courage and enthusiasm — a *real* man, a man of the rebirth of the light, of the emerging new consciousness. He was pioneering the new and is an example of the new, not of the old. He is for the future, for the younger generation and for those not yet born — always empowering others through his own example. His hope was that everybody embarking on the road of transformation should realise that the serpent — the transforming energy — really has bite in it. Peter himself was certainly bitten many times in his life. If one is earnest in the quest, one has to learn to recover from each bite. Whatever Peter went through, he learned the lessons gracefully, without complaining.

He was indeed a deeply knowing one, not only with his head but with the whole of his being. Come what may, Peter never lost his humour or his *peace*. He was free. And then — there is no end of service.

With courage, wisdom and compassion as companions he is travelling on...
With the sun as his sign
Peace as his armour
Truth as his sword
Love as his shield
'I serve' as his crown
With joy as his key
and faith as he steps into the unknown...

* * *

These are Shri Mishra Vishnu Dutt Shastriji's words about Peter, who found him dear and close like a brother:

> *A very pure heart, he was and is a great soul, a very old soul, an ancient soul who has done much work for humanity throughout time. He was free — awakened — a free soul.*
>
> *With his bright eyes and his joyful heart, he was always very strong, solid and handsome in his body throughout his life. He was like an ocean of knowledge, a genius, very intelligent — and very hardworking.*
>
> *Peter's work was worship, as Shri Krishna taught. In the Bhagavad Gita, Krishna told that work is the real worship. By hard work, done with the mind fixed on God, a person achieves lasting happiness in life.*
>
> *This is the real definition of karma yoga — that all peace, joy, love and perfection come naturally from constant work, dedicated to God — Peter was a living example of this. He was a great karma yogi indeed.*
>
> *Peter has done a lot of meditation in past lives. His karma yoga was meditation — meditation was his karma yoga.*
>
> *There was much peace in his heart and he wanted entire peace for the world.*
>
> *He came to Earth for the benefit of his generation and when his work was finished, God called him to Heaven.*

* * *

The Message of Peter's Life

I feel that the message that Peter gave through his life is this:

1. Have faith in God, be guided by God. Have absolute faith. To have faith is to allow the love of God.

2. Think big. The universe is big. Whatever you think, you will bring about. Always see the positive in everybody and everything — thus drawing it out. Affirm love, affirm light, affirm power.

3. Love whatever you do. Learn to love the place you are in, the people you are with and the work that you have to do.

4. Work is love in action. Whatever you do, do it with love and therefore perfectly — and have fun doing it.

5. Remember the three P's: patience, persistence, perseverance.

6. Always aim to be in the right place at the right time, doing the right thing.

7. Be at peace. Be the healer of all troubles. Be not troubled by troubles but be peaceful — peace heals.

8. Be fearless. Fear is tantamount to the denial of God, and no good comes from it. It is unnecessary and a hindrance to the workings of spirit. There is no need for fears of any kind — as they belong only to a realm of illusion and ignorance, and the incapacity to relax into the arms of God.

9. Have courage. Be true to your visions, be inspired and guided by God. Follow that guidance, even if you think it takes you to the brink. Go to the brink and look over — you might see the face of God!

10. Therefore love God, love life, be still within and know God.

11. Be happy. Be joyful in the service of God, in the service of humanity, in the service of life. Joy and a sense of humour are hallmarks of the spirit and the freedom it gives.

12. Do your best and then trust God to do the rest.

Appendix

Leadership and Morale

By Squadron Leader Peter Caddy[1]

[1] Reprinted from Royal Air Force Quarterly April 1952, pp.145-9

INTRODUCTION

Dynamic leadership, with the resultant raising of morale, is the greatest need of this country. Upon a fuller examination it will become evident that the qualities required for such leadership are essentially moral and spiritual in nature.

The democracies lack not only leadership but the potent ideology with which their enemy is armed. In democratic countries this lack of this positive faith creates a vacuum in which Communism flourishes. Not only can leadership raise the morale necessary to withstand this onslaught but it can lead the country to rearm morally and spiritually as well as materially in defence of her threatened liberty.

THE NATURE AND EFFECT OF LEADERSHIP

What are the nature and effect of leadership? They are primarily a gift of character which can be developed but not created. Leadership is a quality of the soul. In the words of Emerson, "Who has more soul than I, masters me, though he should not raise a finger. Round him I must revolve by the gravity of spirits. Who has less, I rule with like facility." It is through its leaders that the human race has stepped up the ladder of evolution. Such leaders can inspire man and draw out his inherent qualities of greatness, courage, faith and initiative. They can co-ordinate and harness all his faculties and energies, thus liberating the individual to express his maximum capabilities. This liberation in turn binds him to his leader.

QUALITIES REQUIRED OF A LEADER

In considering the qualities required of the leader it will be evident that first and foremost there must be self-mastery. Lack of this essential foundation to a strong character will hamper or even nullify whatever other qualities of leadership a person may possess. From self-mastery springs self-forgetfulness and unselfishness. The secret of such leadership is revealed in the words "Whosoever would be first among you shall be the servant of all." Self-mastery is the prerequisite to this ability to dedicate oneself wholly to service.

Secondly, the leader must have the ability to inspire others. There is in all men, even the lowest, a spark of the divine, something which is capable of rising superior to pain and loss, superior to seeking after gain, superior even to death. The true leader evokes this. Montrose appealed to that god-like something in his rough soldiers so that they followed him blindly. Not only must a leader fan the flame of the divine in his followers but he must inspire their perfect confidence in himself and in his undisputed authority. This requires a strength of character that will dominate others.

Thirdly, a leader must have moral courage, which is often preached but rarely practised. The final test of moral courage is the ability to stand alone and take sole responsibility for one's decisions. A striking example of this can be seen in the decision which rested with General Eisenhower as to whether or not to postpone, owing to unfavourable weather conditions, the invasion of Normandy.

Fourthly, there must be fortitude and resoluteness, the power to endure sufferings, hardships and reverses unflinchingly. Courage is the quality necessary for attack. Fortitude or resolution is the quality necessary for endurance. Both are essential to leadership. Churchill's memorable speech on the eve of what seemed to the onlooker absolute disaster has already become an immortal example of fortitude. It might be pointed out here what an effect one great leader can have on a situation. Britain was at her lowest ebb, disaster seemed inevitable, and all she was promised was "blood, sweat and tears." Yet such was the power of her leader, such was his inspiration, courage and fortitude that the whole nation rose at his call to face with a similar courage and resolution whatever the future might bring.

Finally, the majority of great leaders have been aware of a sense of mission, which has been the driving force of their lives. This sense of mission seems to arise in the heart of a man who sees a need to be met or a work to be done, for which he feels himself to be especially fitted and chosen. It is this sense of mission that fortifies the will to achieve the aim regardless of hardship, obstacles or even seeming impossibility. Field-Marshal Montgomery has said: "If a commander has a righteous cause and gives his soldiers success, he will gain the complete confidence of his men: and then there is nothing he cannot do."

These qualities of the soul require adequate development of the heart, mind and body through which to express themselves. If the latter become degenerate through power of corruption, the leader, no matter how great his qualities of leadership, is bound to deteriorate.

The heart must be developed through experience, sensitivity and imagination in order to have the necessary understanding to handle men and their affairs wisely. The following attributes are by no means exclusive to leaders, but they are necessary for effective leadership. One is sympathy, which may be described as the opposite of that magnetic quality in a true leader through which he can make his followers identify themselves with him, his will and his aim. Sympathy, on the contrary, enables him to identify himself with them, with their needs, their outlook and their way of thinking.

Another heart quality essential to the good leader is loyalty, loyalty both to his superiors and his subordinates. John Buchan, when writing of Montrose, said: "Loyalty is one of the greatest of our mortal virtues, and loyalty is not devotion only to a cause but to men, or to a man in which the cause is embodied." Abuse of those above and criticism of orders received from superior authority always recoils eventually on the critic and undermines his authority with those below him.

The intellect of a leader must be sufficiently developed in order to maintain intellectual superiority over at least the majority of his following. A stupid man can never be a great leader. Nevertheless, many a poor scholar in early life turned out to be a great leader. To mention only a few: Eisenhower, Roosevelt, Einstein, Edison and Churchill were all considered of poor-to-average intelligence at school.

THE NEED FOR MORAL AND SPIRITUAL LEADERSHIP

This century stands out from the past as one of change, upheaval and disintegration in every department of human life. Science has moved forward by leaps and bounds and changed our whole manner and tempo of living. War has disrupted the stable pattern of Victorian England, opening the door to so-called "free thinkers," who, in the vacuum of discarded religion, have sown the seed of many "isms," societies and creeds. Social disruption has followed. Implicit loyalties have been forsaken and the motto has become "Self-service." Not only nationally but internationally is this state of flux and chaos prevailing. Solemn agreements are repudiated. Promises are made without any intention of fulfilment, and the accepted usages of international diplomacy have been spurned.

Surely in such times as these the great need of this country, as well as of the world, is for leaders with unshakable convictions who will harness the energies of the people into constructive purposes and who will light their souls with the ideals they have lost. The urgency of this need is underlined by the state of the world today. It is being divided rapidly into two belligerent camps, each with an opposite way of life, conflicting principles and opposing policies. On one side is the ardent ideology of Communism which is incessantly practised and preached—with a goal towards which all plans, all energies and all activities are directed. This challenge to authority, to the accepted religions, becomes increasingly strong, enticing the adolescent and the idealist as well as the disaffected. In this camp everyone is either a whole-hearted and implicit follower or is coerced into an abject obedience.

What opposes this potent force? Where is the faith to combat this ideology? "It takes a faith to defeat a faith," and we shall never defeat the faith of Communism unless we have a faith more real and dynamic. It is the belief of the writer that Christianity is that faith, for through this faith Britain has risen to her greatest achievements and without its guidance and inspiration she is bound to fall from her position of moral leadership in the world. Mr. Arthur Bryant, the well-known historian and writer, in a lecture on "British Character" at Cheltenham in 1950, said that in his opinion by far the most important factor in the forming of the British character was the daily reading of the Bible. This reading of the Bible has now almost ceased. We are living today on the spiritual capital accumulated in our years of greatness. General Sir Bernard Paget, in his opening address to the courses held at Ashridge, affirmed that our great Christian heritage, which has been handed down from generation to generation, is being dissipated; thus we are undermining the greatest bulwark against Communism in the world today.

The qualities of leadership may lie dormant until awakened by some great need or emergency. There can be no doubt that the conditions existing today urgently require qualities of leadership perhaps to a greater extent than ever before. These conditions have produced such leaders as Churchill, Eisenhower and the outstanding men in our three Services. But leaders are all too few and are insufficiently backed because of the lack of leaders at all levels of the community, in industry, government, education, as well as the Forces. The qualities are no doubt there, but the urgency of the times is not sufficiently realized, nor is the desperate need for these qualities made clear to the nation. The man in the street pursues his lethargic way wrapped comfortably in the blanket of the welfare state and sustained by the soothing syrup of specious promises. His myopic eyes are unaware of the storm that threatens not only his welfare but his very life. He is like a sheep without a shepherd, a boat without a rudder, a compass without a needle.

The Christian way of life in this country has been handed down from generation to generation. But the youth of today has been robbed of this inestimable advantage by two world wars which have impoverished the lives of their parents as well as themselves. These youths are Britain's coming generation and her destiny is in their hands. They have been brought up in broken homes with little or no family life. They have been evacuated from blitzed homes and cities to new and strange surroundings. The resultant malaise has sprung from the individual's sense of no importance, of not being part of a pattern and, probably most significant of all, of not being necessary to anyone or anything. This belief, which is indeed the exact opposite of the teachings of Christianity, breeds the evils which are so rife amongst the young people now in their late teens or early twenties. They have left whatever homes they had and are now forced to spend two years in one of the three Services. We, as the older generation, must accept some responsibility for the state of the world in which they spent their childhood. The three Services are thus given the unique and far-reaching opportunity to discharge this responsibility.

A PATTERN, AND ITS PRACTICAL APPLICATION BY THE COMMANDER

Having considered the spiritual and moral aspects of leadership, let us conclude by studying its practical application by the commander. As we have seen, this age has presented him with a bigger problem than his predecessors. He must be father and mother as well as leader and teacher to the young Service men in his charge. How can he accomplish such a task?

We have said that the Founder of Christianity gave us the supreme example of leadership. How did He set about His work, which has revolutionized world history? First of all, He prepared Himself by a complete dedication to His mission, by continually seeking God's guidance, and by setting an example that all should emulate. This can be followed in the Royal Air Force today by leaders at all levels. The commander also can thus prepare himself by putting his whole heart into his job, by daily seeking for guidance, and by setting an example to his men.

Jesus then chose a team, trained them, inspired them with His spirit, and put them to work in the environment prepared for them. The commander's second task, then, is to build up a team. He must have the right man in the right job. Those who are unsuited for their work must be replaced. The commander must understand and be understood by his officers and non-commissioned officers. This team must then be trained to work in harmony both with their leaders and themselves.

Having welded his officers and non-commissioned officers into a single team, the commander's next task is to create the right environment and atmosphere throughout his unit or command.

The most important condition is enthusiasm. You can do anything with a man who is enthusiastic. Those who wish to inspire others with vitality and enthusiasm must themselves possess these qualities. Men cannot be talked into enthusiasm; they can only be infected by it.

He must then build up *esprit de corps*. The real leader inspires his men to a pride in themselves and in their unit. This can be helped through drill and parades, particularly with a band, and team games. Thus the men gain self-respect; they gain a pride in their bearing and work, a pride in their unit and Service, which should lead eventually to a real patriotism which Britain so sadly lacks today.

The commander should make himself readily accessible to his men. They need to sense a personal regard for their welfare and a personal knowledge of their characters and circumstances. In this way the commander can to a great extent counteract the lack of effective parenthood. He can prevent the magnification of imaginary or petty grievances before they assume serious proportions. Every opportunity must be taken in attending to the welfare of the men, improving conditions, and removing small and needless irritations. He can almost eliminate absence without leave.

Further, the commander must produce an atmosphere of success, for nothing succeeds like success. A man who never receives a word of praise becomes resentful and acquires a sense of inferiority. Morale can be heightened by giving praise when it is earned, by encouraging men who, while slow to learn, are obviously doing their best, and by preventing the intimidation of such men.

Provision also must be made for keeping the men abreast of events and their implications. A man will be more valuable if he understands clearly what is going on in the world and, when at war, if he knows why he is fighting. This can be done with the help of an information room or, more effectively, by the commanding officer giving instruction in person. This provides a valuable opportunity for contact with his men, and does much to build up individuality and make the men part of the social community, aware of the trend of events and conscious of their responsibility towards life.

Finally, there must be built up a sense of fellowship. The self-seeking, self-protective point of view prevalent in civilian life must be replaced by one of mutual co-operation, support and confidence. Individuals accustomed to competitive living must be fused together to form a group.

If such leadership is compared with the leadership of German or Russian officers it will be realized that the latter exercise their powers through force and fear, whereas Christian leaders exercise their powers through confidence and love. In the one the individual depends on the state; in the other the state depends on the individual. The writer has proved that Christian leadership can raise the condition of a unit from that of low morale, poor discipline, lack of enthusiasm, indifferent work and an unhappy spirit to that of a thoroughly successful and happy unit.

THE NEED FOR TRAINING IN MORAL LEADERSHIP

What is being done in the Royal Air Force to develop these qualities in its leaders? The Air Council realized the importance of this aspect by inaugurating a course in moral leadership followed by a conference at the Chaplain's School at Dowdeswell Court in November, 1950. The course was attended by all home commanders-in-chief as well as two officers of air rank from each command. The Bishop of Croydon, assisted by the Archdeacon of Lewes, were the speakers. One result of this course has been a programme of week-end courses at Dowdeswell Court for officers, particularly station commanders, and non-commissioned officers.

.The Commander-in-Chief, Technical Training Command, has introduced training in Christian principles throughout his command. The syllabus for every course includes a weekly period for this instruction. Further, he has inculcated the importance of the subject in all his officers through conferences, letters and above all, the influence of his own convictions. The results have been spectacular and are borne out by statistics.

But this is not enough, and no other steps appear to have been taken in this direction. Training in moral and spiritual leadership is neglected almost entirely in such establishments as the Royal Air Force College at Cranwell and the Staff Colleges, despite the fact that these are the sources from which our future leaders are drawn.

If the Royal Air Force has gone too far along the road of material endeavour, surely much more could and should be done to restore the balance by arming our leaders spiritually and morally as well as materially—not only against the armed might of Russia but against the insidious propaganda and distorted half-truths of Communist ideology which is threatening the foundation of our national morale.

Findhorn Press titles connected to this book

—— the Findhorn Foundation Community ——

SIGHTS & INSIGHTS (£2.40) isbn 1 899171 50 9
A Guide to the Findhorn Foundation Community
Compiled by Cally and Harley Miller

This booklet is intended to give those of you who have only heard or read of this near-mystical place a clear and up-to-date picture of what the Community is like and of what there is to see and do here.

Illustrated with line drawings of the most striking buildings of the Community, this booklet will take you through the various developments of the last 34 years; it also places the Community in its local surroundings with listings of local events, places of interest and nature walks.

THE KINGDOM WITHIN (£8.95) isbn 0 905249 99 2
A Guide to the Spiritual Work of the Findhorn Community
Compiled and edited by Alex Walker

This collection of writings about the history, work, beliefs and practices of the Findhorn Foundation and its associated community of spiritual seekers offers a vision of hope, inspiration and encouragement. With contributions by David Spangler, William Bloom, Roc, Dorothy Maclean, Peter and Eileen Caddy amongst others, this book covers topics which include nature and ecology, the art of living in community, the relationship of 'new age' thought to formal religion, and co-operation with the spiritual worlds. The world is hungry for the hope and inspiration this book brings.

THE FINDHORN GARDEN (£9.95) isbn 0 905249 63 1
Pioneering a New Vision of Humanity and Nature in Co-operation
by The Findhorn Community (Foreword by Sir George Trevelyan)

The story of the early days of the Findhorn Community and its communications with the nature kingdoms. Peter and Eileen Caddy's experiences as co-founders of the community, Dorothy Maclean's contact with the devas, R. Ogilvie Crombie's (Roc's) meetings with Pan and the Elemental Kingdom, and the wisdom of David Spangler and others combine to give a unique perspective on the relationship between humans and nature.

THE FINDHORN COMMUNITY (£8.95) isbn 0 905249 77 1
Creating a Human Identity for the 21st Century
by Carol Riddell

The author traces the Community's development over the years and gives a clear picture of the community and the new businesses and independent projects springing up around it. The second half of the book includes a number of intimate and revealing interviews with members, both young and old, who share their lives and experiences of living in this incredible community.

SIMPLY BUILD GREEN (£9.95) isbn 1 899171 90 8
A Technical Guide to the Ecological Houses at the Findhorn Foundation
by John Talbott (Foreword by Jonathan Porritt)

Simply Build Green offers a detailed description of the theory, practice and products used in the Eco-Village project at the Findhorn Foundation and is presented both as a working and reference document which will be of help both to people with a general interest as well as specifically to those in the building profession.

———— **Eileen Caddy's guidance** ————

OPENING DOORS WITHIN (£6.95) isbn 0 905249 68 2

Eileen's bestseller — 365 pieces of guidance received in her meditations, one for each day of the year. They contain simple yet practical suggestions for living life with joy, inspiration and love.

THE LIVING WORD (£3.95) isbn 0 905249 69 0

A pocket-sized book of short meditations given to Eileen in times of silence and used by her over the years for the deepening of her own spiritual life.

GOD SPOKE TO ME (£5.95) isbn 0 905249 81 X

Eileen's first book of guidance received during the early days of the Findhorn Foundation Community. Its message affirms the inherent wisdom and intelligence of all life and the ability of each one of us to contact it by turning within.

FOOTPRINTS ON THE PATH (£5.95) isbn 0 905249 80 1

Sequel of *God Spoke to Me.*

FOUNDATIONS OF A SPIRITUAL COMMUNITY (£5.95)
isbn 0 905249 78 X

Guidance that helped the Caddy family, living in a tiny caravan, grow into the international spiritual community called Findhorn.

THE DAWN OF CHANGE (£5.95) isbn 0 905249 87 9

A selection of daily guidance on human problems relating to work, relationships, purpose, health, inner life, etc. Eileen tells how all of us may experience 'the dawn of change'.

THE SPIRIT OF FINDHORN (£5.95) isbn 0 905249 97 6

This book offers a brief history of how Eileen gave up everything to follow her inner voice as well as sharing much of the guidance and wisdom which supported Eileen throughout the early days of her spiritual transformation and the birth of the Findhorn Community.

EILEEN CADDY MEDITATION SERIES
audio-tapes (£6 each — £25 for the whole set)

- THE CHALLENGE OF CHANGE
- BE STILL — MEDITATION FOR THE CHILD WITHIN
- LOVING UNCONDITIONALLY
- WHY MEDITATE
- FAITH AND THE POWER OF PRAYER

Eileen shares intimate and challenging aspects of her inner life and leads us in meditation and prayer

OPENING DOORS WITHIN *video (PAL format £14.99)*

A deeply moving sixty-minute video combining Eileen's life experience with meditation, affirmation and guidance.

——— Nature spirits: Pan, devas and elementals ———

• THE ELEMENTAL KINGDOM
• CONVERSATIONS WITH PAN
by R. Ogilvie Crombie (Roc) *2 audio-tapes (£6 each)*

Roc talks of his contact with Pan and the elemental realms.

COMMUNICATION WITH THE DEVA KINGDOM
by Dorothy Maclean *1 audio-tape (£6)*

Dorothy shares her personal experiences of the garden experiments in the early days of the Findhorn Community.

THE GOLDEN WEB (£6.50) isbn 1 899171 25 8
A New Partnership with Nature
by Gwennie Armstrong Fraser (Foreword by Dorothy Maclean)

This book describes the urgent need of a new partnership with Nature through messages from the Devic level of consciousness. The Devas explain how each being and life-form has its place in Nature within the interconnected whole. The Devas urge us to step forward together, to deepen our connection with the natural world, and to take active steps to begin the process of ecological restoration.

————— St Barbe Baker —————

MY LIFE MY TREES(£5.95) isbn 0 905249 63 1
Richard St Barbe Baker

The autobiography of the founder of 'Men of the Trees' — from his boyhood in Hampshire to the three and a half years he spent roughing it in Canada, followed by his work as a forester in Kenya, his work with President Roosevelt to establish the Civil Conservation Corps involving six million youth, and the 'Save the Redwoods' campaign... He was instrumental in the planting of 26 trillion trees internationally by organisations he helped or founded.

———— The New Troubadours ————

• HOMELAND
• LOVE IS
2 audio-tapes (£7 each)

Naomi

A WORLD WITHIN A WORLD — X-7 REPORTING (£7)
Telepathic transmissions from Russia on the Practice of Solar Light Radiations
isbn 1 899171 55 X

The messages received telepathically by Naomi, not from a disincarnate source but allegedly from prisoners of consience held underground in Russia; they tell us how, semi-starved and deprived of all physical support, driven to the point of despair and near death, they prayed and, to their amazement, a light appeared... For some time, they took this to be a hallucination induced by their physical weakness; it continued, however, increasing in strength until it drew from them a response which gave them new life and hope.

David Spangler

All books and publications by David Spangler mentioned in this book have been out of print for some time. However, Findhorn Press will publish in 1996 his latest book:

PILGRIM IN AQUARIUS isbn 0 905249 83 6
David Spangler

David leads us through a process of deconstructing the New Age, asking questions about it and challenging some of the ideas and images that have grown up around it. After doing this, he helps us reimagine the New Age as a spiritual process and practice, looking to see how we could use that idea as a tool to enhance our everyday lives and to enable us to make our contribution to the emergence of a loving world.

Index

A

B

C

D

E

F

G

H